The History of Prestwick

THE
HISTORY
OF
PRESTWICK

JOHN STRAWHORN

JOHN DONALD PUBLISHERS Ltd
EDINBURGH

The device on the title page is the seal of the burgh of barony of Prestwick.

© Kyle and Carrick District Council 1994
All rights reserved. No part of
this publication may be reproduced
in any form or by any means without
the prior permission of the publishers,
John Donald Publishers Ltd,
138 St Stephen Street, Edinburgh, EH3 5AA.

ISBN 0 85976 405 2

A catalogue record of this book is available from the British Library.

Phototypeset by
ROM-Data Corporation Ltd., Falmouth, Cornwall.
Printed in Great Britain by Bell & Bain Ltd., Glasgow

Preface

*I*T is now a hundred years since publication of Rev. Kirkwood Hewat's *A Little Scottish World* which reviewed Prestwick's history at a time when the ancient burgh was beginning its transformation into the modern town. It is now possible and desirable to reassess his contribution and carry forward the story of Prestwick into more recent times.

Like many local historians of an older generation Hewat was a man of considerable erudition, but some judgments need to be be reconsidered when the evidence is reexamined by 20th century eyes. In particular, Hewat misunderstood the wording of the 1600 charter to suggest that the burgh of Prestwick originated 617 years earlier in the year 983. That historical myth has found some local acceptance, even though others before and since Hewat's time have more credibly dated the foundation of the burgh to the 12th century, sometime between the years 1136 and 1173. This allows Prestwick sufficient reason for pride, as the earliest burgh on the west coast of Scotland and first in Ayrshire. Hewat in his earlier chapters carefully examined the constitution and character of the medieval burgh and the life of the freemen who worked and lived in Prestwick. He derived most of his information from *Records of the Burgh of Prestwick* which were published by the Maitland Club in 1834. These covered the years from 1470 until 1610, with a few extracts from the 18th century added. Close examination of these published *Records* has allowed a more realistic assessment of how the little burgh operated. One conclusion (reached in Chapter 2) is that "The idealised picture of a kind of democratic commune of peasant landowners cannot be sustained". An analysis of land ownership within the community shows otherwise. The circumstances in which the burgh failed to develop is of particular interest. History is normally an account of success stories, whereas here we have an opportunity to study one burgh which suffered centuries of stagnation. To trace the course of developments it was hoped to pursue reseach in those manuscript burgh records which in five volumes covered the period from 1726 until 1906. But these and other burgh papers disappeared sometime after 1970, presumably lost around the time of local government reorganisation in 1975. Yet from those few later extracts in the published *Records* and from other sources it has been possible (in Chapters 6 and 7) to define significant developments. Annual redistribution of lands to the freemen had been abandoned in 1572. By 1757 freemen were allowed nine years' tenure of the lands then allocated to them, these being a series of small plots dispersed throughout the arable areas. This runrig system was abandoned in 1766 when the freemen were allocated consolidated plots. In 1780 new arrangements were made, fixing the number of freemen at thirty-six and allowing them tenure for twenty-one years. Arable lands were redistributed in 1801, the remainder of the common lands were divided up in 1814, and these holdings became permanent in 1833 when 999-year tenure was introduced. Finally in 1850 legal restrictions were removed so that freemen thereafter possessed their holdingss as heritable property, which they were free to dispose of as they desired, so that all the lands of Prestwick thereafter belonged to individual small proprietors. The remaining functions of the burgh were operated by those few resident freemen, until changing circumstances required new arrangements.

Hewat was able to draw upon the memories of older inhabitants to provide useful details of the little Prestick of earlier times. He was conscious of changes in process and in one chapter he described "The New Era". When he came to Prestwick as Free Kirk minister in 1881 there were just over one thousand people living in the town; when he died in 1927 there were more than eight thousand. Incomers came to settle in what had become a popular holiday and residential town, but many then and since became (like Hewat) interested in the traditions of Auld Prestick. What Hewat had to tell about the 19th century has been supplemented by files of the local press, other contemporary sources, and it is now possible to examine the structure of the changing community with the aid of those census returns which have become available for examination. For the twentieth century, the continued and considerable expansion of Prestwick can be traced in the minutes of Prestwick town council which was statutorily established in 1903 as successor to the old burgh of barony; Prestwick's new importance as international airport can be assessed through various publications, reports and press items; aspects of local life and traditions have been commendably recorded on audio-tape by the enthusiastic members of Prestwick History Group.

In an appendix are listed all sources of information, with notes for each chapter. Help of various kinds has been supplied by numerous persons, including Ken Andrew, Sheena Andrew, Alisdair W.R.Cochrane, Charles Deas, Margaret Foulds, W. Iain Foulds, John Hope, Fred Horton, Ian Lawson, Ian Levitt, David W. Purdie, Margaret Sanderson, Ian Welsh, C.A. Whatley. In particular, invaluable assistance was rendered by Sheena Andrew and her colleagues in the Reference Department of Ayr Carnegie Library. Many of the illustrations are from the Carnegie Library. Ken Andrew supplied photographs from his own extensive collection and took others for this special purpose, his contributions being marked (*KA*). Others were provided by Iain Foulds (*IF*), John Hope (*JH*), and the airport (*PIK*). All the colour photographs are by Ken Andrew. The colour maps were devised by the author, superimposed on Ordnance Survey plans. Special acknowledgment is due to Kyle and Carrick District Council, who suggested preparation of this volume, and generously financed its publication from the Prestwick Common Good Fund. Local historians in Ayrshire have good reason to appreciate such continued patronage by our local authorities.

JOHN STRAWHORN

Contents

	Page
Preface	v
PART ONE: AULD PRESTICK	1
CHAPTER ONE Origins	2
CHAPTER TWO The Medieval Burgh	10
CHAPTER THREE The 16th Century	27
CHAPTER FOUR The Charter of 1600	38
CHAPTER FIVE The 17th Century	48
CHAPTER SIX The 18th Century	57
CHAPTER SEVEN The Early 19th Century	78
CHAPTER EIGHT The Mid 19th Century	89
PART TWO: MODERN PRESTWICK	107
CHAPTER NINE The Late 19th Century	108
CHAPTER TEN The Early 20th Century	137
CHAPTER ELEVEN Between the Wars	161

CHAPTER TWELVE
The Second World War 186

CHAPTER THIRTEEN
The Mid 20th Century 201

CHAPTER FOURTEEN
The End of the Burgh 224

CHAPTER FIFTEEN
The Late 20th Century 241

Sources of Information 253

Chapter Notes 257

List of Provosts 268

List of Events 270

Index 272

Town Plan 278

Colour plates between pages 136 & 137

Part One

AULD PRESTICK

CHAPTER ONE

Origins

*P*RESTWICK first appears in written records of the 12th century, but the name is several hundred years older, and the area was inhabited long before that.

Sometime after the last Ice Age, which ended ten thousand years ago, the first few arrived. Along the Ayrshire coast and beside Loch Doon, traces of mesolithic people have been found, the earliest perhaps around 6000 B.C. These Stone Age people are so called because stone artefacts are all that survived to mark their presence. At eight sites between Heathfield and Monkton there have been found

Five thousand years ago the sea level was higher than now, and the coastline then extended along the length of the airport runway. (*KA*)

flints which had been worked for use as blades, scrapers, and corers – at Monktonhill in a cache of more than fifty. These sites were located near the shore as it was around 5000 B.C., when the sea reached a maximum of forty feet above its present level. Mesolithic settlements would be camp-sites, each occupied on a temporary basis at some time during the long period from 6000 – 2000 B.C. The small groups of mesolithic folk earned a bare subsistence from the sea by fishing, and from the forested interior by collecting nuts, berries, wild fruit, and by hunting. Hides would be worked to provide not only clothing but covering for their rude temporary shelters. All this is deduced from flint remains by archaeologists, who as they re-examine the evidence, continue to revise their estimates of dates and the significance of the finds.

Pastoral and arable farming was a feature of the New Stone Age which spread northwards through Britain after 3000 B.C. No traces of such neolithic presence have been found in this immediate area, but it has been guessed that in course of time mesolithic people became more settled, learning to raise crops, herd domesticated animals, weave woollen clothing, and engage in trade. Certainly by 1000 B.C. a permanently-settled community is confirmed by discovery of a Bronze Age cemetery at Whiteside with urns containing cremated remains, and at Monktonhill other urns containing human bones. In this low-lying area there were no Iron Age forts such as those on some upland sites in the neighbourhood, which mark the immigration of Celtic people in the first century B.C. But there is evidence of continued local occupation on a series of sites, whose age cannot be dated, each with an enclosure of some kind, several encircled by a palisade, one at Nethermuir containing remains of a timbered homestead.

The first thousand years of the Christian era include what have been termed the Dark Ages. There are some written records, but these are sparse, incomplete, and unreliable. What was happening in this part of the world is conjectured from stray references made by persons who lived far away, sometimes at a much later date. Among the Celtic people whom the Romans called Britons were the Damnonii who inhabited the west of Scotland. But little credence can be placed on the assertion by an 18th century minister that Julius Agricola sent Roman forces here "with a view of invading Ireland"; and the so-called "Roman Bridge" over the Pow Burn is of much more recent date. The Welsh-speaking Damnonii formed what was the kingdom of Strathclyde, which was exposed to attack by several enemies: the Novantae of Galloway who also were Welsh-speaking Britons; the Gaelic-speaking Scots from Ireland and those of them who established their kingdom of Dalriada in Argyll and adjacent territories; the Anglians, Teutonic people speaking Old English who crossed the North Sea to form on the east coast between the Humber and the Forth their kingdom of Northumbria; and later from across the sea came Viking raiders. We can conjecture peaceful immigration as well as warlike invasions. Christianity was introduced, with missionaries from Whithorn in Galloway, from Ireland direct, from Iona in Dalriada, and from Lindisfarne in Northumbria.

The name Prestwick is derived from Old English *preost wic* (or *preosta wic*), the

St Cuthbert's Church at Monkton originated as a chapel set up in the 8th century by priests from Lindisfarne, after whom the place was named Prestwick. Parts of the surviving building date from the 13th century. (*KA*)

habitation of a priest (or priests), and belongs to a series of place-names which must have originated about the 8th century. A near-contemporary Northumbrian chronicle records that Edbert of Northumbria in the year 750 added to his kingdom the plain of Kyle, and other districts. It would appear likely that church-men arrived here during the subsequent brief period of Northumbrian ascendancy, and the land they were granted was then given the name Prestwick. Their church was the one which was then or later dedicated to St Cuthbert. Cuthbert (c.631 – 687) was a monk at Melrose who ministered there and in other parts of Northumbria. He was buried on Lindisfarne, and his cult became widespread in the 8th century. It would seem safe to conclude that the priests who gave Prestwick its name came from Lindisfarne, arrived shortly after the year 750, and dedicated to St Cuthbert the little church they erected on the rising ground north of the Pow Burn.

Northumbria's westwards expansion was shortlived, and before the end of the 8th century Kyle was again part of the kingdom of Strathclyde. But a new threat came from Viking invasions of the British Isles. Their first raid on Lindisfarne came in 793. Iona was sacked in 795, 802, and 806. Attacks were followed by settlement. In the 9th century Danish dynasties were set up in the Hebrides, Ireland, Galloway, and Northumbria. Conflict continued between the rival states. In 870 a Danish fleet from Dublin sailed up the Firth of Clyde, after a four-month siege took Dumbarton, capital of Strathclyde, and carried off a great host of prisoners in two hundred longships. It is unlikely that the Ayrshire coast was undisturbed.

Viking pressures forced the Scots of Dalriada into union with their Pictish neighbours during Kenneth Macalpin's reign (840 – 858). The kings of that Scottish kingdom exerted influence over the kingdom of Strathclyde, which from 889 became a satellite state, ruled by members of the Scottish royal family. Kenneth II, King of Scots (971 – 995), extended Strathclyde to include Cumbria, which was held for nearly two centuries; and he also asserted control over the Lothians and the east coast as far south as Berwick. Scottish ascendancy there was confirmed by Malcolm II (1005 – 34) through victory at Carham c.1016. In that battle there was killed Malcolm's cousin Owen who was king of Strathclyde. He was succeeded by Malcolm's grandson Duncan, who when he inherited the Scottish crown in 1034 incorporated Strathclyde in the kingdom of Scotland. The reigns of Macbeth (1040 – 57), Malcolm III (1057 – 93), and their immediate successors continued a period of confused dynastic struggles, and conflict with their southern neighbours in what now formed the kingdom of England. In the troubled time of the later Dark Ages we can only guess at local circumstances. Dundonald may have taken its name from a fortification made by one of several Donalds who ruled over Strathclyde in the 9th and 10th centuries, or from an unknown sub-king of Kyle who bore that name. Perhaps it was that Donald who was king of Strathclyde during an English invasion in 945. Everyday life always continued, with people fishing, farming, and trading. But this was not a period when burghs were created, at Prestwick or anywhere else in Scotland.

Royal control was asserted over what was still a tribal kingdom during the reigns of Malcolm III's younger son David I (1124 – 53), and the latter's grandsons Malcolm IV (1153 – 65) and William the Lion (1165 – 1214). To institute a feudal system similar to that imposed upon England following the Norman conquest of England in 1066, these kings invited into Scotland land-hungry military adventurers from England and the Continent. They were granted estates on which they and their dependents settled, building wooden castles on natural or artificial mottes. As vassals of the king they provided him with military support as required, assisted in bringing under effective royal control outlying parts of the kingdom, and undertaking administrative and judicial duties. That is how it happened in this locality.

During the reign of David I, about 1136 a Breton called Walter, son of Alan, otherwise Walter Fitzalan, was appointed Steward of the Royal Household, making him progenitor of the Stewart family. To Walter was granted Renfrew, Paisley, and adjoining lands on the south bank of the lower Clyde; also that part of Kyle bounded on the north by the River Irvine and on the south by the River Ayr and its tributary waters of Lugar and Glenmuir. David I also transferred to Walter his own burgh of Renfrew, one of the eighteen king's burghs newly established in the first half of the 12th century. It would seem reasonable to suppose that Walter, though having Dundonald as a fortified site, preferred to create at Prestwick a

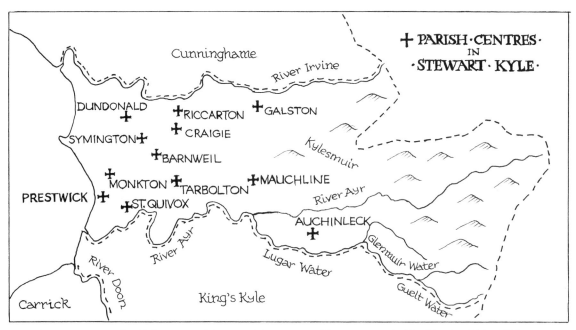

Stewart Kyle: In the 12th century this part of the county of Ayr was awarded by King David I to Walter Fitzalan the High Steward and became known as Stewart Kyle. Walter made Dundonald Castle his local residence and established Prestwick as head burgh of Stewart Kyle. Kylesmuir was donated by Walter to the monks of Melrose, who made Mauchline their local headquarters. Monkton and part of St Quivox were granted to Paisley Abbey, and the Red Friars became established at Fail near Barnweil.

burgh of his own to serve as judicial headquarters of his bailiery, which was called Walter's Kyle and later Stewart Kyle. If Walter had a formal charter creating Prestwick burgh it did not survive. The foundation must have been some years after 1136, when Walter came to Scotland; and before 1173, for in a document drawn up sometime between 1165 and 1173 he mentions "my burgh of Prestwick". It is impossible to be more precise than date the origin of Prestwick burgh to the middle of the 12th century, which is a respectable antiquity. There were then fewer than thirty burghs in all Scotland, and Prestwick was the earliest on the west coast.

While the kingdom was being feudalised, there were parallel developments in ecclesiastical organisation. Christianity in Scotland derived from various sources, and this for long influenced the character of individual places of worship, which might be dedicated to saints from Whithorn, Iona, Lindisfarne, Ireland, or elsewhere. Uniformity and orthodoxy were brought about by the bishop of Glasgow, whose diocese covered the same area as the former kingdom of Strathclyde. The bishop of Glasgow in 1114 is recorded as holding church lands in Kyle – Sanchar (St Quivox), Camcachecheyn (Camsiscan), and Carcleuien (Carcluie). Malcolm IV's queen (c. 1070 – 1093) had sufficient impact on religious life to earn her canonisation as Saint Margaret; the 12th century kings and their feudal followers were equally involved in enhancing the status of the church. For political purposes, they resisted English claims that the Archbishop of York had jurisdiction over the

Scottish church, to which Pope Celestine III extended his favour in 1192, confirming it as autonomous and the "special daughter" under Rome. For more pious reasons, they were generous in support for the church, developing its diocesan and parochial system, and amply providing for the monastic orders. Following the example of David I, his royal superior, Walter Fitzalan brought from Shropshire Cluniac monks who (c. 1163) set up Paisley Abbey, which his gifts of land made the richest house in western Scotland. He donated to it a tenth of the produce of all his estates save those in Kyle. Kyle was included by a series of awards, the first made soon afterwards (as recorded in that document between 1165 and 1173 which mentioned Prestwick burgh). To Paisley Abbey was given those lands of Prestwick lying between the Pow Burn and the Rumbling Burn; and its church, then called Prestwick Church, but soon to be known as Monkton. At the same time Paisley was awarded the church of "my burgh of Prestwick".

Monkton was included as one of the parish churches within the deanery of Kyle which was formed before 1175, as a division within the diocese of Glasgow. David I had enacted that such churches be maintained by teinds, the tenth part of the produce of all lands within the parish. What became known as the parish of Monkton and Prestwick included not only the local lands belonging to Paisley Abbey but also the barony of Adamton, Prestwick burgh, and Newton-upon-Ayr. Teinds from these adjoining properties, plus the rents payable by those who farmed on the church lands of Monkton, went to support Paisley Abbey, with a portion reserved for maintenance of Monkton church. This was an allocation (made in 1227) whereby the vicar of the church of St Cuthbert's should have six chalders of meal annually and altar offerings. The dedication to St Cuthbert we presume to have been made at a much earlier date, though this is the first documentary mention.

Statutes of the 13th century required that parish churches should be built of stone. The surviving ruins of Monkton church retain certain features of that date. The richly-moulded south doorway has been identified as from the early 13th century. The walls, 1.1m thick, enclosed a rectangular building 13.8m x 5.6m with later alterations. Prestwick burgh church, now also ruinous, is presumed also to have been built in the 13th century, having two moulded capitals apparently of that date. It is of comparable dimensions (13.15m x 6.05m within 1m walls) and also with later alterations. This church was dedicated to St Nicholas (as noted first in 1227). St Nicholas was a 4th century bishop of Myrna in Asia Minor, a miracle-worker whose cult became very popular in the 12th century. The Church of St Nicholas was certainly built by Walter Fitzalan, to serve his new burgh and as a place where the head courts of his bailiery might assemble. It was served by a curate, provided by the parish church of Monkton.

There were other places of worship within the parish of Monkton and Prestwick. The foundation of Kingcase is often attributed to Robert Bruce. But it gets mention in William Wallace's exploits a generation before. And on the coast nearby, Spetelcrag was listed in the Dalmilling charter (1219 x 1230). That suggests that there was a spittal (otherwise hospital, hospice, or leper-house) then as later

St Nicholas Church, the place of worship within the burgh and a meeting place for the courts of Stewart Kyle. A wooden structure in the 12th century, it was rebuilt in stone in the 13th century, and was still in use in 1834 when this drawing was made.

attached to the chapel which was dedicated to St Ninian. This raises an interesting possibility that the chapel at Kingcase might have been founded at a very early date by missionaries from Whithorn, which would make it the oldest religious site in the locality. The same Dalmilling charter indicates also the existence in the early 13th century of a chapel dedicated to St Mary, situated beside a newly-established township (*novam villam*); this, soon to become known as Newton-upon-Ayr (*Neuton juxta Are*, c.1280), remained in the possession of Walter Fitzalan and his descendants. At the opposite end of Monkton and Prestwick parish was Adamton. This was possessed in 1210 by Henry de Nes; it may originally have belonged to and taken its name from Adam, son of Gilbert, who obtained Tarbolton and some adjacent lands from Walter Fitzalan. At Adamton there may then have been a chapel, where later in 1337 a royal marriage was celebrated, and which was listed in 15th century written records as Our Lady Kirk of Kyle.

David I, who granted to Walter Fitzalan the northern part of Kyle which became Stewart Kyle, retained in his own hands the remaining part, King's Kyle, which extended as far south as the River Doon. Beyond lay Galloway, against which Malcolm IV launched a campaign in 1160. William the Lion reasserted control over that dissident province in 1177, detached Carrick from it in 1186, and for more effective command of the south-west had a royal castle erected in 1197 at Ayr. In 1205 he created his burgh of Ayr, head burgh for the sheriffdom of Ayr which was formed in 1207. This comprised Cunninghame, the bailiery north of the River Irvine granted by David I to Hugh de Morville, first hereditary constable of Scotland; Stewart Kyle now held by Walter Fitzalan's grandson and namesake; King's Kyle; and Carrick, which after 1186 was converted into an earldom, with Earl Duncan as vassal of the king. As these areas which formed Ayrshire became settled, new developments were possible in the 13th century.

Walter Fitzalan (who died in 1177) had made one other major grant by awarding to Melrose Abbey the great stretch of Kyle which extended from Mauchline to the upland eastern border of the bailiery. His grandson, who succeeded in 1204, extended that grant. This second Walter Fitzalan, "inspired by the divine instinct, since I realise that there is no zeal to compare with zeal for souls", made also the generous offer (sometime between 1219 and 1230) of Dalmilling to the Gilbertine monks of Sixhills near Lincoln. When they failed to take this up, the properties concerned were transferred to Paisley Abbey which thus acquired the church of Sanchar (St Quivox); the lands and mill of Dalmilling in that parish; the church of Dundonald and its chapels at Riccarton and Crosbie; and additional properties within the parish of Monkton and Prestwick – two tofts in Newton-upon-Ayr; the mill of Prestwick; rights of taking peat from Prestwick; and a half-share in the fisheries on the coast between Ayr and Irvine, at Wohar (by Newton-upon-Ayr), Spetelcrag (by Kingcase), Selecrag (by Troon), and opposite Irvine.

Walter's letter offering Dalmillling to the Gilbertines is particularly interesting as revealing how farming in the area had advanced. Dalmilling was stocked with 300 cows and 2,000 sheep. There were 650 acres (five ploughgates) of arable land, with corn mills to process the grain. A charter of 1280 defined the boundaries of Dalmilling with the lands of Sanchar, then held by William, son of Hugh Porter. It indicated properties separated by six-foot wide ditches; crosses erected as markers; and fields were enclosed during the growing season to protect crops from grazing animals. Farming in parts of Monkton and Prestwick must have been as well advanced. Perhaps more so, for the place names in this parish are almost universally English in origin; and lowland cultivation by the mould-board plough was introduced into this part of Scotland by those Anglians who came as colonists as distinct from the 8th century invaders. However, only the best land in Kyle was as yet farmed. Part of Ayr, Alloway, and St Quivox parishes were still wooded in the 13th century; Melrose Abbey's lands of Mauchline were almost entirely forest, providing some pasture, and only a little land fit for improvement. And, of course, there was sandy land along the coast that would long defy cultivation. In that unpromising area, the burgh of Prestwick was situated.

CHAPTER TWO

The Medieval Burgh

WHEN Walter Fitzalan decided, sometime about the middle of the 12th century, to establish a burgh at Prestwick, the plan adopted was a simple one. A coastal area of some 700 acres south of the Pow Burn was allocated – bordered to the north by the lands of Monkton which he had granted to Paisley Abbey; to the east by the lands of Sanchar (St Quivox); to the south by the lands of Newton-on-Ayr which Walter retained in his own hands. South of the Pow Burn, on a knoll dominating the surrounding plain, a church was built, probably of timber, but reconstructed in stone a century or so later. On the landward side of the church was a site suitable for settlement. It was sheltered by the sand dunes. It was near the Pow Burn, which may then have flowed more directly westward into the sea; and it was also far enough from the beach for wells to be sunk which provided a good supply of fresh water. Not far off there was soil fit for cultivation. About a furlong to the south east of the church a market place was sited, indicated by a mercat cross, originally of wood and later of stone. Between church and market was laid out a short broad straight street (*the kingis streyt*, 1470), later known as Kirk Street, along which plots of ground were available for incoming settlers. There was, perhaps at a later date, another set of plots beyond the market area, extending southwards towards and beyond the Puddock Sheugh (that little stream which flowed down the present Ladykirk Road and on past Kyle Street). Each plot within the burgh roods (*the rodis*, 1470) was here sometimes called a place (e.g. *Jok Brounyis plas*, 1470) and never a toft as elsewhere. Each place or toft was protected by a back dyke, and by the late 15th century entry into the settlement was through four gateways (*the foure portis of the toun*, 1484).

One can only guess at the location of these gateways which defined the limits of the burgh roods where the people of Prestwick lived. The first gateway must have been on that road still known as Seagate, which allowed access to the shore, and presumably also a route over the the Pow Burn towards Dundonald and Irvine. A second gateway was almost certainly on the highway which led directly from the market cross towards Monkton, and on this principal route the Pow Burn was later bridged (*Paullis brig*, 1593). The other two gateways would be at the other end of the little town, one on the route to Ayr via Kingcase and Newton-on-Ayr, the other on the equally-important route to St Quivox and the interior of Kyle. Since the area of settlement in the 15th century was still quite small, one gateway may have been on the main street at or near the Puddock Sheugh, the other on the present Crofthead Road. An alternative possibility is for a gateway further south on the Ayr

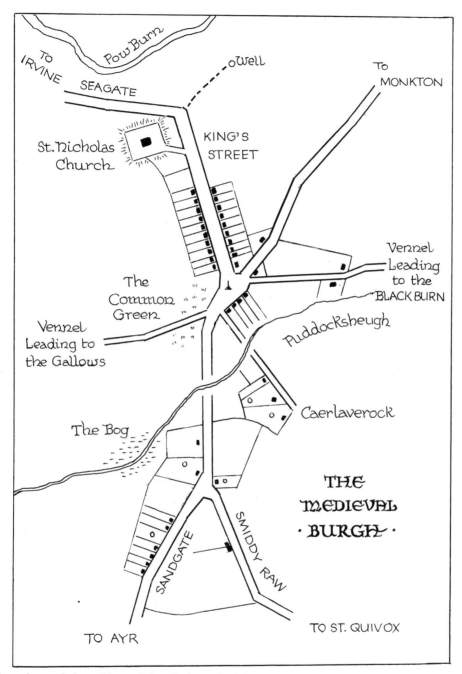

This conjectural plan of the early burgh shows the 'King's Street' laid out beside St Nicholas Church, followed by development to the south along the Sandgate. It is possible that before the burgh was formed an earlier settlement was located east of the Puddocksheugh at what was later called Caerlaverock.

road before Grangemuir Road leads to the shore, for the main street from Boyd Street as far as Grangemuir Road retained until 1904 the old name of Sandgate;

What is now called Kirk Street was the original part of the burgh. (*KA*)

the corresponding fourth gateway would be on Boyd Street, formerly called Smiddy Raw and reputed to have once been a main exit from the town. Though the four gateway ports are nowhere named in the records, they possibly bore the appropriate titles of the Seagate Port, the Monkton Port, the Sandgate Port, and the Sanchar Port. In addition to those gateways on the main thoroughfares, there were lesser outlets on lanes called vennels. There was one which passed along the line of Station Road towards the sea (*the venale, passand down to the galous*, 1470). Another (*the common venal passand doun to the furd of the burn*, 1470) was still in the 19th century called the Vennel, following Alexandra Avenue inland towards the Black Burn.

Privileges enjoyed by those who lived in a burgh would entice craftsmen and others from near and far to come to Prestwick. William of Newburgh in 1197 reported that "the towns and burghs of the Scottish realm are known to be inhabited by English"; and it is known that in some burghs there were early inhabitants who had come from the continent. We have no evidence for Prestwick before the 15th century, but it is possible to deduce the local situation during the burgh's first three centuries.

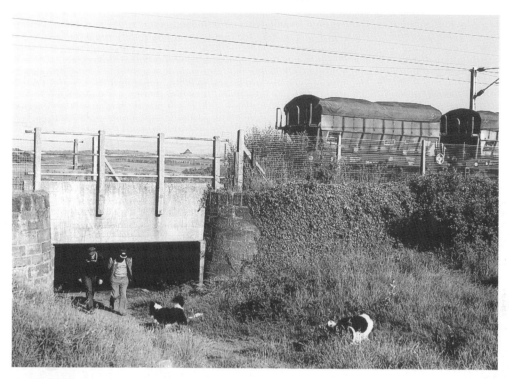

Seagate, one of the main entrances to the burgh. (*KA*)

Each incomer, awarded his toft of ground, with a frontage of some twenty feet along the main street of the burgh, would construct a turf and timber house with a thatched roof as home for his family and servants. After a year and a day he was required to pay that annual due of three pence which entitled him to be accepted as a burgess and freeman. To maintain himself and his dependents the toft included for cultivation a strip of land to the rear. In burghs sited on good agricultural land the tofts might extend for several hundred feet in length and provide sufficient subsistence; but there were variations elsewhere. When Ayr was founded in 1205 the charter allowed each burgess six acres of land in the burrowfield to supplement tofts of limited length on the infertile soil where the town was sited. At Prestwick, each toft was even more truncated, less than 100 feet in length. The sandy soil was quite unfit for productive cropping. More fertile land was available elsewhere, and brought into cultivation. These arable areas (*labourit lande*, 1470; *commoun teill land*, 1473) were situated inland beside the Black Burn; to which was added later another area on the lower reaches of the Pow Burn. The first included lands called Wra-ends and Newdykehead, eventually amounting to thirty-three acres. The second, with holm and meadow land by the ford beside Monkton hall (as Orangefield was originally named) and Burn Crook, would extend to twelve acres, 8 acres of which were located outwith the burgh, beyond the Pow Burn and at some time before 1470 annexed to be included within the "liberties of Prestwick". Such infield or indale land, manured with dung and seaweed, was cropped each year without intermission. That could be supplemented by catch crops which were taken at intervals from parts of the 300 acres of outdale or outfield land which extended along the burgh's eastern boundary. Those parts of outdale which were uncultivated in any one year, plus the remaining 300 acres of moss, waste, and sand hills, provided some pasture land. At Prestwick, the best land was remote from the town, unlike most other places where the settlement was bordered by indale land, with outdale and pasture further away.

The prime purpose of creating a burgh was for the encouragement of crafts and commerce; providing the inhabitants with sufficient land to feed themselves was a subsidiary consideration. Those who came to reside in Prestwick failed to develop a viable trading community, for reasons which must be later examined. While features of a burgh were retained, this survived as a community whose interests were largely agrarian.

Each freeman was allocated riggs within the indale and outdale lands, The indale land was divided into quarters and each burgess seems to have been allowed one rigg in each, these four roods providing him with an acre or so; supplemented by more of the less fertile outdale. There was, until 1572, a reallocation of riggs each year. Ploughing was done on a cooperative basis, since not everyone would have horses, oxen, or his own plough. Crops grown were oats, coarse barley, rye (*corn, ber, or ry*, 1476); peas (ordered to be sown, 1470); and also some flax and hemp. During the growing season, a herdsman was employed to prevent livestock encroaching upon the crops, for such dykes are there were served only to mark the boundary of the riggs. Each burgess was allowed his *soum*, that proportion of the number of beasts which the pasture was deemed able to support. As well as cattle and horses, the inhabitants kept sheep, pigs, and poultry. Some freeman would also be fishermen, and at least one (in 1562) kept bees. They were thus able to supply themselves with foodstuffs – meal, meat, fish, eggs, milk, cheese, ale, honey. Water was obtainable from St Nicholas well (1476) and the Common well (1480). Clothing and footwear could be provided from wool, linen, hemp, and hides. Peat from the moss supplied fuel. This could be supplemented (1479) by coal, which was principally used (1470) in the production of salt at the several salt-pans. One essential commodity missing was timber, for there was a lack of woodland within the burgh boundaries.

The burgh records which commence in 1470 are principally concerned with management of agrarian affairs and disputes between neighbours. Only incidentally do they reveal the existence of bakers, brewers, a few weavers, at least one tailor, shoemakers, and a blacksmith. The fragmentary annual accounts include income from stall-holders, so small as to suggest that the markets and fair were of limited importance. Beside the market cross was the tron, to provide standard weight. Dry and liquid measures held by the bailies had to be displayed at the head court (*the stoupis to be brot to se thar measour*, 1473); but these were apparently so little used that one one occasion they were mislaid and the heirs of two bailies were approached for their recovery (*refound to the towne the common pynt and the common forlot*, 1478). Again, the burgh apparently could not yet afford to build a tolbooth, for the head courts were held at the cross (1470), within the church (*apud ecclesiam de Prestwik*, 1471) where the bailiery courts were always held, sometimes outside the church (*at the kirkend*, 1472), and for several years in various dwelling houses (*in Jonat Cunyghamis hows*, 1572).

These burgh records were irregularly kept. It was not thought necessary to minute each of the head courts which were held quarterly – in September (Michaelmas), December (Yule), Easter (Pasche), and May (Beltane). Accounts were only occasionally engrossed. But it is clear that at the Michaelmas head court each year the burgh officials were chosen. Two bailies were responsible for administering justice when cases were brought before these courts. Another burgess was made the sergeand, with responsibility for burgh security (*warnyng of the toune nytly*, 1481). Two or three were appointed as cunnars to test the quality of ale brewed and fix its price. Four liners or quartermen were chosen to measure the divisions of arable land and make the annual allocation of riggs to burgesses. The bailies who originally were also responsible for the burgh finances delegated that function (from 1484) to a treasurer known as the bursar and conservator of the money of the common good. There is mention of market officials (*stentaris of the stallangearis*, 1480). An appointment was once made of a peat-seller (*sellare of common and daili of pettis*, 1481). No emoluments derived from these appointments, save for the bailies who might (1490) claim a fee of four pence daily when administering justice. There were two paid officials. One freeman was employed as clerk. One who wasn't served as the common herd, recompensed by part of the fee that all who kept beasts had to pay.

Within the burgh records are listed those statutes which were in force in 1470, and others were added from time to time. Most of these concerned regulation of agrarian operations. No one might acquire land contrary to accepted custom of the burgh, under penalty of forty shillings toward repair of the church. No one might without permission lease any part of the common land, else he would lose his burgess rights and be permanently exiled. If livestock were allowed to stray and damage a neighbour's crops, recompense had to be made. Poultry, including cocks, capons, hens, and geese, would be confiscated if they interfered with growing crops. This applied also to swine, and since they could be particularly destructive, each freeman might keep only one pig, which had to be tethered. No sheep could be kept within the town. The taking of peat was strictly controlled. Sale of peat or turf was prohibited; with heavy penalties, a fine of ten shillings and exile, a burgess for a year, others forever. Anyone who cut turf for fuel in the precincts of the town (*in the common gate within the foure portis of the toun*, 1485) would be fined (*a galoun of aile and a lafe*); and those who had dykes were required to maintain them or pay twelve pence.

Commerce was so limited in Prestwick as to require no statutes save for one regulating the quality and price of ale. A check would be made by inspectors (*ane of the cunnaris sall fill a cop of quhat pechar he plessis*) and if satisfied (*as it is availe of gudenes*) would chalk up (*calk apoun a dur*) the price as determined by that in Ayr. Ale brought in from Ayr was charged extra (*for ilke galoun thar sal be a penny allowit to the bringar hame of it*). A fine of four shillings was imposed upon those who refused inspection, and confiscation for alterating the price. Five statutes were devoted to admission of burgesses, their exemption from other courts (*lowsin of the commissioun*), the keeping of burgh accounts, and bailies' fees. One statute prohibited contact with the sick folk of Kingcase under pain of exile. Public order was protected against persistent disturbers of the peace (*thrice a tulzeour, a fechtar or a disobear within a yer*) with a fine of forty pence for each offence till the fifth which earned exile for a year and a day. For those (*rebellouris*) who flouted authority penalties varied: such burgesses might never thereafter hold office; guilty wives were fined a gallon of ale and a loaf, doubled, trebled, then at the fourth time exiled (*expellit the toune for evir mar*); guilty stallholders were permanently excluded from the town.

Just over seventy cases are reported as having come before the burgh court in the years between 1470 and 1500. Several concerned disputed occupation of land, (e.g. *the wrangwise occupacioun severaly of the brygg greyne*, 1480); straying animals, especially pigs (*wrangwis swyne in grete distroctioun to the toun*, 1477); wrongful taking of peat; overcharging for ale (*brekin of the price of hir aile eftir it was prisit be the cunnaris*, 1497). Most cases concerned theft, debt, or default of payments, and the items involved are usually so trivial as to indicate the relative poverty of the community, but interesting as providing mention of items of everyday use. Furnishings included a chest (*a kist*, 1473), a bench (1474), a sideboard (*dischburdis*, 1474), a girdle and stool for baking (*girdile and a bakstule*, 1473), wooden doors (*ii duris of tre hungin without irne*, 1474), bedclothes (*a pair of schetis*, 1479), and other domestic materials (*a cloak*, 1473; *small lynyn yarne*, 1479; *claytht wevying*, 1477; *quarteris of quhit claith*, 1499; *a quhit elne of claith extendan till elne breid and elne lyntht*, 1480). Some prices afford comparisons – eighteen shillings for three bushels of barley, nine shillings for a pot, two shillings for a pan, fourteen shillings and four pence for a horse, a shilling for a pair of shoes (1473, 1481). Thefts included a basket and sledge-cart (*creill, kar*, 1473) and removal of a hut (*a berne of twa cupile*, 1473). Kale and other garden crops were ruined by sheep from Monkton (*all the fre menis yardis, in caile, erbis, and all uthir thair gudis*, 1500). Several court cases indicate that burgesses were involved in salt making, outwith the two saltpans near Kingcase which were held (in 1470) by Thomas Crawford and his father who was laird of Previk, a small estate by the River Ayr in Tarbolton parish. There is note of interference with a tub at the pans (*Johne Simsounis saye in the pannis*, 1472); a theft (*wrangwis disponyn and sellin of Jok Clerkis salt*, 1476); and reference to a saltpan whose construction injured neighbourly relations (*Anne Kerd accusit in court Andro Walcar that he kept not hyr nychburscape, in the biggin of a salt pane hous betwix them and byrnt hir colis*, 1481).There were few offences (*strobillans of the toun*, 1473) against public order. In 1473 Sandy George accused John of Galston (*for the wrangwise cumin on him in his modderis hous without his waponis*) who made a counter-accusation (*that wrangwisli he strobbillit hym and drew his knif in Elene Georgis house and wad haf strikin hym*). Later that year Willi Jurdane caused damage to the mercat cross (*the breking of the corse*) which was probably still a wooden one. In 1474 Anne Kerd was attacked by Jok Smytht (*strak hir and distrublit hir*). In 1486 George Symsoun was threatened by Richy Cristole (*he tuk his knyf out of his scheitht*). In 1497 Jonat Adame attacked Rob Riche (*drew his bluid withoutin ony cause*) and Willi Symsoun, the common herdsman, assaulted Elene Broune (*distroyit hir gudis, and syne, quhen scho reprevit him, he kest stanys and strak hir in the hed quhil scho blede*). Other offences involved a slanderous accusation that children stole flax which was growing on someone else's pasture (*sayande hir barnis brocht ham lynt in gers of other personis,* 1473); four persons cited for anti-social behaviour (*commoun rebellouris and appressouris of that nychboris and common sclanderirs,* 1474); an unspecified breach of authority (*rebelling agane the hale communite,* 1475); and an unsupported accusation (*Johne Symsoun a oppressour of the pur pepill in the burgh,* 1477).

A particular problem arose from persons associating with the sick folk in Kingcase spittal, which was prohibited by a burgh statute. Anne Kerd and Andro Sauer were reported as going there (*reparis to Kingcas,* 1477). When the offence was repeated, it was obvious that they did so because among the leprous (*lipper*) were some of their relatives (*Andro Sauer reparis till Kingcase daily and nytly, and his wif and his barnis. Anne Kerd apoun the samyn wise, and hir seik soun, at is lipper reparis daili in hir house. Marioun Sym reparis to Kingcase apoun the samyn wise, and hir dochtir,* 1479). Andro Sauer continued daily visits to Kingcase which jeopardised public health (*abill till infect the hale toune, and weris the seik folkis clathis and bonnettis,* 1481). Later still Anne Sauer the elder, Marioun Myller, Elane Browne, and Anne Duncane were cited (*for the selling of ale and intromettin of the folkis of Kingcais agane the statutis of the towne,* 1496). Elene Broun was again accused (*that scho reparyt in Kingcas and sald thaim hir gudis and cost thar mele and thare gudis,* 1497) and found guilty, while Marioun Myllar was acquitted.

In all those court cases where guilt was proven, an unspecified fine was imposed (*unlaw* or *amerciament*), and sometimes confiscation of goods (*escheat*). On that occasion previously mentioned when four persons were found guilty of anti-social behaviour they were sentenced to exile (*that thai be banisit the toun and remuv the boundis of it withtin xxiiii houris,* 1474). But though they might never return (*nocht in tyme to cum*) three of them appear in the records within the next two years. Powers of enforcement were obviously limited. And though there was a gallows near the sands it is unlikely it was ever used save for judgements made in the bailiery court. Election to office in the burgh was not always sought, for authority exercised over neighbours was inevitably sometimes resented, One freeman was fined for threatening the sergeand (*forssit the sergeande,* 1474). A stall-holder objecting to market fees slandered various officers (*and speciali of the stentaris of the stallangearis,* 1480). One sergeand was fined (*that he defaltit in his office,* 1481), as was a successor (*for not doing his office,* 1496). The bailies were themselves accused (*the said bailies was foy takaris, and held na courtis na did na justice of thr office in the toun to the nyburis,* 1497). Bailies would continue to be abused (*injurius worddis said to our balye Jhone Gottray and strykin of hym in the executione of his office,* 1556).

The Church was an essential feature of the burgh. It was served by a curate or chaplain appointed by Paisley Abbey, The fabric of the church was the responsi-

The mercat cross, which dates from 1777, replaced earlier versions made of wood, and marked the site of weekly markets. (*KA*)

bility of the burgh council. Each new burgess paid an entry fee (*burgess fine*) of five shillings to the church as well as three shillings and fourpence to the common good of the burgh (*vs to the kirk werk of sanct Nicholas kirk in the said burgh and iiis iiiid to the commoun profat of the town*). Forty shillings towards church repair was demanded of anyone who took unauthorised possession of land, and similar penalties were probably exacted for other offences. The accounts for 1472–73 include payments for a chalice, vestments, and wax for the church. The church was enhanced by donation of altars to St Nicholas, to Our Lady, to St Andrew, and to the Holy Cross. These were supported by annual payments derived from burgesses who held certain properties. The altar to St Nicholas was most favoured, with annual payments amounting to nine shillings and fourpence, coming from two saltpans (1s each), two meadows (2s, 5s), and two *places* in the town (at 2d each), plus one pound of wax from Kingcase. Annuals for Our Lady were four shillings and four pence from eight *places* plus rent of a piece of land (*Our Lade akir liand in the bog cruk*); for St Andrew two shillings and four pence from four *places*; for the Holy Cross only tenpence from two. Pious burgesses made such donations (*of annuele yerly for evir mar*) and sixteen of the fifty-seven *places* which formed the town in 1470 were so burdened, three requiring contributions to two altars, and one to three (*Jok Broun in stat of a porciunkle of commoun land, quilk acht yerli, at the conceptioun of our lade, iid till our lade of Prestwick; iid to sanct Nicholas lycht, and iid to sanct Androis lycht in the said kirk*).

Among such annual payments were several to other chapels – three at six pence each to Our Lady Kirk of Kyle; two providing eightpence and sixpence to Our Lady Chapel of Newton. There were four Templar properties, which has inspired the mistaken belief that some of these military monks lived in Prestwick and a myth that several are buried in St Nicholas churchyard. In fact, such properties were never occupied by Templars. Their organization received financial support from the rent of certain properties in all parts of the country – a hundred of them in Ayrshire. Two of their local properties gave eighteen pence each, and two gave sixpence each. These and the Temple Acre west of the town, following the dissolution of the Order of Knights Templars in 1312, passed to the Hospitallers, the Knights of the Order of the Hospital of Saint John of Jerusalem, whose local agents (in 1474) were John Craufurd of Kilmarnock, a principal Templar bailie, and his deputy Andro Fair of Braidhurst.

The names of certain chaplains of St Nicholas Church find passing mention in the burgh records. Sr William Wallace (1470) seems to have been followed by Sr Thomas Makison (1473). Such priests were not knights – they were designated "Sir" (*Sr*) just as their successors are commonly called "Father". Others who were university graduates were entitled "Mr" (*master, magister*). It is elsewhere recorded that Makison was followed by Martin Bannatyne (1474), Bartholomew Galbraith (1474), Robert Grieve (1507), Robert Wilson (1510), possibly John McTere (1531), and Robert Leggat (before 1525). The medieval parish priest was a central figure in the community. He presided over his parishioners from baptism until burial. He celebrated the sacred festivals which punctuated the year. These provided the calendar for secular events. Head courts of the burgh were held at Pasche (Easter), Beltane (May), Michaelmas (September), and Yule (December). Crops had to protected from straying animals in the period from Our Lady's Annunciation in March till St Luke's Day in October (*Fra the anunciacioun of our lady, or fra the borow landis be sawyn quhill Luxmess or quhil the corne be innyt*). In particular, swine had to be tethered after Beltane, poultry kept in check at seed time until St John's Day in June and from Our Lady's Assumption in August until St Michael's Day in October. Peats had to be cut before St Lawrence's Day in August. Certain beasts were wintered indoors from All Hallows in October till St Patrick's Day in March. Other saints' days mentioned in the records are those of St Matthew, St Kevok, and St Thomas (*sanct Tomas day, the fayr day of Glasgow*).

Remains of St Ninian's Chapel near the south end of the burgh. (*KA*)

It is difficult to assess the size of the burgh population. 15th and 16th century burgh records include lists of freemen whose numbers range from twenty-eight to eighty. The former may fall short of the total at that time, the latter seems to include persons added at various dates. From such uncertain evidence the population in 1470 has been estimated as perhaps two hundred. At that date the town contained 49 roods on the west and 69 roods on the east, with several other plots (*porciunkles*) on either side. There were then fifty-seven holdings, seventeen of these being one rood, the others larger, with one of ten roods. It is not clear whether each rood defined a specific area of one quarter acre, or referred to original separate plots. If the latter, then the number of freemen in the first centuries of the burgh must have been much greater than by the 15th century. It is possible that many persons who came to settle in Prestwick flitted later into Ayr to enjoy the superior attractions of that thriving royal burgh, while the extinction of some families by natural or other causes also reduced the number of freemen. The fifty-seven holdings of 1470 were shared by some who had obviously extended their possessions. Twenty-eight freemen held individual plots, mostly of one or two roods. Seven other freemen held all the rest. Several of these had acquired one or two extra plots. Two men had eight plots each, some very large, and together they held in area half of the property in the town, as well as plots in the common lands. John George had his house on three roods of land on the west side of the town, where he had also 1½ roods rented to John Riche, another plot rented to Andro Sawers, and a fourth plot with the adjoining Hog Croft; on the east side he had Langcroft of six roods, a plot of four roods, another of two roods, and ten roods in life rent to Elen George. Huchoun Wallace of the Newton had eight roods and one rood on the west side, and on the east a consolidated block of six holdings which together made up seventeen roods.

Wallace of Newton was not unique in being a non-resident freeman. Others were listed as such in 1470 – John Smyth of Riccarton; Alexander Crawford of Langholm; Jock Dale of Newton; James of Blair, son of the laird of Adamton, who also appears (indistinctly) on the list. Subsequent lists include landowners like Huchoun Wallace of Smithston, son of Huchoun Wallace of Newton; George Wallace of Ellerslie; John Blair of Achindrayne, son and heir of David Blair of Adamton. There were also tenant farmers like Allan Hall in Sanquharmure; John Gref in Whiteside; John Oglaucht, Christopher Johnson, Finlay Taylor, and John Wyllie, all in Monkton. There were John McCarde in Ayr; Richard Cristell and John Symsoune, unidentified. There were four churchmen, Sr William Snelle, and three others also non-resident even though they became (at dates specified) chaplains in St Nicholas Church, Sr Robert Wilsoune (1410), Sr Marton Bannachtin (1474), and Sr Robert Gref (1507), son of the afore-mentioned John Gref.

To become a freeman was apparently an attractive proposition for those who could afford to do so. A widow, son, daughter, or son-in-law might inherit as freeman by token payment (*quhilk sall gef to the bailies and the communite the spyce and the wyne*). So in 1497 Marioun Myller who kept an ale house made an appropriate contribution (*ix galounis of aile for hir fredome*). For others to be enrolled required the considerable payment of five shillings to St Nicholas Kirk plus three shillings and fourpence to the burgh. Residence of a year and a day was a necessary preliminary to enrolment, and freemen were expected to make a home in Prestwick (*cum and duell betuex and mychelmes, or ellis bruyk na fredome*, 1549). But this requirement could not be enforced. Moneyed men from outwith Prestwick had by the end of the 15th century become freemen, bought up town plots, and derived from each an allocation of arable riggs and rights of pasture. They recompensed themselves by rents from tenants, who were not freemen, and who formed a greater part of the burgh population. The idealised picture of a kind of democratic commune of peasant landowners cannot be sustained. Much of the land had already passed into the hands of outsiders. In 1446 there was a futile complaint by some freemen (*lieges borderond with thaim occupiis wrangwyfly wyth thr katal and uthrwayis bath the common and the propyrte pertenyng to the said burgh*). That the independence of the burgh was already a fiction is indicated when David Blair of Adamton arranged the division of arable lands in 1473 (*be the command and chargis of the larde of Adametoun and the communite of Prestwik*). A year later at the head court he was appointed oversman for life, taking precedence over the two bailies. In 1487 this became a hereditary appointment when he nominated his son and heir John Blair to succeed him as oversman for life.

The burgh records include some particulars of transfer of land. On one occasion there is a clear description of the process of sasine by which a property, relinquished into the hands of the community, is bestowed to a new possessor who takes sasine, which is, literally, the seizing of earth and stone. In 1493 George Wallace of Ellerslie in Riccarton parish conveyed to John Smith, formerly in Crosbie, two roods on the north side of the town, bounded by land of his brother Alexander Wallace on the south and of Huchoun Wallace on the north. George Wallace resigned this land in the customary manner (*be staf and batoun as maner is*) into the hands of Bailie Sandy George, who then granted sasine to John Smith (*be erde and stane gaf heretable state and possessioun*). This procedure was also required when a toft was inherited, as in 1487 when the two roods of the late Will Hunter of Whiteside were conveyed to his son Rob Hunter. Two church properties within the burgh are noted as changing hands. In 1485 William Pethende, rector of Our Lady Kirk of Kyle, conveyed through the burgh bailie to Steven Synclere and his heirs a rood which had the kirkland to the north and Huchoun Wallace's to the south. In 1474 two roods in the Temple Moss were transferred from John Syncler to Willi Hunter and his heirs, sasine being granted by the Temple bailie, whose order must have held in perpetuity this part of the common lands, which were not normally available for heritable possession. Lands outwith the burgh but regarded as within the "liberties of the burgh" could be feued. In 1473 five roods of moss north of the Pow Burn, held by John George and his heirs, were bestowed upon Sr Thomas Makisoun and his heirs; to whom from Christopher Johnsone two adjoining roods were tranferred the following year. Nearby, in 1486 John Symsoun conveyed to Alexander Symsoun lands beside the Pow Burn east of Gledhill. Again, within the "liberties of the burgh", just outwith the burgh's boundary with Newton, were a meadow and moorland which in 1478 Huchoun Wallace of Smithston inherited from his late father Huchoun Wallace of Newton. Feuing of common land within the burgh was only rarely permissible. In 1487 Huchon Wallace of Smithston was granted heritable possession of one rood for operating a corn mill (*ane myll sted with water gang and dammyng*). In 1489 John Wallace of Craigie took over the saltpans, which had previously in 1470 been held by the laird of Previk and his son. To fuel them he obtained from Prestwick burgh the right to work coals in the vicinity (*fra the gallous and gallous hill of Prestwic doun to the sey proporcionaly and up fra the gallous hill to the moss*). Provided this right was exercised within three years, the grant was in perpetuity (*the said balyeis and communite haif enfeft me heretabily be chartyr and seisiing undir thar comun sele*).

For the first three centuries of the burgh there are fragmentary hints of incidents which may have inhibited its development. The establishment by William the Lion of a king's burgh at Ayr in 1205 must have had a deleterious effect on Walter Fitzalan's baronial burgh at Prestwick. The weekly markets at Ayr attracted customers from all parts of Kyle, to the disadvantage of Prestwick. The growth of manufacturing within Ayr must have persuaded craftsmen from Prestwick to flit to the more prosperous larger burgh. Ayr with its estuarine harbour could develop fishing and coastwise trade, as well as foreign commerce which its royal status allowed. Prestwick had merely an open beach.

One can guess at the local impact of successive wars. When King Haakon of Norway brought his fleet into the Firth of Clyde in 1263, Ayr was attacked, and Prestwick possibly ravaged, before the threat was removed by King Alexander III at the Battle of Largs. After that king's death in 1286 the disputed succession was followed by English occupation and the Wars of Independence. Both Wallace and Bruce had associations with Prestwick.

A tale of Wallace's Dream in Monkton Kirk was included in Blind Harry's long poetic biography. That work, written two centuries later, is sometimes historically incorrect, often fanciful, but exhibits accurate and detailed local knowledge. It is narrated that Sir Reginald Craufurd as sheriff of the county called an assembly at Monkton, attended by his nephew William Wallace. After the meeting Wallace entered the church, said his prayers, and fell asleep. In a dream, Wallace was presented with a sword by an aged man, a wand and a book by an angelic figure. When Wallace awoke the figures in his dream were interpreted as St Andrew and the Goddess of Fortune. The sword denoted strength, the wand represented power, and the book prognosticated wars for the restoration of freedom. Wallace then went with his uncle to pass the night at Crosbie. The following morning they travelled towards Ayr. At Kingcase Wallace turned back. Sir Reginald Craufurd went on to Ayr where he was killed. His death has been dated as 1297. Wallace was not created Guardian of Scotland till 1298, not earlier at Monkton as the poem suggested. Yet Blind Harry seemed familiar with the names of Wallace's local associates, and the places around. In particular he assumed that Kingcase existed before the time of Bruce, who is sometimes credited with its foundation.

Robert Bruce after becoming king as Robert I was afflicted with a skin complaint of some seriousness, and at that era all so affected were described as lepers. According to one tradition Bruce after a day's hunting fell asleep on Prestwick moor, contracted leprosy, and founded the spittal or leper-house of Kingcase. It is more likely that this institution was already in existence, known as Kilcase and Kincase before it became Kingcase. Bruce in search of relief presumably sampled the supposedly healing waters of what would become known as Bruce's Well. For the support of the lepers isolated at the spittal he certainly awarded the lands of Spittalshiels (Shields) in St Quivox and Robertlone (Loans) in Dundonald parish. Bruce was ailing when he made a pilgrimage to Whithorn early in 1329, and it may be that he then paid his visit to Kingcase, just a few months before his death.

One other local tradition is that the burgh of Newton-upon-Ayr (which was within Monkton and Prestwick parish until 1779) was created by Bruce when he held parliament in Ayr in 1315, granting burghal privileges to forty-eight persons who had distinguished themselves at the battle of Bannockburn. But if Robert I had been the founder it would have been recognised as a royal burgh. The land of Newton belonged to the Fitzalans, Stewarts as they were now known; the constitution of the new burgh was similar to that of Prestwick; so it is safe to deduce that the burgh of Newton like Prestwick was a creation of the lords of Stewart Kyle, and before that family became royal. Walter Stewart married Robert I's daughter Marjorie in 1315, died in 1327, and their son who was born in 1316 succeeded his

Bruce's Well. (*KA*)

uncle David I to become King Robert II in 1371, first of the Stewart kings. Newton must have been created a burgh by Walter between 1314 and 1327 or by Robert who followed him as lord of Stewart Kyle between 1327 and 1371. As a result, the parish of Monkton and Prestwick now contained two baronial burghs.

This was a time when the perils of war were followed by a different kind of scourge. The Black Death, an epidemic of bubonic plague, reached Scotland in 1349, and it has been calculated that one third of the Scottish population died. The creation of a burgh at Newton may have been an attempt to attract scarce labour to settle there. As far as Prestwick is concerned it seems likely that such a small community would suffer severely from the plague, resulting in what was possibly irrecoverable depopulation. There were half-a-dozen more outbreaks of bubonic plague in the next century. While danger of infection from the leprous folk at Kingcase was always a concern, special measures were required when plague was rife. Thus in 1499 trading at Prestwick might not be done except with healthy acquaintances (*kennyt and clene folk*) and a night watch was instituted, the sergeand and two other men searching the town for strangers, this to continue until the plague disappeared, and at least until Yule (*quhill the plaig ces and speciali quhill yule*). Similar epidemics would recur for the next two centuries, certainly with considerable loss of life on some occasions. A presumed reduction of the population in the 14th and 15th centuries may have left vacant plots in Prestwick, an opportunity for surviving freemen to obtain additional roods, and for neighbouring landlords to acquire a stake in the burgh.

Another threat which emerged towards the end of the 14th century was the blowing of sand, occasioned by heavy western gales. This seriously affected Ayr (*Dum noster burgus de Air, per motionem et agitationem arenae sit quasi totaliter annihilatus et destructus*, 1380), Prestwick must have suffered similar inundations, which would wreak havoc, on the western side of the town especially, burying fertile soil beneath layers of sand, and perhaps diverting the course of the Pow Burn. The local impact of other climatic effects is not easy to assess. It has been calculated that average temperatures which were high from the 9th till the 13th century thereafter declined, and there were also years of heavy rainfall that brought bad harvests and famine conditions. By the 15th century winters had become long and severe, summers short and cool, and western Europe would endure this climatic phase for more than three centuries. In Scotland it had been possible to grow sufficient crops to maintain large herds of cattle, so that meat and dairy products were the

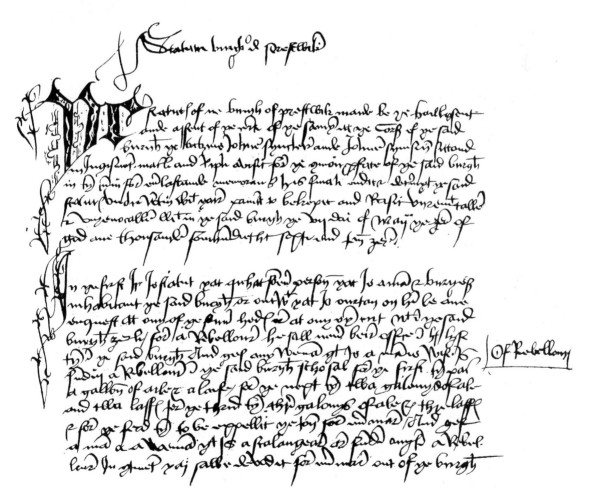

A page from the burgh records which portray local life in and after 1470.

25

principal items of everyday diet; by the 16th century it became necessary to concentrate on growing grain for human consumption rather than for fattening cattle, and so a national diet based upon oatmeal became prevalent.

Wars and threats of war with England must have been a constant concern. Such may have occasioned a panic in 1481 (*anentis the Inglis men*) when a night watch was ordered (*the kingis statute anentis the warning of the toune nytly*) but inefficiently implemented (*Andro Sauer sergeand that he defaltit in his office*). Political uncertainties, recurring pestilence, and natural disasters punctuated the history of the medieval burgh.

CHAPTER THREE

The 16th Century

LIFE in 16th century Scotland was disturbed for a variety of reasons. Among these there was one which particularly affected the little burgh of Prestwick. Throughout the century it suffered from interference in its affairs, and an attempt by the freemen to assert their independence proved ineffective.

Prestwick burgh was brought under control of a neighbouring laird in 1474 when David Blair of Adamton was appointed oversman for life. In 1487 this was made a hereditary appointment when he nominated as successor his son and heir John Blair, who continued as oversman till his death sometime between 1510 and 1514. After an interval, his son David Blair was made freeman in 1523, became oversman from 1533 till he died in 1540; his son David Blair followed from then till 1570. Thus for eighty years, from 1474 till 1514 and from 1531 till 1570, the principal post in the burgh was occupied by successive lairds of Adamton.

Adamton was acquired in the 14th century by James Blair of Blair in the parish of Dalry, whose possession in the year 1363 is recorded. That north Ayrshire family had been rewarded for support of Bruce by some grants of forfeited properties. It may be that Adamton was thus obtained by the Blair family. If not a direct grant from Robert I, then perhaps it came from his son David II (1329 – 71) or most likely from Robert the Steward who would succeed as Robert II (1371 – 90). As Steward from 1327 till 1371, he was lord of Stewart Kyle, and in or about 1347 he was married to Elizabeth Mure of Rowallan "by Roger McAdame, priest of our Lady Marie's Chapel", which has been identified as Our Lady Kirk of Kyle. After becoming king, he elevated Irvine to become a royal burgh, and spent his last years at Dundonald Castle, where he died in 1390. John Blair, second son of John Blair of Blair, was laird of Adamton by that year, when his name is noted as holding lands which included the chapel at Ladykirk (*terras de Adamtoun in baronia de Kile-Stewart, vic. Are, unacum advocatione capelle B.V.M. de la Grace in communi pastura dict. terrarum situate*). This chapel found mention in a letter of 1446 to the Pope: "the chapel of St Marie the Virgin of Adamton, called St. Mary Grace, because of many miracles through the merits of the Virgin. A multitude resort to it daily." The chapel at Adamton enjoyed the patronage of successive kings. James IV, on his frequent pilgrimages to Whithorn, regularly visited Lady Kirk and was generous in his gifts. In 1497 he gave 13 shillings to "Our Lady Kirk of Grace", later in that year provided £5 for its priests to offer "messis for the King", with a further 16 pence for "the poor folkis at our Lady Kirk of Kyle". The lairds of Adamton seemed well situated and firmly established. John Blair, second laird, built a town-house in Ayr. David Blair, third laird, was alderman of Ayr in 1480 and became first oversman of Prestwick in 1484. Succeeding generations of the family maintained themselves within the parish of Monkton until the eighteenth century. But younger sons had to seek a living elsewhere. And the Blairs failed to prevent the rival Wallace family from eventually displacing them as oversmen of the burgh of Prestwick.

John Wallace of Riccarton in 1371 married Margaret Lindsay, heiress of Craigie, and settled in that parish. He or one of his successors became Bailie of Kyle Stewart, and holding this as a hereditary post the Wallaces of Craigie as chief local representatives of the crown became dominant local landowners with branches of the family possessing properties throughout central Ayrshire. In particular they early asserted influence over the burgh of Newton-upon-Ayr, later claiming to have built and occupied Newton Castle since the year 1400. In 1452 Hugh Wallace of Smithston in the parish of Tarbolton obtained possession of the spittal house of Kingcase and the lands of Spittalscheils, being appointed as Hospitaller, which entitled him to rents from which he paid eight marks and sixteen threaves of straw for the maintenance of inmates at the spittal. By 1470 Huchoun Wallace of Newton (perhaps the same person) had become a principal holder of property within Prestwick burgh. In 1487 another of the same name (perhaps a son), proprietor of Smithston, obtained a rood of land in Prestwick to establish a corn mill. In 1489 John Wallace of Craigie obtained a lease to work coals near Kingcase; among the witnesses were his brothers Hugh, Adam, and Matthew Wallace, and another Hew Wallace of Newton. Despite difficulties interpreting the Wallace geneaology, it is clear that by the beginning of the 16th century the family was well established within Prestwick burgh.

Confusion following the disastrous battle of Flodden in 1513 allowed Wallaces temporarily to replace Blairs as oversmen of the burgh. Beside King James IV there died in battle a considerable number of Ayrshire lairds. Among them was a John Blair, perhaps the laird of Adamton rather than his kinsman who had recently acquired Middle Auchindrane in Maybole parish. In any case his son David Blair who succeeded to the estate about this time was a minor, who was not admitted as freeman of Prestwick until ten years later. John Wallace of Craigie was another who was killed at Flodden. He was succeeded by his brother Adam Wallace, who as Bailie of Stewart Kyle took over the post as oversman of Prestwick in conjunction with his namesake Adam Wallace of Newton. The following year this second Adam Wallace established personal control over the area. He was already master of Newton. In 1515 he was appointed oversman for life in Prestwick. Also in 1515 he was made alderman of Ayr and remained in charge of the royal burgh for the next decade. In 1516 he received Kingcase from his brother Hugh.

But upset came during the reign of James V (1513 – 42). In his early troubled years local rivalries became intermixed with nationwide conspiracies. The Wallace family became involved in the Ayrshire feud between Campbells and Kennedys. In September 1527 Gilbert Kennedy, 2nd Earl of Cassillis, returning home from Edinburgh, was ambushed and killed when passing through the sandhills of Prestwick. Sir Hugh Campbell of Loudoun, Sheriff of Ayr, was implicated; it was

Newton-upon-Ayr remained part of Monkton and Prestwick parish until 1779, and Newton Castle was held by Wallaces of Craigie who competed with Blairs of Adamton for control over the burgh of Prestwick from the 15th until the 18th century.

alleged that the assassination was planned by his wife Dame Isabella Wallace; and Adam Wallace of Newton was among the accomplices. On 3 December 1527 at the Prestwick Head Court it was reported that he and his supporters were facing criticism (*rabakin the ovirsman and balyeis behynd thar bakis*). Adam Wallace would continue to be an influential man, promoting coal mining at Alloway in 1528 and reappointed alderman of Ayr 1530 – 33. But he lost control over Prestwick. In 1533 David Blair of Adamton was chosen as oversman for one year, after which he was reappointed for three years, and this pattern was continued. When he died he was succeeded in 1541 by his son, another David Blair. That year John Wallace of Menfurd and James Blair of Auchindrane were appointed as his deputies; the following year that Wallace nominee was excluded and David and James Blair operated as joint oversmen till the latter died at the Battle of Pinkie in 1544. Next year David Blair was appointed for three years; and annually thereafter until 1570.

Meantime there were continuing difficulties for the Wallaces. Their ascendancy in Kyle was facing a challenge from Sir William Hamilton of Sanquhar. The eldest son of John Hamilton of Macnairston in the parish of Ayr, he entered royal service and there gained prestige, power, and wealth. In 1516 he married Katherine Kennedy, daughter of the 1st Earl of Cassillis. They made their country home at Barbieston in the parish of Dalrymple. In 1527 he acquired lands in St Quivox parish, and thereafter other properties throughout Ayrshire. From Adam Wallace he obtained Newton Castle and Kingcase. All these were in 1540 erected by royal charter into the barony of Sanquhar-Hamilton. Newton Castle became the "tower and place of Sanquhar-Hamilton". From there Sir William exercised control over Ayr as alderman between 1539 and 1543 and, taking the new title of provost, from 1547 until his death in 1560. Conflict between Hamilton and the Wallaces may have commenced with the assassination of his brother-in-law in 1527; there was a dispute regarding boundaries between St Quivox and Prestwick in 1530 when Adam Wallace was oversman; and a quarrel of some sort in 1548 between Hamilton and John Wallace, tutor of Craigie. On 17 November 1559 John Wallace of Craigie and some forty followers occupied Newton Castle. This was recovered and possessed by Sir William's heirs until 1584 when this and other Hamilton properties were acquired by James Stewart, Earl of Arran.

Wallace fortunes revived after the death of Sir William Hamilton in 1560. John Wallace, who in 1570 succeeded his father as laird of Craigie, had himself elected the following year as oversman and provost of Prestwick. When the Earl of Arran lost his power as Lord High Chancellor and his properties were escheated, Wallace benefited. He acquired the Hamilton lands in St Quivox, recovered Kingcase, obtained possession of Newton Castle in 1588, and inherited properties in Newton and Prestwick which had belonged to James Wallace of Newton, last of that cadet branch of the family. He became involved in various feuds and legal disputes. Though he continued as oversman of Prestwick till 1592, it seems clear that his control was not absolute, for he would be challenged in the last years of the century.

During the reign of Mary (1542 – 67) and James VI (1567 – 1625) the church was transformed. The Reformation was the result of religious, economic, and political factors. Criticism of church doctrines was expressed as early as 1494 by a number of lairds known as the Lollards of Kyle. In 1533 opposition was demonstrated in Ayr to what was regarded as idolatry. During the next two decades the reformers George Wishart and John Knox undertook preaching tours in Kyle. As well as criticism of church doctrine there was dissatisfaction at secularism within the church, and in particular the wealth of some churchmen. Parishioners were required to pay teinds, a tenth-part of their produce, towards support of the church, and this became especially burdensome because of inflation. Meanwhile some lairds were in process of securing possession of church lands and their revenues. In 1545 John Hamilton, abbot of Paisley, feued to his kinsman David Hamilton of Bothwellhaugh the land of Monktonmains. In 1553 the abbot's nephew Claud Hamilton, ten-year-old son of the Duke of Chatelherault, was made commendator of the abbey and later acquired all its revenues. Wallace of Craigie was made bailie for Monkton and all other Paisley lands in Ayrshire. Political events of the 1550s precipitated a crisis. The young queen was in France, and her mother Mary of Guise as regent was extending French influence in Scotland. Among the Scots magnates was formed an anti-French opposition which became pro-English and also anti-catholic. In 1560 these Lords of the Congregation took control and protestantism was formally recognised.

A few early 16th century events find an echo in the local record. In 1522 when a Scottish raid on the Solway was organised, the inhabitants of Prestwick were mobilised on 31 July, ordered to be equipped for fighting (*bodyn*) in eight days' time (*that al the induellaris wythin the burghe, baitht fre and unfre, be reddele bodyn wythin aucht dais*). Some years later two men who had been on that campaign disputed ownership of a horse (*ane gray meyr of his at the raid of Soulway bygane*, 1531). By 1542, at the time of the later battle of Solway Moss, Ayrshiremen were apparently showing little enthusiasm for continuing war with England. In 1545 when there was a further call to arms, Bailie John Miller was deprived of his rights as a burgess of Prestwick for refusing to contribute towards the king's wars (*he has dissabeyyt his*

Our Lady Kirk of Kyle: its remains etched by Robert Bryden.

ovirsman and comunitie in special at he wald not geyf thame thyr comoun geyr to sustene the kyngis weris). There are no references in the burgh records to suggest that such a political protest involved matters of religion. But the widespread enthusiasm for ecclesiastical change which was affecting people in Ayr and inland Kyle presumably extended to Prestwick. The sole index of local opinion is that the last priest to occupy St Nicholas Church in Prestwick became its first protestant pastor.

Robert Leggat first appears in 1524 as a chaplain witnessing a contract made in Ayr by Adam Wallace of Newton. At various other places he later performed a similar duty for Wallace, suggesting he may have been his private chaplain and clerk. As oversman of Prestwick Adam Wallace may have engineered the installation of Leggat as curate of Prestwick sometime before October 1525. Leggat also became clerk of the Prestwick burgh court, recorded as such in October 1528 and retaining that post for forty-two years. In 1530, when his ageing patron Adam Wallace was losing control over the burgh, Leggat had a serious dispute with Bailie George Simpson (*concerning the wounding of said George and effusion of his blood accidentally, committed between them*); and Simpson was resentful (*expressly confessed that he never wished to be nor could be in friendship with Sir Robert, nor reconciled in any way with him*). Dr Margaret Sanderson, who has made a particular study of Leggat's career, when listing a curate's duties reminds us that some of these could made him unpopular. Such were "enjoining confession and meting out penance just before the Easter communion"; reminding them "almost simultaneously, of the Easter offerings (which) did nothing to create a cooperative mood"; and "carrying out disciplinary measures against parishioners" which might involve 'letters of cursing' and even excommunication for those defaulting in payments to the church.

In October 1544, the year when George Wishart was preaching reformed doctrines throughout Ayrshire, Leggat was for some unexplained reason replaced as burgh clerk for one year by the curate of Monkton, Sr David Neill. Then in 1548 Leggat was appointed as vicar of the Church of St John in Ayr. Both the rector and the vicar of such a church derived their fees from the teinds; they were seldom if ever required to officiate, delegating their duties to poorly-paid curates. Leggat, now vicar of Ayr as well as curate of Prestwick, was personally benefiting from the much-criticised abuse of pluralism. He could, however, devote some time to both of his parishes by residing in Newton, in a house on the east side of the main street. In May 1558 when Ayr town council was actively sponsoring protestantism, Leggat replaced Sr Richard Miller, the Ayr curate who was unwilling to cooperate. He thus became vicar-curate of Ayr, and retained that post when in 1559 the local protestant congregation chose as the burgh's first protestant minister, Christopher Goodman, an Englishman who had been with John Knox in Geneva.

When the reformed Church was formally established in Scotland in 1560, parishes were where possible staffed by priests who were prepared to conform. Robert Leggat continued at St Nicholas kirk in Prestwick. Sr David Neill who had in 1556 or 1557 left Monkton for Largs, became Protestant reader there. At St Cuthbert's in Monkton, Neill was succeeded as curate in 1557 by John Wylie who was preceptor of Our Lady Kirk of Kyle, and continued to minister at Monkton after 1560. Financial provision for the clergy of the reformed church proved awkward. In 1562 it was decreed that those who held benefices within the old church might retain life-rent of two-thirds of their emoluments, which left only one third for maintenance of the those appointed to charges within the reformed church. Leggat continued to receive two-thirds of the vicarage fees of Ayr. But his salary as curate of Prestwick, previously paid by Paisley Abbey, may not have been continued. Prestwick burgh seems to have taken pity on him, for in 1562 he was given the special privilege in taking peat (*for al days of his lyftyme*). Robert Leggat remained at Prestwick till his death in 1571, and was until shortly before the end also burgh clerk, making his last entry in the burgh records in October 1570. During the last year of his life there were two notable but apparently unrelated local incidents. In August 1571 John Mure, kinsman of Mure of Rowallan, riding from Ayr was slain at the well near the kirk of Prestwick by a party of the Boyd family from Kilmarnock. In November 1571 John Wallace of Craigie superseded David Blair of Adamton to become oversman of Prestwick.

Though kirk sessions were formed in or around 1560, more than twenty years passed before presbyteries were constituted. The Presbytery of Ayr, one of the early ones, was established in 1581. Until then, superintendence was exercised as in 1565 when the minister of Perth was appointed "to visit the Kirks and Schools of Kyle, Carrick, and Cunninghame, and to remove or suspend ministers or readers as he found them offensive or incapable". In the burgh records the clerk continued to designate himself as Sr Robert Leggat, once calling himself minister (1570) as he did with Wylie (*mynister in the kyrk of Monktoune*, 1563). Each however may well have been a reader or assistant minister, competent to conduct protestant worship but debarred from celebrating communion and other sacramants. Dr Sanderson has indicated that "where ministers were few and the incumbent was the former parish priest or other cleric familiar with the parish, who already knew his parishioners well, these official rules were sometimes breached; people were grateful for the prompt service of a pastor in the matters of marriage, baptism and burial, especially if he was already known to the family." She concludes of Robert Leggat that "his continuous local service does much to redeem and perhaps helps to qualify the reputation of the sometimes maligned parish curate".

In 1571 after Leggat's death, John Wylie who was in charge of Monkton took over Prestwick as well, and probably from this time dates the long-continued practice of services at St Cuthbert's church for two Sundays in succession and at St Nicholas each third Sunday. In 1575 John Nisbet, a qualified minister, was put in charge of the parishes of Tarbolton, Barnweil, St Quivox, Monkton and Prestwick, in each of which there was a reader, John Wylie continuing in this capacity till 1591. The parish of Monkton and Prestwick thereafter was served by fully-qualified graduate protestant ministers: Ninian Young (c.1594 – 98) then Claud Hamilton (1599 – 1613).

While the parishes were thus served, most of the other religious foundations ceased to function. Nothing more is heard of St Mary's chapel at Newton, whose inhabitants became parishioners of Monkton and Prestwick. Kingcase survived as a spitttal with latterly eight inmates lodged in huts beside the disused chapel, and Wallace of Craigie possessing its lands. Similarly Our Lady Kirk of Kyle was abandoned; its lands were acquired sometime before 1597 by James Blair, possibly a younger son of Adamton; Ladykirk thus became a separate estate, whose owners continued to include in their charters patronage of the former chapel. As for the lands of Monkton which were possessed by Paisley Abbey, these were in 1587 converted into a temporal lordship held by Lord Claud Hamilton, who was entitled to rents, teinds, and all other dues previously belonging to the abbey. Burgesses of Prestwick who innocently hoped that annual dues were no longer required when a chapel ceased to operate were disabused (*Sr Jhone Wyle to be obeyt of his anuell pertenand to our Lady kyrk in Kyll of al termys bygane*, 1565). They also found discipline being enforced by the reformed church, whose kirk session collaborated with the civil authority. In 1565 when Gilbert Henderson slandered Sandy Knight and his wife, the burgh court required public penitence (*orderis hym to cum apone sonday next to cum befor the congregatione and ask hyr and hyr husband bayth forgefnes apone his kneys*). The following year he was again in trouble, accused by William Wylie of assault (*dinging and hurting of him and his wyif*), and sentenced to appear dressed only in his shirt (*apone sonday cum viii days to cum to the kyrk sakalane*).

The burgh records throughout the 16th century continue to list a variety of misdemeanours. There were thieves and thieving (*pikaris*, 1521, 1525; *spuilzie*, 1593). The disturbed times required each burgess who possessed a horse to equip himself with a choice of weapons (*steyl banot and ane stot staf, or ane pow axe, suerd and buklar*, 1561). Yet there is evidence that despite such difficulties, Prestwick this century was enjoying a limited economic progress.

Efforts were being made to increase the productivity of the arable lands. The use of lime to counteract soil acidity was becoming common in Ayrshire. In 1584 Michael Wallace of Cunning Park took a lease to quarry lime and limestones within the bounds of Prestwick. As fertiliser, seaweed seems to have been increasingly used. So much so that in 1545 for the first time a statute had to be enacted restricting the collection of wrack (*na man sal medin wrek at the se syd quhyll the sun be rasen in the morneyn*), and there were further limitations imposed in 1554, 1567, 1568, 1570, 1586, 1594, 1597, 1600, and 1601. There were similar constraints on taking of peat, which suggests that the supplies were proving inadequate for a population which this century may have increased to three or four hundred inhabitants.

Cultivation of arable land benefited from abandonment of annual allocation of plots in 1572 in favour of occupation for nineteen years (*ilk daill to be set in tak for the space of nyntene yeris*). This allowed each freeman to initiate improvements for his own profit in subsequent years. It also persuaded him to take more pains in constructing dykes (*for sawete of theyr awin stufe and keiping gud nyburheid*). Mention of various corn mills in the vicinity indicates that grain crops were substantial. There was Monktonmiln, otherwise the monks' mill of Monkton, which served the farms which had belonged to Paisley Abbey. It was powered by the Pow Burn before it changed its course, perhaps in the early 14th century; after which it was for a time fed by an "ancient aqueduct" which brought water through Adamton estate (*trahendi aquam per terras de Adamton ... ad molendinum dictorum monachorum de Monkton, per antiquum aqueductum*, 1390, 1396). There was also the Pow mill, which was probably that Prestwick mill which was awarded in the 13th century by Walter Fitzalan for support of the projected settlement of Gilbertine monks at Dalmilling, then transferred by him to Paisley Abbey. This mill would be the one held by Hugh Wallace in 1487 and occupied by Adam Leppar in 1510. It was joined by a second mill held by Mertyn Myllar (*myllar of the new myll of Prestwik*, 1514). There were others further up the Pow Burn, at Shaw farm (*the myl of Prestwikschawis*, 1562, also known as *the Sand mill*, 1774) and certainly later the Adamton mill near Brieryside, as well as Helenton and Heugh mills outwith this parish. In the 17th century additional facilities were provided by a windmill erected on an elevated site above Monkton village. Grazing for animals was proving awkward. There were repeated complaints against enclosures on the pasture land (*hirsels*). It was difficult to maintain the practice of a stipulated number of beasts, all under the care of a common herdsman (*ane comone hyrd yerle feyt ... and the comone gers to be somyt ... and na by hyrsalis to be halden*, 1560).

It may be that Leggat as burgh clerk was more precise than his predecessors;

From the 16th century coal was worked near Bellrock in deep quarries, now filled with water. (*KA*)

certainly the records he kept give passing mention to a wider range of beasts – a black cow and stirk (1511), a farrow cow and a milk cow (1514), oxen (1523, 1534); a grey mare (1534) a scabbed horse (1541), a black horse (1565); and pigs continued to be a nuisance, especially in 1527 when they found their way into the kirkyard. Surplus cattle were slaughtered each November at Martinmas to provide salt beef (*twa martis of salt beiff*, 1575) and the hides could be sold in Ayr (*price of ylk hyde viii s*, 1549). There is mention of implements – a spade (*speid*, 1507), a plough (*plewch*, 1556) and harrows (1511); baskets for carrying peat (*crells of pettis*, 1509), barrows with one wheel (*trinnyll of ane quheybarow*, 1513), cars which were sledges, and at least one which was wheeled (*a pair of car quhelys*, 1501). Theft of a net (*deppyne*, 1521) indicates some fishing. There seems to have been some increase in textile manufacture – as suggested by note of various materials (*iii quartaris of woll*, 1570; *twa pund of lint and twa pound of hemp*, 1575), preparation of flax (*lynt of the wattir*, 1512), spinning (*ane speneyn quheyl*, 1566), laying of yarn in a trough (*ane warpene fat*, 1565), weaving (*ane wovin luyme wyth al graith at pertenis to the said lwym*, 1535), waulking (*wouk wark*, 1507), and a variety of finished products (*ane wob of leneyn claith*, 1541; *ane tannyn hayk of claith*, 1541; *tuay sekis of tuyll*, 1561; *ane wob of blew clayth contenand viii ellis*, 1570; *ane wyndou clayth*, 1570).

There was certainly an extension of coal-working. Michael Wallace of Wasfurd the oversman obtained in 1576 a nineteen-year lease for taking out coals from beside the salt-pans (*the coilheuch besyd the panis*). No one else might work coal within

Prestwick, which gave him a monopoly for unspecified twice-yearly payments. In 1584 his son and heir, Michael Wallace of Cunning Park (formerly provost of Ayr), took over the working of coal, and also the right to quarry stone and lime (*querrel and querrel stanis, lyme and lyme stanis*) for the remaining eleven years of the lease, paying forty shillings yearly. One further example of progress was construction of a bridge, possibly in the 15th century (*brygge greyne*, 1480), certainly a century later (*Paullis brig*, 1594). This would replace a ford across the Prestwick burn, which was becoming known as the Pow burn (*poll* or *pow*, a slow-moving ditch-like stream).

There was an affluence which was not earlier apparent. More currency was circulating (*unicornis, crownis, grottis*, 1523; *merks*, 1543; *fourte pownd mony of this relme*, 1569). Jewellery and an expensive cloak and gown were inherited (*ii ryngis price xiii s iiii d, ane hayk and ane kyrtyll price xl s*, 1523). Another legacy of 1565 included a loom (*ane volene lwyme*) which was valued at 4 merks, i.e. £2 13s 4d, and worth rather more than all the rest of the items: a big pot (*ane mekyl pot*), a grain chest (*ane ark*), a table (*ane met burd*), a sideboard (*ane weschel burd*), a warping trough (*ane warpene fat*), a high stool (*ane cheyr stuyl*), and a mortar (*ane morter stane*). Other items appeared in the records (*ii hoghed of wyne*, 1562; *ane sylvir ring*, 1568; *ane payr of hoys, ane douplat*, 1570). If some of the burgesses could afford luxuries, it is probable that they were now housed in more substantial dwellings. The quarry was providing stones (*querrel stanis*, 1583) which may have been used also to provide the burgh's first tolbooth sometime around the end of this century. There must have been a gaol of some sort by 1575, when for the first time it is recorded that certain persons were sentenced to imprisonment (*to be haldin and put into prissoune*). Between 1572 and 1578 meetings of the burgh court were held in various dwelling houses, and from 1587 till 1591 in the kirk. In 1601 three freemen were appointed (*keperis of the tounis keyis*), possibly to take charge of a newly-erected tolbooth.

When John Wallace of Craigie made himself oversman of Prestwick in November 1571 he adopted also the new title of provost (*ovirsman and provest*). To ensure firm control, in April of the following year he appointed as his deputy Michael Wallace of Wasfurd, joined in 1573 by John Wallace in Monktonhill, with Edward Wallace in Ayr becoming a third deputy in 1574. Sterner punishments (*puniest to the rigour*) were imposed in 1575 – imprisonment for two thieves who had fled, threat of whipping and banishment if resetting of stolen goods was repeated. When annual allocation of arable lands was superseded in 1572 by a division for nineteen years, some freemen may have been dissatisfied. In 1580 a more drastic innovation was made, by instituting heritable possession (*that everie freman within the said burgh sall haif, be equall divisione, heretable infeftment of thair landis quilk ar teillable*). If, as seems likely, the oversman and his dependents had advantageous allocation, this would be sufficient reason for widespread resentment. Dissension is reported in 1583 (*thair wes differance amangis the neboris of the toun anentis the cheising of theyr officemen affoir the ovirsman forsaid wes present*). The assembled freemen then agreed – no doubt reluctantly and perhaps under duress – that no court might be held in the absence of the oversman. In 1586 this rule was relaxed to allow the bailies on their own to judge certain cases (*contrauversies and actiounes betwix nybour and nybour*), but they were subject to surveillance (*ansuerable to he ovirsman for theyr administration*). In 1589 an attempt was made to prevent forcible seizure of lands (*ordanit that na freman, etc., sall tak the ryt tak nor possessioun of another freman without the guidwill of the possessour*). Such transactions would later, in the charter of 1600, be specifically condemned (*pretended charters, infeftments, sasines, and other donations and dispositions*) and restitution promised (*to call and prosecute for restoration and annulment*). Opposition to Wallace aggrandisement was overtly expressed on 16 October 1592. When the oversman sought reappointment, he failed to obtain the usual unanimity. It is reported that he was chosen not by the whole community, but by a majority (*for the meist parte being examinat upoun thair consienceis*). Three months later action was taken against disturbance of the peace (*personis sclanderis uthris or invadis uthris in bluid*) with a fine of £5, half of which was to go to Wallace, and later in 1593 an example was so made of one freeman. Between 1594 and 1597 no entry is made in the records. John Wallace of Craigie died about this time, which may have allowed opportunity for the freemen to revolt. In the last years of the century there is no further mention of an oversman. In November 1597 the bailies of Prestwick on their own authority made a series of new statutes, and in the absence of any documentary evidence of their rights sought a royal charter.

Parallel protests were made in the adjoining burgh of Newton. There the burgesses raised the substantial sum of £500 Scots to obtain in 1595 a royal charter defining their rights, in particular their freedom to elect bailies without interference from Alexander Lockhart of Boghall in St Quivox parish. The example of Newton was followed in Prestwick, where a new charter was obtained in July 1600, whose expense was met by a levy that year of £6 from each freeman. Also in August 1600 the freemen countermanded Wallace's previous allocation of lands by ordering a redivision (*ane new daill of thyr said fre land arabill to be devydit and fewit at michelmes nixtocum*) which was to remain unaltered for a stipulated period (*for xvii yeiris now to cum*, 1602). In October 1600 a former bailie was appoined as chancellor (*Johne Mertene canceller*), supported by two bailies, four liners and cunnars, and two officers. In 1601 and 1602 John Martin was succeeded as chancellor by Lambert Hay and William Blair.

But this rule of independent freemen was short-lived. Soon after Sir John Wallace of Craigie succeeded his father, he obtained in 1599 a charter of the lands of Dundonald, in which he got inserted a phrase suggesting his possession of both burghs (*duas villas et terras de Prestick et Newtoun de Air*). This was repeated in 1603 when he obtained a general charter for all his lands. Thus he obtained some legal recognition as superior of the two burghs, something which went unmentioned in the charters of these burghs. He was elected oversman of Newton in 1603 and of Prestwick in 1605.

CHAPTER FOUR

The Charter of 1600

*T*HE charter granted on behalf of King James VI in 1600 is a document which defines in lengthy detail the constitution of Prestwick burgh. It is presented in translation from the Latin, with headings and numbered subdivisions added to guide the reader through the text, and followed by an explanatory commentary.

I: INTRODUCTION, CONFIRMING PRIVILEGES PREVIOUSLY GRANTED

James, by the grace of God, King of Scots, to all honest men of his whole realm, clergy and laity, greeting. Know that as father, lawful guardian, tutor, and guide to our most dear son Henry, Duke of Rothesay, Earl of Kyle, Carrick, and Cuninghame, Lord of the Isles, and Prince and Steward of Scotland, and also for our own proper right, title, and interest in the burgh and lands undermentioned,

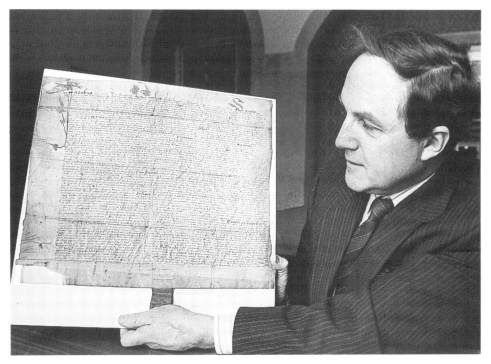

The charter of 1600, inspected in 1986 by the Secretary of State for Scotland, George Younger, MP, now Lord Younger of Prestwick.

we perfectly understand that our most noble progenitors of good memory of old beyond the memory of man by the period of six hundred and seventeen years past for various good considerations did (1) erect and create the Town and Burgh of Prestweik, lying within the Bailiery of Stewart Kyle, into a free burgh of barony; with all privileges and immunities of a free burgh; and (2) granted and disposed to the freemen, burgesses, and inhabitants of that Burgh, and to their heirs and successors, various and sundry lands, held as property or by the community, which should remain with them and their successors for ever. These lands have been very often walked over to establish the boundaries between themselves and their neighbours, and their limits and bounds are well known; also (3) the Bailies of Stewart Kyle by the erection of the Burgh of Prestweik are required to hold the courts of the Bailiery and Barony of Stewart Kyle within that burgh; and (4) all the inhabitants within the Barony of Stewart Kyle by right and custom are bound to present their goods for sale at the Cross and Market of the Burgh of Prestweik, and there pay their customs; and at that burgh receive their pound-measure, and other weights and measures, by use and wont; and (5) the burgesses and inhabitants of the said burgh are bound by their commission, if they be arrested or detained, to be repledged by whatever judge or agent of the law, to the freedom of their burgh and their own proper courts and there to submit to justice and not elsewhere.

II: RATIFICATION OF ALL PREVIOUS GRANTS

And we, from experience of the said good, faithful, and gratuitous service performed and spent for us and our predecessors by the burgesses and inhabitants of the Burgh of Prestweik and their predecessors, and that we may give to them and their successors better occasion for continuing there in the future, therefore and for various other great reasons and good considerations moving us, we have ratified, approved, and for us and our successors forever confirmed, and by the tenour of our present charter we approve, ratify, and for us and our successors for ever confirm all and sundry ancient charters, infeftments, erections, instruments, donations, titles, licences, and privileges whatever, made and granted by us and our most noble progenitors to the Burgh of Prestweik, burgesses and inhabitants thereof, and their predecessors and successors; with all lands, held as property or by the community, with annual rents, privileges, and immunities specified therein, and all contents thereof, of whatever dates or date, which we wish to be held as if expressed in this our present charter.

III: NEW GRANTS

Moreover we from certain knowledge and proper motive have once again made, constituted, created, erected, and incorporated, and by the tenour of our present charter, for us and our successors make, constitute, create, erect, and incorporate all and whole the said Town and Burgh of Prestweik; with all and sundry lands, houses, buildings, tenements, yards, acres, wasteland, tofts, crofts, and others lying within the Burgh Roods and territory thereof; together with all other and sundry lands, held as property or by the community, belonging to them, into (1) a free burgh of barony, to be called the Burgh of Prestweik in all time coming; and (2) in like manner we have once again given, granted, assigned, disponed, and incorporated, and by the tenour of our present charter, for us and our successors give, grant, assign, dispone, and incorporate to the said burgh and freemen, burgesses, inhabitants thereof, and their successors, in property and heritage, all and sundry, the lands, houses, buildings, tenements, yards, acres, wasteland, tofts, crofts, and others lying within the Burgh Roods with territory thereof; together with these Burgh Roods, namely infield and outfield lands; and also with all and sundry other lands and possessions, held as property or by the community, far and near, the parts, pendicles, and pertinents thereof, which belong to them or can be so proved; and with all and sundry privileges, immunities, and liberties which the burgesses and inhabitants of the said burgh, or their predecessors, had in use, custom, or possession, any time in the past before the day and date of the present charter, within whatever bounds, boundaries, and limits, and wherever lying; and (3) especially we revoke, cancel, and annul all and whatever pretended charters, infeftments, sasines, and other donations and dispositions which were made and granted by us to any person or persons, of the said lands, held as property or by the community, or any part of the same, which had belonged to the Burgh of Prestweik, burgesses and inhabitants thereof; and to the freedom of the said burgh in any time past preceding the day and date of the present charter; and we declare, and for us and our successors pronounce and ordain that they shall be of no effect or value in or out of court in any time coming; as also, for us and our successors we give and grant full power to the burgesses and freemen of the burgh, and their successors, to call and prosecute for restoration and annulment of the pretended infeftments, sasines, and other dispositions, in their own names or by the assistance of our advocate, before such judge or judges as are qualified in the appropriate law; (4) with special and full power, also, to the burgesses and freemen of the said burgh, and their successors, of making, electing, constituting, and creating a Provost, Bailies, Treasurer, Councillors, Burgesses, Deacons of Crafts, and other members as necessary, and officers within the burgh for its regulation and government; making, electing, constituting, and creating, and each year changing or retaining all or any of these; (5) with power also to the burgesses and freemen of the burgh and their successors, of pak and peill, and of selling and buying all merchandise and what are commonly called staple goods; and within the said burgh and its freedom, of buying and selling pieces of cloth, woollen and linen, broad and narrow; and all other merchandise and staple goods; (6) as also with power to the provost and bailies and councillors of the burgh and their successors, of having, admitting, retaining, and receiving within the burgh, bakers, smiths, butchers, sellers of fish, tailors, tanners, weavers, craftsmen, carpenters, and all other tradesmen necessary respecting and belonging to the freedom of a free burgh; (7) and of building, holding, and having within the burgh a Court Hall and Market Cross and a weekly market on Tuesday; together with a fair once a year on

St Nicholas Day and continuing for two days; (8) and admitting, levying, bringing in, collecting, and applying the common levies, namely the tolls and petty customs of the burgh, at the markets and fairs, towards the Common Good of the said burgh; (9) moreover with power to the provost and bailies of the burgh, and their successors, of receiving resignations of all and sundry lands, tenements, annual rents, yards, tofts, crofts, and others lying within the burgh and its freedom; and of delivering and disponing the same to such person or persons having right or title thereto, with all infeftments, charters, sasines, and other evidents necessary; receiving and entering and giving sasine to heirs of persons deceased, both by document and by hasp and staple, earth and stone, or by any other arrangement observed within the burghs of our kingdom; (10) stating, affixing, beginning, affirming, holding, and, as often as there shall be need, continuing Burgh Courts within the burgh and its freedom; creating clerks, sergeants, adjudicators, officers and all other necessary members of court; punishing transgressors according to the laws of our kingdom; levying, receiving, and applying to their own proper use the decisions, fines, penalties for blood-letting, and forfeiture of property by the said courts; and poinding and seizure of goods for the same if need be; making and ordaining acts, laws, and statutes for the observance of good order within the burgh and its freedom; attaching, arresting, imprisoning, and punishing all transgressors according to the laws of our kingdom;

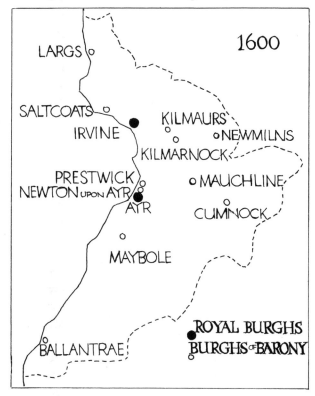

Ayrshire Burghs in 1600.

IV: RECOGNITION AS A BURGH OF BARONY

And generally, making, carrying, and using all other and sundry things, in like manner and as freely in all respects as any other free burgh within our kingdom; (1) having and holding all and whole the said Burgh of Prestweik, with all and sundry lands, houses, buildings, tenements, yards, acres, waste tenements, tofts, crofts, and others lying within the Burgh Roods and territory thereof; together with these Burgh Roods, the infield and outfield lands; also with all and sundry other lands and possessions, held as property or by the community, far and near, pendicles and pertinents thereof; with all common pastures, free entry and issue; and with all and sundry privileges, immunities, and liberties of which the burgesses and inhabitants of the burgh, or their predecessors, have had use, custom and possession, any time past before the day and date of the present charter, within whatever bounds, limits, and boundaries, wherever they lie; (2) to the said provost, bailies, councillors, burgesses, and freemen of the said burgh, and their successors, the said Henry, Prince and Steward of Scotland, and his successors as princes and stewards of Scotland, grants in hereditary feu-farm and as a free burgh of barony forever, as they lie in length and breadth the houses, buildings, bothies, plains, moors, marshes, roads, paths, waters, pools, streams, meadows, pastures and pasturages, mills with their multures and sequels, hawkings, huntings, fishings, peats, turves, coals and coal mines, rabbits, doves and dovecots, workshops and smithies, heathland and broom, woods, groves, and bushes, timber, quarries for stone and lime; with courts and their decisions, herezelds payable on inheritance, bloodwits payable when blood is shed, and wives' merks payable when a woman inherits; with common pasture, free entry and issue; and with all other and sundry liberties, commodities, profits, easements, and their just pertinents whatever, both named and unnamed, under and above ground, far and near, relating or that can justly belong to the burgh, lands, houses, buildings, tenements, tofts, crofts, and others, particularly and generally, respectively above written, with their pertinents whatsoever way in future, freely, quietly, fully, entirely, honourably, well, and in peace, without any revocation, contradiction, impediment, or obstacle whatever;

V: ANNUAL DUES

Rendering therefore yearly, the said provost, bailies, councillors, burgesses, and freemen of the burgh, and their successors, to the Prince and Steward of Scotland and to his successors as princes and stewards of Scotland, the sum of three pennies of usual money of our kingdom, for every Burgh Rood of the said lands, at the term of Whitsun, together with the service required from a burgh of barony only.

VI: AUTHORISATION

In testimony whereof, we have ordered our Great Seal to the affixed to this our present charter, before these witnesses,our well-beloved cousins and counsellors:

(1) John, Marquis of Hamilton, Earl of Arran, Lord Avon, etc., (2) John, Earl of Montrose, Lord Graham, our Chancellor, (3) George, Earl Marshall, Lord Keith, etc., Marshal of our Kingdom; our beloved serving counsellors: (4) Sir James Elphingstoun of Barntoun, our Secretary, (5) Sir Richard Cokburn, junior, of Clerkingtoun, Keeper of our Privy Seal; (6) Mr John Skene, Clerk of our Royal Register and Council, (7) Sir John Cokburne of Ormestoun, Clerk of our Justiciary, (8) Mr William Scott of Grangemure, Director of our Chancery at Holyrood House, the nineteenth day of the month of June in the year of Our Lord One Thousand and six hundred, and of our reign the thirty-third year.

COMMENTARY

This royal charter was granted by James VI on behalf of his six-year-old eldest son Prince Henry, who would die in 1612, after which a younger brother Charles would succeed as heir to the throne. Though the charter was issued by the king, it is most unlikely that he had a hand in its compilation, or was even aware of its existence; then as now ordinances issued under royal authority do not imply a monarch's personal involvement.

The author of this official document was presumably the lawyer Sir John Skene. He was Clerk of the Register and his name appears among the witnesses to this charter. Skene was at this time preparing for publication in 1609 an edition of the laws and constitution of Scotland. In his researches he readily accepted mythical accounts of the origins of the Scots people and their kings, as propounded in the historical works of John Major (1521), Hector Boece (1526) and George Buchanan (1582). Skene attributed to Kenneth II, king from 971 till 995, laws which in fact originated some three hundred years later. Similarly in this charter we are taken back to the middle year of that king's reign.

Title of the Liber Communitatis, the manuscript burgh record, returned to Kyle and Carrick District Council in 1994 after conservation and restoration work by the Scottish Record Office.

The reference early in the charter to "beyond the memory of man by the period of six hundred and seventeen years" (*ab antiquo ultra hominum memoriam per spatium sex centorum et septem decem annorum*) has sometimes been misunderstood. It is in fact applicable to the "most noble progenitors" of James VI, whom Skene was glorifying by emphasising his long lineage since the time of Kenneth II. The charter implies that one or several of those progenitors of James VI had originally agreed to the creation of Prestwick as a burgh. But the wording is ambiguous, and has sometimes been misinterpreted to suggest that the burgh was 617 years old, However, to date Prestwick burgh to the year 983 is to provide a spurious precision to something for which there is no justification in the charter or elsewhere.

Nevertheless this claim for Prestwick burghs's incredibly early origin has been often propounded. Mitchell (writing in the 1790s) thought that the 1600 charter "expressly says, that it was known to have been a free burgh of barony beyond the memory of man, for the space of 617 years before its renewal", though he admitted that "there are no papers beside the charter, that can instruct it to be so ancient". Chalmers (1824) thought the early date as "far beyond the epoch of record, and still further from the truth". Fullarton (1834) argued that "there is no probability that these pretensions rested on any authority other than vague tradition". Burns (1837) simply defined the burgh as "very ancient". Paterson (1852) described the charter as "fabulous, in reference to matters of antiquity". Hewat (1894) was willing to accept a 10th century origin, and Murray (1932) argued that Prestwick was "a burgh before the age of charters". That distinguished authority on Scottish burghs, Pryde (1955) described as "merely stylistic" the phrase in the charter claiming a remote antiquity. Following Chalmers, Fullarton, and Paterson he concluded that the burgh was founded in the 12th century by Walter Fitzalan. The people of Prestwick in 1983 celebrated the millenium of the burgh in a harmless and quite enjoyable occasion. The historical truth is that it is not quite so ancient, though undoubtedly the oldest burgh in the county of Ayr.

I. 1: Prestweik is the spelling uniformly throughout the charter of 1600. In the earliest 12th century written records it appears as Prestwic. In the burgh records of the 15th and 16th centuries there are no fewer than eighteen variant spellings. Though this part of the charter claims an original erection into a free burgh of barony, that precise designation was not given to any burgh before the 15th century, when it was introduced to differentiate baronial burghs from royal burghs, which had a monopoly of foreign trade,

I. 2: The burgh contained freemen (who were burgesses) and inhabitants (who were not). As indicated here and later, land within the burgh might be held as property (i.e by individual persons) or by the community (*tam in proprietate quam comunitate*). The boundaries of the burgh, though not here specified, may be identified from the burgh records and from maps of much later date. To the south, Newton-on-Ayr was bounded by a line from St James Cross near the sea to large boulders known as Hare Stanes or Grey Stanes; so towards the moss, an eastern boundary which was sometimes disputed; the north boundary was formed by the

Prestwick Burn (later called Pow Burn) for part of its course. Some lands beyond the northern and southern boundaries of the burgh were annexed and regarded as within what was called "the liberties of the burgh".

I. 3: Prestwick was established as head burgh of Stewart Kyle, and the place where its courts were held. In the bailiery court justice was administered by a local landowner appointed by the king (or the High Steward) to be Bailie of Stewart Kyle. This was quite distinct from the burgh court (III. 10).

I. 4: Prestwick was the only recognised market within Stewart Kyle. Those bringing goods for sale had to pay a levy called the petty customs, and accept as standard those weights and measures held by the burgh. In practice, Ayr became the centre for the whole of Kyle, and even within Stewart Kyle, markets were authorised at Mauchline (1266, confirmed 1510) and Auchinleck (1507).

I. 5: Those resident within a burgh might be tried only within that burgh, and if arrested elsewhere could claim the privilege of being returned for trial (re-pledged).

II: As well as ratifying those grants previously noted, recognition would be given to any others if documentary proof turned up.

III. 1: Though Prestwick was already a burgh it was necessary to provide it with this formal recognition by royal charter. It was confirmed as a burgh of barony, subject not to the king but to the king's son as later indicated (IV, V). The Steward's other burgh of Renfrew, created as a king's burgh by David I, then granted by him to Walter Fitzalan, was promoted to become a royal burgh following Robert II's charter of 1396, as confirmed by James VI in 1575 and 1614. But Prestwick was not similarly elevated, retaining the lesser status of a burgh of barony.

III. 2: The lands of the burgh comprised three categories: the Burgh Roods,

The charter allowed for a mill, and the Powbank Mill survived till the 20th century.

which were tofts where burgesses dwelt; Infield and Outfield cultivated lands; and Waste, which was pasture land.

III. 3: This is a particularly interesting section, implying that the burgh had suffered recent encroachments on its lands.

III. 4: As in any burgh of barony those inhabitants who were burgesses had a franchise to elect a burgh council. An act of 1469 established a secure system of councillors selecting their successors, but this apparently applied only to royal burghs. Popular election by burgesses continued in burghs of barony; in some cases those elected had to be approved by the superior of the burgh; no such stipulation was indicated in this Prestwick charter.

III. 5: One prime purpose of a burgh was to provide a market for buying and selling; including the (inexplicable) right of *pak and peill.*

III. 6: The other prime purpose of a burgh was to foster manufactures by craftsmen, working in wood, leather, and textiles.

III. 7: The Prestwick records first note a cross on 13 October 1473, "*the quhilk day Willi Jurdane come in will for the distrubillans of the toun, and the breking of the corse*". It is possible a tolbooth or court hall was erected shortly before 1601 when keepers of the town keys were appointed; it is first definitely mentioned in 1722 as "out of repair". Though provision was made for a weekly market and an annual fair, these could never have attracted much custom because of the proximity of the royal burgh of Ayr, and had fallen into disuse by the 18th century.

III. 8: The burgh council's income was derived principally from the petty customs levied on those displaying goods for sale at the markets, which with other receipts formed the fund known as the Common Good of the Burgh.

III. 9: All transfers of property in the burgh had to be made through the agency of the council, which took receipt from one party before making grant to another; by the same process as any landlord would grant a new tenancy. At a formal ceremony possession of a house would be symbolised by handing over hasp and staple for the door, and of land by seizing a handful of earth and stone, which procedure of sasine (seizing) continued till 1845. This was accompanied by written documentation of property transactions, as appear in the 15th and 16th century Prestwick records. There was instituted in 1617 the Public Register of Sasines, which continues to provide a uniform national system of compulsory registration of land transfers.

III. 10: An essential feature of a burgh was the judicial power which the bailies exercised. All who dwelt within the burgh were subject to the jurisdiction of the burgh court, and might seek to be repledged there (see I. 5). The burgh records contain details of meetings of this burgh court (which met in the same place but was distinct from the bailiery court; see I. 3). Its officials were annually appointed. Burgh laws were formulated to regulate the everyday businesss of what was essentially a farming community, and infringements were penalised. The court was also empowered to make exactions when property changed hands. It dealt with criminal as well as civil cases. The charter here and later (IV. 2) mentions penalties for blood-letting (*bloodwits*). The records for 1470 note the vennel on the west side

of the town "*passand down to the galous*". The gallows may have been to acccommod-
ate those condemned by the bailiery court; there is no record of its use by the
burgh court.

IV. 1: Legal cover is provided for the burgh, by indicating a full range of
properties and privileges.

IV. 2: Tenure was feu-ferme, exclusive possession in perpetuity granted by the
king's eldest son as Steward of Scotland, in return for the annual payments later
stipulated. Not all of the items listed were necessarily applicable to Prestwick.

VI: The burgh was required to make, for each burgh rood, an annual payment
of three pence. With approximately 120 roods (according to the 1470 inquest)
that would generate annually less than £2; comparable with Ayr which from 1400
made a fixed annual payment of £10 to the crown, plus another £10 for Alloway.
The description "of usual money of our kingdom" is ambiguous, perhaps deliberately so, for there was currently in the royal burghs opposition to demands for
payment of burgh-fermes in pounds sterling, twelve times the cost of payment in
pounds Scots.

VI: The charter was witnessed by three noblemen who were ministers of the
crown, and five others who were employed as civil servants. One copy was included
in the Register of the Great Seal, another held by the burgh.

CHAPTER FIVE

The 17th Century

URING this century of ecclesiastical conflict, management of Prestwick was retained in the hands of the Wallaces.

John Wallace of Craigie who in 1605 became provost of Prestwick reasserted his family's ascendancy over the burgh. He did not long enjoy personal control, for he died, possibly in 1610, certainly before 1614. His son and heir Hew being a minor, Sir John Wallace of Carnell, who was a kinsman, was chosen as provost in 1610 and until 1616, in which year the surviving records cease. Hew Wallace reached his majority by 1631 when he had sasine of the Craigie lands. He and his successors are presumed to have continued as provosts of Prestwick for the rest of the century, though, as will appear, wider concerns must have diverted their attention from parochial affairs.

National politics, which were largely concerned with ecclesiastical matters, had inevitable impact upon the local community. From 1560 till 1690 there was dispute, and at time armed conflict, as to how the Reformed Church should be governed. Was it to be a church controlled nationally through bishops appointed by the king, and locally by the landowners who as patrons nominated the ministers; or an independent presbyterian church governed by its General Assembly? Andrew Melville in the Second Book of Discipline, 1578, argued that "na person be intrusit in ony of the offices of the kirk contrar to the will of the congregation, or without the voce of the eldership". But though a presbytery of Ayr was formed in 1581, an episcopal system operated save for brief interludes, 1592–97 and 1649–60. Choice of parish ministers involving some popular participation was obtained only during those two periods, as later in 1690–1712, and since 1874. In 1599 Rev. Claud Hamilton was appointed to the parish of Monkton and Prestwick, followed in 1615 by Rev. Robert Hamilton. On each occasion choice was made by the patron, who was obviously favouring his kinsfolk. That was Lord Claud Hamilton, commendator of Paisley Abbey, whose lands were converted into a temporal lordship in 1578, who thus had the patronage of several Ayrshire parishes, and who had as bailie for his Ayrshire lands Wallace of Craigie. As such they were supporters of the establishment, and on one occasion in Craigie Kirk Hew Wallace threw a dagger at the minister who dared criticise him.

There was local resistance to the imposition of episcopacy by James VI and Charles I in the period after 1597. When Rev. George Dunbar, minister of Ayr, refused to submit to bishop's authority, he was deposed. Though sentenced to banishment, he took refuge in Prestwick, where there was sufficient sympathy to allow him hold services within St Nicholas Church. In 1625 it was noted that "the said Maister George hes not as yit given obedience, bot still remaynis within this kingdome, preachis ordinarlie in the kirk of Prestick". Rev. Robert Hamilton, the established minister, was the sort of man to report this to the privy council, and Dunbar was exiled to Ireland.

There was increased opposition to the policies of Charles I who succeeded to the throne in 1625. Landowners faced possible confiscation of lands they had acquired from the church, worshippers were antagonised by introduction of a new liturgy. The National Covenant of 1638 won widespread support, and armed conflict broke out the year after. The cause of the Covenanters against the king was supported by David Blair of Adamton, his son James Blair of Monktonmains, and another James Blair in Monkton hall. Led by Blair of Adamton, a contingent from the parish prepared to "venture themselves and estates for the defence of the Gospel". When the Marquis of Montrose raised his standard on behalf of the king in 1644, a Monkton contingent was sent against him and participated in his defeat at Philiphaugh in 1645. On the other side, among royalists supporting Montrose was Sir Hew Wallace of Craigie, who was taken prisoner after the battle of Philiphaugh. Rev. Robert Hamilton of Monkton and Prestwick, who was also a royalist, resorted to verbal abuse against his opponents, which contributed to his eventual deposition.

When the Blairs of Adamton and Monkton were chosen as military officers of the parish "for leading the people of God in such public service as suld occur", they were denounced from the pulpit by Hamilton as "drunken blasphemers, profane and debosht companions" and "the curse of God wold light upon all who followed such leaders and commanders". The following Sunday the minister was refused entry into Prestwick kirk. Adam Blair accosted him, saying, "Ye sall not come heir to preach" and at the same time "strak Jonnet Duncan in Prestwick with his rod, because she refused to give him the key of the kirk". In 1640 Rev. Robert Maxwell was appointed to share the charge. Accusations were made against Hamilton, and after Montrose was defeated and the Covenanters triumphant, the presbytery of Ayr took action against this dissident minister, and deposed him on 13 Jan. 1646 for "various misdemeanours".

He was accused of failing to support the cause of the Covenant, for "in these sad and melancholick tymes he did never come towards them of his charge that were in the fields, nather to exhort nor encourage them to stand in the defence of the Lord's cause against the public enemie, as the rest of the ministers did, and as was desyred by the committee of the shyre". More generally, his conduct as a preacher was found wanting. There was the serious charge that for twenty-six years "he had preached by reading of Commentaries and bringing no Byble to the Kirk at all". When ordered so to do, he "did bring a great Kirk-Bible with ane silk covering thairon, and in the samin had an quair of paper or thairby tyed therin, wherin his preachings were wreatten, and immediately after reading the text, goes to the said paper, and turneth the leafs thairof, sometymes ten or twelf, sometimes moe, or fewer, as occasion serveth, and so insisteth in reading of the same, till the time of sermon be past." Then while the concluding psalm was being sung he took his script from the Bible, to take away hidden in his plaid. Reading of sermons was regarded as objectionable, so that when Hamilton was preaching, "in tyme of sermon the most part of the people do nothing, but lay wajours upon the turning of the pages". He was also charged with lack of gravity in the pulpit, using vulgar expressions which amused some of the congregation but offended others. He was also accused of, for his own profit, watering the wine supplied for the sacrament. His private life was also the subject of criticism. After his second wife died, he proposed marriage to his maid servant, Grizel Black, who was already engaged to another. Rev. Robert Maxwell, who was his colleague, and several other local ministers refused to officiate at the marriage ceremony, which was in 1645 performed by a Cambuslang minister who was himself under censure. Hamilton died in 1647, aged about 64.

Rev. Robert Maxwell who had been his colleague continued in sole charge of the parish. He was a more devout man, serving Monkton and Prestwick through the period of the Commonwealth, and concerned when the restoration of Charles II in 1660 threatened the presbyterian character of the church. When episcopacy was then restored, Maxwell was one of those staunch presbyterian ministers who refused to submit to bishops, was confined to his parish in 1662, and deprived of his charge in 1665. When the government sought compromise, he was offered an indulgence in 1672 but refused a transfer to Craigie. He continued illegally to conduct those private acts of worship called conventicles, and for this was imprisoned for a time in 1677. He retired to Cathcart where he died in 1686 at the age of 75. In 1676 the charge of Monkton and Prestwick was awarded to a conforming minister, Rev. Alexander Cunningham who was transferred from Colmonell. But dissident Covenanters continued to distance themselves from episcopal services in the established church. In 1678 field conventicles were being held at Prestwick, and John Muir, sometime provost of Ayr, worshipped alongside David Blair of Adamton and the two bailies of Prestwick burgh, James Blair and William Neill. At such services the preacher could have been a minister called Muirhead, about whom nothing is known which can be authenticated. He might have been inducted in 1683 as an indulged minister to succeed Maxwell, but was apparently ejected from that charge for harbouring a proscribed preacher. Thereafter Muirhead continued to hold conventicles in his own house or among the Prestwick sandhills. At a prayer meeting beside the bed of a dying parishioner he was seized by Captain Grierson and his dragoons, taken off to Dumfries, and on the way was wounded and drowned while attempting to escape. During these unhappy times there were armed risings of the Covenanters. In 1666 Colonel James Wallace of Auchans led 2,000 armed Covenanters from Ayr towards Edinburgh and defeat at Rullion Green in the so-called Pentlands Rising. No local names are found among those proscribed. After 1679 when the Covenanters were victorious at Drumclog but defeated at Bothwell Brig, two men of this parish were denounced as fugitives: John Henryson in Newtoun of Ayr and William Wilson in Prestick.

In 1685 Charles II was followed as king by his Roman Catholic brother James

VII and II, and indulgences followed which allowed a measure of religious toleration. The indulgences allowed those who objected to episcopacy to form their own congregations. Rev. Matthew Baird, who had been preaching in Ayr, was called in November 1687 and in March 1688 ordained as presbyterian minister of Monkton and Prestwick. It is likely that he officiated in St Nicholas Church in Prestwick, while Rev. Alexander Cunningham continued as established episcopal minister at St Cuthbert's Church in Monkton. The Glorious Revolution of 1688 which expelled James VII and brought William and Mary to the throne was followed early in 1689 by the ejection of episcopal ministers from many parishes. Cunningham was so removed from Monkton and Prestwick, and Rev. Matthew Baird confirmed as parish minister in a Church whose presbyterian constitution was guaranteed by an Act of 1690.

Throughout the 17th century there were various changes in ownership of the local estates. At Adamton, David Blair succeeded his father in 1647, was one of the Committee of War for Ayrshire in 1648, supported the Covenanting cause, in 1689 was with his son amongst the commissioners appointed by parliament to order out the county militia, and was soon afterwards succeeded by that son, John Blair. Ladykirk was bequeathed by James Blair to his son and namesake, who succeeded in 1616 to an estate which later in the century was disposed of to John Gairdner. Monkton estate, formed of lands which had previously belonged to Paisley Abbey, was possessed by Lord Claud Hamilton until his death in 1621. His grandson, James, Earl of Abercorn, inherited, but these lands (with patronage of the parish church) were disposed of, and passed through several hands. They were acquired in 1650 by John Hamilton, first Lord Bargany; in 1674 by John Cunninghame of Enterkine; in 1688 by Hugh Cunninghame, an Edinburgh lawyer; and in 1695 by William Baillie, a Kilwinning man who had become an Edinburgh merchant. A tower house, built in Lord Claud Hamilton's time and depicted on Blaeu's map as Monkton Castle, would become known as Monkton hall and later Monkton House. Overmains, part of the Monkton estate disposed of in the 16th century, was held by three generations of the Hamiltons of Bothwellhaugh, then early in the 17th century was obtained by James Blair, a younger son of Adamton. His family would for a century keep possession of Overmains, whose 18th century purchasers would rename it Fairfield.

The Wallaces of Craigie continued influential. Hew Wallace in 1626 gave up to the crown the family rights as hereditary bailies of Stewart Kyle. He was promised a surrender value of £20,000 Scots, which was never paid; but he was rewarded (before 1634) with a knighthood. Sir Hew fell into disfavour as a royalist who actively supported Montrose against the Covenanters. Yet he survived to welcome Charles II's restoration to the throne in 1660, and died in 1665. All his sons predeceased him, and Sir Hew was succeeded by a grandnephew, son of William Wallace of Failford. This was Thomas Wallace, a lawyer and pillar of the establishment, who was created baronet in 1670, appointed a Lord of Session in 1671 and Lord Justice Clerk from 1675 till his death in 1680. Wallace control over the burghs of Prestwick and Newton-upon-Ayr seems to have become relaxed because of Sir

Detail from the Map of Kyle. Timothy Pont surveyed the whole of Scotland at the beginning of the 17th century, and his maps were published in Amsterdam in 1654.

Hew's military adventures and his successor's legal duties in Edinburgh. When Sir William Wallace of Craigie succeeded his father in 1680 an effort to reassert authority was particularly resented because he was a Roman Catholic. The freeman of Newton claimed that they held of the Prince of Scotland and had been "constantly in use of choiseing their oune bayllies" until "the late Craigie, by his power without any right, sought to oppress and inthrall them". Wallace argued that he and his predecessors were "heritably infeft in the lands of Newtoun of Air and Prestick" and were "in constant use and possession to preside at the annual election of magistrates". We know that neither of the Newton or Prestwick charters mentioned a superior other than the king's eldest son; and Hew Wallace had in 1626 given up "the offices of the baillierie of Kyle and regalitie of Newtoun" upon which Wallace claims were hitherto based. But the privy council dismissed the freemen as "disorderly and factious persones" and decided that "Craigie had right for what he clamed". That authority on the Scottish burghs, G.S.Pryde, has concluded that "The oppression of the tiny burghs by the Wallaces of Craigie makes a sordid and shameful tale".

After the Roman Catholic James VII succeeded in 1685, Sir William Wallace of Craigie extended his influence, becoming provost of Ayr in 1687 as well as continuing provost of Newton and of Prestwick. He became an absentee laird by following James VII into exile and supporting the Jacobite cause. In 1696 he was allowed to return, though attacked by Ayr Presbytery as a papist. His brother, an advocate who had managed the estates in his absence, inherited in 1700 to become Sir Thomas Wallace of Craigie.

St Nicholas Church had a bell cast in Holland in 1619, now at Kingcase School. (*KA*)

With the burgh records for this period lost, it is not possible to assess changes within the bounds of Prestwick. There are, however, fragmentary references which hint at developments within Monkton and Prestwick parish throughout the 17th century. St Nicholas Church in Prestwick was enhanced by a new bell, cast in Holland in 1619. At Monkton the medieval bell inscribed "Sancte Cuthberti ora pro nobis" continued in use, but the church itself was remodelled around 1650, with lofts installed by the lairds of Adamton and Crosbie. The Fullarton family had their own chapel at Crosbie; in 1651 James Fullarton of Crosbie persuaded Ayr presbytery to have Crosbie disjoined from Dundonald parish and attached to Monkton and Prestwick; but in 1681 the chapel was rebuilt and Crosbie was in 1688 re-united with Dundonald parish.

The protestant Church, in order to recruit ministers and more generally to encourage widespread reading of the Bible, sought in 1562 to obtain "maintenance of schools for the instruction of the youth in every parish". There may have been a school in Prestwick before the Reformation. The only evidence is slender, being a mention of payment in 1382 to William of Prestwick for the cost of two scholars from Bute. An act of 1496 instructed "all barronis and frehalderis that ar of substance put thair eldest sonnis and airis to the schulis". But this was not implemented. After the Reformation there was a series of acts, in 1567, 1616, 1633, 1646, and 1696, which attempted to create a universal system of parochial schools. It is possible that after the Reformation some of the Readers appointed to parishes lacking a minister provided some secular instruction. The first definite mention of a school in this parish comes in 1616 when John Shiringlaw was appointed as schoolmaster, session clerk, and beadle, "to instruct the young, as also to do and exercise the ofice of Bedell in all poynts within the Kirk and parochine of Mounktoun". In 1639 John Hunter, schoolmaster at Tarbolton, followed as schoolmaster, session clerk, and precentor, "to read and taik upe the psalme in the Kirks of Mounktoun and Prestuike and to enter to the teaching of the school at Candelmas nixt and to have for his pynes quarterlie the sowme of aucht marks, besyd his wantage of the bairnes," which was annually thirty-two merks plus fees. Those who followed as session clerks continued also as teachers. In 1651 the kirk session of Monkton resolved to provide "ane able young man to train up the children at school in the knowledge of the Latin and English tongue". The following year one such was appointed, but in 1653 he could be paid only £40 Scots, less than the minimum stipend of one hundred merks (£66 13s 4d) required by the Act of 1646. This was supplemented by fees of "everi ane of his scholars 13s 4d quarterli" – which few could afford. Lessons were originally taught within St Cuthbert's, as in 1644 when "the sessions apoyntes the schoole to be at the Kirk till a school be provided elsquhar". This was satisfactorily accomplished in 1655, when the session paid £9 2s "to Johne Gottray for his work in bigging the schoolhouse." The parish school at Monkton contrived to survive, for the presbytery of Ayr was assured in 1698 that "they had a schoolmaster". He was apparently not yet being paid the minimum salary, whose implementation was recently urged in the 1696 Act, though it was hoped "that he should be sufficiently provided". There is one possible explanation for the parish school sited in Monkton lacking support. The Act of 1646 imposed "a stent upon everie ones rent of stock and teind in the paroche proportionallie to the worth thereof" and that of 1696 more specifically required this to "conform to every heritors valued rent within the paroch, allowing each heritor relieff from his tennents of the half of his proportion". Defaulting payment was not uncommon, especially if those being taxed were too distant from the parish school to enjoy any advantage, or if they chose to make alternative provision. It is known that the freeman of Newton had established their own school by 1643. It is possible that in Prestwick also there was in the 17th century as later a freemen's school, meeting in the town house.

The kirk session continued its concern for discipline. Absence from public worship could not be excused by distance from church, even when the weather might be inclement. In November 1641 non-attenders were visited by elders and the session rebuked "all these within the newtoun that keeps ther doores fast apon the Sabbath day when the visitours comes and choapes therat." Again in October 1664 "a greate number of Newtoners who had absented themselfes from the Kirk were calt upon by their names severalli and sharpli rebuked". Sinners were called upon to repent, as in 1698 when Margaret Wood was accused of calling Agnes Cuthbertson a "witch-bird". The church's continuing concern for poor relief extended to a collection in 1620 "for the captives of the Turks" and in 1622 "for the french Kirk". When at the end of the century times were particularly difficult,

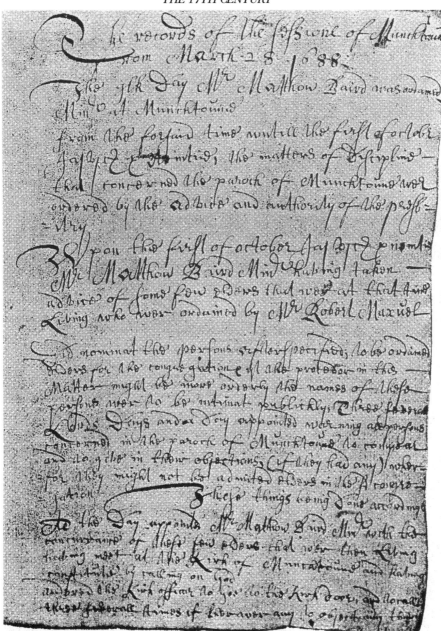

Throughout the troubled 17th century the kirk session exercised discipline and provided for poor relief and schooling. After bitter struggles by the Covenanters, parishioners were in 1688 free to choose their own minister, as this extract from the Kirk Session Minutes reveals.

in 1698 certain beggars were licensed and provided with "badges with the inscription of Muncktone on the one side and Prestwic on the other, and that conform to the list given them or to be given them by the minister". Kingcase, of course, continued to operate as a spittal, with the Wallaces of Craigie as bailies retaining patronage, the right of presenting pensioners. Those admitted were, according to a contemporary account, lodged in huts or cottages. They were supported by rents payable to the bailie from the two farms in neighbouring parishes which had long been allocated to Kingcase. Inmates were still described as lepers, though they might now have been persons suffering from other ailments. They were, however, in 1693 fit enough to gather timber and wrack from the shore, dig peats, and collect other materials "for building and repairing their houses without liberty asked", to the displeasure of the Prestwick freemen.

While there are no surviving burgh records to illustrate 17th century Prestwick, there were some general developments which must have affected local social life. Scotland was enjoying an expansion of overseas trade, and increased demand for staple commodities. We have noticed how the local economy in the 16th century was showing signs of vitality, and we can guess that the 17th century brought some continued growth. More intensive use of limited farmland may have been reason for disputes concerning the precise boundaries of Prestwick with Newton in 1605, 1634, 1635, and with St Quivox in 1698. Working of coal and manufacture of salt seems to have continued, and a search for coal in St Quivox by Sir Thomas Wallace in 1672 suggests there was an increased demand. Ayr's fishing fleet was busy supplying herrings for export, and smaller vessels along the Kyle coast would have a minor share in the trade: levies of seamen in 1672 and 1690 required men from all coastal places, including Monkton and Prestwick, and Crosbie. The craftsmen of Prestwick would continue to supply textiles and hides to merchants in Ayr. But the burgh remained quite insignificant. When in 1693 it was proposed to extend participation in foreign trade from the two royal burghs in Ayrshire to twenty burghs of barony and market towns, Prestwick was not included in the list. Perhaps the most impressive development affecting Prestwick was improvement of the great highway passing through the town, for the convenience of troops on the way from Glasgow to Portpatrick for Ireland, for commercial traffic by pack-horse, and for the long-distance postal service which was instituted in 1662. An act of 1669 for repair of roads required of "all tennents and coatters and their servants ... sex days for man and horse yeerlie for the first three yeers and four days yeerly therafter." When this was re-enacted in 1686 Sir William Wallace of Craigie then took advantage to renovate the highway through Prestwick and Newton into Ayr.

Prestwick apparently did not share in the general growth of Scottish population in the 17th century. This occurred elsewhere despite a deteriorating climate and a series of bad harvests culminating in famine conditions between 1695 and 1699; despite the plague which affected Ayrshire in 1606 and 1647; and despite the ravages of civil war. Prestwick could not escape the other general trend of the period, that of massive inflation. Rising prices brought advantage to lairds, who could charge increased rents while continuing to pay fixed feu-duties; to ministers, whose stipends were based on the price of grain; to merchants, lawyers, and craftsmen who could always charge more; and to the freemen of Prestwick who enjoyed heritable tenure. Less fortunate were tenants and labourers whose standard of living deteriorated, and for whom a diet based largely on meat and dairy products was replaced by one in which oatmeal predominated.

CHAPTER SIX

The 18th Century

*T*HIS was the century when the freemen secured their independence, though with little immediate advantage.

In 1723 an inquiring visitor provided a brief but informative account of Prestwick. It was described as "a long village called the toun of Prestick with a tolbooth and toun council and twa Bailies". It was still the case that "the familie of Craigie are proprietors of both Newtoun and Prestick and can not elect magistrates with (out) his concurrance and hes the naming of the leit". The kirk of Prestwick "stands on a rising ground closs by the sea, where the minister of Monktoun preaches every Sabbath". Prestwick remained "the head brugh of the Principalitie of Koyle Stewart, here the Prince and Steuart of Scotland keeps 2 head courts in the year, where all his vassals in the principalitie of Koyle-Steuart are oblidged to appear." On the way to Newton (which – unlike Prestwick – was described as a "hansome village") there was "ane old Hospitall called the Kings-Case closs by the sea ... where lepers are mentain'd and hes lands of ther own doted by one of the Kings of Scotland a leper". Nearby "Sir Thomas Wallace of Craigie hes very hansome salt pans". In the opposite direction was "the kirk and village of Monktoun which stands in the midle of the most publict road in the west country leading from Edinburgh and Glasgow to the Brugh of Air and on forward to Portpatrick in the shire of Wigtoun where passingers are transported to Donochadie in Ireland". Monktoun had "a handsome litill church with ane Isle and buriall place for Blair of Adamtouns familie." That Blair family "hes possessed this place 400 years and upwards" and were "patron and first famelie in the parioch". Adamtoun was a "big old house with a grate dale of old planting, stands a short mile E of the kirk, hes orchyards, 2 woods, and severall hansome inclosures". Beyond was "Ladykirk called in old chartors the grace of Koyle has been a large building and old monastrie now ruinous". South of the kirk "about 3 or 4 bows draught" was the house of Monktoun, which "belongs to Baillie of Monkton, formerlie to the Earls of Abercorn and was the place of ther residence now and then". Very close to Monktoun House was "the Pow Bridge over a considerable burn of that name; hes only one arch".

Sir Thomas Wallace of Craigie, fifth baronet, an advocate like his predecessors, was the last of the family to control Prestwick. He attended the Michaelmas meetings of the burgesses in 1726 and 1730 and the records designated him as hereditary provost. But the two bailies and thesaurer (treasurer) chosen at that latter meeting proceeded to draw up, with twenty-eight other burgesses, a lengthy statement of objection. "Sir Thomas Wallace of Craigy advocate hath ... assumed the office of hereditable provest ... to which heritable office we conceive he hath not a sufficient right ... pretends right to the burgh itself and to the lands in the possession of the burgesses and freemen or their tennents, and threatens diligence against them for payment of the rents mails and duties ... to which we apprehend he hath no right." The signatories indicated that they had already protested "against his sitting and acting as provost" and bound themselves to "maintain and defend the said town of Prestick their rights against all incroachments" and be at the expense of necessary legal action. Their complete success is apparent when on 22 December 1731 the "freemen and burgesses proceeded to the election of bayllies and thesaurer and in order heirto to choyse ane chancellor to preside at and oversee the election; and by plurality of votes, James Neill is choysen chancellor, as hath been the ancient custome: who being sett, and the freemen being called to vote and choyce there bayllies and thesaurer William Neill and Andrew Caldwall were elected and continoued bayllies, and William Hunter was elected and continoued thesaurer by plurality of votes; who have accepted and given there oaths de fideli." When those extracts from the burgh records were later published, the editor added a note: "This seems to have put an end to the *hereditary* pretensions of the laird of Craigie – neither he nor his descendants ever afterwards appearing as provosts of Prestwick. On what this extraordinary assumption rested it is difficult to conjecture". At a following meeting, on 22 May 1732, among four men admitted as honorary burgesses "for good services done and to be done thereto" was a young advocate who may have assisted against Wallace pretensions, Alexander Boswell, who would later become Lord Auchinleck. Yale University holds twenty-six burgess tickets awarded to him later in his career by other burghs, but if he received any such document from Prestwick it has unfortunately not survived.

Sir Thomas Wallace similarly lost control over Newton-upon-Ayr burgh. Newton Castle had been storm-damaged in 1701, and though it was apparently still habitable in 1723, soon after that Sir Thomas built Craigie House, a new mansion in St Quivox parish further up the River Ayr. He provided himself with a new town to control by laying out about 1760 a community called Wallacetown. But there were family misfortunes: Sir Thomas's wife seems to have left him; his eighteen-year-old daughter eloped in 1748; his only son died, aged twenty-seven, in 1756; when he himself died in 1770, the baronetcy was inherited by his grandson Thomas Dunlop, who in 1783 sold off the estate of Craigie and most of his other lands.

Let it not be assumed that throwing off the yoke of the Wallaces of Craigie resulted in Prestwick becoming a commonwealth of independent peasants. William Neill, one of the bailies in 1726 and 1730, who engineered the expulsion of the Wallaces, was connected by marriage to the Blairs of Adamton. His son, James Neill, who took office as chancellor in 1731, was a merchant in Ayr who becamea bailie there, was wealthy enough to acquire lands in the parishes of Ochiltree (Shaw) and Tarbolton (Drumley), and in 1754 purchased that part of Alloway which became Doonholm estate. He remained chancellor of Prestwick from 1731 until 1743, was reappointed for shorter spells in 1750–54 and 1760–65, and died at the age of eighty-eight in 1774. His son, James Neill, writer in Ayr, was clerk to Prestwick burgh from 1758 until 1766 when he became one of the freemen. In 1784 he purchased Barnweill, part of the Craigie estate, from Sir Thomas Dunlop Wallace; his son, Major William Smith Neill of Barnweill and Swindridgemuir, would continue the family interest by appointment as chancellor of Prestwick in 1830. Though ascendancy of one family was diminished from 1731, those who from time to time occupied the position of chancellor were nearly all like the Neills, persons having outside interests: James Blair in Monktonmill (1743–48, 1766–70); Charles Dalrymple of Orangefield, sheriff clerk (1754–60); William Fullarton of Rosemount, surgeon returned from India (1770–80); James Campbell, junior, Irvine merchant (1780–82); Robert Doak, formerly of Townhead of Monkton, later in Struthers (1782–84); Captain John Hamilton (1784–86); Colonel William Fullarton of Fullarton (1792–1802). The only locally-resident chancellor was David Andrew in Prestwick (1748–50), and possibly David Boyd (1786–92, 1806–10). The successive burgh clerks were Ayr lawyers: James McDermeit (1748–54); James Neill (1758–66); William Gairdner of Ladykirk (1754–58, 1766–80); Robert Miller (from 1780).

The burgh records faithfully report appointments made and decisions confirmed, but like some other records, they conceal as much as they reveal. In 1770 it was noted that there was "a competition for the chancellorship" with William Fullarton of Rosemount being preferred to Charles Dalrymple of Orangefield. It was also cryptically remarked that the election had to be adjourned from 31 October until 29 November "in consequence of an interruption of the proceedings". Another source unexpectedly presents evidence that on this occasion there was outburst of violence and continued bitterness. On the eve of the election there was a riot, in which Fullarton hit a bystander and was detained in the tolbooth for three hours. Several lawsuits followed, one a complaint against Dalrymple that he refused to come from Orangefield in the middle of the night and as a justice of the peace secure his rival's release. Fullarton lost his case in the Court of Session. We know all this because Dalrymple engaged in his defence James Boswell of Auchinleck, every detail of whose career has been so fully investigated. Among Boswell's legal papers is an enigmatic reported remark by one of the judges at the trial, which may explain the election riot: "Casual commotion all owing to advent of girls". Andrew Paton, one of the Prestwick bailies seems to have been somehow involved, for when nominated as an elder, the kirk session minutes indicate that there were "certain deficulties anent the ordination".

A longer dispute, in which the above was perhaps only one episode, also went to the Court of Session, and necessarily required mention in the burgh records. In 1766 it was "putt to the vote, whether or not the old custom in dividing their dales, which was run rigg and rigg about, so that no freeman had two riggs of his freedom lying together, should continue, or whether or not the land divisable amongst the freemen for their dales should be ordered to be planned and laid down in thirty six loats, so that each freeman might have his loat lying together, and injoy and possess the same for the space of twenty one years as freemen of

Prestick." A majority agreed to abandonment of runrig in favour of introducing consolidated holdings. A former chancellor David Andrew protested on behalf of himself, those who had voted with him, and those freemen who were minors or otherwise could not attend the meeting. Despite this opposition, in 1767 the arable land, 200 acres in extent, was divided into thirty six dales, which were allocated by ballot; and equal shares were made in the pasturage and the peat holes. An action was led by John Guthrie and David Andrew against the chancellor James Blair and those freemen who authorised the innovation; but in 1772 the Court of Session rejected the objections, and the particular complaint that no distinction had been

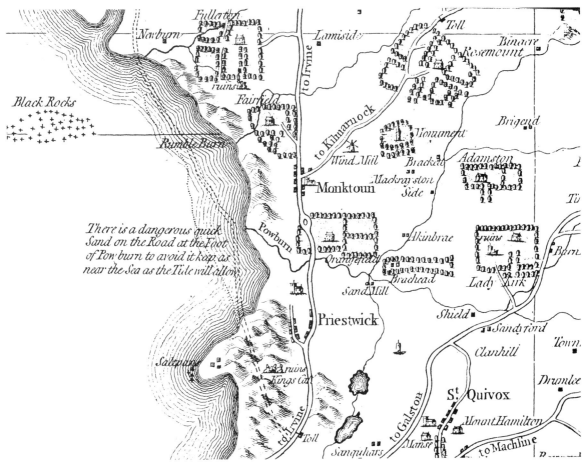

Detail from the map of Ayrshire published in 1775 by Andrew and Mostyn Armstrong. Prestwick and Monkton remained small communities. Landowners were improving their estates – Fairfield, Orangefield, Adamton, and Ladykirk in this parish, Fullarton and Rosemount nearby. But the sandhills of Prestwick were not yet levelled, nor the Newton loch drained. The monument to James Macrae of Orangefield is shown; the nearby windmill is an indication of increased production of grain; on the coast are Oswald of Auchincruive's salt-pans; Kingcase had become ruinous; and east of Prestwick the Shaw Tower is depicted, though unnamed. The new turnpike roads are delineated, with their toll-houses; and there is indicated the coastal route to Irvine used by those who wished to avoid payment.

made between the infield and outfield parts of the arable land. But opposition persisted. Ten freemen were fortunate enough to be allocated plots in "what is called the infeild, or in other terms the croft land, which are situated close or hard by the town of Prestick ... lands on which the freemen of Prestick were alwayes in the use of laying out their dung and mannure made within the burgh": these lands were known as the Stripe, the Holm, Twenty-elns, Inches, and laigh Wraes. All the other freemen were less lucky, receiving plots in the "outfeild, or what in other terms are called feild land, which ly at a greater distance from the town ... these never received any dung or manure from the freemen save a little wrack or sea ware": these were lands known as the Bull-yeat, Newlands, Cranliehill, and the Path. Discontent continued until by legal process two advocates were in 1780 appointed as arbiters. They drew up a sett of the burgh, defining its constitution in thirteen clauses. The arable lands were reallocated, with boundaries of the thirty-six arable plots marked on a carefully-drawn plan.

By the constitution of 1780, the number of freemen burgesses was fixed at thirty-six, each entitled to an equal share in the arable and pasture land, and in electing magistrates and other officers. No others might participate, and no honorary or nominal burgesses should be admitted, as had previously occurred. The burgh records list forty-three honorary burgesses so created between 1726 and 1772, including James Blair and Charles Dalrymple, each of whom by this means became eligible for election as chancellor. Legitimate procedure had been followed when William Fullarton of Rosemount succeeded a freeman who was (conveniently) disposing of his freedom, paying £40 sterling to the burgh and Fullarton was admitted in time for his election a few months later. It was now defined that a freeman might bequeath his freedom to descendants, failing whom only to the issue of an elder brother or sister. If there were no legal successor, or if a freeman wished to dispose of his freedom, it must revert to the community. The magistrates and council must then sell it to the best advantage of the community, preference being given to persons who were or would become residents, or those existing honorary freemen, providing they matched any other offer.

Affairs of the burgh were to be managed by a chancellor or provost, two baillies, a treasurer, four councillors, a procurator-fiscal, with two liners who could also be councillors. They must all be freemen, except for the chancellor whose sole function as now defined was to preside at meetings. Elections would be held each second year on the first Tuesday in November at noon in the court-house, with freemen previously advised by the burgh-officer to attend. Only those who were freemen might vote; females might be represented by a husband or eldest son; minors were excluded. All must be elected at this meeting by majority of those freemen present, except for two of the councillors who were nominated by the baillies.

The method of allocating arable land among the thirty-six freemen was prescribed: "The numbers of the said lots shall be written on different slips of paper or pieces of card or parchment and put into one bag or box, and the names of the said thirty-six freemen shall be wrote in the same manner and put into another

The modern landscape with plantations and hedges was a creation of 18th century improving landlords, illustrated on this view of Ladykirk. (*KA*)

bag or box, and the bags or boxes being shaken, the name of a freeman shall be drawn promiscuously from amongst their names by such proper neutral person as the majority of the freemen present shall chuse; and after his name is marked, a number shall be drawn promiscuously from amongst the numbers of the lots by another proper neutral person also chosen by the majority of the freemen present; and the possession of the lands in the lot of which the number is so drawn shall belong and be allocated to the freeman whose name has been previously drawn as aforesaid." The thirty-six divisions were apparently as previously made in 1767, marked on the prepared plan, "pitted, marked, marched and laid off upon the ground conform to the divisions on the said plan" and the liners appointed were "in time coming to have the lines of said marches and divisions duly observed and distinguished." Most of the divisions were just over five acres in area; seven were less than five acres, one only 3 acres 2 roods 25 falls; the four largest ranged from 6 acres to 6½ acres; variations presumably to some extent an attempt to compensate for the character of the land.

The freemen were also entitled to their share in the pasture land, and the magistrates and council, who might seek "the advice of skillful persons", should determine the "soums of grass", that is, the number of horses, sheep, and cows that could be maintained. The number of soums divided into thirty-six shares would determine each freeman's soums. In 1767 it had been assessed "that the ground would keep to the extent of sevinty two sums upon the same, being two sums to

62

each freeman, and the sums to be at the rate following, viz., each cow of three years of age to be a soum, each three queys or stirks of one year old to be a soum, a quey of two years of age and one of one year old to be a soum, each horse above three year old to be one soum and one half, each mare and foal to be two soums, every five ews and lambs to be ane soum, each six yeal (mature) sheep to be one soum."

Allocation to the freemen was also made of the Peat-holes, which were divided into thirty-six lots, each exactly of 1 acre 1 rood 24 falls. In 1767 it had been instructed that "if any persons shall not fill up all the holes in the lot he gets and bring in the same to be arable ground within ten years after martinmas next he shall forfeit the sum of five pounds sterling upon his freedom." The plan made in 1780 shows no sign of any of the forty-eight acres of peatland converted into arable, but seven continuing peat-holes with each freeman possessing the right to dig in one or more.

The number of freemen being fixed at thirty-six, no one could subdivide his freedom, or acquire others. Any freeman might lease his arable land, his share of the pasture, and his right to peat, granting it to unfreeman whether resident or stranger, or to another freeman, who would have prior claim. But such leases could not extend beyond the date of the next ballot. From 1780 that would be in 1801, after an interval of twenty-one years; and beyond that, allocations each nine years were planned; but these last proposals would be superseded.

When those arrangements were made in 1780, massive changes were under way on Ayrshire estates, where innovations in agrarian techniques were being made. The peculiar cirumstances obtaining in Prestwick militated against local experimentation or improvement. Temporary tenure of a plot of arable land inhibited investment of capital even if a freeman had the necessary resources; and it was difficult to arrange within six acres an effective rotation of crops. The pasture allowed for the whole community a maximum of 216 cattle or 360 sheep, it was of poor quality, and there was no opportunity for anyone to build up a substantial herd or flock. The situation was exactly as in the neighbouring burgh of Newton, where a critical assessment was made: "In regard to their property, That a considerable tract of ground, belonging to them, remained in common; and, that no favourable presage could be drawn, from the manner in which their small possessions were cultivated; for, that in a much inclosed country, their acres remained open, were kept constantly in tillage, and consequently, in a state greatly inferior to the lands of those who held a larger extent of ground in their possession, and whose rights were not liable to the same system of restriction". In the *Statistical Account* it was confirmed that "The grounds are mostly enclosed with ditch and hedge in the Monktown part of the parish and properly subdivided into parks, with extensive belts of planting. In Prestwick, the enclosures are few, the soil sandy, and the tenure by which they hold their freedoms unfavourable for such improvements."

In the Monkton part of the parish, it was noted, even the poorer soils were utilised where "as it approaches the sea, is sandy and benty downs, that answer for the pasturing of young cattle; and from saltness of the water, and warmth of the

Monkton House was rebuilt and renamed Orangefield by James Macrae after his hero, William of Orange. (*JH*)

climate, judged conducive to the recovery of weak sheep. Snow and frost are of short duration in the winter, and the pasture open". Inland the soil was "deep and loamy", comparable to that of the Prestwick arable plots; but even the higher ground of Monkton with its "earthy clay" had achieved higher productivity than at Prestwick.

The same reporter (Rev. Andrew Mitchell), who was writing in the 1790s, revealed that in Monkton "The most of the enclosing and planting has been made within these 60 years, and there are people still alive, who remember when it began." Farms had been divided and new farm houses built. The rotation pioneered by Alexander Fairlie of Fairlie had been adopted: two years oats, then barley, bear (coarse barley), peas and beans, or another crop of oats, laid down with grass seed, one or two years of hay, then grass for four to six years. As manure, seaweed was used on farms near the sea; all applied lime, imported from an adjacent parish. An Engish type of plough was now in use, drawn by two or three horses. Oats was sown in March-April, barley and bear in May; hay was harvested in June-July, grain crops in August-September. Grain was milled, and being of high quality, fetched good prices at Ayr market. Some wheat was sown, and produced good crops. Potatoes were mostly planted for family use, about thirteen acres in Monkton, only ten acres in Prestwick. The cultivation of turnips was recently introduced; not yet grown in Prestwick, though at Monkton one farmer sowed six or seven acres, found them useful for fattening black cattle and for sale at Ayr. The landowners, who among them owned the thirty-seven Monkton farms, were able to charge higher rents. In the 1730s ground rents ranged from 2s 6d sterling per acre (outfield) to 13s 4d (croftland); by the 1790s the cheapest was 25s, the dearest above 40s per acre, and grass land could be let for pasture at 21s to 30s per acre. The freeholds at Prestwick were then valued at 50s yearly, meaning that if rented they would yield less than 10s per arable acre. From what we learned earlier of the capacity of its pasture land, Prestwick could have supported only a fraction of the 220 cows, 250 sheep, and 92 horses which the whole parish contained in 1793.

Agricultural improvements often imposed financial strain upon owners of small estates such as those in Monkton parish. For this and other personal reasons we find numerous changes in ownership, with established families often impoverished and replaced by moneyed men. In the 17th century Ladykirk passed out of Blair ownership into possession of John Gairdner; then his son, William Gairdner, writer in Ayr, who was involved in Prestwick burgh as its clerk in 1754 and from 1766 until his death in 1780; whose son Alexander Gairdner would eventually sell Ladykirk to R.A.Oswald of Auchincruive. In 1740 Fairfield was acquired by William Campbell, whose family for several generations had been merchants in Ayr; his son William Campbell became an advocate and was provost of Ayr in 1783–85. In 1783 Adamton passed out of Blair hands. That estate, worth two or three hundred pounds a year, was inherited by Catherine Blair. When she was eighteen years of age, her guardian Lord Auchinleck thought she would made a good match for his son, James Boswell, who paid court to her. So did her neighbour William Fullarton, whose father had acquired Rosemount in Symington parish, an estate he inherited and improved after returning in 1766 from service as a surgeon in India. But Catherine rejected both in 1768, and eight years later married her cousin Sir William Maxwell of Monreith. In 1783 she sold Adamton to Robert Reid, of whom little is known save that he had made his money in business, being described as "the architect of his own fortune". Monkton estate had been acquired in 1695 by William Baillie, an Edinburgh merchant; his son, the advocate Hugh Baillie, built a new Monkton House, but financial reverses forced him to dispose of this estate in 1734. It went to James Macrae, a poor Ayrshire lad who rose to become Governor of Madras in India where he amassed a large fortune. He returned to this country in 1731, purchased Blackheath estate in Kent, and came home to Ayrshire two years later. Monkton House he renamed Orangefield, after William of Orange, whom he also commemorated by erecting a statue in Glasgow. He also assisted Glasgow to pay for the levy imposed by the Jacobite army which occupied the city in 1745. After his death in 1746 the Macrae Monument was erected on a prominent site overlooking the estate; it was built in 1748, collapsed and re-erected in 1750, perhaps intended as a mausoleum for his remains which were interred in Monkton churchyard. Being a bachelor, during his lifetime he enriched distant surviving relatives. For Hugh McGuire, a carpenter in Newton who eked out a living by playing the fiddle, he purchased the small estate of Drumdow in Stair parish. His son James McGuire got Houston in Renfrewshire and took the name of James Macrae. The three daughters received similar awards. Elizabeth McGuire was presented with Ochiltree estate, and a handsome dowry when she married the impoverished 13th earl of Glencairn. Margaret McGuire similarly obtained Alva estate in Stirlingshire and the hand of James Erskine, later Lord Barjarg and Lord Alva. Governor Macrae's favourite, the youngest daughter, Macrae McGuire, inherited Orangefield and in 1750 married Charles Dalymple, who was Sheriff-Clerk of Ayrshire. Their son, James Dalrymple of Orangefield, succeeded in 1785, and was one of Robert Burns's patrons. In 'The Vision', Dalrymple is described as "The owner of a pleasant spot, Near sandy wilds", which suggests that the poet was familiar with Prestwick and may have visited Orangefield. Dalrymple would squander his inheritance, went bankrupt in 1791, and had to sell Orangefield before his death in 1795. Despite the changing fortunes of many who possessed the estates in the parish, it is clear that they devoted considerable efforts to making improvements, as compared with the freemen of Prestwick who seldom had resources and in any case lacked incentive to develop their temporary holdings.

It would seem that similarly there was little expansion of the town of Prestwick in the 18th century. The burgh, originally conceived as a place where trades might be fostered, remained a community devoted almost exclusively to cultivation. The number of inhabitants, estimated as around 200 in the 15th century and above 300 a hundred years later, had declined in the 17th century. In 1791 the parish population was only 717, with the town of Prestwick containing 266 persons, Monkton village having fewer than 200, and the rest in the countryside. By comparison, Newton-upon-Ayr, disjoined from Monkton and Prestwick Parish in 1779, had then a population of around 800, which doubled in the next twenty years. Newton burgh retained its agrarian character but the town was rapidly growing as an industrial suburb of Ayr.

By the end of the 18th century the town of Prestwick extended south of the Cross for less than half a mile, with most of its sixty-six dwelling-houses straggling along the long road through the sand dunes, towards Newton two miles distant. Within this community most families' livelihood depended upon agriculture, for there were (in 1791) only sixteen weavers, two stockingmakers, four wrights, one mason, and one blacksmith. There was however some indication of improving prospects. The market cross was restored in 1777 and the tolbooth rebuilt in 1780. In 1791 it was reported that thirteen new houses had been erected within the previous seven or eight years. Monkton village, though smaller than Prestwick, could boast (in 1791) a wider range of crafts: four wrights, four shoemakers, two tailors, two tobacco manufacturers, one cooper, one weaver, one mason, one blacksmith. Eight new dwellings had been recently erected, as well as two premises to house a novel industrial development. To the customary weaving of woollens was added this new textile manufacture, operated within two cotton houses, one containing nine and the other six spinning jennies, and employing "a considerable number of hands".

Prestwick's only significant industrial development was in saltmaking. Because of increasing 18th century demands, efforts were made to increase production, even though the processes were laborious and expensive. Sea water brought in at high tide was trapped in reservoirs cut in the rock, then transported to saltpans

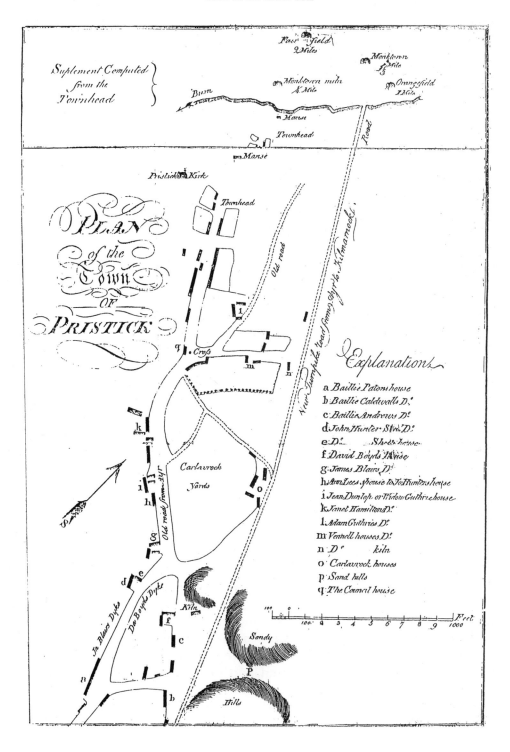

Prestwick burgh in 1780 contained fewer than 300 inhabitants.

where the water was boiled off by coal fires underneath. At best a poor-quality salt for domestic use could be produced – fish-curing needed superior imported salt. The sea water on this part of the coast, diluted by fresh water from the River Ayr, had a relatively low salt content, so that much fuel was required. The local salt industry also suffered from the huge extent of smuggling of salt from Ireland. Nevertheless, during the 18th century there were several saltpans in this locality. There were the long-established Craigie pans at Bellrock Cottage, operated by John Guthrie (1720) and Robert Wilson (1750). Also on Craigie property were Allison's pans at Bentfield; and a further set of pans still further south beside the Bellrock pit near the Newton boundary. Each of these could for a time be supplied with coals extracted in the immediate neighbourhood. To the north at Maryburgh other pans were established by Richard Oswald who acquired Auchincruive in 1764. From the freemen he obtained in 1765 "a liberty for erecting a salt pan, one or more, on the sea coast within the liberty of the town of Prestick, with some grounds for building houses on and yeards for the salters and other workers". Nine acres, known as the Clak, were feued at £20 grassum on entry and £1 annually thereafter. Oswald had hopes of developing those coalworks which were already established in St Quivox parish at East Sanquhar, and sought permission from the freemen to construct several roads through the lands of Prestwick. One such coal road was to supply the saltpans at Maryburgh. A second road was authorised "through the lands belonging to the burgh in that dale called the Aitkinhead, of twenty four foots wide" by which coals might be more directly conveyed to Prestwick, Monkton, and points north. Oswald also obtained permission to cross part of the burgh lands with "a wagon road of thirty foots wide from his coalworks in the estate of Auchincroue, straight to the harbour of Ayr". This was first in a network of waggonways which would lead from the coalworks of St Quivox parish towards Ayr harbour. This waggonway crossed from Prestwick into the lands of Newton at Heathfield, and though no coal was then being worked on the lands of Prestwick, prospecting in the southern parts alongside the waggonway led in 1791 to "appearances that indicate that such may be found in process of time, and will undoubtedly turn out to great advantage". However, transport of coals from Sanquhar to the Maryburgh saltpans seems to have proved impracticable. Concurrently, following the death of Sir Thomas Wallace in 1771, his grandson Sir Thomas Dunlop-Wallace relinquished control of the Craigie saltpans. By the early 1770s the Craigie-Maryburgh saltpans were being managed by a Mr Alexander, possibly Robert Alexander from Edinburgh who in 1769 inherited the Blackhouse estate in St Quivox parish and engaged John Beaumont to expand coal production on his estate. Beaumont was a business associate of William and John Caddell who came from Cockenzie and were involved in various industrial enterprises. By 1776 the Caddells were managing the Craigie-Maryburgh pans. They were advised, "I do not know if your Pans here are upon a good construction; and if you have good Salters, or not; but I know it requires great care and attention, as well as skill, and that the bringing the Pans to salt, is a nice operation." They brought from the east some men of experience, Robert Stein and David Bryan as master salters, James

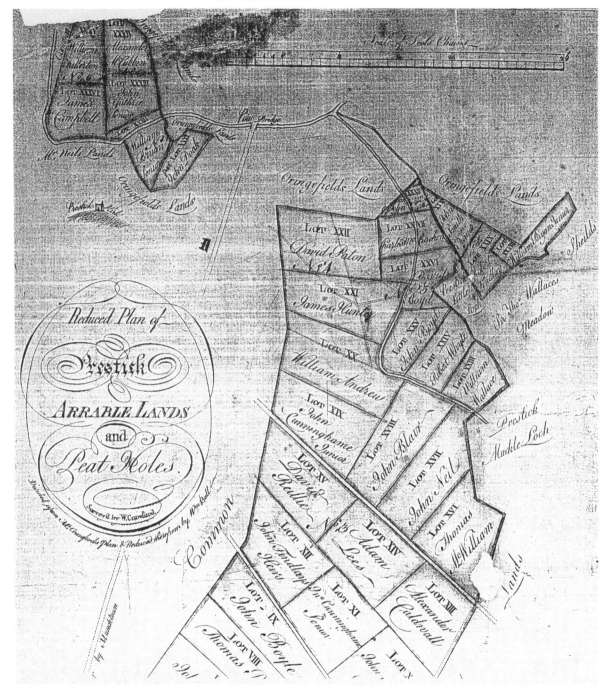

Detail from a plan of 1780, in which year the number of freemen was fixed at thirty-six.

Clark as blower man, James Morrison as agent, and employed local workers as part-time assistants. Supplies of coal they obtained from Dr John Campbell of Wellwood, who was now sole partner of the Newton Coal Company. There were problems. Coal could be purchased from Campbell at one shilling a ton, but it cost more than that for carriage (1s 6d) plus the charge per cart (4d) at Prestwick toll. The road from Newton past the toll was "pretty good" but the carts could not take more than 5 cwt loads through the "heavy sands" to Maryburgh. To save the "exorbitant expense of Carriage and Tolls", shipping coals along the coast in lighters was suggested in 1776. In 1777 at the Newton colliery there were labour disputes "betwixt Dr Campbell and his Coliers part of whom have left" and indeed production ceased there in 1780. Alternative supplies were obtainable from Robert Alexander of Blackhouse and Richard Oswald of Auchincruive. In 1779 there were plans to improve the Maryburgh road to allow loads of 10 cwts, with a consequent reduction in costs, but the consent of the proprietors of the ground would be required, and these were "the Lords of Prestock, a very willful ignorant set" It was hoped to operate four pans – presumably the two Craigie pans and the two at Maryburgh – for there was a ready market, with George Black, an Ayr retailer, taking bulk orders. Further, "if a method could be fallen upon to suppress the smuggling of Irish salt it would turn out to Great Advantage". There was a change of cirumstances in the next decade. In 1786 John Taylor from Edinburgh reopened the Newton colliery and the following year bought the Blackhouse estate. By this time Sir Thomas Dunlop-Wallace had been forced to sell off his Craigie estate, and that Prestwick portion containing the Craigie saltpans passed into Taylor's posses-sion. He and his sons had by 1816 ten pans operating at Newton, and it seems unlikely that after 1786 he would wish to continue leasing the Craigie pans to the Caddells. In 1787 they decided to give up their lease of the two remaining Oswald pans at Maryburgh. An inventory made in 1790 describes Maryburgh as a stone building containing two pans with accommodation for salters upstairs, and that house (which still survives) had then stables and a smithy adjoining. In 1791 Dr Mitchell in his report for the *Statistical Account* made no mention of salt pans. But if production had then ceased, it was renewed, for Mr Oswald's Pans are named on plans of 1814 and 1831, while those of Craigie, Bentfield, and Bellrock are described as ruins.

One 18th century enterprise in which some of the folk of Monkton and Prestwick participated was what was euphemistically described as "the free trade". A century later it was recalled that "the inhabitants of Monkton were notorious for their smuggling exploits". It was reputed that illicit imported spirits were concealed at a house called Rum How, in a nearby field named Brandy Hill, or within a tomb in St Quivox kirkyard. Several farmers of the time allegedly transported smuggled goods, and one is said to have been killed in an affray. Tradition has suggested that Rev. John Fulton, a young man who was minister of this parish from 1720 till his early death in 1730, was involved. He is supposed to have acted as decoy by drinking with the tidewaiters, whose responsibility as customs officers was to keep watch for landings. Later in the century a more efficient service was established, and by 1791 Monkton had a resident customs officer. Nevertheless, in the early 19th century loads of Arran whisky were being illicitly landed on Prestwick sands and supplied to reputable customers at eleven shillings a gallon.

The so-called Roman Bridge was possibly built in the 18th century to provide crossing of the Pow Burn for a turnpike road planned to bypass Prestwick. (*KA*)

Evading another form of payment was also practised following the establishment of turnpike roads in Ayrshire. By the Ayrshire Turnpike Act of 1767 the roads through Monkton and Prestwick parish leading from Ayr towards Kilmarnock and Irvine were among those designated for improvement. Previously roads were imperfectly maintained by tenants, cottars, and servants, who were expected to devote several days each year to this unwelcome task; and by landowners, who were supposed to supervise and make financial contribution. By the 1767 Act, such statute labour was commuted into money contributions to the Ayrshire Turnpike Trust, which was composed of landowners devoted to road improvement. But the principal source of income was from those using the roads, who paid when passing the turnpike gates at tollhouses erected at intervals along those roads. In 1769 Prestwick Toll was established. The trustees in 1767 originally favoured a route "by the back of Prestick" through "Prestick arable and meadow". Part of this road was laid out, for it appears on a plan of 1780 following the line of Sandfield Road and Caerlaverock Road, and went on to cross the Pow Burn by the so-called "Roman Bridge"; and indeed Sandfield Cottage was built to provide a hostelry for travellers on this route. But the bypass scheme was soon abandoned, and the turnpike road followed the traditional but awkward passage through the town of Prestwick. When Prestwick Toll was set up, the Turnpike Trustees suggested that "to guard against evading of the said Tollbar there ought to be built a sufficient stone Dyke from Newton Loch to one end of the said Bar, and from the other end of the Bar along the said march to the sea ... and appoint the minds of the Baillies of Newton and

Prestick to be asked as to said Dyke." But this was judged too expensive to construct, so that some of those who travelled up the coast from Ayr evaded paying by leaving the road before Prestwick Toll and following the shore as far as Irvine. This route was sufficiently wellknown as to be marked on Armstrongs' Map of 1775, with the warning: "There is a dangerous quick Sand on the Road at the Foot of Pow burn to avoid it keep as near the Sea as the Tide will allow". The parish minister of Dundonald wrote in 1792 that "a strong temptation is presented to pass from the one town to the other along shore" but repeated that this route "on account of its quick sands, is very dangerous to travellers". He added that several persons had been buried alive at that spot, and advised against passing at high tide. While the shore route was convenient for wayfarers on foot or horseback, the turnpike roads were essential for the coaches and growing number of carriers' carts plying between Ayr and Irvine, and to Glasgow via Kilmarnock.

Glimpses of 18th century social life appear from stray references in contemporary and later documents. Though the little town of Prestwick was larger than the village of Monkton, the latter as parish centre had more facilities. Monkton village was provided with five public houses (as compared with only two in Prestwick). Village life in Monkton was enhanced by establishment of a masonic lodge in 1762, and (as noticed in the kirk session minutes) a dancing school in 1769. Within the parish the farmers from 1797 till 1887 maintained a Wreck Brethren Society, electing a president and two baillies to regulate the carting of seaweed (wrack) and maintaining the roads from the shore; this society met usually in Monkton Inn or the schoolhouse, which was located within Monkton village.

The Church took responsibility for provision of education. The heritors, who were supposed to provide the finance, were notoriously unwilling to do so. In 1727 the schoolmaster at Monkton was receiving only forty pounds Scots, equivalent to £3 6s 8d sterling and less than the minimum of one hundred merks (£66 13s 4d Scots, £5 11s 1d sterling) as required by the Act of 1696. Following representations from Ayr Presbytery, the laird of Adamton expressed "his willingness to concurr with the other heritors about redressing what is wanting of a sallary for a schoolmaster". But the Monkton school continued to be poorly provided. Classes were conducted in a cottage where in 1766 "a partition is necessary to separate the school-house from the schoolmaster's house". There was also a school at Prestwick, though the only notice is in 1762 when William King left it to become schoolmaster at Monkton. Quite soon he was followed as parish schoolmaster by David Thomson, who demitted his charge in 1772 and died leaving his family "in very straitened circumstances"; David Neil who left in 1776 to teach in Ayr; then John Wallace who resigned to better himself as a clerk in Glasgow. Robert Carson who was appointed in 1783 obtained a basic salary of £100 Scots, above the legal minimum, but hardly enough to cope with the now-inflated cost of living. He enjoyed a free house and garden, and income from school fees but, as the parish minister admitted, "the wages for teaching are very small." His charges were 1s 6d a quarter for reading, 2s for writing, 3s for arithmetic and church music. He had forty scholars, but they usually attended only three quarters in the year, being absent when working in the fields at seedtime and harvest. It is not surprising that teachers did not stay long in Monkton parish school.

The landowners as heritors were by law also required to maintain those aged and infirm persons who had no other means of support, but in practice poor relief was also left almost entirely to the church. In 1698 licensed begging had been authorised by the kirk session, but sometime during the 18th century this practice was abandoned. Church collections and various fees were devoted to building up a Poors Fund, which amounted to £68 in 1767 and increased to £130 by 1791. About £22 was that year collected at church, sufficient to meet expenditure. Twelve aged or infirm parishioners were each paid three shillings a month to augment their own meagre resources, with rather more to those who were quite destitute. There were also eight poor persons lodged at Kingcase, until 1786 when it was purchased from Sir Thomas Dunlop-Wallace by Ayr town council. The magistrates of Ayr then acquired "the sole and absolute right of presenting pensioners to the hospital". But they allowed the cottages to fall into ruin, and the contributions from the farms of Shields and Loans went to support the poor of Ayr parish.

Poor relief at three shillings a month provided an annual subsistence of less than £2 a year, at a time when inflation was causing problems. Local wages in 1791 were recorded in the *Statistical Account*. Male farm servants earned from £8 8s to £10 a year, female servants from £3 10s to £4, in each case with bed and board. Day labourers' pay ranged from 10d per day in winter to 1s 4d at harvest, so if fully-employed they might take in £15 a year. Craftsmen could with luck take in twice that, with masons at 1s 8d to 3s a day, wrights at 1s 4d to 1s 6d; tailors got only 10d a day but as they travelled around making up garments they could claim their meals. Less fortunate than many craftsmen was the parish schoolmaster, whose income would be about £20, plus free house and garden, and small fees as session clerk and as precentor leading the singing of psalms at public worship. By comparison, the parish minister's income was more than £100, with a manse and glebe, and £5 for communion elements. Just over £25 was computed on a cash basis, but the most valuable part of his stipend was a stipulated quantity of grain – more than 50 bolls of bear and 29 bolls of oatmeal – which, based on fiars prices, yielded in 1790 a monetary equivalent of nearly £80, which sum continued to increase in line with grain prices.

After the Patronage Act of 1712, the chief landowner of a parish (or the Crown in some cases) was made responsible for appointment of the minister when the charge fell vacant. In the parish of Monkton and Prestwick the right of presentation went to the lairds of Adamton. After the death in 1718 of Rev. Matthew Baird, Adamton nominated Rev. John Fulton, who had been Baird's assistant. Certain parishioners resented this appointment of a minister not of their choosing, and protested to Ayr Presbytery that Fulton was an alcoholic who consorted with smugglers. It was charged that he was "a deep drinker" and "could fill three companions drunk while he himself kept pretty sober". Yet Fulton was ordained in 1720. Five further presentations would be required to replace three ministers who died in their forties and two others who after a few years here chose to be

Sandfield House, erected beside the projected road to by-pass the town, survived two centuries to become Prestwick's last thatched house, demolished in 1958.

translated to other parishes. Fulton died in 1730 after ten years; his successor Rev. Thomas Andrews died in 1734 after serving only three years; Rev. James Stirling left in 1742 after five years; Rev. William Walker in 1760 after twelve years; Rev. John Cunninghame who was ordained in 1762 died twelve years later.

The Presbytery of Ayr showed concern in 1737 for the condition of the manse – possibly that old building which was sited between St Nicholas Church and the Pow Burn. Only one of its walls had been built with lime mortar; the other three were held together by mud; and the south side wall was bulging nine inches from the plumb. "We think the house can by no reparation be made sufficient, unless these insufficient walls be taken down and rebuilt from the foundation, which in all probability would occasion the falling of the other parts." A better manse was now constructed, presumably the one at Monkton, and in good condition when, after the unfortunate sequence of brief ministries, there arrived Rev. Andrew Mitchell, whose tenure was more satisfactory in length and character.

Andrew Mitchell was second son of the laird of Dalgain, a small estate in Sorn parish. After study at Glasgow University he was presented to Muirkirk parish, ordained in 1751, and held that charge for twenty-four years. In 1775 he was translated to Monkton and Prestwick, following presentation by Catherine Blair of Adamton, perhaps on the recommendation of Mitchell's cousin, William Campbell of Fairfield. When he was inducted to Monkton, Mitchell was a fifty-year-old bachelor, a man of means who had acquired the small estate of Avisyard near Cumnock and was wealthy enough to lend £470 in 1785 to James Boswell of

Auchinleck. He was made doctor of divinity by Edinburgh University in 1784, was conservative in theological views, and critical of Rev. Dr. William McGill of Ayr who was charged with heresy but exonerated in 1791. For his opposition to McGill, Robert Burns in 'The Kirk's Alarm' satirised Mitchell as "Andrew Gowk", telling him, "Ye're rich and look big". In conducting worship, Mitchell is said to have suffered from occasional confusion in expressing himself, and in 1810, an old man in his eighties and with only one more year to live, he could not sign the minutes of the kirk session "on account of his Imbicility and failure of sight". But for thirty-six years – as Hewat was informed by those who had known Mitchell – things seem to have moved "quietly and smoothly", the people "kept well together", and dissent was "almost unknown".

Early in his ministry, Newton-on-Ayr was in an amicable manner disjoined to become a separate parish. Dr Mitchell in his contribution to the *Statistical Account* explained: "Before this disjunction and erection took place, the inhabitants of Newton were distant from the parish church of Monktown, about 4 English miles, and were the most numerous part of the parish, amounting to between 800 and 900 persons. The valuation of the burgh being small, they had only a seat in Monktown church that could contain 12 or 14 persons at most." The community of Newton made use of their burgh funds to build in 1777 a church which was recognised by Ayr Presbytery as a chapel of ease. In 1778 they appointed as their minister Rev. William Peebles, having purchased the right of presentation from

Prestwick from Ayr Road · Mar. 97

Prestwick in the 18th century remained a rural village, with the main street little changed by 1897 when sketched by T. Smellie for Steven's *Guide*.

Sir William Maxwell, who by his marriage in 1776 to Catherine Blair of Adamton became patron of Monkton and Prestwick parish. He and the other heritors in 1779 agreed to recognition of Newton as a separate parish.

While the population of Newton increased to 1,689 in 1791, the truncated parish of Monkton and Prestwick then contained no more than 717 persons. The church at Monkton was considered now central enough to cater for parishioners in Prestwick, who lived only a mile distant from it. That church was the pre-Reformation building dedicated to St Cuthbert, which would continue as a place of worship until 1837, though in the 1790s the walls were already "bended off the perpendicular on one side, and rent in the west gable". The church of St Nicholas at Prestwick, where services were conducted every third Sunday until 1779, was subsequently less regularly used for public worship.

The kirk session throughout the 18th century met sometimes in Monkton, sometimes in Prestwick. Minutes of meetings record arrangements for annual celebration of the Sacrament. Before 1721 it was normally in April or May but then changed, "it being the very throng of the labour"; for a time the third sabbath in July was chosen, though sometimes a later date was preferred. Always the sacrament was preceded by examining the roll of communicants to purge those deemed unfit to participate; members of the session themselves submitted to privy censure; and there were days of fasting and humiliation. The elders' devotion to their responsibilities is variously revealed. In 1722 "the minister proposed to the Session that besides the usual meetings for prayer with him they would divide into two classes for prayer among themselves"; a year later these exercises were being performed; and in 1725 the elders were studying church law and practice, the minister having provided books and "it was agreed that each member should have them to peruse a month by turns".

The kirk session's responsibility for parochial discipline appears most prominently in the record of those cited to be examined for moral lapses, and if found guilty required to appear before the congregation for rebuke and absolution. Marriages were announced by proclamation of banns; this was customarily preceded by celebration in an ale-house to which the session clerk was invited. The kirk session in 1716 legislated: "Finding that the people, in giving in their names to be proclaimed in order to marriage, sit frequently too late upon the Saturday night att drink, and incroatch upon the Lord's Day, therefore they have made an Act discharging any bookings to be upon the Saturday, in all tyme coming." Weddings, which were considered irregular unless performed in church, were accompanied by other customs, including a horse race called *the riding of the broose*.

Rev. Kirkwood Hewat committed to print several other items based on what he called "word-of-mouth information", which we should now define as oral history, and so reported traditions of some antiquity. In his day, dancing around a bonfire on Midsummer Eve was still practised, a posssible relic of pagan worship. Though he had no evidence of continuing belief in holy wells, he could remark that "there is still the Lady Well – though not used now – behind the Kirk knoll, which the old wives said contained fine water for making tea." He recounted a tale regarding superstitious belief in the appearance of Satan, taken from an earlier writer who placed the incident "about the end of the 17th or beginning of the 18th century" and located at the Prestwick tolbooth. There a freeman could be incarcerated, but not locked in; though if he let himself out he lost his privileges as a freeman. The story however relates to a boy who was locked in on the charge of stealing peas. "David Rankine (afterwards smith in Kilmarnock) then apprentice to the bailie, and who had also made free with the pease, found means to steal the key of the prison, from under his master's pillow, and to liberate his companion. Observing a bull-stirk at hand, he incarcerated him, locked the door, and deposited the key where he had found it." The next morning the magistrates "found in prison, a bull roaring for want of food, which from their ignorance of the trick that had been practised, and the superstition of the times, they imagined to be the devil, who they thought had destroyed the prisoner." In order to *lay the devil* they sent for the parish minister. "Having learned the truth from Rankine, and none of the magistrates or barons having the hardiness to look Satan in the face, the minister easily succeeded in *laying* him. The terrified bailies and barons, happy to find that their prisoner had escaped from so formidable an enemy, inflicted no further punishment on the delinquent."

We might have known more about Prestwick in the 18th century and earlier, for Prestwick's history was explored, though never written, by that distinguished literary figure, James Boswell of Auchinleck. Early in 1773 as an Edinburgh advocate he was involved in that Court of Session case concerning a disputed Prestwick burgh election. Later that year, after conducting Dr Samuel Johnson on their famous tour to the Hebrides, he brought the great lexicographer to Ayrshire. On Monday 1 November 1773 they may have visited Prestwick when returning from Auchans to Treesbank; certainly the burgh's curious constitution was discussed by them. Johnson had certain items sent on to him in London, but complained, "No account of the little borough"; which Boswell explained (in his *Life of Dr Johnson*) referred to "The ancient Burgh of Prestick in Ayrshire". Some years later Boswell contemplated writing a history of Ayrshire. When Johnson advised him to "inquire into the old tenures and old characters of Scotland" Boswell recalled that "I have some hereditary claim to be an antiquary; not only from my father, but being descended, by my mother's side, from the able and learned Sir John Skene". The history was never written. Boswell however continued an association with Prestwick, from his courtship of Catherine Blair of Adamton in 1767; borrowing money from Rev. Andrew Mitchell in 1785; and on five occasions between 1787 and 1794 he returned to Adamton as guest of its new owner Robert Reid.

CHAPTER SEVEN

The Early 19th Century

*D*URING the first four decades of the 19th century Prestwick began to show signs of a limited growth.

In 1834 when the burgh *Records* were published, the preface described Prestwick as still "a mere country village ... The houses are chiefly thatched cottages of one story; and but for the presence of a market cross by the side of the public road in front of the main line of dwellings, there is no external object whatever, to intimate the rank or authority of the community." Yet there had been significant growth, with three times as many residents as those 266 of forty years earlier. In 1814 a dozen small plots were feued for building, beside the road north of Prestwick Toll, forming "a modern-built village for mechanics." In 1831 Prestwick's population was 758, and there were another 327 in New Prestwick, as the community at Prestwick Toll was sometimes designated. The population of the entire parish in 1801 at the first census was 986, and increased in the following decades to 1,340, 1,744, 1,818, and 1,933 by 1841. Monkton with 376 inhabitants in 1831, and the country parts of the parish with 346, showed more limited growth. Rev. Thomas Burns in his contribution to the *New Statistical Account*, written in 1832, revised in 1837, supplied other details. Most of the inhabitants were involved in the cotton trade, and some of the handloom weavers had come from Ireland to settle here. There were also a few shoemakers, whose products went for export. In the 1830s there were between 150 and 200 handloom weavers in the parish, most of them working in cotton, though a few specialised in weaving silk handkerchiefs. There were also many women employed in Ayrshire needlework, known locally as Flowering web, executing intricate patterns in muslin and cambric.

Analysis of the Census Returns for 1841 provides a more detailed picture of the local economy. Of those 770 residing within Prestwick burgh, 302 were gainfully employed. More than half of these were engaged in the cotton trade, with 103 male and 17 female handloom weavers, 27 women sewing muslins, and another 20 working in auxiliary jobs like pirn winding. One man was still weaving at the age of eighty, one boy of twelve was already so employed; a girl of that age had begun sewing, a woman of seventy-five was working at the winding. There were only 8 persons employed in shoemaking, 5 masons, 3 wrights, 3 tailors, 3 shopkeepers, one blacksmith, and a dozen others including one salmon fisherman. That the burgh retained its traditional agrarian aspect is evident from 17 residents listed as farmers, and most of the 46 men and 25 women designated as labourers and servants were agricultural workers. The only professional persons resident within the burgh were Thomas McCrorie who taught in the Freemen's School; and Robert Cruikshank who offered medical provision. New Prestwick, where 149 of its 313 inhabitants were gainfully employed, was similarly dependent upon cotton, with 47 weavers and 28 sewers. There were also 28 coal miners (the youngest an eight-year-old boy), 5 quarrymen (one of them eighty years of age!), 4 shoemakers, a few assorted tradesmen, the farmer at Braehead, twelve agricultural workmen, and eight female servants. No longer was anyone employed in saltmaking: the Maryburgh pans were occupied by two families, containing two men and three boys employed as salmon fishers. At the other end of the parish, Monkton village among its 496 inhabitants had 14 weavers, 24 sewers, and 4 others working in cotton. There was one solitary silk weaver (with another settled in New Prestwick). Adjacent to the village there were also 3 weavers at Watsonhall and 2 at Corsehill. Monkton as the parish centre also possessed a wide variety of trades (the parish total for each being given in brackets): 9 shoemakers (23), 3 tailors (8), 3 dressmakers (4), 2 wrights (7), no fewer than 8 blacksmiths (10), 3 carpenters (6), 6 masons (12), 4 carters (6), 6 quarrymen (11), 2 publicans and spirit dealers (8), 1 grocer (3). Monkton had (alone in the parish) a cooper, a tea dealer, and a lodging house keeper. Also in the village lived the parish minister, Rev. Thomas Burns, and the parochial schoolmaster, James Gibson.

For the rural part of Monkton parish, the 1841 Census Returns listed 363 inhabitants. These included 17 farmers, and 59 male and 46 female servants nearly all of whom were farm workers, as were some of the 37 male and 9 female servants resident in the village. There were millers at Powbank and Adamton Mills, but Monkton Mill had ceased operating as such. At Adamton House, Robert Reid's 74-year-old widow had several relatives as house guests, served by 7 indoor servants, a coachman, and a gardener. At Fairfield House, William Gunning Campbell (aged 57) lived more modestly with two servants. Ladykirk, owned by R.A. Oswald of Auchincruive, was tenanted and farmed by William Gemmell. Orangefield was in 1841 unoccupied: after Charles Dalrymple had to dispose of it in 1791 it passed eventually to Thomas Wilson who died in 1829, after which it was held by non-resident owners, Alexander Murdoch followed by James F. Murdoch, both lawyers in Ayr. The Census Returns of course did not list non-resident landowners; but a Land tax roll of 1837 includes lands in the parish owned by the Duke of Portland (as part of the Fullarton estate); Lord James Stuart (who now owned Rosemount); with two minor proprietors, General Sir J. Barnes (High Monktonhill and Fairleys) and Robert Andrew (Townhead).

From the Census Returns it is possible to abstract information regarding ages and sex of the population. Prestwick Burgh in 1841 appears as typical of the times, with a high proportion in the younger age groups. 29% of the inhabitants were children under the age of ten, and indeed 50% of all were under the age of twenty. The death rate was universally high, affecting young and old. Only 5% in Prestwick had survived beyond the age of sixty. The sex ratio of 11 females to 10 males was the same in Prestwick and New Prestwick as the Ayrshire average, but rather higher in Monkton village (14) and parish (13). The growth of population in the first decades of the 19th century was only partially due to natural increase. The Census Returns for 1841 do not provide information about migration within the county, but indicate some residents born in other parts of Scotland, a few from south of the border, and substantial numbers from Ireland. A score of those Irish-born were in their twenties, some of whom were likely recent arrivals; but most were in their forties or over, suggesting they had been here for some time. In New Prestwick natives of Ireland formed a significant 15% of the population. In Prestwick burgh there were as many of Irish extraction but formed a less obvious 7% of the inhabitants. They were less in evidence in Monkton village (5%) and the rural area (3%). Of those 134 Irish-born within the parish, 61 were gainfully-employed, 41 in the cotton trade.

The thirty-six freemen continued to possess the lands of Prestwick. At least fifteen of them were (in 1829) absentee owners whose holdings were farmed on their behalf. Several of these outsiders were among those elected as provosts: James Hunter (1802), David Boyd (re-elected 1806), William Fullarton of Skeldon (1810), John Guthrie (1814, 1827), Major William Neill of Barnweill (1830). In the published *Records*, the Prefactory Notice confirmed that in 1834 the burgh was still governed "by a chancellor or provost, two baillies, treaurer, clerk, and other inferior officers, who are all elected annually except the chancellor, whose appointment is for two or more years". Bailie John Smith, who had been a magistrate for seventeen years, explained that "there are four stated quarterly courts or meetings of the whole freemen, (as instituted in the year 1785, and continued ever since,) which meetings are in general pretty well attended by them, to hear and see how the affairs of the burgh are managed by the magistrates and council, and to give such directions to them concerning the management of the funds of the burgh, and any other matter that may affect them as a body: Every matter of any consequence is laid before these meetings, and discussed by them, and their proceedings are entered in the minute-books of the burgh". Bailie Smith provided some details of his experience as a magistrate, dealing with summons for debt and cases of assault. He never required to exercise severity. A few hours incarceration in the burgh prison (where freemen might be confined but not locked in) was sufficient and "generally brought the most refractory to a sense of duty." The prison was principally used as a lock-up for more serious offenders who were then transferred to the county gaol in Ayr for trial before the sheriff. Such was John Withrington, a highwayman, who in 1815 robbed two Monkton farmers at Jeanfield on the road past Symington, who was apprehended, lodged in Ayr gaol, tried in Edinburgh, and brought back to be hanged at the scene of his crime. One of the "inferior officers" was the burgh officer, who until the 1820s "by tout of drum, would make announcements to the lieges". When the Prestwick Drum then ceased to be used, the occasion was celebrated in verse. The drum was formed of "Twa guid sheep skins, wi' oaken sides, An' leather lugs aroun' ", and it was reputed to date from the 13th century "When to our shore, For aid the gallant Bruce did come, His lieges leal Did tak the fiel', An' march'd to Prest'ick drum."

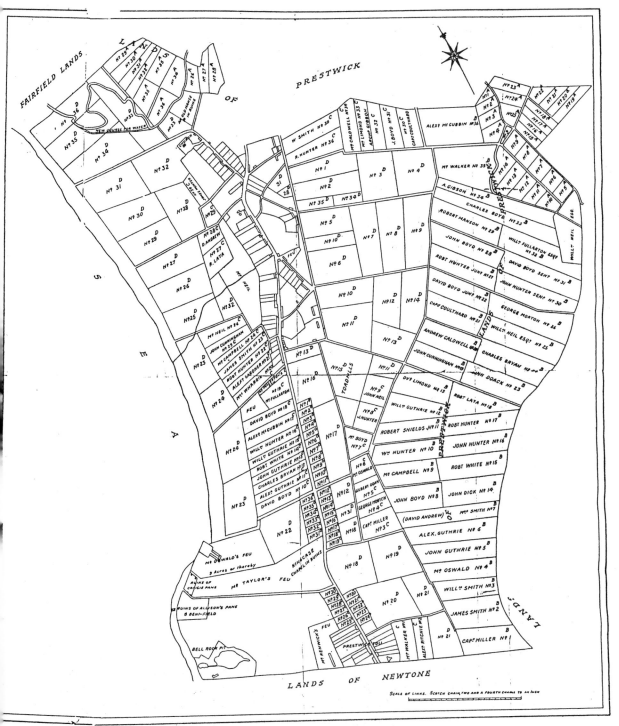

PLAN OF THE LANDS OF PRESTWICK, 1814,
BY A. AND R. KENNETH, SURVEYORS, KILWINNING.

In 1814 this plan was made when the common lands were divided up, each freeman obtaining two plots (C and D) to supplement those of indale (A) and outdale (B) land already held. In 1850 all these became heritable properties.

81

Bailie John Smith, who personally financed publication of the *Records*, was owner of Swindridgemuir estate in the parish of Dalry. There from the year 1785 he had made notable improvements, in particular by reclaiming moorland for arable farming. It would seem likely that he had some responsibility for innovations made at Prestwick, but which surprisingly find no mention in the Prefatory Notice to the *Records*. In 1767 the traditional reallocation of runrig holdings after nine years was abandoned and thirty-six new consolidated holdings were allocated to the free-men, to be held for twenty-one years. A redivision was made thirteen years later in 1780, when boundaries and process of allocation were more strictly defined. At the next occasion in 1801, a fairer distribution was made, when each freeman received a portion of indale (the former croft or infield land), another of outdale (outfield land deemed inferior). It was proposed that this arrangement should continue until the next division in thirty-eight years' time; but two years later in 1803 that was extended to ninety-nine years. In 1814 it was decided to divide up the remainder of the common lands. Each freeman was provided with two additional individual plots, which hopefully might be converted into arable land by following the techniques which John Smith had published in 1797. Each freeman also received in feu one sixteenth of an acre beside the highway to allow for possible future building north of Prestwick Toll. Then, copying a decision made by the freemen of Newton in 1828 to introduce 999-year holdings, such tenure was in 1833 established in Prestwick. Thus from 1833 each freeman obtained perma-nent possession of from fourteen to sixteen acres for farming, two of his four plots containing arable land, the other two being sandy land nearer the shore which would never prove to be of much agricultural value.

The Freemen's Cash Account Book from 1824 has survived to provide some particulars of the burgh finances. Income was derived almost entirely from feu duties, some rents, and money paid by those entering as freemen. Feu-duties were often in arrears, so that in the year 1827–28 only £41 was collected; though in 1834–35 it had risen to £143, which included that year a major contribution of £42 from George Taylor of Newton. Regular expenditures included statutory payments to the County Commissioner of Supply – cess, rogue money, bridge money, and as assessment for rural police in 1842; there were also required contributions towards repairs at the church, minister's stipend, parish schoolmaster's salary; also annual payments to the burgh schoolmaster, the burgh officer, the treasurer, and the molecatcher. The freemen supplied coals for the school, candles for the Sunday School, paid expenses of an annual ploughing match, repaired roads and bridges when necessary. In 1832 they paid James McDerment £8 12s for making a plan of their lands, in 1836 they repaired the cross, and in 1864 reprinted one hundred copies of the burgh charter (previously issued in 1794). In 1832 they spent £1 13s 7d "treating the people" when Mr Oswald was elected to parliament, next July four shillings on a bonfire, in 1838 thirteen shillings celebrating Queen Victoria's coronation. There was a regular outlay on meetings, in particular around £6 on the annual "Election Dinner and Drink". There were donations towards the deserving poor, and during trade depressions in 1825, 1837, and 1848 generous help was provided for the "distressed operatives" in the form of meal, potatoes, and alternative employment. Finances were sufficient to allow from time to time bank deposits (21 July 1846, "To Ayrshire Bank, £90) and dividends to freemen (1 June 1838, "To four pounds Divided to Each freeman, £144").

The *New Statistical Account* commented on improvements made in the first three decades of the 19th century. One striking change was that the arable lands throughout the parish were raising an increased amount of farm produce. More oats and barley were being grown, the cultivation of wheat had been successfully extended, and no fewer than 215 acres were now annually devoted to root crops. Potatoes were in demand for food. Turnips provided winter fodder for animals, especially for sheep which could feed off the turnip crop on the ground. It was agreed that "the state of husbandry in the parish may be said to be in a very advanced stage of improvement". One contribution was that "surface-draining, in every alternate furrow, with tiles and stones, has been adopted with the best effects in some of the best land in the parish". The average rent of land on the Monkton part of the parish was over £2 per acre; that of land held by the freemen was less than half of that. But while their 400 acres near the shore were (as yet) of minimal worth, those other 150 acres of arable fields which the freemen now held in secure tenure were in good heart.

At the south end of Prestwick burgh were most of the remaining 150 acres, those portions which had been previously feued. At Maryburgh, the last surviving saltpans were possessed by Richard Alexander Oswald of Auchincruive, and apparently still in use when James McDerment made his plan of the lands of Prestwick in 1831; but production had ceased before his cousin James Oswald succeeded in 1841. On the Newton border was the property once held by the Wallaces of Craigie, since acquired by John Taylor of Newton, his son George who succeeded in 1810, and George Taylor Gordon from 1832. The saltpans on this property were now abandoned, but the coal seams in the area were being exploited. Within Newton, the Ann pit at Heathfield worked an upper seam of poor quality for three decades until 1830; in the same era there was also the short-lived Williamfield pit at Bellrock. At New Prestwick, a deeper seam of better quality was wrought from about 1815, and this Prestwick Pit was further developed after 1832 by J.T. Gordon. It is uncertain when the Williamfield and Prestwick pits were abandoned, but there were 28 colliers resident at New Prestwick in 1841, reduced to 12 a decade later. All these coals went to Ayr harbour for export, utilising the 18th century Oswald waggonway. This became more fully operational after the freemen between 1840 and 1843 made several investments "for ground to Mr Oswald's railroad". Fuel for local consumption was obtained from Newton, St Quivox, or Kilmarnock, each horse cart load costing from five to six shillings.

At Prestwick Toll, by the parish boundary, the dozen small plots which formed the nucleus of that new small community had been feued before 1814. In that year, as previously noted, the freemen allocated to themselves thirty-six feus along both sides of the highway to the north. No doubt they hoped to emulate the new building developments in Newton, where the highway was by 1837 lined with "small

Prestwick Toll, where in 1814 a dozen plots were feued to form what became known as New Prestwick. Some of the old cottages survived until the 1960s. (*KA*)

well-cultivated inclosures, neat cottages and gardens, and handsome villas with ornamented avenues and shrubberies." By then there was "a small extent of sandy hillocks, in the neighbourhood of Prestwick, and it too is fast disappearing in the progress of improvement". But it would be some time before the freemen's building plots would be occupied.

This new spirit of optimism was apparent also in the church. After the aged Dr Mitchell died, Rev John Steel Oughterson was translated from West Kilbride, a rather frail man who was inducted to Monkton and Prestwick parish in 1812. A new manse was provided at Monkton, with a glebe of eight acres which could be let at around £40 a year to supplement his stipend. This was now seventeen chalders of victual, half barley, half meal, plus £8 6s 8d for communion elements. Building of an impressive new parish church was accomplished during the ministry of his success or, Rev. Thomas Burns. A nephew of the poet, his distinguished ministerial career commenced in 1826 at Ballantrae. He became engaged to a niece of the Monkton minister, and in 1830, after Oughterson's death, he married her and was presented to this charge. Then an energetic thirty-four-year-old, it was due to his efforts that in 1834 authority was granted for construction of a new place of worship. The site chosen was a convenient one between Monkton and Prestwick, beside the Pow Bridge on land purchased from Orangefield. The architect was the

The new St Cuthbert's Church, erected in 1837. (*KA*)

celebrated David Bryce and this was one of his earliest commissions. He provided, according to Rev. Thomas Burns, "one of the handsomest churches in the west of Scotland", which with its commanding situation "forms one of the most striking objects in the surrounding landscape". Opened on 14 May 1837, it cost around £2,500, which compelled some to describe it as "Burns's Folly". The two ancient churches dedicated to St Cuthbert and St Nicholas were now abandoned and fell into ruin. The new parish church could accommodate 825 persons, and about 600 regularly attended, including about 400 communicants.

The established church continued its traditional responsibility for poor relief and education. In the 1830s there were from fifteen to twenty paupers in the parish receiving three or four shillings a month, and others obtaining occasional aid, though, as Rev. Thomas Burns noticed, "There is still remaining among the poor a considerable reluctance to apply for parish relief, if it can by any means be avoided." Unlike larger towns where the church was finding difficulty in coping, in this parish expenditure was still adequately met by £35 from the church collections, £10 in voluntary donations from heritors, and £5 from fines and dues. The same minister was also gratified to record that "there are very few, if any, in the parish unable to read, and parents in general are very much alive to the benefits of education." An Education Act of 1803 raised parish schoolmasters' salaries, which had not been adjusted since 1696, and allowed for further revision each twenty-five years. In 1824 the parish school at Monkton was a two-storey building with a schoolroom measuring 30 by 17 feet on the ground floor, and accommodation above for the master, who was also provided with a garden, as required by the Act. James Edie, the schoolmaster at that date, was paid the maximum statutory salary of 400 merks (£34 4s 4d) which with school fees (£33 15s) and his duties as session clerk (£2 2s plus payments for proclamations, baptisms, etc.) gave him an annual income approaching £70. School fees had been increased in 1817, with quarterly payments for Reading, 2s 6d; with Grammar and Writing, 3s 6d; Arithmetic, 4s; also on offer were Latin, Greek, French, and "all branches of practical Mathematics", at 4s 6d each. There were just over one hundred scholars, between twenty and thirty of them admitted free because of parents' poverty. Of those ninety who paid fees, many were kept off for farm work so that "the harvest quarter is, in a great manner vacant". A decade later, the roll had increased towards 130, fees remained the same, though the choice of foreign languages was limited to "when pupils offer, the elements of Latin." The parish schoolmasters were James Gibson (1828–44) then James Cowan (1844–73). At Prestwick there was the Freemen's School, which was held in their Town House. Since this was not a parish school, the teacher was not entitled to any salary, but the freemen – who were required to contribute around £2 a year towards the parochial schoolmaster's salary – provided rather more than this for their own burgh schoolmaster, even if it was only enough to rent a dwelling house. He had never more than fifty pupils, and had to rely entirely upon their fees, so his income was very small. Thomas McCrorie was so employed in 1820, and continued till 1844, during which period he was paid £3 annually. New Prestwick lacked educational facilities. Though the freemen in 1832 contributed £5 towards "Building a schoolhouse at the Toll", the only mention therafter is of sixty-year-old John Anderson who was listed there in 1841 as "Teacher of deaf and dumb".

In the *New Statistical Account* Rev. Thomas Burns reported an innovation, for which he himself was probably responsible: "There are also two Sabbath evening schools, attended by from 160 to 180 or 200 children, most of whom do not regularly enjoy any other means of education." The purpose of the Sunday Schools was not only to offer secular education for those not otherwise provided, but to operate as missionary agencies serving the growing number of people outwith the established church. Some of these had left because of their opposition to appointment of parish ministers by patrons. Of Rev. Andrew Mitchell, it was later asserted, "During the 37 years he was Minister of this Parish, the people kept well together. Sound in the faith himself, he was opposed to any tampering with the fundamentals on the part of others. ... Dissent accordingly was almost unknown here." It seems to have increased in the time of his successor, with immigration a contributory cause. Rev. Thomas Burns in the *New Statistical Account* of the 1830s listed "about 200 Dissenters, young and old, of all persuasions, in the parish; of these about 60 are Roman Catholics." No group was strong enough to form any local organisation, but had to resort to chosen places of worship in neighbouring parishes. Seceders belonging to the Anti-Burgher sect met at Wallacetown in St Quivox parish (from 1770), Burghers at Tarbolton (1776) or Wallacetown (1799); there were Relief Churches in Irvine (1773) and Ayr (1814); Ayr provided also for Episcopalians (from 1744), Moravians (1765), Methodists (1785), Roman Catholics (1822) and Reformed Presbyterians (1828).

If religious dissent in the early 19th century was limited in local expression, political protest was more widespread. In Ayrshire, complaint was made that the franchise was restricted to substantial landowners when a county member of parliament was elected, and to commissioners representing five royal burghs who chose the member for Ayr Burghs. The roll of county freeholders entitled to vote in 1830 contained the names of 202 persons, only one of whom was resident within the parish of Monkton and Prestwick. That was Robert Reid of Adamton, which was the only local property which qualified. None of the freemen of Prestwick was entitled to vote unless he had a property qualification elsewhere. Such in 1830 were R.A. Oswald of Auchincruive, John Smith of Swindridgemuir, William Neill of Barnweil, William Fullarton of Skeldon, David Limond of Dalblair, and the recently-deceased William Campbell of Craigie.

Demands for reform came from Radicals and in 1819 weavers from Prestwick joined a county demonstration for universal suffrage which assembled at Wallacetown. More effective action was pursued by liberal-minded voters who accepted the necessity for a limited extension of the franchise. At the General Election in May 1830 the whig R. A. Oswald of Auchincruive obtained 36 votes, but failed to unseat tory William Blair of Blair, who received twice that number, and continued as MP for Ayrshire. Nevertheless, T.F.Kennedy of Dunure, M.P. for Ayr Burghs since 1818, was committed to parliamentary reform, and helped pass the Reform Bill of 1832 which extended the franchise to most landowners, many well-off tenants, and some householders in the major burghs. At the next General Election in December 1832 the new voters enthusiastically supported Oswald with 2,152 votes against Blair's 324. Oswald retired from politics in 1835, and was followed by another Liberal, John Dunlop of Dunlop, who held Kilmarnock Burghs 1832 – 34 and was MP for Ayrshire from 1835 until his death in 1839. When R.A.Oswald died in 1841 his estates were inherited by a cousin James Oswald, another enthusiastic reformer, who represented Glasgow in parliament 1832 – 37 and 1839 – 47. The Ayrshire seat was taken by Conservatives in 1839, held by Viscount Kelburne until 1843, followed by A.H. Oswald, then from 1852 by J.J.Blair, this Conservative ascendancy continuing for twenty-nine years. By contrast, Liberal support wss maintained in Ayr Burghs from 1818 until 1874; for when T.F.Kennedy retired in 1834, Lord James Stuart succeeded, to be followed in 1852 by H.J.Crawford.

Prestwick lay within the county constituency, but for many people the 1832 Reform Act was a disappointment. Not many inhabitants had the necessary qualifications entitling them to acquire a vote in the subsequent parliamentary elections. Owners of property valued at £10 annual rental included W.G. Campbell of Fairfield as an elector, as well as James Sinclair when he acquired Orangefield. though Mrs Reid of Adamton as a woman was disqualified. Concerning the Prestwick freemen, whose average rental in 1834 was £8 10s, few would qualify initially, and by 1857 only eight of the resident freemen were on the voters' roll. Tenants paying an annual rent of £50 also qualified, and in 1857 these comprised sixteen Monkton farmers, five residents in Monkton village, and eight others in Prestwick in addition to the freemen. Fourteen others who were non-resident were on the roll by virtue of land they held in this parish. But with just over three hundred adult males within the parish of Monkton and Prestwick, fewer than forty of them were as yet enfranchised. Popular demand for universal suffrage led to the formation in 1839 of a Prestwick Chartist Association, one of nineteen in Ayrshire, but nothing has been discovered of its membership or activities.

In the early 19th century Prestwick was benefiting from the improved system of roads that the Turnpike Trust had created. Within the parish there was the main highway from Ayr to Kilmarnock and Glasgow, with that other principal route branching off at Monkton towards Irvine. Monkton was reached from the interior by a road coming past Adamton from Tarbolton and Mauchline, and another passing Sandyford and Aitkenbrae coming from Coylton and Cumnock. Prestwick was served by two lesser roads, one coming past Shaw from Adamton, the other past Sanquhar from St Quivox. The *New Statistical Account* suggested how busy the roads had become by the 1830s: "Beside the mail-coach, six public coaches pass through Monkton and Prestwick every day, three early in the morning from Ayr, two of them to Glasgow, and the other to Edinburgh; and three in the afternoon to Ayr, one of them from Edinburgh, and the other two from Glasgow. Besides these, a regular diligence leaves Kilmarnock for Ayr in the morning, and returns in the afternoon, and another, three times a-week, leaves Irvine for Ayr in the morning, and returns in the afternoon." There were also those travelling independently, like Hew Ainslie who when touring the Land of Burns in 1820 stopped at the Black Bull in Monkton. There were four such public houses in Monkton, four or five in Prestwick, and four at Prestwick Toll. As Rev. Thomas Burns commented: "a number much greater than required, and certainly not favourable to the moral habits of the people." But these obviously catered not only for thirsty residents, but for the refreshment of the considerable passing traffic, coach passengers, horsemen, carters, carriers, and vagrants. Along the great highways were brought news from the outside world. In 1815 victory at Waterloo was celebrated by Monkton boys with wooden swords, and Prestwick was bedecked with red and blue colours. In 1828 news of the arrest in Edinburgh of Burke and Hare for body-snatching resulted in a local society being formed to protect new graves. In 1832 came word of the the passing of the Reform Act. In 1837, as before in 1820 and 1830, the death of a king was announced. Quite soon afterwards, early in the reign of the young Queen Victoria, Prestwick gained a new and more effective link with the outside world when the Glasgow and Ayr railway opened in 1840.

CHAPTER EIGHT

The Mid 19th Century

THE middle of the 19th century brought several important innovations to Prestwick, none of which however had significant immediate effect on the character of the community. The parish population remained static, 1,933 (1841), 1,960 (1851), 1,937 (1861).

The Glasgow – Ayr Railway was opened in 1840. Services between Ayr and Irvine operated from 5 August 1839, but Prestwick station attracted so few passengers that it was closed after two months. Monkton station proved more useful for goods traffic. Prestwick station was reopened in June 1841 but again after six months "the stoppage of trains was discontinued there". On 1 July 1846 it was permanently reopened, though for many years it continued to be little used. The track ran west of the burgh through land which was mostly waste, so that acquisition of land by the railway company offered the freemen an unexpected and welcome windfall. The Freemen's Account Book records several meetings regarding the railway but, since extraordinary payments were not there listed, it is impossible to ascertain the precise financial arrangements. Presumably, as at Newton-upon-Ayr, a lump sum was paid to the community. With this it was possible to erect in 1844 a fine new Freemen's Hall, with a graceful spire later added. For many years afterwards, "At the great Annual Meeting of the Freemen, when a sumptuous dinner is provided after the business sederunt is over, the vicinity of this building, with the Burgh-Officer standing at the door in his uniform, and the bell ringing merrily from the steeple, is a scene of considerable animation." The freemen were affluent enough to commence levelling the sandhills on their plots beside the railway. Access to lands west of the railway had been provided in 1840: at Monkton and Kingcase by bridges over the line; within Prestwick burgh by underpasses, which would prove awkward in later times.

In 1850 legal restrictions were removed so that freemen thereafter possessed their lands as heritable property, which they were free to dispose of as they desired. Immediately afterwards a Prestwick Golf Club was formed, leasing ground between the railway and the shore from twelve freemen at a cost of £6 per year, and allowed private access from the station to the course by a wicket gate. Before this time a few gentlemen had paid an annual contribution of ten shillings to Prestwick burgh for permission to play upon the links beside the sea, teeing off beside the salt pans and finishing play by the Pow Burn. The initiative to form Prestwick Golf Club came from one of them, James Ogilvie Fairlie of Coodham, Captain of the Royal and Ancient Club of St Andrews in 1850, who persuaded fifty-seven gentlemen

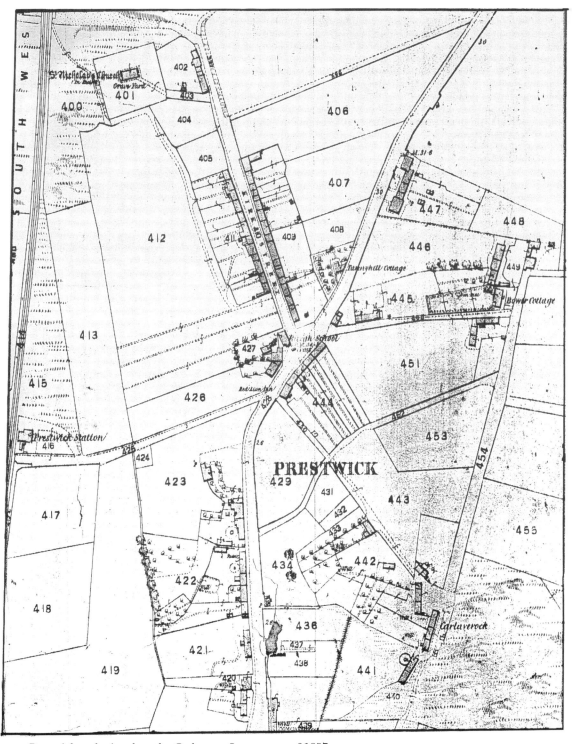

Prestwick as depicted on the Ordnance Survey map of 1857.

from the west of Scotland that it was desirable to establish a course on this side of the country. The inaugural meeting was held in the Red Lion Hotel, Prestwick, on 2 July 1851, when the 13th Earl of Eglinton was appointed president and Fairlie was chosen as captain. Tom Morris was brought from St Andrews to lay out a twelve-hole course, and was employed as greenkeeper, initially paid £25 a year. This he supplemented by sale of gutta-percha golf balls, recently invented in 1848, which he preferred to the traditional balls of leather filled with feathers. He and his family lived in a little cottage opposite the Red Lion; next door in another cottage the gentlemen members of Prestwick Golf Club stored their clubs and clothing. On 3 November 1851 twenty-eight less affluent local enthusiasts for the game (including Tom Morris) formed their own club, with an original entrance fee of sixpence, and were allowed to play over the Prestwick Club course. This artisans' club was known as "The Mechanics" until 1858 when they adopted the name of Prestwick St Nicholas Club. They too acquired a club house at The Cross, beside that of Prestwick Golf Club, in Alexander Hutchison's grocery shop. The artisans in 1863 also had a hut erected upon the links, which became known as the Luncheon House.

The railway, opened in 1840, bisected the town and created problems of access. (*KA*)

Of more local concern was schism within the established church. The Ten Years' Conflict regarding state intrusion in ecclesiastical affairs culminated in the Disruption on 18 May 1843. Rev. Thomas Burns was one of those who "came out". He took with him all the elders save one, and most of his congregation, including Mrs Reid of Adamton, who greatly aided the cause of the new Free Church. To begin with, things were difficult for parish ministers who gave up their stipends and their homes. One of Rev. Thomas Burns's daughters remembered as a child leaving Monkton manse and its attractive garden; the family found accommodation in what had been a public house at Prestwick Toll; as neighbours they had colliers who were "no better than heathen, and riots generally took place on Saturday nights"; food and fuel were scarce; many old friends who remained within the established church were bitter and scornful. Adherents of the new Free Church held their first act of worship at Tippery's Brae (a mound near the Pow Burn). Not far from that spot, their first communion was celebrated in West Orangefield stackyard. Jane Burns remembered that "The rain fell in sheets all the day: still there were 1,000 people present. They came long distances from other

A new Town House was erected in 1844. (*KA*)

92

parishes, and not one went away till the services were over. ... I can shut my eyes yet to picture the long tables, with the white cloths dripping with wet, and the raindrops in the wine cups, and the saintly Mr. Stevenson (of Newton-on-Ayr) standing beside our father with an umbrella to shield their uncovered heads, and keep the Bible dry." Rev. Thomas Burns was given responsibilty for organising throughout Ayrshire the congregations who were valiantly raising funds to support the Free Church. Only six months after the Disruption, in December 1843 at Monkton the first Free Church in Ayrshire was built. Rev. John McFarlan, a young man of twenty-seven, was ordained as its first minister, and provided with a stipend. In 1844 a manse was built for him. In 1845 Monkton Free Church School was opened, under James Gibson, the former master of the parish school who was not permitted to continue in that post when he joined the Free Church; followed before 1851 by John P. Duncan. In 1846 a meeting place was acquired so that Free Church services might be conducted within Prestwick as well. By 1851 the Free Church had a local membership of 430 who attended services. Rev. Thomas Burns in 1844, after staying a few months in New Prestwick, found more suitable accommodation in Newton, until 1846 when he was inducted to the Free Church in Portobello.

While he was concerned in promoting the Free Church throughout Ayrshire, from 1843 Burns was otherwise involved in planning, as his major enterprise, a settlement in New Zealand under Free Church auspices. Proposals for Scottish emigration to the Otago peninsula on the South Island of New Zealand were first put forward by George Rennie, sculptor and politician, supported by William Cargill, a retired army captain. In July 1843 they visited Rev. Thomas Burns who was then still residing in Monkton Manse. Burns, with his fiercely evangelical and sectarian outlook, advocated that the projected settlement should be a Free Church colony. This was not to the liking of Rennie, who lost interest, leaving Cargill and Burns, with the support of the Free Church, to complete lengthy and complex negotiations. Eventually on 2 November 1847 the expedition was ready. One ship carrying stores and a few passengers left from London. A larger vessel set sail from Greenock with the bulk of the emigrants, 287 Scots under the supervision of Rev. Thomas Burns. 144,000 acres had been purchased from the New Zealand Company, to be resold to settlers at £2 per acre. On the Otago peninsula they founded Dunedin. William Cargill was appointed resident agent of the New Zealand Company and managed the settlement in its first difficult years. By 1860 Otago contained 4,000 households with about 7,500 individuals, more than 80% of them Scots. From 1848 until 1854 Burns was the colonists' sole minister. In 1860 Edinburgh University awarded him the degree of doctor of divinity, and in 1869 he became first chancellor of Otago University. He died in 1871 and is commemorated by an impressive monument in Dunedin. By that time the Free Church character of the settlement had been diluted by prospectors who in 1861 came to search for gold. But it remained predominantly Scottish through-out the 19th century, as did another South Island settlement, Invercargill founded in 1857 by James Wilson from Prestwick.

In 1851 Prestwick Golf Club was inaugurated at a meeting in the Red Lion Hotel. (*KA*)

Born in 1814 at Prestwick Toll, James Wilson was eldest in a family of eleven children. His father James Wilson was a shoemaker, his mother Ruth Kerr did muslin hand sewing, and they could afford to send young James daily through Newton-on-Ayr to Wallacetown Academy. After leaving school, he hoped to become an estate factor, but could find employment only as a farm servant. In 1841 he emigrated to Australia, and in New South Wales worked on the land, becoming overseer of a government agricultural station, then tried his fortune in the new goldfields. His wife whom he married in 1848 died four years later. After corresponding with Rev. Thomas Burns of Dunedin, in 1856 James Wilson and his two young daughters sailed for New Zealand. Shortly after arriving in Dunedin, Wilson went south to find a suitable place to settle, and Invercargill was established, to become capital of the province of Southland. Wilson in 1858 found some gold in the area, but farming proved to be more profitable. The family at home left Prestwick sometime in the 1840s, but Wilson maintained contact, for a younger brother Thomas joined him in 1859, followed soon afterwards by a married sister. James Wilson was a prominent member of the Southland Provincial Council until 1870 when the province was reunited with Otago, and for the next six years was a member of the Otago Council. He died in 1898, aged eighty-four, and was buried in a cemetery a few miles from Invercargill at Wallacetown, named after the place near Prestwick where he had gone to school.

Two years after James Wilson had left home, to the vacant charge of the established church in Prestwick, Rev. Dr George James Lawrie was presented in 1843. Four generations before him had ministered to Ayrshire parishes, and this son of the manse, after a brilliant career at Glasgow and Oxford, and service as a chaplain in India, was inducted to St Cuthbert's Church just before his forty-seventh birthday. He served the parish for the next thirty-four years, described as "a shrewd, upright, kindly man", who helped restore the reputation of the established church locally. Dr Lawrie was last of the parish ministers who personally farmed the glebe. This he had to abandon when, after caring for a sick parishioner, he contracted an illness which incapacitated him, and a succession of assistants provided pulpit supply for ten years until he resigned in 1877, and died a year later. In 1879 there was posthumous publication of his *Songs and Miscellaneous Pieces*, a slender booklet of sixteen pages, containing his song "Hae ye mind o' lang, lang syne" which recalled his boyhood days in Loudoun parish. There his grandfather and father had been ministers, both close acquaintances of Robert Burns. A generation later Rev. Kirkwood Hewat in his history of *A Little Scottish World* listed all those persons in Monkton and Prestwick who shared a link with Burns. They included a great-grandson of Douglas Graham who was prototype of Tam O' Shanter; descendants of John Davidson – Souter Johnnie – were also settled in

Tom Morris, who laid out Prestwick golf course, and his equally-famous son, Young Tom.

Prestwick; there were others whose forbears had known Burns in Tarbolton or Mauchline; one was in fact related to Burns, for her grandfather had been brother to Burns's mother.

The established church no longer held the dominant position within the community. The Disruption increased that proportion who worshipped elsewhere, and there were others who had lost any church connection. The established church could no longer effectively exercise its role in providing poor relief, especially during that decade appropriately designated the Hungry Forties. Government intervention proved necessary and the 1845 Poor Law Act established Parochial Boards to provide by levying a local assessment on owners and occupiers of property. But the Act failed to stipulate a minimum standard of relief or clearly specify which groups were entitled; and the Parochial Boards, composed of major property-owners, representatives of the kirk session, and some elected ratepayers, were unable to cope satisfactorily. Records of the Monkton and Prestwick Parochial Board have not survived, but the kirk session minutes report its establishment in February 1846, and James M. Cowan, parochial schoolmaster, became also Inspector of Poor. In 1849 there were within the parish 57 persons on poor relief, plus 13 casual poor, 2 described as fatuous, and 5 orphans who were also maintained. Just over £400 was raised by assessment, providing an average of £5 for each pauper. Similarly the established church's role in providing education was diminishing.

Rev. Thomas Burns gave up his charge in 1843 to join the Free Church, and in 1847 led a party of emigrants who established Dunedin in New Zealand.

The parochial school at Monkton under James Cowan (1844–1874) was joined by the Free Church School there. Within Prestwick there was the Freemen's School, which however was finding difficulty retaining teachers, even though the basic salary was increased from £3 to £5. William D. Wood (1845) was followed there by a Mr Hunter (1848), Robert Adams (1849–53), Thomas Reid (1854), Mr Bryan (1855), Mr Armstrong (1858), Andrew Campbell (1860), James Stewart (1861–62) and William McIntosh (1864–67). Of a school at Prestwick Toll which the church and freemen tried to maintain, the only only mention is when Samuel Hillas resigned in 1845 to go to Glasgow.

Such records as survive provide glimpses of varying aspects of social life in mid-century. One old resident told Kirkwood Hewat of his schooldays at Prestwick, where the only text books were the Bible and the Shorter Catechism, and he remembered having to learn by heart large portions of the Book of Proverbs. They attended school six days a week. Fees were supplemented by money gifts to the dominie at New Year, the boy bringing the largest sum being nominated king and the girl the queen. There was rivalry between the inhabitants of Prestwick and Monkton, with particular feuds at the time of the Disruption, when there was stone-throwing by boys and girls. Within each church the traditional forms of worship were maintained, with a precentor leading the singing of psalms, each kirk session disciplining adherents who were found guilty of ante-nuptial fornication and similar "sins of uncleanness", and purging the roll before issuing communion tokens to those allowed to share in the Sacrament. Despite initial differences, there were instances of co-operation, and in 1848 Rev. Dr Lawrie and Rev. J. McFarlan agreed that each church should celebrate the Sacrament twice-yearly on the fourth Sabbath of July and the third Sabbath of December. One institution which failed to survive was the Monkton and Prestwick Parish Library Society which was instituted in 1839 by Rev. Thomas Burns, operated by a committee of management, and open to any resident in the parish paying two shillings annually. It was designed "to promote the great objects of moral and religious improvement" and allowed "No Novels or Plays, and no political publications, nor controversial Works". Books purchased and donated were available for borrowing from the Monkton schoolhouse every second Monday evening, and for a time it flourished, even adding a juvenile section. But there is a gap in the minutes for 1843 (the year of the Disruption), membership therafter declined, Rev. Thomas Burns wrote to insist that certain books should be returned to him, and not till 1851 did Rev. Dr Lawrie become involved in the library, which foundered in 1856.

The Census Returns for 1851 reveal that handloom weaving of cotton remained the principal occupation, with 126 weavers in Prestwick, 53 in New Prestwick, 15 in Monkton village, and 3 nearby at Watsonhall. Those 197 weavers and 22 in auxiliary occupations showed hardly any change in numbers over the previous decade. There was however a substantial increase among those variously designated as flowerers, handsewers, seamstresses, and dressmakers, with 67 in Prestwick, 22 in New Prestwick, 34 in Monkton, and 10 in country homes. This was an era when Ayrshire Needlework was enjoying its greatest popularity. Tambouring

– embroidering of muslins on drums called tambours – had been introduced to the west of Scotland in the later 18th century; in the early years of the 19th century point lace fillings were introduced, and this technique was so widely practised in Ayr and neighbourhood as to earn by 1834 the name of Ayrshire Needlework. Glasgow cotton agents commissioned work, marketing throughout Britain and overseas ladies' dresses and babies' robes and caps. In the nearby parish of Riccarton in 1839 "the wages vary from 9d to 3s 6d per week; but this latter sum can only be earned at the best work; and by the most expert sewers, and at the expense of comfort to themselves. The employment, we believe, is very injurious to the general health of those employed, but especially to their chest and eyes". This was evident when flowerers might work fourteen to sixteen hours daily, with candle-light their only illumination in winter. The industry, locally known as "Flowering Web", reached its peak in the 1850s. Kirkwood Hewat was informed that products from Monkton and Prestwick went for sale in France, Germany, and Russia.

The number of handloom weavers elsewhere was declining drastically, faced with competition from power looms and periods of trade depression in the 1840s. Those in Monkton and Prestwick survived with difficulty, in many cases supported by wives' and daughters' embroidery work. One of the cotton weavers in New Prestwick had an elder son take up carpet weaving. Another in Monkton village had three sons who were turning to silk weaving, more successfully, for this was fine work which the power looms could not tackle. If prospects for cotton weaving were poor, other traditional trades were also in decline. Within Monkton and Prestwick parish there were 23 makers of shoes in 1841; ten years later there were only ten. The fishing trade was virtually extinct – in 1851 only one man, at Prestwick Toll, is named as a fisher. Hewat later referred to "the Salmon Fishings, which today might have brought a considerable revenue to the Burgh, as they extend from a point near Kingcase, not far from the mouth of the Ayr water, to the mouth of the Pow, but that the Freemen one unfortunate day bartered them away to a neighbouring laird for a bowl of toddy! Such, at least, is the local tradition." He also mentioned a midcentury attempt at starting a ship-building industry, and three or four ships-carpenters are in fact listed in both the 1841 and 1851 Census Returns. According to Hewat, "several remember a schooner of about 150 tons burthen being built and launched at the Salt-pans. Her timbers were from the Montgomerie Castle (Coilsfield) grounds." More exact details can be added from a news report in the *Ayr Advertiser* (25 June 1846): "A schooner of about 110 tons burthen, built of timber grown at Coilsfield, and fitted for the coasting and foreign trade, was launched by the Coilsfield Timber Company, from their ship-yard at Prestwick, on Monday last. This is the first vessel they have turned off the stocks. She is named *King Coil*, and her build reflects great credit on the company." Hewat believed that "it was an Aberdeen Company that built the vessel, but luck at the first was against them, as she stranded or toppled over immediately after being launched." There is no record of any other ships built at Prestwick. Hewat also mentioned that "There used to be a Colliery in the New Prestwick neighbourhood". That Prestwick Pit may still have been in operation in 1851, when 12 colliers are listed in the Census Returns; if so it closed soon afterwards, for is not shown on the Ordnance Survey map of 1857.

Though the Census Reports for 1841 and 1851 show no significant difference in numbers, comparison of the Census Returns for these years reveals a substantial alteration of personnel; a social change no doubt reflecting current economic problems. Of the 185 households in Prestwick burgh in 1851, only 72 can be identified as occupied by persons living here ten years before. More than half of those who lived in Prestwick in 1841 had disappeared; some had died, but many more had left the town. Numbers were sustained by births and by incomers who came to occupy vacated houses. Many of these were Irish. Immigration into Ayrshire reached its peak in 1851 when 11% of the county population was Irish-born. By that year the proportion in Prestwick burgh who had been born in Ireland was 10%. More however had come from other parts of Scotland, 27% of the total, and most from neighbouring Ayrshire parishes. However, 63% of Prestwick's 827 inhabitants were locally-born, including some who had flitted in from Monkton, and some who had returned to their native burgh within the previous ten years. In New Prestwick, by contrast, only 39% of its 315 inhabitants had been born within the parish; 12% were Irish-born; the remainder, almost half of the total, were incomers from neighbouring parishes. In Monkton village, with

James Wilson from Prestwick Toll, who emigrated to Australia in 1841, moved to New Zealand and founded Invercargill in 1857.

415 inhabitants. 50% were natives of the parish, the rest incomers, fewer than 1% from Ireland. Of those 405 persons living in the rural area, 30% were natives of the parish, with the labour force mainly incomers, though only fifteen (0.4 %) were Irish-born.

The Census Returns, which are so helpful in tracing family histories, are equally useful for analysing the complex patterns of migration and social change, as some samples from 1851 reveal.

Living in Prestwick burgh was a.Irish-born handloom weaver (aged 45) who with his wife (41) from Bellshill in Lanarkshire had settled here more than twenty years ago, for two sons (22, 15) and a daughter (18) who were also working as weavers had been born in Prestwick, like a younger daughter (11) who was attending school. A stone mason (47) born in Moffat had a wife (46) who had been born in Prestwick; before settling here they had lived in Dumfriesshire and Lanarkshire where their two sons (15, 5) were born, the elder now an apprentice millwright. Powbank mill was occupied by a miller (36) who with his wife (32) came from Stair; a daughter (2) and son (8 months) had been born here; there were two servants, a local boy (19) and a girl (19) from Coylton. A shoemaker (32) and his wife (32) who was a hand sewer came from Newton with two sons (7, 2) and a daughter (4) who had been born there; they were recent incomers to Prestwick, for a baby girl (6 months) had been born here. With them came a woman lodger (30), a hand sewer with a daughter (7) born in Newton. A Glasgow man (47) who had left the army was now a handloom weaver, married to a local woman (35) who did hand sewing, and had a daughter (11). A handloom weaver (29) from Maybole lived with his Symington-born wife (29) who was a hand sewer, and his sister from Maybole who was also a weaver; they had recently lived in Dundonald where one child (3) was born, whereas the second (11 months) was born in this parish. An Irish labourer (33), with his Girvan-born wife (33) who was a weaver, lived here when a first daughter (5) was born, then in Cumnock for the second (3), before returning here. A joiner (40) from Stair, with his wife (41) from Dalmellington, lived for a time in Kirkmichael where two daughters (13, 11) were born, with other two (5, 1) born here. They had fallen on hard times, being designated as paupers. One of the bailies of Prestwick may be noticed, if only because in 1851 he gave his age (59) and that of his wife (59) whereas at the census ten years before they stated they were 45 years old; similar discrepancy in ages attributed to their children indicates how uncertain people might be before compulsory registration of births was introduced in 1855. This freeman cultivated his farm of 50 acres with the aid of his youngest son (11) who acted as herd boy. His other three sons (34, 29, 25) and three daughters (24, 19, 17) were all farm servants, apparently working for other farmers. Within the household was a schoolboy (5) described as a grandson, but who were his parents is not specified.

Among those who inhabited New Prestwick in 1851 was a miner (47) from Lochgelly in Fife who had settled here, with a locally-born wife (46) and two daughters (21, 6) who both worked as seamstresses. One family from Newton which had recently arrived comprised a handloom weaver (62), his wife (61) who was a

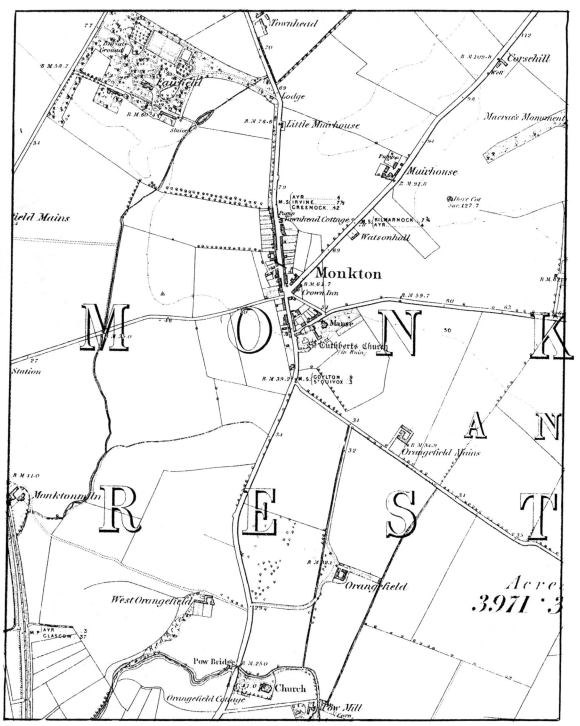

While Prestwick was enjoying growth, Monkton always remained a small village, as the Ordnance Survey Map of 1857 shows.

pirn winder, a daughter (21) who was a seamstress, two sons (27, 16) who were weavers. The elder son's wife, also from Newton, was a flowerer, and they had two baby daughters (3, 1) born in St Quivox. A far-travelled family was that of a labourer (54) from Ayr. He had been in Ireland where his wife (43) was born and also their first son (20), now a handloom weaver living with them in New Prestwick. Two daughters (17, 14), now seamstresses, had been born in England; another son (12) and daughter (10) in Paisley; the youngest daughter (5) nearby in St Quivox; since when the family had settled here. A recent innovation was the building of several new larger houses in New Prestwick, and these formed the nucleus of Prestwick's first residential area. In Thymefield Villa lived a retired army officer (73) who had been born in Ayr, married an English wife (67), had a daughter (37) born in Leith, whose children, a boy (7) and girl (5), had been born in Prestwick and attended school here. Broomfield housed a 65-year-old spinster from St Quivox who was an innkeeper and took in lodgers. Ghazepore House had been quite recently built (and named) by Robert McWhinnie (61), a native of Maybole who had served with the East India Company, and whose young wife (29) and son (5) had been born in the East Indies; with them lived a niece (13, born locally) and a nephew (10, born in East Indies), and two servants; McWhinnie now farmed the adjoining 22 acres with the aid of six labourers. Nearby was a fourth new house – Pleasantfield, occupied by a 67-year-old Glasgow man, his wife, daughter, and two grandchildren who had been born in India; he is described as a house proprietor, no doubt as builder and owner of Logan's Place near the Toll.

In Monkton village, the Post Office was occupied by the postmistress (28), whose younger sister (20) was the letter deliverer, her two brothers (32, 25) being shoemakers. All were natives of the parish, and unmarried; with them lived a niece (7) from Lanarkshire, who was at school. The parochial schoolmaster, James McKinning Cowan (52), was born in Kirkmichael, and had been in Dalrymple, where he married his wife (54) and had a daughter (23) and son (16), then moved to Wigtownshire where another daughter (13) and two sons (11, 8) were born. The Free Church teacher was John Paton Duncan (36), who came from Fife, having been in Perthshire where he married his wife (29) and a son (5) was born. The blacksmith (58) from Renfrewshire had a wife (62) from Monkton, where there had been born two daughters, one a dressmaker (28), the other a seamstress (21). The son (26), who also worked in the smithy, was married but seemingly widowed. In the household there were also a grandson (3) and a grand-daughter (3 months), presumably children of two absent married daughters. In one group of single-end dwellings there lived separately a seamstress (55) from Glasgow; a locally-born dressmaker (57), widowed and maintaining her little grand-daughter (8); an Irishwoman (73), formerly a pirn winder, now pauper; a seamstress (45) from Dailly; an agricultural labourer (50) who was a bachelor from Ochiltree.

In the rural part of Monkton parish there were eighteen farms. The largest of these, Aitkenbrae, covered 260 acres. It had been tenanted by Matthew Paterson, who was with Robert Burns a member of Tarbolton Bachelors Club; his wife was Anne Ronald of the Bennals whom Burns had briefly courted. Aitkenbrae was by

1851 in the possession of the eldest of three unmarried daughters, Mary Paterson (49), Grace (47), and Martha (45), and managed by their nephew Alexander (23). They had a house servant (18), a dairymaid (20) from Kirkmichael, and two lads (16, 12), one from Tarbolton, who were farm servants living on the farm. Another eight men were hired as agricultural labourers. In the neighbourhood of Monkton village were four other fair-sized farms – Whiteside, 170 acres; Laigh Monktonhill, 164 acres; Hobsland, 120 acres; Muirhouse, 135 acres. Ten of the others ranged from 50 – 100 acres. Many smaller units had been incorporated within the larger farms, and their steadings survived to provide accommodation for agricultural labourers and their families. Such were Townhead, Rumhowe, Mount William, Corsehill, and Old Aitkenbrae. The last of these was occupied by three families: an agricultural labourer (35) from Wigtownshire with a wife (34) from St Quivox, and a family of six, all of whom had been born here; an old woman (72) of this parish who was still working on the land; a third agricultural labourer (51) from Tarbolton, quite recently returned to the area with his elder daughter (20) who kept the house; she had been born in Kirkcudbright, the other daughter (9) in Ireland, and a son (4) in Straiton.

Various agrarian changes may be detected by comparison of the Census Returns of 1841 and 1851. West Orangefield, 75 acres, at the earlier date was partly cultivated by an old farmer (75) and his wife (73); the rest by a younger man (40) from Maybole and his wife (45), with the assistance of two male and one female farm servants, and a boy (10). Ten years later the younger farmer was on his own, apparently widowed, and assisted by three male farm servants. The old couple had gone, presumably dead, and in their place was a family with five young children; the husband (38) was a shoemaker and the wife (40) described as a "Bower of Cows". This was a west of Scotland term for a person who rented some cows and grazing. In 1841 the ten-year-old boy was employed as a herd – an indication that hedges were not yet sufficiently grown to contain cattle; by 1851 hedges must have matured, for herd boys were no longer required on the Monkton farms. Of the eighteen farms in 1851, four had been let to new tenants over the previous decade, and only seven remained in the hands of natives of the parish. An incomer (45) to Monkton village from Maybole had begun by 1851 a new marketing business as a dealer in potatoes and kail plants. A generation later, Hewat reminded his readers of what had become "an extensive and remunerative industry". In the spring months, many acres of young kail and cabbage plants were lifted and put into bundles – providing seasonal employment to many hands – and sent off to customers in various parts of the British Isles. It was said of the local people that "they could talk of nothing but kye, kail, and cabbages".

The Census Returns for 1851 list occupants of the several mansion houses. Adamton was still possessed by the aged Barbara Reid (84). With her were residing her brother, his wife, and two children; also a niece, a grand-nephew, and three grand-nieces. The servants were a cook and under cook, a table maid, a housemaid, a laundry maid, and two nursery maids – none of them local women. At Adamton Gates lived a coachman, a gardener, and two local men, a saddler and an agricultural labourer. Ladykirk, recently acquired from the Auchincruive estate by William Paterson of Monkwood, Maybole, was tenanted by William Gemmell (68), described as an army lieutenant on half pay, a native of Dailly; his wife (60) came from Edinburgh; at the time of the census they were entertaining five house guests; they employed three servants, who came from neighbouring parishes. Fairfield still belonged to William Gunning Campbell, but he was not present at the time of the census. The *Ayr Advertiser* (21 Nov. 1850) reported that Mr and Mrs Campbell would soon be leaving to vist Ripley Castle in Yorkshire; before doing so they visited Monkton Parish School to provide eighty-six books as prizes and arranged for thirty carts of coals for distribution among the poor. In residence at Fairfield in 1851 was a Mary Menzies (50) from Aberdeenshire, with a housekeeper (born in India), an undergardener (from England), with two local girls employed as housemaid and to keep the poultry. The gardener (from Ireland) lived in Fairfield Cottage, and his English wife was employed as laundress. Orangefield had again changed owners, and the new proprietor was James Sinclair (64) from Perthshire. His wife, Isabella Bruce (54), could claim family acquaintance with Ayrshire's two great literary figures. Her father had left the employ of James Boswell of Auchinleck, who expected him to become estate overseer as his father and grandfather had been. Her mother was a Ronald of the Bennals, whose sister (later in Aitkenbrae) was briefly courted by young Robert Burns in Tarbolton. The household at Orangefield was a modest one, requiring only one maid servant; and six acres adjacent to the mansion house were farmed by two labourers.

The *Ayr Advertiser* in mid-century provides little information about Prestwick. Most of its columns were devoted to national and foreign news; events were recorded for Ayr itself, Kilmarnock, and places as distant as New Cumnock and Largs. But Prestwick was still too insignificant to be frquently reported. There were only occasional items as when a public dinner in the Red Lion Hotel honoured William Raeside, farmer in Hobsland (9 Dec. 1841). Among a score of Ayrshire teams competing at curling for Lord Eglinton's Prize, there was one from Monkton (27 Nov. 1851) — we know there was another for a medal (donated to Prestwick town council in 1954) was "Subscribed for in the year 1847 by the Prestwick Curling Club to be played for annually". Among advertisements there was "To Let, for one year, from Martinmas first, A Bowing of 24 Cows, on Fairfield Mains" (9 Oct. 1834). Annual meetings of the Prestwick freemen were seldom recorded. One such (6 Nov. 1834) listed William Neill (Chancellor), William Smith and Andrew Caldwell (Bailies), Charles Boyd (Treasurer), William Cunningham, John Smith, Charles Bryan, John Hunter (Councillors), Robert Manson (Fiscal), David Boyd and William Harris (Liners). William Smith continued as chief magistrate, so listed in the 1851 Directory. William Neill of Barnweill, who served as chancellor of Prestwick from 1830, inherited Swindridgemuir from his maternal uncle John Smith in 1838, assumed the name of Smith, and died in 1850. His son and heir, born in 1810, became Brigadier-General James George Smith Neill who died a hero's death in 1857 at Lucknow during the Indian Mutiny and is commemorated by a statue in Wellington Square, Ayr. Previously, after inheriting his father's property in Prestwick he had advertised it for sale (11 Sept. 1851) as "Separate Lots including a Freedom Lot situated near the Burgh of Prestwick, which belonged to the late Col. William Smith Neill and at present possessed by Robert Paton, and other tenants or Vassals." He was among the first who took advantage of the change of tenure approved in 1850 which allowed freemen to dispose of their lands, and eventually transform the face of Prestwick.

Part Two

MODERN PRESTWICK

CHAPTER NINE

The Late 19th Century

*I*N the second half of the 19th century "Auld Prestick" finally emerged from its
long history of somnolence and commenced a period of steady and sustained
growth to become Modern Prestwick.

The signs at first were not promising. The parish population actually suffered a
sharp decline in the fifties and sixties – 1,960 (1851), 1,937 (1861), 1,744 (1871).
Thereafter numbers began to increase, and at a substantial rate – 2,121 (1881),
2,608 (1891), 3,854 (1901). This was altogether the result of growth within
Prestwick itself. The burgh's temporary decline – from 827 (1851) to 750 (1871)
– was followed by a quite spectacular expansion – 1,064 (1881), 1,479 (1891), 2,766
(1901). Within one generation, in the last three decades of the 19th century,
Prestwick's population enjoyed a fourfold growth, having doubled within the last
ten years.

The drop in numbers between 1851 and 1871 is easily explained. Hewat in 1894
wrote that "in recent years the weavers have become almost extinct. While there
were from 150 to 200 in the parish some sixty years ago, there is just about
half-a-dozen now." These last survived only because, as he noted, "the weaving of
silk handkerchiefs was a speciality, and happily that, though now to a very limited
extent, still continues". The once-flourishing cottage industry of Ayrshire Flowering was also in decline, despite Hewat's hopes for "the revival of home industries
in our ancient parish." The collapse of the domestic cotton trade in Scotland,
accelerated by shortage of raw material during the American Civil War (1861–65),
was ultimately caused by competition from factories employing power looms. Lack
of local employment resulted in emigration. The *Ayr Advertiser* throughout this
period publicised schemes of emigration. Passage to Australia could be had for
£12; and for £50 there was on offer free passage and 50 acres of freehold land (11
Sept. 1851). A few young men enlisted in the army, like George Fechney and David
McLean who served during the Crimean War. Many of those who remained at
home must have suffered impoverishment. Helen Steven, writing in 1897, remarked that "besides the local tradesmen there is no special industry to employ
the population unless growing of young plants" – referring to the cultivation of
kail around Monkton which Hewat mentioned as a continuing seasonal occupation.

These economic difficulties affected particularly some of those freemen who
held the burgh lands. In earlier chapters it has been noted that many of these lands
had already passed into the hands of absentee owners. The 1851 Ayrshire Directory

In the late 19th century houses were built along the sea front.

listed in Prestwick only fifteen resident freemen. It is certain that some of these (as well as non-resident freemen) took advantage of the provisions of 1850 which allowed them to dispose of their freedom lands. When an official Return of Owners of Lands and Heritages was published, listing for 1872–73 the names and addresses of every owner of one acre and upwards, only nine persons resident in Prestwick can be identified as the freemen of 1851 or their descendants. The lands they retained ranged from nine to forty-eight acres in extent, and occupied altogether 219 acres. Another 215 acres were possessed by twenty-one other residents, the larger properties mainly older feus, but there were a dozen owners of one, two, or four acres. Some of these had come to build houses and reside in Prestwick, known to the natives as "new-comers" or "saut-water folk". According to Hewat, "the earliest of all was the late Rev. Dr. McQuhae of St Quivox who built a cottage at Maryburgh near the sea". This was more likely his son, Rev. Stair Park McQuhae who retired because of illhealth in 1859, and purchased the saltpans-house at Maryborough (as it was now more often spelled) before going south to Hampshire where he died in 1872. Though, as noted in the previous chapter, several incomers had in the 1840s selected New Prestwick to build new residences, McQuhae was first to choose a home at the sea front. Here too came first of the summer visitors, for after McQuhae left, his saltpans-house was let for the season by Dr Mathew Foulds who came down from Mauchline with his family of six. The 1872–73 Return indicated Maryborough (48 acres) as possessed by McQuhae's heirs. It also revealed more recent builders of new houses – James Bell of Craigview (18 acres);

Thomas Manson of Boydfield (1 acre); and Thomas McCulloch of Grangemuir, the first villa built at the sea-front (4 acres held by heirs). Hewat mentioned by name others who had arrived from Kilmarnock and Glasgow. William Wilson, a wholesale draper and Glasgow bailie, built Ardayre. Thomas Mack, a Kilmarnock bailie, built Seabank (renamed Stonegarth c.1920). James Keppie, a tobacco merchant from Glasgow, settled in Haddington Park West in the 1870s: his son John Keppie (1862–1945) became architect and artist. Charles Rennie Mackintosh joined his firm of Honeyman and Keppie in Glasgow, and was for a time engaged to Jessie Keppie, herself an artist of note. John, his sister Jessie, and other members of the family are buried in Prestwick Cemetery. In 1872–73 there were, in Prestwick, in addition to those 400 acres held by thirty owner-occupiers, another 300 acres possessed by non-residents, whose properties would in due course unexpectedly appreciate in value.

Exactly how Prestwick was enlarged can be measured by comparison of the Ordnance Survey Maps of 1857 and 1897. Gap sites within the old town were being filled up. New houses were built at intervals along the main highway between what were later known as Grangemuir Road and Maryborough Road. A major development was feuing of plots west of the railway, with access by Station Road or by Grangemuir Road: Ardayre Road and Marina Road provided prime sites fronting the sea, and the area south of Links Road was filling up. Building was commencing on land between the railway and the Main Street. On the landward side of the town there were also new houses, along and beyond Caerlaverock Road. Census Returns

Marina Road, Prestwick

The area west of the railway was developed.

indicate the stages of development west of the town where there were no houses in 1861, twelve in 1871, seventy-six in 1881, 106 in 1891. The Valuation Roll for 1899, the earliest available, shows that the villas near the front were nearly all owner-occupied. The numerous new cottages behind them, on the main street, and on the east side of the town were mostly occupied by tenants – building houses to rent was then a worthwhile investment.

All the towns along the central Ayrshire coast were enjoying substantial growth. During the period 1871 – 1901 Ayrshire population followed the general Scottish pattern of gradual increase (by a ratio of 1.3) but above-average increases in population were registered in Ayr (9,093), Ardrossan (2,232), Saltcoats (3,496), Stevenston (nearly 5,000), Irvine (2,732), Troon (1,974). Prestwick's population increase (2,016) gave it an outstanding rate of growth (a ratio of 3.68). In all of these other towns industrial development played some part in their expansion. Those who chose to settle in Prestwick did so because of its particular residential attractions.

Kirkwood Hewat, describing in 1894 "The New Era", explained why Prestwick had recently become "a popular resort for summer visitors, and a favourite residence for retired people". It was such a healthy place because with "no factories, coal pits, or public works of any kind, with objectionable smoke or refuse, the air

New shops were opened to cater for the growing population.

is always pure and wholesome." One particular feature then, as later, was that "Fogs are unknown", which he attributed to the sandy soils and lack of trees preventing damp, mist, or vapours. One might enjoy quiet walks inland or along the shore, and he quoted from the *Scots Magazine:* "Paradise can contain no sight more beautiful than what we behold any summer day from the coast at Prestwick" so that "twenty years have transformed this lonely desert into the haunt of beauty and fashion – the recreation ground of men of distinction in the higher walks of life, and the favourite health-resort of all classes of Her Majesty's subjects". Hewat pointed out the advantage of "the almost unequalled service of trains", with, in summer, thirty stopping each day on the lines from Glasgow and from Kilmarnock to Ayr. "The Glasgow merchants who sojourn here do not need to be told of the excellence of the 4.15 p.m. train from 'the Second City' which comes down at full speed, stopping only at Paisley, and by an ingenious method when in rapid motion disengaging its later part at Irvine." This was the only slip-coach service operated by the Glasgow and South Western Railway Company, and operated from 1888 until 1901. In 1892 a railway extension which marginally enhanced Prestwick was the opening of a Monkton and Annbank branch for goods and mineral traffic, diverting from the main line past Prestwick those trains carrying coals from central Ayrshire to Troon harbour. In listing the advantages the railway offered Prestwick, Hewat might have mentioned the situation of the station, which was so uniquely convenient for the shore and for the town, with feus for new houses available within easy walking distance, and hardly anyone more than half-a-mile away from the station. This was particularly suited for businessmen who travelled daily to Glasgow, and for their sons who in many cases – like John Keppie – were sent for schooling at Ayr Academy.

Progress was not without problems. Hewat noticed that "at intervals there have been halts in the forward movement. We have had our building manias and their reactions." Failure of the Glasgow Bank in 1878 ruined shareholders, and in particular interrupted building of Queens Terrace, whose houses were sold off at £250 each. This was told in 1991 by an old resident who had heard the story from his parents. He also told how William Atkinson, a freeman who was a potato merchant, hired spare-time workers to build, at a cost of £450 each, eight houses for rent in Regent Park (which he named after a variety of potato!). Parcels of lands which were part of the former freemen's holdings were built upon with no overall plan. The result was a street layout whose awkward irregularities inevitably became a permanent feature of the town. Also, on the western side of the town, where the railway bisected the new housing areas, there would always be difficulties in access and intercommunication. In 1900 the bridge under the railway at Station Road was only 8' 6" high and 11' 9" wide, which was described as "preposterous". During the initial period of building there was another problem with roads. As Hewat complained, "The new town is of mushroom growth, and the builders of it have just gone on the plan 'out west' of erecting the houses in the expectancy that the roads will follow. And they will; they are indeed beginning to appear; though we could wish that those who have their dwellings near the 'roads' and are experimenting in road-making would either study Macadam's principles or have some concerted method in their operation instead of each doing what he thinks best in his own eyes – one laying the foundations for the coming traffic in ashes, another in pieces of soft sandstone, a third in wood-shavings, while a fourth boldly ventures on the remains of decayed cabbage-stalks." The lack of a water supply or sewage system had also detrimental effects, which, as the *Ayr Observer* reported (26 July 1881) "injured the prosperity of the place as a summer resort." At the height of the season, "Many valuable properties and furnished houses of all classes were standing unlet." Some visitors from Glasgow brought their own supplies of water, when Prestwick wells were proved to be "quite unfit for drinking." Analysis indicated that they contained the equivalent of "a mixture of 100 gallons of pure water with one gallon of average Glasgow sewage".

To remedy such deficiencies proved difficult. Throughout the 19th century legislation was enacted to deal with various sanitary and social deficiencies, but the acts were difficult to implement because an appropriate system of local government was wanting. In the larger burghs and other populous places efforts could be made to secure improvements; there were more formidable obstacles to overcome in Prestwick. A burgh of barony lacked any statutory powers to provide public services. After 1850 when the lands of the freemen became their own individual heritable properties, the burgh of Prestwick ceased to have any significant remaining function. It was noted (*AA* 13 Nov. 1902) that "for fully a century their powers and duties have been practically confined to the collection and distribution among the freemen of the revenues from the Common Good of the burgh". Office-bearers were elected annually. They maintained the Burgh School. The Freemen's Hall was otherwise let for various public functions. Such funds as were available supplied the freemen with banquets and the indigent poor with coals. They continued to employ a burgh officer, who acted as town-crier, but they had long since discontinued appointing a constable. The gaol on the ground floor of the Freemen's Hall was apparently disused.

A County Constabulary was established in 1841, under control of the Commissioners of Supply, a committee of the county's major landowners, responsible for assessment and collection of national taxes and other levies from owners and occupiers of heritable property. Originally the force comprised only fourteen men. The constable for Ayr District visited Prestwick only once a week, relying on the aid of part-time parochial constables who were recruited to assist. A more effective police presence became possible after 1857 when the force was increased from thirty to sixty men. By 1891 Prestwick had a resident sergeant and constable, but as yet no local police station.

The Monkton and Prestwick Parochial Board, set up in 1845 to provide poor relief, was by the Public Health Act of 1867 given additional responsibilities. Though it was empowered to operate as a Local Authority and make provision for water and drainage, no action was as yet felt to be necessary. Following the Education (Scotland) Act of 1872, a Parish School Board was elected, and to meet its requirements, the Parochial Board was required to add a school rate to its poors rate. In 1867 the Commissioners of Supply were made responsible for a general assessment for county purposes; and from 1878 an additional levy was made when road tolls were abolished. There was inevitable objection to such increased impositions, and reluctance to incur additional expenditure. So, in Prestwick, despite a new urgency in extending sanitary provision, the Parochial Board as Local Authority repeatedly in 1881 refused to initiate a Water and Drainage Scheme. Those who resisted the scheme were satisfied that they had "abundance in their wells"; and argued (more convincingly, as it has turned out) that "the beach would be spoiled by the sewage which would be discharged in it". In 1882 however, at a special meeting, by a vote of 68 against 48 the Local Authority agreed to form the town of Prestwick and adjacent area into a special water district. In 1883 a reservoir to hold seven million gallons was formed on the Raith Burn beyond Ladykirk and the town supplied with piped water, while at the same time a drainage scheme was carried out. Monkton and Prestwick Parochial Board now levied (in 1885) a poors rate (7d in £), school rate (6d in £), water rate (1s 9d in £), drainage rate (6d in £). While the two former were collected from all owners and occupiers of property, the two latter were only from those who resided within the areas served. Appeals against the water assessment, from persons who claimed they did not want to use the new public supply, were dismissed.

By end of the century, to manage the several public services so haphazardly developed, legislation provided a more efficient system of local government. In 1890 Ayr County Council was created, elected by ratepayers, assuming most responsibilities previously exercised by the unrepresentative Commissioners of Supply. In 1894 the Parochial Board was similarly replaced by a Parish Council entirely composed of elected members. Prestwick water district was now managed by a subcommittee of the county council composed of two county councillors and all members of the parish council. To improve the water supply to Prestwick, in 1899 the Raith Burn reservoir was enlarged by raising the earth dam, and sand filters were installed nearby at Ladykirk. But during the work of construction, reserves were drained by an estimated thousand summer visitors, which produced a "Prestwick Water Famine". Consumers were served by a cart going round the town with a barrel from which jugfuls of water were obtained. An indignation meeting exhibited dissatisfaction with the arrangements.

Those councils newly established complemented others which had already been formed in the larger towns within the county. In Ayr, Irvine, and Kilmarnock, the burgh councils had in 1833 become elected bodies with powers to operate local public services. Acts of 1850 and 1862 allowed other populous places to become police burghs, with elected councils providing certain services. In the latter part of the century this opportunity was taken up in twelve Ayrshire communities. Three of them were burghs of barony which, like Prestwick, still functioned as such (Maybole, Newmilns, and Girvan); four of them had previously allowed their charters to lapse (Cumnock, Largs, Ardrossan, Saltcoats); the other five had never been burghs (Darvel, Galston, Stewarton, Kilwinning, Troon). When they applied to become police burghs, each of them (except Darvel) had a population of two thousand or more. Prestwick would not join them till 1903. Yet by the 1890s Prestwick had sufficient inhabitants to justify initiative, as Hewat forecast: "We have sometimes had to inform visitors that a good many things that ought to be done, for the good of the place, are not done owing to our having either too little oversight from public bodies or too much. It has in fact to be explained that things are rather 'mixed', owing to this being a very modern and a very ancient place. We have the Council of the Freemen, the Parochial Board, the Local Improvement Committee, and, over all, the County Council. Now, the only observation we should like to make regarding these bodies is this, that if a place like Prestwick, which cannot be called very populous as yet, is able to furnish such worthy representatives to so many and so diverse bodies, when the time comes for one united Board or Council to look after its interests there will surely be plenty of excellent material for its formation."

There was no lack of political enthusiasm in Prestwick. Disappointment at the limited extension of the franchise in 1832, and failure of the Chartist movement, did not inhibit local agitation for further parliamentary reform. In 1850 a banquet was held in the Council House to present Hugh Dunlop McLellan with a clock "for his public services, and advocacy of civil and religious liberty." A native of Prestwick, a handloom weaver, then aged forty-four, with an English wife and a family of seven, he had as a young man participated in the Reform demonstrations of 1832. He continued as an activist, reported as addressing a reform meeting in Ayr in 1861. He remained without a vote, for by 1857 only fifty-four persons from Monkton and Prestwick parish were so entitled, eighteen of them living within Prestwick. In 1867 renewed agitation resulted in the Riot Act being read in Prestwick, just before a second Reform Act was passed. That resulted in few additions to the voters roll. Small proprietors like McLellan were included, and as numbers of new properties in Prestwick increased so did the number of voters. So long as the franchise remained restricted, the Ayrshire parliamentary constituency was held by Conservatives, J.H.Blair (1852–54), and after his death, Sir James Fergusson of Kilkerran (1854–57); briefly by a Liberal, Lord James Stuart (1857–59), then again by Sir James Fergusson (1859–68). After 1867, when the franchise was extended, the Ayrshire constituency was divided. Prestwick was included in South Ayrshire, which returned a Liberal, Sir R. Wedderburn (1868–74), then a Conservative, Sir Claud Alexander of Ballochmyle (1874–85).

The political parties required to adapt their tactics after introduction of the secret ballot in 1872. By chance there have survived two electoral rolls for the South Ayrshire constituency with annotations by agents of the Conservative party between 1877 and 1884. These allow insight into political opinion in Prestwick. Allegiance of those who had voted in the open elections before 1872 was on record, and opinions of some of the others was known. Opposite each voter's name was listed church membership (especially useful since Rev. W.F.Lorraine was a member of the local Conservative committee) and there was note of estates to which tenant farmers were attached (hopeful of covert intimidation). In 1877 there were 152 electors for Monkton and Prestwick parish: sixty-two of these were non-resident owners of properties; the others comprised sixty living in Prestwick and thirty in the Monkton area. The political balance was then seventy-two Liberals as against fifty Conservatives, with the remaining thirty uncertain; among the resident Prestwick electors thirty-nine were known to be Liberals and only thirteen Conservatives. By 1884 the total had increased to 262, entirely the result of new properties acquired within Prestwick, which had now 122 resident and 99 absentee owners. The arrival of these incomers helped narrow the local Liberal majority to fifty-two versus forty-seven. The ninety-nine non-resident electors, many of whom had holiday homes in the town, were predominantly Conservative (forty versus thirty-eight, the rest unknown); as were the resident and non-resident electors of Monkton (eighteen versus twelve); so that by 1884 the previous Liberal ascendancy had given way to uncertainty, for of the 262 electors there were 105 Conservative and 102 Liberals.

A change in political circumstances came when the Reform Act of 1884 substantially increased the electorate. It was preceded by another great demonstration in Ayr, when among the Prestwick contingent were two veterans of 1832, now in their seventies, Hugh McLellan who was a weavers' agent, and Andrew Bryan who had been a wood and metal worker. The Reform Act which followed increased to 447 the number of voters in Monkton and Prestwick. To woo the new working class voters, a Liberal Association was formed in Prestwick in September 1885. A month later at the General Election 364 of the 447 persons now enfranchised in Monkton and Prestwick cast their votes, and we can guess that most of those in Prestwick helped elect the Liberal Eugene Wason (1885–86). But the Liberal Party became split over Irish home rule. Wason was defeated by a Liberal Unionist, Hon. G.R. Vernon (1886–92), recovered the seat (1892–95), only to lose it again to Sir William Arrol (1895–1906). The Conservatives were cooperating with, and ultimately merged with the Liberal Unionists to form the Unionist Party. It was strong enough locally as to afford the opening in 1899 of a Prestwick Conservative Club, in premises designed by James A. Morris which would later become a town hall.

In the latter part of the 19th century the face of Prestwick changed. The public highway passed through what had previously had the appearance of a country village but now alongside the old thatched cottages appeared two-storey tenements with shops and other new buildings. A modern town centre extended from north of the Cross as far as Grangemuir Road; and beyond, as Hewat observed, it was now difficult "to detect where Ayr ends and Prestwick begins, as houses line both sides of the road nearly the whole way from Ayr Bridge to Prestwick Cross". The highway itself, he compared favourably with the unsatisfactory newer side streets. The turnpike and the parish roads are excellent as any Jehu will testify. A friend, who had travelled over a great part of the world, praised them to us very highly." Notice that he continued to refer to "the turnpike" even though tolls had been abolished some twenty years before he wrote, understandably since the name of Prestwick Toll has survived for another century. Until 1878 the Road Trustees annually auctioned collection of tolls at the various tollbars throughout the county. At Prestwick Toll, the charge for a springed vehicle was 4d, 3d for a cart, and appropriate amounts for cattle and sheep. Mark Kerr, the toll-keeper, in 1867 paid £337, for which he occupied the tollhouse and pocketed all receipts from those passing between Prestwick and Ayr – and augmented his income by sale of beer and spirits. Replacement of tolls by an annual levy on all ratepayers allowed the growing traffic less restricted passage. The Road Trust (and the County Council after 1890) was responsible for the former turnpike roads, from Ayr through Prestwick, and those from Monkton towards Irvine, Kilmarnock, and Tarbolton. They also were concerned with upkeep of parish roads. One inland route led from Prestwick Cross past Shaw, Brieryside, and Adamton Mains; another from the south end of Prestwick towards St Quivox. There were three roads from the main highway to the sea – those which would become Maryborough, Grangemuir, and Station Roads. They also maintained the street from Prestwick Cross to the Kirkgate; the West Wrack Road in Monkton from the village as far as the station; and the road north from Monkton Station towards Fairfield.

Where the public highway passed through the town, the street was as yet unlit at night. Newton-on-Ayr Gas Company, established in 1845, extended their supply to Prestwick. In 1863 gas-lighting was introduced into the burgh school and council house, but the streets were still dark in 1884 and the first gas lamps were not installed till around the year 1890. Initiative was taken by a Local Improvements Committee, about which little is known except for a series of concerts held in 1891 to fund improvements, an indication of voluntary enterprise. That incomers took the lead is suggested by Hewat's comment that "some of the natives looked coldly on this undertaking and refused to subscribe ... An old man told us he would give nothing, as 'folk should bide at hame at nicht'."

The arrival of so many incomers required, and enabled, the provision or augmentation of other facilities, as churches, schools, shops, and recreations.

Within the established church, when Dr Lawrie resigned his charge of St Cuthbert's in 1877, he was followed briefly by Rev. Walter Fotheringham Lorraine (1878–80) and Rev. John Patrick (1880–87). The former died after a chill contracted from preaching in the open air; the latter left for another charge and then a chair in Edinburgh University. In Fotheringham's first year, evening services were introduced, and for this purpose the session resolved in instal gas-lighting; in the same year the building was enhanced by a bell, cast in Glasgow, and costing nearly £100. After Patrick's translation from Kilmarnock, the interior of the church, which had acquired "a very dingy appearance", was in 1881 extensively renovated. At the same time the manse was repaired (followed by a legal dispute of which more later). A major innovation was made in 1884 when an organ was introduced. Praise had always been led by a precentor, the last one being James Howat who taught in the public school. In 1883 he was succeeded by Alfred Hart who came from Coatbridge, tempted by an offer of £40 annually to serve as organist and choirmaster, and who continued in that post until 1940, and died a year later at the age of eighty-two. In the early years of Rev. David Reid's long ministry (1888–1923) further changes were reported in the kirk session minutes: collections to be taken within the church instead of at the door (1889); church to be heated

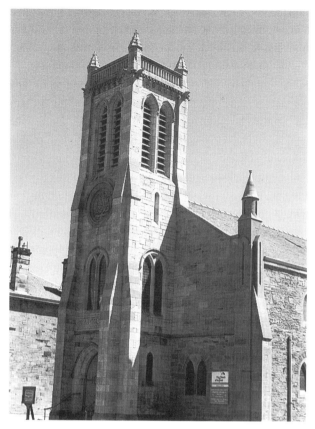

The North Church, built in 1874 for the Free Church congregation. (*KA*)

(1889); social gatherings proposed (1894); Mr John Keppie, architect, recommended improved ventilation (1896); copies of new Church Hymnary for the choir (1899). Throughout the period of change, the minutes record provision of public worship also at New Prestwick; some parishioners still being censured for moral lapses; and an expanding communion roll, with incomers transferring from other parishes.

The Free Church congregation under Rev. John Macfarlan (1843–54) and Rev. William Wilson (1855–64) continued to worship in their small church at Monkton. During the ministry of Rev. Alexander Stirling (1865–81) it was found necessary to provide a larger place of worship. Nearer the town centre, a site was acquired on Monkton Road, where Prestwick Free Church was built in 1874 at a cost of £1,600. It was designed by Messrs James Salmond and Co., Glasgow, and built by local tradesmen with freestone from the Bellrock quarry; a tower designed by John Keppie was added in 1896. This church, with 450 sittings, was large enough to accommodate a local congregation whose numbers had not significantly increased, and provide for summer visitors. The former place of worship in Monkton continued in use as a church hall, where services were conducted on Sunday afternoons. A new manse was built in 1885, following the ordination of Rev.

The South Church, built in 1884 by the United Presbyterians. (*KA*)

Kirkwood Hewat (1881–1909). Educated at Edinburgh and Leipzig, he was a man of wide-ranging interests, as his several publications reveal. Author of books and articles on subjects ranging from church history to foreign travel, he is best remembered for his local history, *A Little Scottish World*, first published in 1894, and popular enough to require a second edition in 1908.

There were other presbyterians who found spiritual comfort in those separate congregations founded by 18th century seceders, which in 1847 had come together to form a United Presbyterian Church, but Newton-on-Ayr was the nearest place of worship for adherents who lived in Prestwick. In 1879 a mission station was established, and in 1880 a little redstone place of worship, designed by John Mercer, was erected on the west side of the Main Street. It was served by visiting preachers, until one of them was called to the new charge and inducted in 1882. This was Rev. Archibald Alison, born in Strathaven sixty-two years before, and minister in Leslie since 1849. He was a tall bearded man with the appearance of an Old Testament patriarch, and attracted a congregation ambitious enough to commission James A. Morris, the noted Ayr architect, to design a church which was erected in front of the mission station. Prestwick U.P. Church, formally opened in 1884, was of Gothic style in grey freestone from Craiksland quarry, Troon, providing 600 sittings. For the minister a manse was provided in Queens Terrace, then in St Quivox Road. The U.P., like the Free Church, attracted not only some incomers and visitors, but an equally-distinguished minister in Rev. Ernest F. Scott (1895–1908), a young man who came to assist when Mr Alison became unfit, and succeed him when he died in 1900. Educated at Glasgow and Oxford, and author of several books on the gospels, he received a doctorate from St Andrews (1909) and went as professor of New Testament Criticism to Canada, then from 1919 in New York, where he died in 1954.

In 1897, in the earliest *Guide to Prestwick*, Helen Steven advised visitors that there were church services each Sunday at 11.30 a.m., and the Free and U.P. churches had also evening services at 6.30 p.m. An assembly of Christian Brethren provided morning and evening meetings in the Freemen's Hall at these times. There were other evangelistic meetings in the Bute Hall at 6.30 p.m. Also, at the Ayr side of New Prestwick, Thomas Young who was a solicitor and member of Ayr Baptist Church began holding kitchen meetings in his home in 1887. Two years later a wooden hut was erected, which became New Prestwick Baptist Church.

The three presbyterian congregations retained their separate traditions. While the illfeeling that had accompanied the Disruption had diminished, there continued to be occasional differences. In 1881 when the heritors called upon property owners to make their statutory contributions towards repair of the manse of the established church, certain adherents of the U.P. church understandably refused to contribute, but were required to do so after due process of law in what was called the Monkton Manse Case. Yet the three congregations were similarly adapting their outlook to changing circumstances. Each provided a new range of social activities for members, with musical evenings, soirees, and Sunday School outings. Some such attracted members from other denominations, like Rev. Kirkwood Hewat's course of lectures in the Free Church schoolroom in 1884. Many of the divisive issues were being resolved. The abolition in 1874 of patronage in the established church meant that Rev. W.F.Lorraine and all subsequent ministers were chosen by the congregation, thus removing one of the principal complaints that had contributed to the secessions of the 18th century and the Disruption in the 19th. The dissenting churches were themselves becoming less rigid in their attitudes, each in particular relaxing its adherence to the Westminster Confession of Faith. Thus Dr Robert Rainy (who opened Prestwick Free Church in 1874) as Principal of the New College in Edinburgh guided those negotiations which led to reconciliation and formation of the United Free Church in 1900. Therefter Prestwick Free became Prestwick North U.F. Church and Prestwick U.P. became Prestwick South U.F. Church, and those distinguished ministers Revs. Hewat and Scott became colleagues within the same communion. Effort by the church to attract young people was evident when in the last decade of the century Colonel J.G.Hamilton, recently retired to Prestwick, formed a company of the Boys' Brigade, which was associated with the North Church, and Kirkwood Hewat served as their chaplain.

The churches had always honoured a commitment to education. But as the 19th century advanced it proved increasingly difficult for them to fulfil their traditional role. The parish and Free Church schools at Monkton, the Burgh school in Prestwick, and the school which the established church tried to operate at New Prestwick could not cater for all children, nor were all parents able to afford fees. For those who as adults regretted their own lack of schooling, a novel experiment was attempted. A Working Men's College was established in Ayr in 1860, copying one founded in London by Rev. F.D.Maurice six years before. This was followed by Prestwick setting up its own College in November 1861. Revs. Lawrie and Wilson attended the inaugural meeting to guarantee support of the established and Free churches. Messrs Stuart, who were teachers at Prestwick and New Prestwick, volunteered to teach, without recompense, classes in writing, arithmetic, grammar, geography, composition, mathematics, Latin, and French. Between thirty and forty enrolled in various classes, paying a fee of a shilling per class per term. In the spring of 1862 the close of a first session was celebrated by a soiree, and forty persons enrolled for the next session. But in 1863 the Colleges in both Ayr and Prestwick gave up this premature provision of adult education.

Establishment of a national system of education followed the Education (Scotland) Act of 1872. This required election of parish school boards, which were charged with responsibility for providing compulsory education for all children between the ages of five and thirteen. Monkton and Prestwick Parish School Board first met on 3 May 1873, with five elected members, of whom John Gray, freemen and Liberal, was the first chairman. It was ascertained that accommodation was

Prestwick Public School, opened in 1882, was embellished with the seal of the burgh. (*KA*)

required for more than three hundred children, 142 in Monkton and 180 in Prestwick. Monkton Parish School was handed over to board control. Its schoolroom (34' 2" x 18' x 10' 3" high) could take 80 pupils; another classroom (30' x 18' x 12') would provide for another 80 children by taking over the adjoining dwelling house of the parish schoolmaster. The schoolmaster, 73-year-old James Cowan, was pensioned off at £40 per annum. John Dinning, whose Free Church school in Monkton closed, was made master of what was now Monkton Public School, at £90 plus house; aided by a pupil teacher and a sewing mistress. In Prestwick, there was no possibility of the board becoming owners of the Freemen's Hall where the Burgh School met. Arrangements were made with the freemen to let the school room on the ground floor and also the council room above. Walter Beaton, who in 1868 had succeeded "Wee McIntosh" as teacher in the burgh school, continued as master of Prestwick pupils. Previously he had to rely on fees from pupils, supplemented only by £18 from the freemen, more than the miserable £5 his predecessors had been granted. The School Board now provided him with a fixed annual salary of £105, plus £15 as secretary and treasurer of the board. He had as assistants a pupil teacher and sewing mistress, posts valued at an annual £15 and £8. To ensure that parents sent their children to school, the board paid an annual £10 as compulsory officer to Douglas Chalmers, post messenger, Monkton.

What made things especially awkward at first was that the parents were required to pay school fees. In Monkton and Prestwick the quarterly fees (to be paid monthly) were assessed at 2 shillings (10p) for Reading, 2s 6d (12p) for Writing and Arithmetic, 3s 6d (17p) for Grammar, Geography, and History, 5 shillings (25p) for Latin and Mathematics. Parliament enacted free education in 1889, but since parents had to continue paying for schoolbooks problems over payments continued. The school board was constantly concerned with defaulting parents. Another problem was truancy, which here was particularly prevalent when boys could seek gainful employment on the golf courses. James Moore, the burgh officer who succeeded as compulsory officer in 1876, was required to prevent "the employment of boys of school age as 'Caddies' ". He failed to do so, and in desperation by 1887 it was proposed prosecuting "gentlemen employing schoolboys as caddies"; a year later, to remedy the abuse, both golf clubs were supplied with a list of all boys of school age.

The school board within its first six months made plans for a new school at Caerlaverock. The Board of Education in Edinburgh deemed this an unnecessary extravagance. But the school in the Freemen's Hall became overcrowded, with 161 pupils in 1879 and 200 a year later. Some parents chose to send their daughters to learn sewing in a private "industrial school" in the Bute Hall; and Hugh Anderson ran a little school, first in Sandgate, later at Prestwick Toll. The Schools Inspector after his annual visit in 1881 agreed that the Freemen's Hall was no longer suitable, and anticipating further expansion of numbers, Edinburgh agreed to provision of a new school building capable of accommodating 350 pupils. The school board feued from James M. Ferguson, publisher of the *Ayr Observer*, an acre of his land at Caerlaverock. Several architects were invited to submit designs, those of John Murdoch of Ayr were selected, and Prestwick Public School was opened in 1882. This was financed by a grant of £2,000 from the Public Works Loan Board. The pupils were marched in procession to the new school by Walter Beaton, a tall dignified bachelor with Dundreary whiskers; supported by his assistant James Howat and the sewing mistress Jessie McWilliam. To pay for the new school, the Parochial Board required to increase the school rate, to provide £350 in 1883 as compared with £120 ten years earlier. To run the schools, the board depended upon school fees and annual government grants based on number of pupils and efficiency of the teachers as judged by Schools Inspectors. In 1883 government grants amounted to £177, not enough to pay the salaries of £247 shared among six teachers, which ranged from £115 to £8 a year.

Monkton Public School, enlarged in 1877, easily accommodated (in 1880) a roll of 128 pupils with an average attendance of 106. As master, Gabriel Muir in 1885 succeeded John Dinning who resigned and died a month later. In 1890 the number of Monkton pupils was almost exactly the same. The new Prestwick Public School in 1890 had still only 214 pupils on the roll and average attendance of 167, little more than attended the old school ten years earlier. In the 1891 Census Returns 265 children are designated as scholars within Prestwick burgh, which suggests that a number of better-off parents were sending their children elsewhere for schooling, often to Ayr Academy. Prestwick Public School served also New Prestwick, which was inconvenient. Some children there attended the small private "adventure achool" run by Hugh Anderson, other boys were accustomed to truanting as caddies at St Nicholas Golf Club. In 1883 parents in New Prestwick urged that the old schoolhouse at New Prestwick be reopened, but when this proposal was ultimately taken up in 1895 the kirk session of the established church was unable by terms of the title deeds to let it as a day school.

Monkton and Prestwick School Board was chaired by John Gray (1873–85); Dr William Hewitt (1885–88); Hugh Peebles, blacksmith (1888–91); then Hugh Macpherson, postmaster. The board was responsible for allocating school holidays. There was a month's holiday in summer, August originally, July from 1887. There was a week at New Year – Chistmas was not yet publicly recognised. There were days off in April and October, superseding the church Fast Days which had fallen into disuse. The only other holiday was on the Queen's birthday, plus a special Jubilee holiday in 1887. From time to time one or other of the schools had to be closed during epidemics of fever or measles. The school board minutes report also the provision from 1889 of silver medals as prizes for deserving pupils. In 1879 it established a Night School, and evening classes were continued in the new school and at Monkton. The school board also provided in its first decades accommodation for night classes for caddies (including formation of a Caddies Flute Band); an Established Church Sunday School; meetings of the Good Templars, the Choral Union, Monkton Dramatic Association, and dancing classes (Rev. Alexander Stirling had objected to these in 1880); balls organised by the Choral Union and the Bowling Club; also bazaars and political meetings.

The growing community was provided with a widening range of facilities. Directories of 1851 and 1867 listed in Prestwick only four grocers, three innkeepers, and one who sold both victuals and spirits. In New Prestwick there was one who was both innkeeper and grocer; plus (in 1867) the tollkeeper Mark Kerr who also supplied spirits. Monkton had three inns (Crown, Wheatsheaf, and Campbell Arms), two grocers, and (in 1851) an undertaker and a postmistress serving the parish. In 1867 the Monkton post office was run by the Free Church schoolmaster John Dinning; Prestwick was now served by an office, where letters had to be collected from George McQueen, the receiving officer. By 1883 Prestwick had its own post office, with money order, savings bank, and telegraphic departments. The Census Returns for 1891 reveal the range of shops and other businesses which by that time occupied the town centre. The west side of the main street contained the Golf Inn (formerly the Craw's E'e), the Royal Hotel (previously Prestwick Arms), the Priest Inn (later Central Bar), a licensed grocer, a temperance hotel, John Silver the solicitor's office, the surgery of Dr William Hewitt (who came as a young man of twenty-eight in 1879), Andrew Dykes's engineering smithy, a seed merchant and florist, joiner, newsagent, stationer, plumber, golf club maker (Charles Hunter), two grocers, butcher, Gilbert Gardiner's bakery (since 1875), with another grocer and butcher near the Cross. On the opposite side, there was the Red Lion inn (familarly known as the Rid Dug) and southwards a physician, the post office, confectioner, licensed grocer, dairy keeper, house painter, shoemaker, plumber, grocer, coal merchant, potato merchant, carrier, and yarn agent. East of the main street, other businesses were sited at or around Caerlaverock – hatter, hosier, tailor, tea merchant, butcher, potato merchant, two builders, four joiners, and John Gray's smithy where he manufactured iron-headed golf clubs. The Valuation Roll for 1899 listed a total of forty-eight main street shops. Nine of these – shoemaker, butcher, hairdreser, draper, jeweller, tobacconist, cabinetmaker, fruiterer, Girdwood's bakery – were in the newly-erected Bruce Quadrant which also housed the Unionist Club, a lawyer's office (John Stewart), and a recently-established branch of the Clydesdale Bank. How facilities were being augmented to cater for the summer trade is shown by two entries in a county commercial brochure published in 1894. The Royal Hotel in Prestwick had been acquired four years earlier by Thomas P. Oliver, listed in the census as a young Englishman. It was advertised that this "handsome structure ... enjoys a very considerable patronage, especially during the golfing season." One room measuring 42 x 18 feet had been adapted to hold two billiard tables, which were patronised by "the leading amateur players of Ayr and the district". Also on the main street, John McClure had recently opened a draper's shop which stocked Manchester goods, dress materials, ribbons, shawls, blankets, quilts, rugs, household linen, and fancy goods; with a dress and mantle department which was "wellknown as a reflection of the latest Parisian styles"; and behind the premises several were employed manufacturing 'Land of Burns Hosiery' on "several machines of the latest modern invention." Prestwick shops were now catering for an extensive clientele, both residents and holidaymakers. Some of the latter, however, it was said, "did little guid tae Prestick". Montgomerie Terrace was known as "Kilmarnock Row", whose summer visitors allegedly "even brocht their paraffin oil and peasemeal wi them".

The 1891 Census Returns further reveal how the old was giving way to new. In Smiddy Raw (Boyd Street) three traditional trades survived. One man worked on his own as shoemaker (like another on main street); one old woman still did white flowering (as did another in Kirk Street); and there were several silk weavers still. They specialised in silk handkerchiefs, but one exceptional product was a silk flag to celebrate the Relief of Mafeking in 1900. Robert Brown would be the last surviving handloom weaver when he died in 1916 at the age of eighty-four. In 1891 he acted as an agent employing those other weavers who lived in Smiddy Raw (4), Kirk Steet (3), and Victoria Terrace (2). The rural character of old Prestwick was still retained, for within the burgh there were thirteen farmers and eight gardeners and nurserymen. Only four of these can be identified as freemen continuing to cultivate part of their freedoms – William Latta of Greenbank, David Manson at Sandgate, Robert Manson at Caerlaverock, David Boyd in Smiddy Raw. Those who occupied the small agricultural holdings required to employ twenty-eight workers. Some were still specialising in growing cabbages, and Pat King (aged 36 in 1891) would be the last to do so. A new line of business was introduced by George Mair, a native of Aberdeenshire who in 1881 began growing gladioli in a nursery beside Queens Terrace. Nearby, out of the smithy at Orchard Villa from time to time emerged one of Andrew Dykes's steam threshing machines, to make its way along the main street to work in neighbouring parishes. The principal employment for men in the burgh was now the building trade, with nearly seventy employees serving the firms which were busily engaged in house construction.

The incoming residents of the many new houses were catered for by fourteen women who worked as milliners, dressmakers, laundresses, and washerwomen, either on their own or with the aid of twenty assistants. The incomers also required to employ domestic servants, most of them – 73 out of 105 — in the new houses to the west of the town. Some were housekeepers; most were maids. Few of the latter were local girls; some came from parts of Ayrshire where jobs for girls were scarce; the rest came from all corners of Scotland. The influx of servant girls produced by 1891 a sex ratio in the burgh of 132 females per 100 males, as compared with the Ayrshire average of 104 per 100, a common feature of the population in all the coastal towns. Many of the large new houses west of the town belonged to owners who had their businesses outwith Prestwick; among them were thirty-four residents who were either retired or had private means. Others in similar circumstances lived elsewhere in the burgh, modestly, and usually as tenants. There were twenty-two in main street houses, where handloom weavers had once worked. There were thirty-three to the east, mostly in the new cottages being built beyond Caerlaverock. This large number of older persons settled in the burgh contributed to Prestwick having 9.5% of its population over the age of 60, as compared with the Ayrshire average of 7.7%, another characteristic common to the coastal towns.

Along Ayr Road and seawards south of Maryborough, there were twenty-eight other modest households containing 128 inhabitants, whom the census enumerators included with New Prestwick but who in fact belonged to Prestwick burgh, whose population in 1891 actually totalled 1,607. Here were five retired persons, five businessmen (like Wallace Allan who had a watchmaker's shop in Ayr), twelve domestic servants, three milliners and three employees, two dairy keepers, four farmers, and eight farmworkers.

New Prestwick itself, with a population of 269, was served in 1891 by two grocers, a publican, and a blacksmith. Workers included two hand sewers and a silk weaver. There was one mason employing some of the eight men who worked in the building trade. Most found work outwith New Prestwick, including (probably) a carpet weaver, three dressmakers, and several of the nine domestic servants – whom none of the four retired persons could afford. At the other end of the parish, Monkton village also remained small, with 387 inhabitants. It retained more businesses, with a contractor, builder, two masons, two joiners, a glazier, and a stone breaker, most of whom would, with their employees, benefit from jobs in Prestwick. The village contained also a silk weaver, shoemaker, tailor, draper, grocer, general dealer, licensed grocer, spirit merchant, and publican. Neighbouring farms provided work for fourteen persons specifically described as employed in agriculture, plus most of the twenty men and sixteen women more loosely defined as general labourers or outdoor workers.

Monkton had a relatively settled population – 45% had been born within the parish, and 36% of the heads of households. Elsewhere it was a different story. In

The first Open Golf Championship was played at Prestwick in 1860, commemorated by a cairn at the first hole. (*KA*)

New Prestwick, the comparable proportions were 40% and 20%. Within Prestwick burgh, only 37% of the inhabitants were natives of the parish, and here too when heads of households were considered each native was outnumbered by four incomers. Among inhabitants of Prestwick were forty-five from England (2.8%), only twenty-nine from Ireland (1.8%), and sixteen from overseas (1%). 74.4% of the population were incomers from other places in Scotland. These statistics are marginally distorted by the fact that the 1891 Census was taken on 5 April during Easter holidays when there were 128 visitors in Prestwick, but this was compensated by fifty-one residents themselves absent at the time of the census, and eighty-one uninhabited houses which would be occupied during the summer months. The general picture is clear by listing heads of households in fifty occupied houses west of the railway. Only two were natives of this parish; five were from Ayr and adjacent parishes; eight came from Kilmarnock; another eight from other parts of Ayrshire. No fewer than eleven were natives of Glasgow, four were from Edinburgh, six from other parts of Scotland. Five were English and one Irish, but the overwhelming majority were Scots-born who had chosen to settle in Prestwick.

Many of the new residents came to enjoy Prestwick's existing facilities and in some cases would enhance them.

Golf contributed to Prestwick's reputation. The exclusive Prestwick Golf Club, though with fewer than a hundred members, was wealthy enough to sponsor in 1860 a competition for a Championship Belt, thus instituting the Open Championship. The first contest attracted only eight entrants, and was won by Willie Park. Tom Morris was successful in 1861, 1862, 1864, and 1867. His son, young Tom Morris, at the age of eighteen won in 1868; by doing so in three successive years gained in 1870 permanant ownership of the Belt; in 1872 he won the replacement Cup, which continues as the Open trophy; then this gifted golfer died while only twenty-five. The Open, after twelve years at Prestwick, went from 1872 in rotation to the Royal and Ancient Golf Club at St Andrews; the Honourable Company of Edinburgh Golfers at Musselburgh, then after 1891 on their new course at Muirfield; and every third year here at Prestwick Golf Club. In 1893 the Open and also the amateur championship were both held at Prestwick, which Hewat described as "an *annus mirabilis et memorabilis* in Prestwick golfing annals, and caused the name of our ancient burgh to bulk largely in the eyes of the British public."

Membership of Prestwick Golf Club increased from the 58 founder members of 1851 to 100 in 1867, to 375 in 1889, and 500 in 1901, when there was a long waiting list of others seeking to join. A clubhouse, built in 1866 (at a cost of £758), was extended by J.A.Morris and J.K.Hunter in 1893 (costing £2,000). Nearby, beside Links Road a cairn unveiled by Henry Cotton in 1977 marks the first hole of the first Open Championship. The course was extended from twelve to eighteen holes in 1883; the land, which was originally leased from freemen, was acquired by a series of purchases between 1873 and 1912. The St Nicholas Club, which originally shared the same course, was in 1877 required to provide a course of its own. In April 1877 they opened a nine-hole course at Monktonmiln, but having failed to secure permission from the trustees of the Fairfield estate it had to be immediately

Charles Hunter and Tom Morris, playing in 1863.

abandoned. Within a few weeks an alternative site was secured on the east side of Ayr Road, and a twelve-hole course opened on 14 July 1877. This catered for a membership which increased from 28 in 1851 to 195 in 1892. Then it was decided to move to the present seaside location south of Grangemuir Road, on an eighteen-hole course which allowed a massive increase in membership. There were 360 members in 1894, and the clubhouse, designed by John Mercer and erected in 1892, was enhanced by a sculpture by W.G. Stevenson. The new St Nicholas course was on land which was originally leased, but by 1911 all had been purchased, including that part where the Volunteers had their rifle range from 1886 until 1904. The course which they abandoned was continued for use by ladies and boys. There the St Nicholas Ladies Club was established in 1893, with a membership of 150 in 1897, and their own clubhouse. Ladies had originally played over a six-hole course, on land which was taken over by Prestwick Golf Club in 1883. In that year the ladies moved south of Links Road to a new course which was "beautifully laid off", but in an area which over the next decade was being filled up with new houses, which required their further move. Popularity of the game was so great that another course was provided when St Cuthbert Golf Club was established in 1899 by a group of working men. Ground was obtained from Fairfield estate to lay out a nine-hole course, and an old cottage on Manse Brae called Beenie's Bower was a first clubhouse, replaced in 1908 with an attractive club-house designed by J. Gibb Morton. The course was then extended to eighteen holes by taking in part of West Orangefield farm.

By the end of the 19th century over a thousand members were playing golf over these four courses. A few were old inhabitants, some were incomers, but many, probably most, were resident in Ayr and the adjoining areas and travelled by train or charabanc to play. This popularity was despite inflated charges. To join Prestwick Golf Club had originally cost £1 admission fee with £1 per year thereafter; in 1897 it was £15 with £2 annually. St Nicholas Club membership in 1851 cost only sixpence; by 1858 this had been increased to five shillings as entrance fee and five shillings annually; in 1897 quite substantially inflated to seven guineas for entry, then £1 5s each year. St Nicholas Ladies charged ten shillings for entrance and ten shillings annually. Hewat hoped that "these large sums will not stagger summer visitors, because such continue to have the usual facilities for playing." For these, St Nicholas offered temporary membership at £1 per month, and St Nicholas Ladies at 2s 6d. St Cuthbert's was formed to cater for those who wanted cheaper golf.

How the game was progressing can be observed from passing references in the local press. In 1861 there was a junior golf club. In that year there was also a challenge match of four rounds of twelve holes between the two champions, with Willie Park scoring 217 and Tom Morris 220. For a wager, H.Smith of the Star Hotel, Ayr, did two rounds at Prestwick in forty-eight minutes. There were annual games between Glasgow and St Nicholas, over thirty-six holes. There was a Tournament at Prestwick Ladies Links in 1885. At this time, Helen Steven reported "large sums easily earned as caddies", and Hewat noted that many local men had found employment as professionals or greenkeepers in various clubs throughout the British Isles. Hewat was himself a keen golfer, and often played with old Alexander Hutchison, who had been baptised by Rev. Dr Mitchell in 1809 and had been an elder in the Free Church session since the Disruption. He was still playing good golf in his eighties and, shortly before his death, at the Open in 1898 he was able to tell Harry Vardon his memories of old Tom Morris. This veteran golfer Hutchison, a founder of St Nicholas, made his own clubs, a set comprising a driver, long and short spoon, one iron, and a wooden putter. Iron-headed golf clubs were then being manufactured by John Gray in Smiddy Raw (Boyd Street). These Johnny Gray clubs had a wide sale, but after he died in 1904 no one continued his work. One other local man who contributed to popularising golf at Prestwick was Charles Hunter. He was one of the eight who competed in the first championship of 1860. In 1864 he succeeded Tom Morris as greenkeeper, after a year went off to Blackheath, but returned in 1868 to serve Prestwick Golf Club as greenkeeper, then professional and clubmaster till his death in 1921, aged eighty-five, a staunch Conservative, and remembered also for his pawky humour. Charles Hunter was so closely associated with Prestwick Golf Club that Mathew Foulds found one of his pupils believing that the three local courses were St Nicholas, St Cuthbert's and St Charlie's!

Clubhouse of Prestwick Golf Club, built in 1866 and extended in 1893.

Another sport could be practised from 1878 when Prestwick Bowling Club was formed. Walter Beaton, John Gray, David Manson, and Thomas McLatchie were the leading promoters. The bowling green was sited on William Latta's freedom, through which Midton Road would later be formed. Tom McLatchie donated turf from his field near Berelands Hill, which proved so acceptable that several Glasgow clubs bought turf from him. By 1897 it had sixty members, paying £1 for a season lasting from May until September. There were also tennis courts in 1894; the location is uncertain, perhaps near the west end of Bridge Street, perhaps nearer Grangemuir Road. Billiards could be played in the Royal Hotel and in the Unionist Club. After the summer visitors had left, and the windows of holiday homes were boarded up for the winter, curling could be played when conditions were suitable. There were ponds near Monktonmill farm and within Prestwick. The earliest at Prestwick was identified by Hewat: "It may surprise the dwellers in the large villas facing the Links to be told that not so many years ago a 'hill' occupied their present flat site, behind which was a sheet of water on which curlers in winter disported themselves". This was presumably the Bog, so-called since the 15th century (*a porciunkle of commoun land ... the bog apoun the south sid*, 1470). That low-lying area was often waterlogged, for the Puddock Sheugh could fill it, and only with difficulty drained into the sea near the foot of Burgh Road. Possibly the drainage scheme initiated in the 1880s required construction of that alternative pond near Manse Brae, sometime before 1894 when "recently a skating pond has been made, close by the Prestwick curling pond, where skaters can follow their bent." Elsewhere in the west of Scotland, during the last three decades of the 19th century the new sport known as association football became immensely popular. There was passing mention in the press of a local team which apparently failed to win much support – "Prestwick v Ayr Doon, 0 – 1", as the *Ayr Observer* reported (22 Feb. 1881), seems to have been a typical result.

The shore was still "pretty much as Nature made it", with as yet so special

St Nicholas Clubhouse was built in 1892 on their new course at the south end of the town. (*KA*)

attractions for day visitors. There were some seats, a few bathing boxes, some rowing boats for hire, and in 1883 Knox's donkeys catered for the youngsters. Hewat regretted that the waters were too shallow for sailing or swimming. "There is a story told of one bather who fancied he heard the Brodick bell ringing – some twenty miles across the sea – before the water conditions were favourable for a good swim." He suggested that "one great improvement which might easily be made, as nature has done so much already, and that is the construction of an esplanade." This would provide a "magnificent drive" along the front by chara-bancs. These, drawn by three horses and taking up to thirty passengers, were recently introduced by Alex. Gemmell of High Street, Ayr, plied between the Red Lion in Prestwick and the Bucks Head in Ayr, and allowed those holidaying here access to the facilities of the county town. In the summer months, the hourly service (as publicised in the *Ayr Advertiser* 24 June 1897) was increased to forty-five minute frequency, with extended trips to Burns Monument five times daily. Two-seater landaus were also available for hire from the Red Lion stables. In 1883 the possibility of a tramway operating between Burns Monument and Prestwick was first suggested.

For residents there was in 1894 a library in the Freemen's Hall and another one in Monkton sponsored by the Free Church. There was also a reading and recreation room in Monkton; a reading room in Prestwick was however little patronised and described by Hewat as "in a languid if not *in articulo mortis* condition". More popular were the winter concerts in the church halls, the Freemen's Hall, and in the Bute Hall, which was founded in the 1870s by that charitable man, William Wilson of Ardayre. In the early months of 1891, for example, there was a series of concerts in the school in aid of the Local Improvement Fund; a sacred concert in the parish church by Monkton and Prestwick Musical Association; a Free Church Soiree; and the annual concert of the St Nicholas Lodge of Good Templars in the Bute Hall. An innovation in 1884 was a summer show, when a travelling company presented a concert in the Bute Hall.

While noticing the emergence of this new community, Hewat devoted a chapter to Superstitions and Legends which were relics of old Prestwick. He repeated old and unsubstantiated tales. The Hare Stane, a large boulder stone on Muirhouse farm, had been dropped from the apron of a witch. Little Bo-peep had visited the parish, for "an old woman who died thirty or forty years ago, at the advanced age of ninety ... once saw a lady-shepherdess tending her flock on the Manse Brae". The bell of St Nicholas church was reputed to have been stolen by foreign sailors and recovered years later by local mariners on a voyage abroad. Hewat also derived from aged inhabitants report of old customs which had fallen into disuse. Until the 1830s, some sixty years before, infirm beggars seeking alms were passed from house to house by wheelbarrow. The last of the licensed beggars was Paddie Carey who died during the cholera epidemic of 1847. Some old practices survived, especially associated with marriage ("washing of the bridegroom's feet by friends on the night before the wedding ceremony") and death ("friends convened at the coffining, with the minister present to offer up prayer"). In former generations there was much drunkenness at these and many other occasions: "Drinking came to be connected with every conceivable event or transaction between man and man." Thanks to the temperance movement, by the end of the 19th century excessive consumption of alcohol was much diminished, though inevitably a small group of drouths continued habitual drinking. Hallowe'en was still generally celebrated: "Old and young in fact then hold quite a saturnalia"; and concerning the "bairns of our natives" Hewat commented that "their ongoings with kail-stalks, candles, nuts, etc., do surprise the stranger who has recently come to reside among us". The other pagan festival of Beltane was also still commemorated locally. Bonfire Monday in Prestwick was celebrated each year preceding Ayr Midsummer Fair, which by the 19th century was being held in July. In 1850 the foot races which had been included in the festivities had been abandoned. Herd-laddies continued to collect half-pence to build the bonfire; they regaled themselves with bread and cheese, and spent their pocket money on dainties displayed in the tents of itinerant dealers. But the occasion was "all but neglected, save by the younger members of the community". A local versifier recalled, "When the bonfire took place in the month o' July, And the herd laddies gather'd bawbees through the toon, On our help and attention they aye could rely, Till the scenes were all ower and the bonfire burnt down." Official participation in the event was noticed: "I like the scenes – they were really amusing, Frae twa muckle baskets o' baith cheese and bread, The bailie, near tumbl'd amid the confusion, Dispers'd the contents 'mong the children like seed." The bonfire, on the first Monday in July, continued to be lit into the first decade of the 20th century. What were called the Bonfire Hills were levelled in the making of Broompark Avenue. Until then, bonfires were also lit at that spot to celebrate special occasions, like the Relief of Ladysmith in 1900.

The verses just quoted were by R. Mackenzie Fisher, a handloom weaver's son born in 1840, who spent only his boyhood in Prestwick, and later published a volume of *Poems* which included several relating to memories of childhood and an appendix containing character sketches of various minor personalities. Fisher's book was popular enough to go through four editions. Interest in Prestwick's past was sustained by incomers. Rev. Kirkwood Hewat, who arrived in 1881, became interested enough in the traditions of the old burgh to produce in 1894 his local history, *A Little Scottish World,* illustrated with photographs by John Mack Wilson who in the 1880s had come from Kilmarnock to inherit his uncle's house of Seabank. Helen Jane Steven, also from Kilmarnock, rented Cathcart Villa in Mansewell Road, and after only a few years there published in 1897 her *Guide to Prestwick and Vicinity,* which directed special attention to the town's history and antiquities. These contributions were particularly valuable since they came at a time when the character of the community was undergoing so many changes. In 1898 the National Telephone Company extended its lines to Prestwick, and other new means of communication would soon follow. Also in this last decade of the 19th century there was a new development on the eastern edge of the burgh. Hewat viewed this with foreboding, for "Certainly no visitor or native will wish for a coal-pit in Prestwick or near it. Some indeed were alarmed by the sinking of a tentative shaft near New Dykes last year".

The landward part of the parish, though not sharing in Prestwick's spectacular expansion in the late 19th century, underwent changes of its own. Monkton village had lost its former importance as a parish centre and continued as a rural village. Its population of 415 in 1851 was reduced to 387 in 1891. Most of the houses were of one or two apartments. There was overcrowding, for in 1891 there were several families of six persons occupying single-ends, and a ratio for the village of 1.8 persons per room. This appears worse than in New Prestwick (1.2) and Prestwick burgh (0.96), but with the newer villas in these places such statistical averages concealed poor living conditions, as in in Kirk Street where there were single-ends as grossly overcrowded as those in Monkton.

In the rural part of the parish the population was in decline, from 405 in 1851 to 345 in 1891. There had been some consolidation of farms – the lands of Fairlees, Syke, and Adamton Mill were now absorbed by neighbouring farms, though Townhead and Monkton Miln, occupied by agricultural labourers in 1851, were operating as independent units by 1891. There were as many people dwelling in farm steadings as before, but a dozen cothouses had been abandoned. Over this period Muirhouse was held by Thomas Andrew, then his son, and grandson, the only farm which continued to be tenanted by the same family. Of the seventeen farmers in 1891, other two had been born within the parish; ten had come from other parts of Ayrshire; four from beyond. Of the farmworkers, only one head of household, a ploughman, was locally born; there were half-a-dozen from Ireland; most of the others were from adjacent parishes. Throughout the period, many farm folk had emigrated to Canada or Australia, and others found new farms in the south of England. Those incomers who took leases of Monkton farms did so at a time of agrarian change. Intensive cultivation of early potatoes was introduced in 1857 along the Ayrshire coast. In 1860 a factory was opened at Newton-on-Ayr to produce superphosphate, which improved fertility of fields in this area. The Ayrshire breed of cattle superseded all others, and while elsewhere the milk was usually converted into cheese, there was in Prestwick a ready market for liquid milk. Much of the local farmland would always be devoted to cultivation of grain crops, but Adamton Mill ceased working, leaving Powbank Mill as the only one within the parish. Near there in 1891 James McEwan was operating steam-driven threshing machines. These were manufactured locally, in the smithy behind Orchard Villa in Main Street, by Andrew Dykes, a Tarbolton man. Some years earlier, the Mauchline correspondent of the *Ayr Advertiser* reported (15 Jan. 1874) their introduction: "For the last two or three weeks one of Mr Dykes's steam thrashing mills from New Prestwick has been travelling from one steading to another in this and neighbouring parishes, thrashing wheat and oats. We learn that the farmers who have employed it are all highly satisfied with its work in thrashing and cleaning the stuffs. Formerly, the farmers had to be at the trouble of uniting together and sending their draught horses to where the mill was last working – sometimes at a considerable distance to bring the mill and its engine, involving a great loss of time of both men and horses. This season, however, to the amazement of both old and young, it goes from place to place, with its engine puffing and dragging it along the highways and byways at an easy pace, going down and up braes and wheeling round and turning corners apparently as easy as a youngster with his toy wheelbarrow. This must be a great saving on the work of farm horses." Press reports of the 1880s noticed annual ploughing matches locally, and a cattle show in 1882 and subsequent years, organised by the Monkton, Newton, Prestwick, and St Quivox Agricultural Society, which was devoted to maintaining and improving standards of farm practice.

There were changes in land ownership. Adamton, after the death of Mrs Reid, was sold by her heirs to John George Alexander Baird (1854–1917), a member of that coal and iron dynasty which had extensive interests in Lanarkshire and Ayrshire. His father, John Baird, had acquired Elie in Fife and Rosemount in Ayrshire; his uncle was James Baird of Cambusdoon. J.G.A. Baird's entry into the ranks of the county gentry was secured by an education at Eton and Oxford, service with the 16th Lancers, membership of the Carlton Club, and marriage in 1880 to Susan Fergusson of Kilkerran. In 1876 he inherited Wellwood at Muirkirk from his uncle, but Adamton became his favoured country seat. The old 18th century house, described as "a large, plain building", was replaced in 1885 by a new mansion "in swaggering Jacobean taste with ornate carved gables". When it was completed, the satisfied owner entertained all the workmen in the King's Arms, Hotel, Ayr. J.G.A.Baird, this "model landed proprietor and country gentlemen", became M.P. for Glasgow 1886–1907, Commanding Officer of the Ayrshire Yeomanry, and Deputy Lieutenant for the county. Within the parish, his estate extended to 685 acres and comprised not only Adamton house and policies, but also the farms of Adamton Mains, Brieryside, Newlands, Woodside, and East Bogside. By the end of the century none of the other estates within the parish were occupied by resident owners. Fairfield from the sixties, after the death of W.G.Campbell, was held by trustees, who operated in behalf of heirs who lived in England. The house was let to a succession of tenants. In 1881 the trustees, noticing the mushrooming of new building in Prestwick, had an ambitious plan drawn up for feuing plots on the seaward side of Monkton station, but the only person tempted was Thomas Thorburn who built a house he called St Andrews. The Fairfield estate was extended by purchase of Orangefield. Soon after James Sinclair of Orangefield died, his widow moved in 1861 to live in Miller Road, Ayr, where she died in 1892; thereafter Orangefield's 106 acres were added to the 685-acre Fairfield estate, which now comprised the farms of Fairfield Mains, Monktonmiln, Muirhouse, Orangefield, and West Orangefield. Orangefield House from the time of Sinclair's death was also let: occupied by George Oswald until 1868 when he succeeded his brother Alexander as laird of Auchincruive; thereafter by James Brown, Collector of Inland Revenue, and his widow; in 1899 by Captain J.C.A. Anstice. Tenancy of Ladykirk House was continued in the sixties by William Gemmell's widow, who took in boarders. For a time, according to Hewat, "that old mansion had so degenerated as to be used for some years as a private asylum for the insane". By the end of the century it was in poor condition and occupied by several tenants, including a farmer, a joiner, and a mineral borer. Of the medieval chapel which stood within the grounds, little remained, save one turret which had survived three centuries of neglect and was incorporated as part of a walled garden. In 1894 when two human skeletons were unearthed, they were reinterred in Monkton kirkyard. Ladykirk estate continued in the possession of William Paterson of Monkwood, and included the two farms of Ladykirk Mains and South Bogside. The Oswalds of Auchincruive, the previous owners of Ladykirk, retained some of their lands in this parish, the farms of Aitkenbrae and New Dykes, Powbank Mill, and various properties within Prestwick. The successors of R.A.Oswald (1771– 1841) were his nephew James (1778–1853), who had a nephew Alexander (1811– 68), whose brother George (1814–71) was followed by his son Richard Alexander (1841–1921). The remaining four farms in the parish, Monktonhill, Hobsland, Townhead, Whiteside, each belonged to owners who resided outwith the parish.

Annually the local gentry donated coals for the deserving poor. In 1881, for example, contributions came from Adamton, Orangefield, Auchincruive, Rosemount, Underwood, and Coodham. J.G.A. Baird also provided Monkton with a reading and recreation room. The schools benefited from their donations of prizes. The school board in 1882 singled out Miss Brown of Orangefield for her special encouragement of sewing instruction for girls in Prestwick Public School. But while the landed gentry continued to be influential and widely respected, within the 19th century the dominance they had exercised over Prestwick had gone forever.

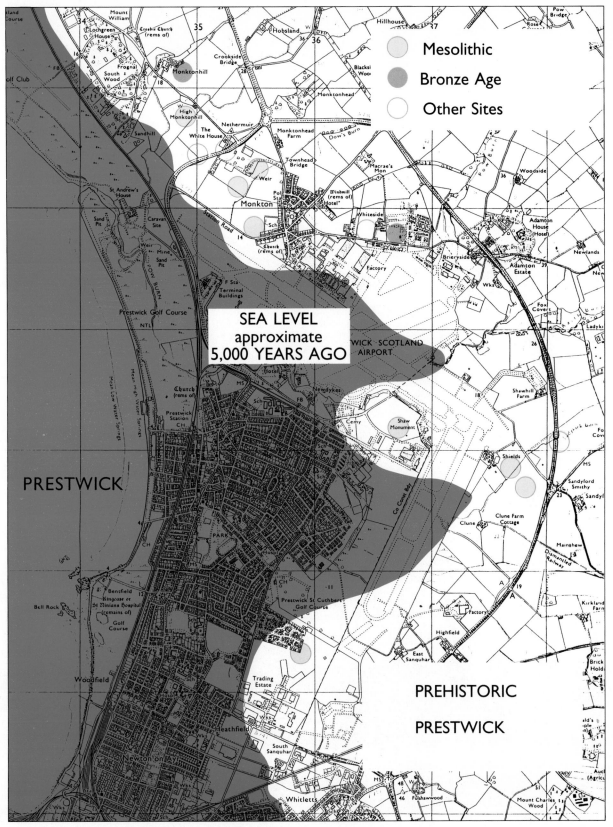

PREHISTORIC

PRESTWICK

C1

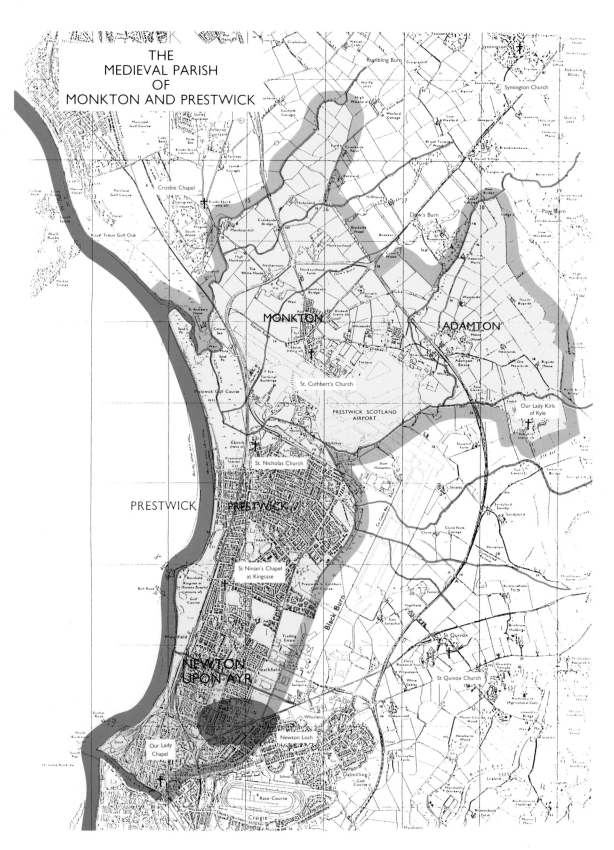

THE
MEDIEVAL PARISH
OF
MONKTON AND PRESTWICK

MONKTON

ADAMTON

St. Cuthbert's Church

PRESTWICK SCOTLAND
AIRPORT

Our Lady Kirk
of Kyle

St. Nicholas Church

PRESTWICK

PRESTWICK

St Ninian's Chapel
at Kingcase

St Quivox

NEWTON
UPON AYR

St Quivox Church

Our Lady
Chapel

Newton Loch

Race Course

Craigie

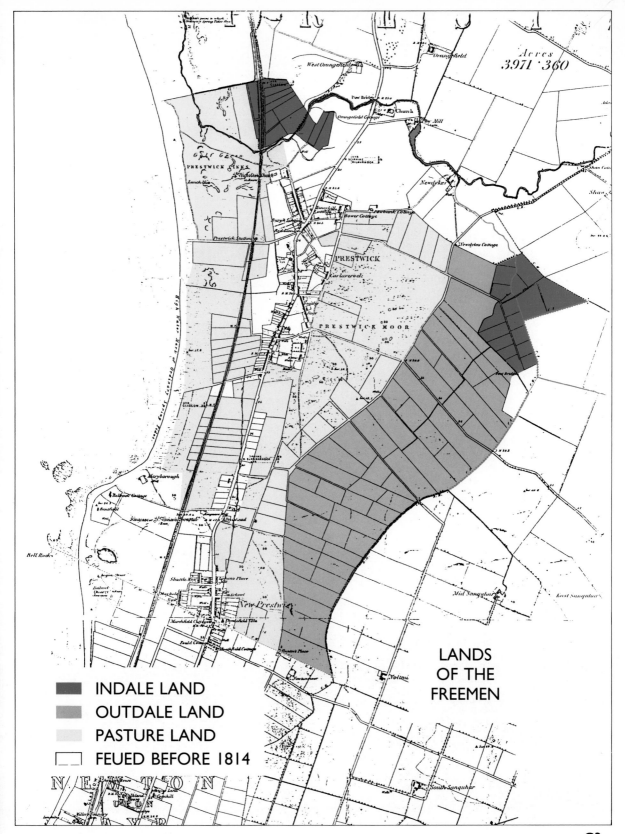

LANDS
OF THE
FREEMEN

INDALE LAND
OUTDALE LAND
PASTURE LAND
FEUED BEFORE 1814

C3

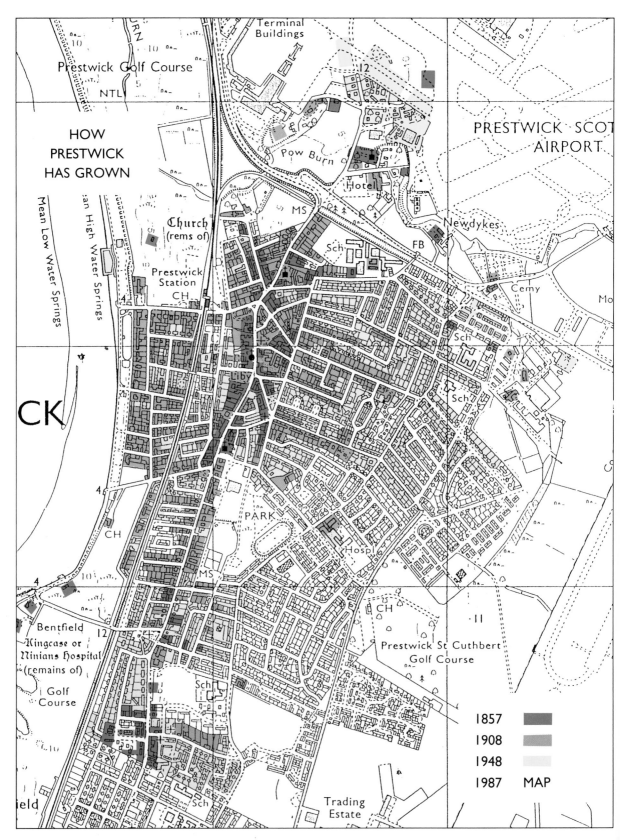

HOW
PRESTWICK
HAS GROWN

Prestwick Golf Course

NTL

Mean Low Water Springs

Mean High Water Springs

CK

Terminal
Buildings

Pow Burn

Hotel

Church
(rems of)

Prestwick
Station

CH

MS

Sch

FB

Newdykes

Cemy

Mo

PRESTWICK SCOT
AIRPORT

Lib

Sch

Sch

PARK

Hosp

CH

Bentfield

Ringcase or
Ninians Hospital
(remains of)

Golf
Course

CH

MS

Sch

Prestwick St Cuthbert
Golf Course

11

field

Sch

Trading
Estate

1857	
1908	
1948	
1987	MAP

All illustrations on pages C5 to C8 are by courtesy of Ken Andrew

Prestwick from the air with the airport beyond

(Far left) The ruins of old St Nicholas Church
(Left) The new St Nicholas Church

Polish War Memorial on its original site

The Shaw
Tower

Macrae
Monument

Saltpan Houses
at sunset

Monkton Windmill
and Doocot

C6

Prestwick beach
in a January
storm

The Broadway cinema

St Ninian's Park

Industry at
Glenburn

Jetstream production

HMS Gannet

Adamton
Flying College

CHAPTER TEN

The Early 20th Century

PRESTWICK Town Council was established in 1903, a most opportune time to meet the demands of a town which in the first decades of the 20th century was continuing to grow, provided with new facilities, developing new characteristics, faced with problems but also with possibilities.

Between 1901 and 1931 the number of inhabitants of the town rose from 3,170 to 8,538. That was a remarkable increase not matched in the rest of the parish, whose total population grew from 3,854 to 9,417, with numbers in Monkton and the rural area rising more modestly from 686 to 889. When one looks at how Prestwick's population grew over this period, some care is necessary in interpreting statistics in the Census reports – 2,766 (1901), 4,879 (1911), 8,516 (1921), 8,538 (1931). The figure for 1901 excluded those 404 persons who then lived in New Prestwick, which was thereafter included; so the comparable figure for 1901 should be 3,170. Then, as later, allowance must be made for visitors present at the time of the census. There were nearly 2,000 of these when the census was taken in 1921 – it was postponed from April till June "on account of extensive industrial unrest" – whereas the number of usual residents in 1921 would be around 6,500. A more reliable graph of the town's rate of growth can be based upon the number of houses – 490 (in 1891), 936 (1901), 1,351 (1911), 1,859 (1921), 2,284 (1931). This confirms that the late 19th century expansion of the town continued through the first decade of the new century. The period which included the First World War showed a slackening in building; but in the twenties the town began to grow faster than ever.

During the first decade of the 20th century, in which Prestwick obtained its town council, the burgh acquired a range of new and improved facilities – a tramway service to Ayr, a rebuilt railway station, a new church, a cinema, another school, a police station, a new cemetery, a laundry company. New organisations were formed, including a merchants' association, a troop of boy scouts, and a masonic lodge. And a mining village was created at Glenburn.

Initiative to secure statutory burgh status for Prestwick came from the Freemen, led by Gray Edmiston, a Glasgow property agent who after only five years' residence was in 1897 elected their provost. Entry as a freeman was now open to anyone holding only one lot, and many were recent incomers, who were dissatisfied with administrative arrangements for the town, for their council of the burgh of barony was an ineffective instrument. Though the Parochial Board was converted into an elected Parish Council in 1894, its powers were limited; the parish had only one representative on Ayr County Council; and there was indignation at their handling of the Water Famine in 1899. In most other old burghs of barony, the council chosen by the freemen had during the 19th century been joined by so-called police commissioners, elected by ratepayers to provide certain local services. The Burgh Police (Scotland) Act of 1892 ended this dual administration, and the subsequent Town Councils (Scotland) Act of 1900 required all such Police Burghs – whether or not they had been previously burghs of barony – to adopt the historic terms of provost, bailies, councillors. This placed the freemen of Prestwick in an anomalous position. As recently as 1896 Troon, that nearby town less than a hundred years old, had secured the status of Police Burgh, and its provost, bailies, and councillors could exercise statutory powers which were not available to those in Prestwick who held similar titles by right of charter. In 1901 there was a dispute in Blairgowrie regarding surviving charter rights, and the law-courts decided that "it is not competent in future to elect any Town Council under the aforesaid charters, or otherwise in accordance with the Town Councils (Scotland) Act 1900". Though the situation in Prestwick was not quite comparable, the Blairgowrie case per-suaded the Prestwick freemen in 1902 that "to set the government of the burgh on a proper footing, steps are being taken by means of a petition to the Sheriff to have the boundaries of the police burgh fixed, and the election of a Town Council proceeded with." The application to the sheriff, made "on behalf of the burgh of barony of Prestwick", would create a Police Burgh with a town council competent to police the burgh (i.e implement *policies*) and administer certain local services like water, drainage, lighting, and cleansing (but *not* maintain a police constabu-lary). Objection was made by Ayr Town Council, on the grounds that it had recently in 1901 inaugurated a New Prestwick water and drainage district which included forty acres within Prestwick; and it owned the tramway which operated within Prestwick. Ayr burgh had in 1873 incorporated the burgh of barony of Newton-on-Ayr, was anxious to retain control of its investments in Prestwick, and was perhaps anticipating a similar annexation, which could be thwarted if Prestwick's petition succeeded. In February 1903 Sheriff Brand issued his findings, rejecting Ayr's objections, and authorising election of a town council in Prestwick, whose bounds were defined as those of the burgh of barony, extending from the Ayr boundary in the south towards the Pow Burn in the north, with an extension beyond that burn to the wall across the Golf Course. The first municipal election was fixed for Tuesday 3 November.

Gray Edmiston, the freemen's provost, just returned from two months in Cairo, had high hopes of becoming first provost of the police burgh. At an election meeting in October, Edmiston explained that the burgh of barony of which he was the provost had taken the steps necessary to form a more effective town council. He proposed that the new town council should call annual ratepayers' meetings to consult on capital projects; that the penny tram fare into Ayr should be reduced to one halfpenny; and the old quarry on St Nicholas Golf Course should be filled up with burgh refuse. Altogether thirteen candidates offered themselves for the nine places on the council. Polling took place in the Public School. There were

Prestwick Freemen, 1900. James Hunter. Standing: Dr Erskine, W. G. Stevenson, David Manson, Bailie Boyd, Jas. Mutter, Bailie Manson, John Semple, Wm. Clark, Walter Beaton. Sitting: A. B. Cowan, Wm. Latta, John Gray, Jas. Andrew, J. Cuttle, Bailie Rae, Provost Edminston. Drummer Wm. McEwan on left.

no burning issues; only two candidates issued handbills; and several candidates "to relieve the monotony of hanging about the booth, had a round of golf over the St Nicholas course". After the poll, boxes containing 696 ballot papers were taken for counting in the County Buildings, Ayr, and Sheriff-Substitute J.C. Shairp as returning officer announced the result. Top of the poll was John Wilson Weir of Craigard; Gray Edmiston came fourth; and James Gibson, joiner, the only native of Prestwick among the candidates, was seventh.

The first meeting of Prestwick Town Council was held in the Freemen's Hall at noon on Friday 6 November, Sheriff Shairp presiding. Gray Edmiston was nominated for appointment as provost, but there was no seconder; choice was made of J.W.Weir who though a recent incomer was obviously widely respected. Two bailies were then elected: James Wilson of Belize, who was current chairman of the Parish Council and of the School Board; and Hugh Macpherson, postmaster, who had previously been chairman of the School Board for thirteen years. Choice was made of persons to act as interim burgh officials until appointments could be made. Subsequent meetings were held in the evenings in the Parish Council Chambers, 2 Bute Place. Four committees were formed concerned with Water and Drainage, Roads and Footpaths, Lighting and Cleansing, and Finance, each containing all the nine councillors; and a Dean of Guild Court of five members was constituted

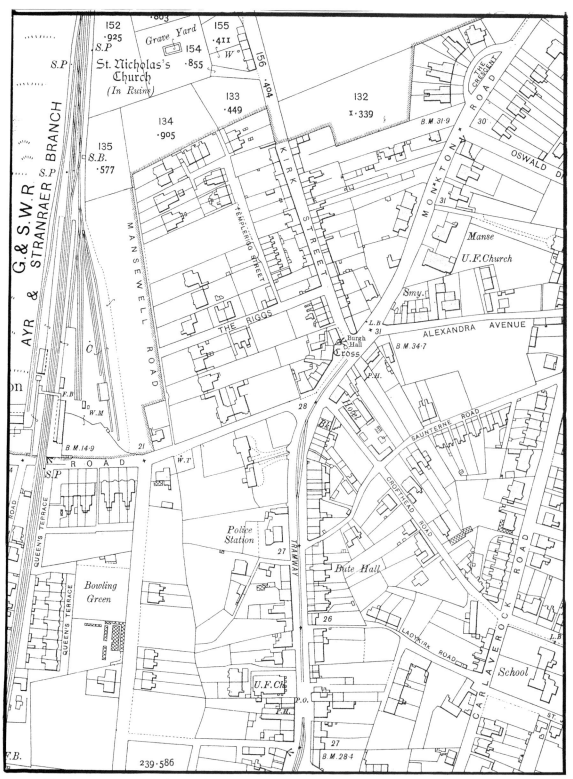

The town centre, on Ordnance Survey Map of 1903, the year Prestwick Town Council was formed.

to monitor buildings plans. In January 1904 the burgh officials were appointed to their paid posts: John Stewart, solicitor, as Town Clerk (£50 per annum) and Clerk to the Police Court ((£5); John Silver, solicitor, as Burgh Prosecutor (£12); Hugh Boyd junior, Parish Council Clerk who had been interim town clerk was continued as Treasurer (£15) and Collector (2% of rates collected); Dr John Highet of Troon as Medical Officer of Health (£12). All were part-time posts apart from John Orr, Burgh Surveyor and Sanitary Inspector (£100). To pay for the services the burgh would provide, rates were payable by owners and occupiers of property, based on valuation: in the first year owners paid 1s 1d in the £, tenants 1s 11d in the £, and owner-occupiers 3s 0d in the £. The rates plus some minor additions (including £192 government grant) produced around £4,000. Most of this went towards paying off loans for water and sewers which were inherited from the county council along with those undertakings (properties in the New Prestwick water and drainage district paid a different rate). The rest was devoted to other local services; an additional charge was added in later years when responsibility for roads was transferred from the county council; and the rates were increased as more money was borrowed to finance a series of improvements.

In the early years the town council faced the awkward problem of its relationship with the freemen. A Minute of Agreement in 1904 conveyed to the Town Council the Freemen's Hall, a shop attached, a plot in Boyd Street (open space), part of Bentfield (where sea wrack had been stored), and the foreshore (if not previously disposed of). There was however uncertainty regarding other items. In 1901 the law-courts had judged that in Blairgowrie the new Town Council "superseded the Town Council elected under the charters of the said burgh" and was thus "entitled to administer the whole funds and property" of the old burgh of barony. But the Burgh Police Act of 1892 had reserved "the patrimonial rights of any body of feuars". To settle who was in fact entitled to income from feu-duties, the Freemen of Prestwick became involved in litigation with Prestwick Town Council which was not settled till 1907 when Hugh Boyd, who was both a burgh official and a freeman, arranged a compromise. The Town Council was entitled to all properties; the freemen retained their right to feu-duties, which would be collected on their behalf by the Town Council. It took some time to resolve the financial complexities; but income became substantially augmented with royalties from mineral rights when Glenburn pit began production and in 1913 £180 became available to provide a first dividend of £5 per freedom.

Before each annual election in November (when one third of the councillors retired) there was a ratepayers' meeting, and indeed a Ratepayers Union was formed, which kept council activities under close observation. Each election was contested; most of the original councillors were defeated when they sought re-election; though several of them were returned after a short period out of office. In 1905 when J.W. Weir resigned from the council, he was replaced as provost by R.H.Steedman (1905–06), then by Gray Edmiston for two terms (1906–12), followed by Thomas McClure. Born in Edinburgh in 1877, as a two-year-old he came to Prestwick where his father set up as a draper, and Thomas McClure now

The town council laid out the esplanade in 1908. The disused saltpan houses are seen in the distance.

managed that family business. Initially a shy young man, he gained confidence in a U.P. church debating society; in 1903 he took sixth place in the poll to become one of Prestwick's first councillors; was not re-elected in 1905, but was successful when he stood again in 1908 and 1910. In 1912 he was the council's unanimous choice to succeed as provost – nephew of a former lord provost of Edinburgh, at the age of thirty-five Thomas McClure was the youngest provost in Scotland.

In its first ten years Prestwick Town Council proved a most active authority. The first act of the Roads and Footpaths Committee was to name the streets within the burgh. Several of the new streets had been already been named after those who had been responsible for building there, which was acceptable. But in the main street in particular, rows of new houses had been also been given such names, which could cause confusion. Some of the traditional names were regrettably allowed to lapse; Smiddy Raw was already called Boyd Street; the Vennel, known also as Shaw Street, was renamed Alexandria Avenue, converted to Alexandra Avenue, possibly by association with Edward VII's queen; Sandgate was incorporated within Main Street. The committee addressed itself to the need to provide kerbing and pavements on the principal streets, with the proprietors required to co-operate. As builders planned new streets, they were now compelled to conform to standards of width and construction. In 1907 work began on tar-metalling the principal throughfares. The Lighting and Cleansing Committee assumed responsibility for improving street-lighting, started by purchasing forty second-hand gas lamps from Partick, and experimented with incandescent lamps. In 1904 there were sixteen of those in addition to 120 of the older type. For economy, lamps were lit only between 28 August and 21 May, and not at all on forty-seven moonlit nights; in 1907 first of the provosts' lamps was installed. The committee also undertook scavenging of six miles of principal streets, and arranged for collection of refuse from all households, daily in summer, every second day in winter. Initially carts were hired from Hugh Gaw and burgh workmen participated in the collection, but from 1906 the entire process was contracted to William Mitchell. Sadly, Gray Ediston's proposal of 1903 to fill up the Bellrock Quarry with refuse could not be implemented and it remained as a deep pond in which several persons were drowned.

The Water and Drainage Committee energetically applied itself to cope with the needs of a rapidly growing community. In 1905 at Ladykirk mechanical filters were introduced to purify the water from Raith reservoir, an innovation for a Scottish local authority. The capacity of one million gallons a day was ample for the time, but future needs inspired a further venture. Troon burgh was finding its supply from Collenan inadequate and planned in association with Ayr County Council to bring water thirty miles from Loch Bradan. When this scheme was implemented in 1908, Prestwick Town Council entered into a contract to take up to 400,000 gallons a day, a measure which would satisfy requirements for the next sixty years. In 1904 Prestwick Town Council invited members of the parish council and school board to inspect the water works, initiating what became the annual Water Trip; it was also agreed that ratepayers might purchase permits to fish on Raith reservoir. Provision of drainage proved an equally expensive undertaking, since all the new houses being built had to be connected to the burgh sewers. One problem which was difficult to solve was that heavy rain was frequently followed by flooding in Station Road, Grangemuir Road, occasionally even on Main Street. In 1908 an improved sea outfall was installed, with 24-inch cast iron pipes extending a hundred yards beyond low water mark. Additional sewers had to be installed in 1912 to serve Glenburn mining village. Yet flooding persisted, and sewage disposal would be a continuing problem. Another inconvenience, an administrative one, was that New Prestwick water and drainage district remained separate, and it was technically difficult to link the sewage systems. Nevertheless the entire community was well enough provided, and it was noted with satisfaction in the sanitary inspector's report for 1910 that few ashpits and dry privies now remained, with consequent benefit to public health.

Prestwick Town Council's desire to publicise the town's attractions was expressed by the formation in 1904 of a House-letting Committee to publish a list of houses available for summer letting, to advertise Prestwick as a health and summer

Esplanade and Pavilion, Prestwick

In 1910 a pavilion for summer concerts was erected at the end of the esplanade.

resort, to draft bye-laws for shops selling ice cream and aerated waters, and the following summer the first of a series of Guides to Prestwick was published, illustrated with photographs by J.Mack Wilson. In 1906 an Attractions Committee was established on a permanent basis. Existing seats on the beach were repaired and new ones provided. Daniel MacMillan of Ayr was granted permission to erect bathing boxes and operate rowing boats for hire. In 1908, with the co-operation of those owning houses fronting the beach, a sea wall was constructed, which protected them from blowing sand; and, with the enthusiastic motivation of Provost Edmiston, an esplanade was provided, which enhanced the beach. In 1910 £800 was borrowed to erect south of Grangemuir Road a pavilion seating 350, replacing an existing entertainments hut. This provided more satisfactory premises for the summer concerts provided by minstrel troupes – in 1903 by "The Niggers" and from 1905 by Alf Laurance's Geisha Boys for twelve weeks each summer. Another £200 was borrowed to erect a kiosk, and franchises were granted for the sale of ice cream and erection of automatic weighing machines. In 1911 the Salvation Army provided Sunday afternoon services, in 1912 a sand-building competition was organised. A putting green was laid out in 1911, but a proposal to make a bathing pool at St Nicholas rock was not implemented. Councillors were not unanimous about these innovations. In 1908, for example, a motion to spend £13 providing band music on the beach was carried only by the provost's casting vote.

Improvements made the town more attractive to residents and holidaymakers alike. In 1908 permission was granted for Ayr burgh to lay electric cables to supply householders within Prestwick; in 1913 couplings to hydrants became available for use in emergency by Ayr fire brigade. In 1903 public subscription provided Matthew Smith, former parish and county councillor, with an illuminated address and at the Cross a fountain and drinking trough dedicated to him was erected, which the town council agreed to maintain. Though decorative, Smith's fountain was said to be "cut down like a pair of breeks", for the former horse trough was three times bigger. In 1911 the town centre was further enhanced by an underground urinal costing £400, "planted out with flowers or flowering shrubs and round the whole enclosure a neat iron railing". Also in 1911 Bruce's Well at Kingcase was taken over by the town council, to be rebuilt and restored the following year. In 1912 a small public park was provided in Newdykes Road – where the Prestwick Ailsa Football Club obtained permission to play. In 1911 following a petition from 165 potential members it was agreed to provide municipal golf, land was acquired at Kingcase, and this fifth local course was opened in 1912, with fees of 10s 6d per annum, and for visitors three shillings a week or threepence a round, managed by the council's new Golf Course and Public Parks Committee.

In September 1907 the council, following settlement of the dispute with the freemen, took over full possession of the Freemen's Hall, and borrowed £800 to convert it into burgh headquarters. Here the provost and two bailies in their capacity as magistrates in the burgh court dispensed justice over minor offences. There is a story often recounted of a drunkard who was incarcerated within the "Black Hole" on the ground floor. His friends kept him supplied through the

The Cross, Prestwick.

The town council, extending facilities for visitors, provided an underground urinal, centrepiece of the Cross from 1911 until 1960.

barred window of that gaol with whisky by means of a straw; for, it is said, he could not be tried until he was sober. The miscreant is alleged to have been Tommy Shields who sold herrings about the town in the early years of the century. But the story may be apocryphal, or relate to some earlier period. As work of the council officials expanded, William Shaw who had succeeded as town clerk in 1906 was provided in 1908 with a typewriter costing £14, and Frank Pritty, burgh surveyor from 1913, was supplied with a bicycle. The council's responsibilities were extending. In 1909 they were required to form a special committee to monitor claims for the old age pensions which the Liberal government had then introduced. They co-operated with the County Constabulary whose Prestwick police station, designed by John Murdoch, was opened in 1903. Police assistance was sought in 1905 for "a number of motor cars pass through the place at a speed apparently greatly in excess of ten miles an hour". One problem, especially at New Year, was "the great incursion of persons from Ayr for the purpose of procuring intoxicants", for the licensing hours differed and the town council had as yet no power to alter them.

By comparison with the busy town council, the Monkton and Prestwick Parish Council had little left to do. Its principal remaining function was poor relief – in 1903 supporting thirty-one paupers, most of whom were granted three shillings a week. With few lairs available in the two old churchyards, the parish council in 1903 feued from R.A.Oswald of Auchincruive ground off Shaw Road for a new cemetery. Little public concern was shown in the work of the parish council. At the elections of 1913 six members from the burgh and five from the landward area were returned unopposed; the same year G.F.Loudon of Orangefield retained his seat on the county council, also without opposition. It was a different story with the school board, however, for in one sample year (1903) the parish council had to raise £460 for the poor, £100 for burial grounds, £50 for its registrar of births, marriages, and deaths, while the school rate required £1,400.

Chairman of the School Board, Hugh Macpherson the postmaster, was in 1903 succeeded by James Wilson of Belize, who was already chairman of the parish council and later that year would be elected to the new town council and become its first bailie; followed in 1915 by Thomas Lindsay of Aitkenbrae farm. There was elected to the school board in 1900 the first woman in Prestwick to serve on a public body: Mrs Christian Aitken, daughter of John Gray, the school board's first chairman, and later affectionately remembered as Grannie Aitken. Monkton and Prestwick School Board at the beginning of the new century found itself faced with the same sort of challenge as confronted the town council, to provide appropriate facilities for a population which had suddenly expanded and was continuing to do so. There was the particular challenge of coping with the raising of the school-leaving age from thirteen to fourteen in 1902.

Prestwick Public School, opened in 1882 to accommodate 350 pupils, had by 1901 just over 400 on its roll. To alleviate the gross overcrowding, it proved necessary to rent again the Freemen's Hall for the two senior classes, until two extra classrooms were added to the Public School in 1905. The board had more

Prestwick High School, opened 1902. (*KA*)

ambitious plans. A site in Newdykes Road was obtained from R.A.Oswald of Auchincruive, and John Eaglesham from Ayr was commissioned to design another school in order, as the *Ayr Advertiser* put it (7 Aug. 1902), "to make some provision for the children of a new class of people who have lately invaded the district, a class who have done much to increase the prosperity of Prestwick by furnishing work-men with labour and local merchants with trade. These people desire for their children a more extended course of instruction and are willing to pay for it." It was pointed out that more than seventy such children were presently travelling daily by train or tram for schooling in Ayr. When Prestwick High School was opened on 5 August 1902 there were 122 scholars enrolled. 82 of these paid fees, ranging from three shillings a quarter for infants to eight shillings for senior pupils; the others were free pupils tranferred from the public school. The building cost £5,000, had accommodation for 300, and contained five classrooms and a drill hall, which was a novelty. The first headmaster, on a salary of £250 per annum, was James Marshall, a graduate of Edinburgh University previously in charge at Mauchline. An Ayrshire Committee for Secondary Education had been formed in 1892 to encourage schools to provide more than elementary instruction, this had been introduced at Mauchline in 1896, and Marshall now had opportunity to apply his experience there to Prestwick High School. Senior pupils, including some transferred from the public school, were offered Mathematics, Latin, and French. In 1905 a school library was instituted; the board agreed to provide apparatus for experiments in magnetism, electricity, and chemistry; and over the next few years part-time instructors were employed to provide classes in needlework, cookery, shorthand, and woodwork. Rooms for cookery and woodwork were built in 1910; and in 1913 a major extension provided more classrooms, an art room, and a science laboratory. Prestwick High School now met the requirements to be desig-nated a Higher Grade School. There was inevitably some inter-school rivalry, as expressed by pupils of the public school: "High Schule pup wi your tail tied up, Swimming in the water like a wee black duck".

Pupils at both schools had "drill" from an ex-sergeant employed by the board. National concern for physical wellbeing of the rising generation prompted "Physical Exercises and Military Drill", and also the introduction in 1908 of medical inspections. The traditional religious inspection of classes continued, undertaken by ministers of the established and U.F. churches. H.M. Inspectors of Schools paid regular visits, and grants were based upon their reports. Local rumour had it that at one school after such a visit the inspector was presented with a basket of eggs, beneath which a half-bottle of whisky was discretely concealed. "Payment by Results" perpetuated rote learning, yet standards were improved. In 1913 H.M. Inspector complained that in Monkton school sixty-five pupils were being taught by one teacher; to improve matters, several pupils from neighbouring parishes were excluded, and a transfer to other classes brought down the number to fifty-eight, which was judged satisfactory. Also in Monkton school that year there was an experiment in replacing slates with jotters. Pupils' academic excellence was rewarded with annual prizes from the board; in 1909 girls won the dux prize at all three schools. There were still defaulting parents to be dealt with, and members of the board were required to visit schools and check the registers of attendance. The board still had to arrange holidays, purchase new equipment for a widening curriculum (in 1919, pianos at £75 each), organise the qualifying examination after which pupils might be promoted to higher grade or supplementary classes, and publicise those competitive county bursariess for pupils seeking higher education. One continuing difficulty was that parents were still required to pay for school books. In 1909 the board considered a proposal to provide free books, but decided that these should be supplied only to necessitous children; in 1914 a commmittee was formed to investigate the possibility of providing these pupils also with meals. One group of parents who continued to feel deprived were those in New Prestwick: in 1909 a petition with eighty signatures for a school there was not followed up.

Walter Beaton, headmaster of the Public School, remembered as "a man of gentlemanly bearing and literary turn of mind", retired in 1906 after nearly forty years' service and died in 1917. His successor as headmaster of the public school was another bachelor, James Howat, who as pupil then teacher spent all his life in the parish, until he retired in 1920. Since 1901 he had been headmaster at Monkton, and was replaced there by John Steele, who in his turn was promoted to Glenburn school. This was the third new school which Monkton and Prestwick School Board was called upon to erect to meet the requirements of a growing community – in this case to cater for children of the new mining village. To provide for an estimated roll of 500 pupils, the architect William Cowie prepared plans for ten classrooms plus a hall, which would cost over £7,000. Glenburn School was opened on 25 October 1915, with an initial roll of 171 pupils. Three years later when the first headmaster, Jack Steele, died, he was replaced by Mathew Foulds.

One who experienced and has written about Ayrshire education in the years before the First World War described "the sheer joylessness of school life for pupils and teachers alike". To cope with the large classes, teachers appointed pupils as monitors to assist them, and some of these on reaching school-leaving age were then employed as pupil-teachers. Two such have already been mentioned. James Howat was born in 1855, son of the Adamton gardener. A pupil of Walter Beaton in the Freemen's School, he continued as pupil-teacher and returned from training in Glasgow to become assistant in Prestwick Public School from 1880 until 1900. A member of St Cuthbert's congregation, he served for a time as precentor, the last to do so. Applying for promotion as Monkton headmaster, he failed in 1885, but was successful sixteen years later. He earned further advancement by appointment as head of Prestwick Public School from 1906 until 1920. He died in 1941, and is remembered as "Cocker" Howat, a strict disciplinarian, fond of golf, bowling, angling, and bicycling. The second renowned pupil-teacher was Mathew Foulds, son of a dental surgeon. Born in 1887, he was a pupil in Prestwick Public School, and his class was one of those which finished its schooling in 1901 in the Freemen's Hall. He was then aged thirteen, a monitor, and in July obtained his Merit Certificate. On 20 August 1901, turned fourteen years of age, he was contracted to be a pupil-teacher, at £15 rising to £25 in his fourth year. Learning his business by example, and attending classes in Ayr, he progressed to appointment as assistant teacher. He was now on a salary scale rising from £90 to £115 — female assistants came much cheaper at £60 – £90. By 1909 he was in charge of the night school, taking classes in English, Arithmetic, and Drawing, while Mr Short from Ayr offered instruction in Shorthand, Typewriting, and Book-keeping. In 1915 he was appointed headmaster at Monkton. A year later he entered the ranks as a private in the Argyll and Sutherland Highlanders. Early in 1918, newly commissioned second lieutenant, the school board appointed him head teacher at Glenburn, where he continued until his retiral in 1951. Between 1922 and 1928 he served on the town council as an Ex-servicemen's representative, and in St Nicholas Church he was elder for fifty-seven years and Sunday School superintendant for twenty years. He is especially remembered for his contribution to the Scout movement. In 1908 Baden Powell founded the Boy Scouts, and in April 1909 some of young Mathew Fould's pupils persuaded him to form a local troop. He agreed to act as scoutmaster "till the summer holidays" but continued and in 1911 also formed "junior scouts", which was Ayrshire's first Wolf Cub pack. In 1935 he relinquished direct control of Prestwick's 14th Ayrshire troop of Scouts to serve as Group Scoutmaster and latterly County Commissioner. After fifty years of scouting in Prestwick, Mathew Foulds was in 1959 made a freeman of the burgh, and he was still actively involved in the Scout movement when he died in 1979 in his ninety-third year.

The era of the School Board came to an end in 1919 when an elected Ayrshire Education Authority was established to manage the service on a county basis, and offer a more uniform and improved system. By that time Monkton and Prestwick School Board was spending more than £4,000 annually, employing thirty-one teachers to instruct 1,181 pupils, with 210 others in evening classes. It maintained four schools, Prestwick High School (James Marshall, 9 assistants, 316 pupils plus 90 in higher grade classes), Prestwick Public School (James Howat, 9 assistants, 368 pupils), Glenburn (Mathew Foulds, 7 assistants, 305 pupils), Monkton School (John Wilson, 2 assistants, 102 pupils). Some school boards had a reputation for mean-ness and petty prejudices. Yet in the four and a half decades of its life Monkton and Prestwick School Board faithfully served the parish, making a notable contribution to provide for expanding local needs of this fast-growing community.

House-building in the first decade of the 20th century was now mainly along Ayr Road and to east of the town. The area west of the railway was by this time largely built-up; and with the beach crowded in summer the sea front was no longer the desirable site it had originally been. More secluded inland spots had previously been only occasionally preferred – as Craigview and Glenburn House – but now there were new villas like Redbrae and Towans, and especially Monktonhead, designed in Elizabethan style by James Miller in 1910. Orangefield House was purchased in 1905 by George Loudon from Kilmarnock, who engaged James Hay to extend it with wings and additions to the rear, and became county councillor for Monkton parish. Ladykirk was rebuilt in 1903 by J. & R. S. Ingram for its new owner, Robert Angus, managing partner of William Baird & Co.'s Lugar ironworks. A senior partner in the same company, William Weir of Kildonan, acquired Adamton. Fairfield continued to be let by the trustees of W.G.Campbell.

The most important housing development was however of a quite different character. In 1903 William Baird's subsidiary Auchincruive Coal Company secured from the Prestwick freemen a lease to the minerals under the burgh provided there was no pit within their bounds. In 1910 a sinking was made just over the St Quivox border and the Glenburn colliery when production began in 1912 was considered the most modern of pits. Its two shafts (Auchincruive 4/5) and the pithead installations were supplied with electricity from two turbines of Auchincruive No. 3 at Mossblown. Glenburn House was acquired to accommodate a manager and offices. 184 houses for miners were constructed in 1912. Made of Sanquhar brick, each comprised one or two rooms and kitchen, laid out in three terraces – the Front Row (60), Middle Row (60). and the Back Row (64). Water, gas, and drainage were laid on, a Wash-house and Recreation Room were provided, so that Glenburn was adjudged a model mining village, even though original plans to provide each family with its own W.C. and bath were not fulfilled. Glenburn Pit worked a seam of Ayr hard, splint coal at a depth of seventy-eight fathoms which extended beneath most of the burgh and eventually was taken under the sea. The miners were not all accommodated at Glenburn; some lived within Prestwck, others came each morning by tram from the Toll and from Ayr. The presence of this community of colliers added a new element to Prestwick's population.

The town centre of Prestwick became a busier place. Though the area near the Cross had a decent appearance, the rest of main street was becoming "an unsatisfactory juxtaposition of commercial and domestic, decent cottages cheek-by-jowl with commercial palaces". Most of the old cottages had by now their thatched roofs

Prestwick Laundry, opened in 1903, with its reservoir storing water for use after filtration.

covered with slates. In the first decade of the century traffic showed a dramatic increase. On 26 September 1901 there was instituted the tramway service, operated by Ayr burgh, and powered by their electricity station in Mill Street. The original track provided a service from St Leonard's in Ayr to Prestwick Cross. Plans to extend the line towards Monkton were never implemented, but in 1902 the track was continued southwards as far as Burns Monument, giving a total length of six miles. Within Prestwick burgh there was a single track, with five loop lines as passing places. The tramway proved popular and profitable. There was a fifteen-minute service in the winter months, increased to a ten-minute service to cope with summer holidaymakers. Some ineffective competition was for a time offered over the same route by a Daimler wagonette with solid tyres, chain drive, and tiller steering, but carrying only half-a-dozen passengers. Some of the wealthier Prestwick residents acquired their own private cars, and applications were made to the Dean of Guild Court for erection of "motor houses" to garage them. A familiar figure in and around the town was Dr Hewitt driving recklessly on a motorised tricycle – his experiment to convert it into a motor boat by floating it in the Pow Burn proved unsuccessful! The town council in 1904 made a futile attempt to have the speed limit within the town reduced from ten to eight miles per hour. What

Glenburn pit operated from 1910 until 1973. (*KA*)

was considered more dangerous than the new powered vehicles was the "furious riding by cyclists going through Prestwick", as reported in the *Ayr Advertiser* (17 July 1902). Horse-drawn vehicles continued to be the norm. In the 1908 *Guide* David Bryson of the Red Lion Stables advertised "First-Class Landaus, Victorias, and Broughams for hire". The Glasgow Drapery Warehouse in the Unionist Buildings included among its wares "motor scarfs, motor veils, motor caps". William Foulds designated himself as "Cycle and Motor Agent" and sold petrol and motor oils; but he had to rely also on sale of "wringers, mangles, sewing machines, talking machines and records, incandescent light fittings, golf clubs and balls." The first motor garage was that of William Allan and Sons, though they were still designated as Cycle Agents in the 1913–14 Valuation Roll.

Shops were now selling a wider range of goods and catering for the holiday trade. John McClure and Sons offered "Bathing Requisites" and "Golf Jerseys"; Stevenson, chemist and optician, was dealing in "Photographic materials"; William Somerville, the printer, advertised his Reading Club, picture framing, ladies' and gent's visiting cards, and postcards, with "Local views in great variety"; James Foulds, former dental surgeon, set up in 1906 a bookshop and antique business. Alexander Bremner's Italian warehouse was stocked with exotic foods from Italy and France – sold in paper bags decorated with a picture of the adjacent mercat cross. The 1913–14 Valuation Roll listed around one hundred shops in Main Street. Restaurateurs, hairdressers, jeweller, china merchant, electrician were

Glenburn village was built in 1911, with 187 houses for miners, and its communal wash-house. (*KA*)

among those who supplemented traders in everyday wares; Italian ice-cream merchants, Carlo Bonnetti and Barlami Lombardi, and Alfredo Tronfi, were among those described as confectioners; there was a branch of the Kilmarnock Cooperative Society; and the Clydesdale Bank had a competitor in the Bank of Scotland, whose agent William Shaw succeeded as town clerk.

In 1902 the Prestwick correspondent for the *Ayr Advertiser* noticed (24 July) that "Never in the memory of the oldest residenters have so many people been in our midst". In 1903 he estimated (5 June) nearly two hundred families here on holiday. In subsequent years the Sanitary Inspector guessed the population was augmented by around one thousand in June and up to three thousand in July. How the town council made provision for this annual influx has already been indicated. The Glasgow and South Western Railway Company met the demand by an increased service of trains, and by rebuilding Prestwick station in 1903 with sidings which would serve for goods and excursion trains. Householders with rooms to let put up appropriate signs each April; shopkeepers and tradespeople welcomed the summer visitors, and message boys were hired to deliver rolls, milk, and newspapers. Also in 1903 J. & R. Thom established their Prestwick Laundry off Briarhill Road, in a building of 157 square feet which by 1934 would extend to 14,600 square feet.

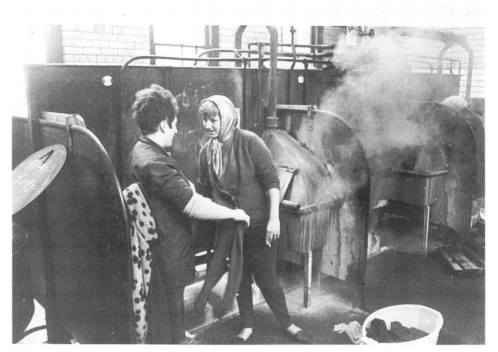

Inside the Glenburn Steamie, 1968.

Glenburn School, opened in 1915. (*KA*)

Prestwick remained a favoured place of residence, whether for retired persons or for businessmen who could easily travel daily by train to Glasgow. Prestwick had been considered in the 1890s as a suitable place for a Nurses Home "not long ago ... opened for the purpose of recruiting fatigued sick-nurses" as Hewat reported. This was followed in 1904 by the Biggart Memorial Home. Intended for cripple children and others from deprived families, it was controlled by the Glasgow United Evangelical Association and sponsored by Mr Biggart, later Sir John Biggart.

The increasing diversity of the population meant that a writer on Old Prestwick (*AP* 4 Feb. 1938) would regret an end of "the delightful spirit of neighbourliness which characterised the habits of the people". Though there was "a plethora of social gatherings" (*AP* 6 Mar. 1903) such societies as existed in the early years of the century appealed to a limited clientele, and not all managed to survive. The Merchants Association formed in 1903 organised an annual dance for members and friends. There was, for a time, a Literary Society, a Male Voice Choir, a Horticultural Society, and from 1903 a short-lived football club. The Band of Hope and the Rechabites continued, but were losing their evangelical appeal. In 1909 Prestwick Masonic Lodge was formed, number 1060 on the roll of the Grand Lodge of Scotland. The first Master of the Lodge was Archibald McEwan, the Deputy Master was Gray Edmiston, both of them then magistrates of the burgh they had also so recently helped institute. This lodge would become more firmly established than a previous one formed in Monkton in 1762. Also in 1909 the Boy Scouts formed a troop in Prestwick, soon joined by a second one, though the local company of the Boys Brigade had by 1912 been disbanded. The curling club met

Biggart Memorial Home, opened in 1904 to accommodate cripple children from Glasgow, was sited on what was then farm land.

occasionally in Monkton School. For the farming fraternity there was still a Cattle Show, but less well-supported as more land along the shore was devoted to cultivating early potatoes. The Unionist Hall was available for larger functions, the schools were let for some other meetings. In 1911 William Alexander from Kilmarnock, one-time gold miner in South Africa, submitted plans to the town council for "a Public Hall in Bridge Street" to accommodate 350 persons. This was opened in 1913 as the Picture House. Sited on the Bog it was in course of time (though perhaps not for that reason) known as the Bug Hut. There had been an occasional exhibition of moving pictures in the Unionist Hall, but this was the beginning of the cinema era.

The Church remained a powerful and popular institution. St Cuthbert's Church was extended during repairs in 1903. But this was felt to be insufficient, and a separate congregation was formed, worshipping in a new St Nicholas Church opened in 1908. It was sited at Sandfield, designed in Norman style by Macgregor Chalmers of Glasgow, largely financed by William Weir of Adamton, and was intended to "meet a felt want in this part of the Parish where there is a large and increasing population." Its first minister was Rev. James Montgomery Crawford, a native of Ayr previously minister in Scotstoun, for whom William Weir also provided a manse. The Mission Hall at New Prestwick was transferred to the new church, and rebuilt in 1912. St Cuthbert's in its turn acquired a church hall in Monkton – the old Free Church School, converted into a Reading and Recreation Room by J.G.A.Baird, was renovated by William Weir who succeeded him at Adamton, and opened for use in 1913. Plans were also made for a church hall within Prestwick, supported by a bequest from the daughter of John Bell of Craigview in memory of her mother, and this hall in Alexandra Avenue opened in 1915. These halls were required for the various organisations which were now proliferating within each congregation. Sunday Schools had previously had to rent rooms in the public schools. About 1915 the local Woman's Association for Missions changed into the Woman's Guild. Also during the long ministry of Rev. David A. Reid (1888–1923) another indication of ecclesiastical change is evident from scrutiny of the records: the kirk session continued throughout the 19th century to discipline parishioners for fornication, but no further cases appear after 1901.

One further example of changing attitudes was increasing co-operation among the several presbyterian denominations. The United Presbyterians and the Free churches had combined to form the United Free Church in 1900. In 1902 during the six months when St Cuthbert's Church was under repair, the congregation worshipped in the North U.F.Church. Rev. Kirkwood Hewat retired in 1915 and died in 1927; followed by Rev. George Ferguson Forbes (1915–21); at Prestwick South U.F., Rev. E.F.Scott was followed in 1909 by Rev. Alexander C. Macmillan, who resigned to go to South Africa, and the vacancy was filled by Rev. Alexander Gibson. By now Christmas was being celebrated more widely. In 1902 St Cuthbert's held its annual Sunday School soiree and Christmas fete in the Unionist Hall; the North U.F. Church had a Christmas tree. In 1903 the *Ayrshire Post* noted that in

Prestwick "the various business premises of the merchants have quite a seasonable look – holly, mistletoe, etc., bulking largely in the way of decoration." Each summer, trips were arranged for children attending Sunday schools – even the Christian Brethren had their annual excursion, in 1903 by tram and brake to the Carrick Hills. In that year the Brethren who had previously held their assemblies in the Freemen's Hall had to find an alternative place of meeting and moved into the Bute Hall. The Salvation Army had by 1911 established itself in the town. Members of the New Prestwick Baptist Church in 1901 were able to replace their wooden hut with a more permanent place of worship. Thomas Young who served as their pastor was replaced by full-time ministers, Revs. George Douglas (1906), James Lamont (1909), James Scott (1912). Members of other religious denominations still had to find their way into Ayr. For such the trams were a convenience, provided the members were not strict sabbatarians, as many still were. When the trams commenced in 1901, Ayr town council decided by twelve votes to three to operate on Sundays. Protest petitions attracted nearly seven thousand signatures from Ayr, and another eight hundred from Prestwick. But on the first Sunday the trams operated they carried three thousand passengers, and a plebiscite of rate-payers in Ayr overwhelmingly agreed to the continuation of Sunday trams.

There was improvement in various forms of communication. Prestwick post office was open daily from 7 a.m. till 8 p.m., and for an hour on Sunday mornings. There were four deliveries of letters each day. In 1912 the post office took over control of the telephone service. As business expanded the post office moved from its original premises near the Bute Hall to another site at the corner of Saunterne

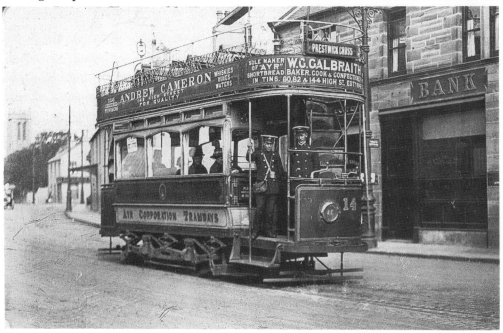

Ayr Corporation Tramways commenced operating in 1901 and until 1931 provided a service between Prestwick Cross and Burns Monument at Alloway.

The railway station, adjacent to Prestwick Golf Club House, was rebuilt in 1903 to cater for increased holiday traffic. (*JH*)

Road, then to the opposite site of Main Street by the Central Bar, until the present post office was opened in 1928. The town obtained better local press coverage. The *Ardrossan and Saltcoats Herald* which in 1897 produced a separate edition, the *Troon Times*, converted this in 1904 into the *Troon and Prestwick Times*; and faced with this competition, the *Ayrshire Post* and the *Ayr Advertiser* devoted more attention to Prestwick news.

Events in the outside world made their local impact. Seven local men volunteered for service in South Africa during the Boer War. Three of them were attached to the Ayrshire Imperial Yeomanry – Trooper J. Peebles and Shoeing-smith James Gibson of Prestwick, and Trooper P. Robertson of Monkton. When they arrived back home on 25 June 1901 they were welcomed by almost the entire population. A grand procession was led by the local members of the Ayrshire Yeomanry, four pipers, the Boys Brigade, then the three heroes in a carriage, followed by decorated lorries and all the schoolchildren from Prestwick and Monkton. William Hewitt, the wee doctor in his top hat and frock coat, made a patriotic speech and presented the veterans with gold scarf pins. There were sports in the afternoon and a dance in the Unionist Hall that evening. In subsequent years, the growing threat of a major European War persuaded the government to

The Picture House, known as the Bug Hut, operated from 1903 till 1957, demolished in 1963. (*KA*)

introduce the Territorial and Reserve Forces Act of 1907. The St Quivox and Monkton Volunteers throughout the 19th century had practised at a rifle range near the Pow Burn till extension of the golf course prompted a move in 1884 to Bentfield. Such part-time soldiers were now recruited into territorial battalions of the Royal Scots Fusiliers to undergo more rigorous training, and the Ayrshire Yeomanry was similarly incorporated within the territorial army.

On 4 August 1914, just after the territorials left their annual summer training camps, war was declared and these soldiers were mobilised. In the fever of patriotism others volunteered, to be joined in 1916 by conscripted men. In the first months of the war the town was little affected. Restriction of street-lighting in coastal towns required a number of Prestwick's 197 lamps to be left unlit, including those sixteen along the sea front. Committees were formed to raise funds for comforts for the troops. Early in 1915 two hundred men of the Royal Scots were billeted in Prestwick High School, whose pupils were housed in those parts of Glenburn School which were completed. When troops from Newfoundland arrived, this new school was itself requisitioned for periods in 1916 and 1917, and its pupils provided with part-time education in the public school. The churches were also affected when the young U.F. ministers were absent as army chaplains. Newspapers, more widely read by the generations benefiting from compulsory education, extended their circulation as a result of interest in progress of the war. The local press printed lengthening lists of casualties. Sunday newspapers were for the first time available – the *Sunday Post* dates from 1914 — and there are memories in Prestwick of queues to buy them outside the newsagents' doors, for shops were not yet allowed to open on Sundays. Public services during the war suffered from the loss of able-bodied men. Temporary staff, including more women, were employed; public bodies like the town council and the school board had the additional expense of making up the army pay of employees on active service. In 1915 municipal elections were postponed for the duration of the war, and vacancies filled by co-option. One such was caused when in 1916 Provost McClure enlisted, even though as a magistrate he was exempt from military service. His first letter of resignation was not accepted by the council, which reluctantly agreed only when he wrote from France – where he was experiencing "the rigours of a private's life" – that Prestwick could not afford an "absentee provost". Alfred James Cochrane, who replaced him as provost, was burdened with so many additional responsibilities that in 1918 a telephone had to be installed in his grocer's shop specially to deal with increased burgh work. Throughout the war the provost was expected to represent the community in every fund-raising venture. In 1915 the council formed a special committee to deal with soldiers' and sailors' dependants who required help. From 1916 a tribunal met to deal with claims for exemption from military service. To prevent profiteering, meetings to limit price increases were authorised, as in 1917 when the town council met with local coal merchants to fix maximum retail price of the various grades of coal at 24 to 27 shillings per ton, or 1s 3d to 1s 6d per hundredweight if sold by the bag. That year when the German U-boat campaign began to threaten food supplies, a Local Food Control Committee was set up containing representatives of the town and parish councils, traders and workmen. Among various measures, forty acres of the municipal golf course were let for cultivation of oats. When early in 1918 rationing of various foods was introduced, this Local Committee was made responsible for operating the system, which was considered particularly difficult since summer visitors continued to patronise the town throughout the war. Here as everywhere there was rejoicing at the Armistice on 11 November 1918. A month later it was announced that a German machine gun and ammunition box would be sent to Prestwick for public display. Plans were made to welcome home those who had served in the forces. On Friday 5 September 1919 they were all entertained to a supper and dance in Prestwick High School. The following day, when the entire nation held its Peace Celebration, Prestwick had a pageant in the form of a procession, led by Dr William Hewitt on his white horse. The proceedings were captured on a twenty-minute film later screened in the Picture House. Another film (sadly, also now lost) showed the unveiling of the war memorial on 23 October 1921. James A. Morris designed this, in the form of a tall shaft crowned with a cross, rising from an octagonal base bearing on its principal front a bronze plaque bearing the roll of honour – those 113 "men of Prestwick who fell in the Great War, 1914–1919".

CHAPTER ELEVEN

Between the Wars

AFTER "the Great War" there was a period of recovery and that postwar world lasted until the end of the nineteen-twenties. Then came some new beginnings, including redefinition of burgh status by the Local Government (Scotland) Act of 1929. But progress was abruptly terminated by outbreak of a Second World War after twenty years of peace.

Transition from war to peace in the years after 1918 proved difficult, with demobilisation, economic dislocation, the influenza epidemic in the winter of 1920–21, and the Geddes Axe of 1922 to reduce public expenditure. There was labour unrest, affecting particularly the coal industry. The miners at Glenburn were inevitably involved in national strikes, the first in October 1920, the longest a seven months' stoppage in 1926 at the time of the General Strike. It was a time of political excitement, when open-air meetings were held in Kirk Street by the Independent Labour Party and the Economic League, and indoor election rallies were organised by the Conservative and Liberal Parties. In 1918 the parliamentary franchise was extended to all men over the age of twenty-one, and also awarded to women over the age of thirty; in 1929 widened to everyone over twenty-one regardless of sex. Until 1918 Prestwick had been part of the South Ayrshire constituency, with W.P. Beale its Liberal MP since 1906. The 1918 Act reshaped a number of constituencies. Ayr Burghs, previously comprising Ayr, Irvine, Campbeltown, Inveraray, and Oban, became a more compact unit taking in Ayr, Irvine, and including Prestwick, Troon, Saltcoats, Ardrossan. South Ayrshire was won for the Labour Party by James Brown of Annbank in 1918 and held at five of the six subsequent elections before his death in 1939. Sir George Younger, MP for Ayr Burghs since 1906, retained that reconstituted seat at the 1918 general election, and so now represented Prestwick. The Conservative ascendancy in this constituency would continue – John L. Baird was successful in the general elections of 1922, 1923, and 1924; when he was appointed Governor General of Australia in 1925 the subsequent by-election was won by Colonel Thomas C.R.Moore, who retained the seat at the nine subsequent general elections until he retired in 1964. There was however a change in political alignments. In 1918 the Labour Party contested Ayr Burghs for the first time, coming third after the Liberals; in 1922 and 1923 Labour came second; thereafter the Liberal Party ceased to contest the seat.

In the annual elections for Prestwick town council party politics played little part as yet. Most councillors were shopkeepers or businessmen, and the principal

The arms of the Burgh of Prestwick were matriculated in 1921. A motto, "Loyalty, Vigilance, Foresight", was added in 1955.

division of opinion was between those who wished to develop the holiday trade and those residents who felt disturbed by growing numbers of visitors. In November 1919 six Labour candidates were nominated: Adam Bond, a miner, was the only one to be elected, but he was displaced in 1925. James Dougan was elected in 1930, and not joined by other Labour members until 1938. A special interest was represented between 1922 and 1928 by Mathew Foulds who stood as an Ex-servicemen's candidate. Though most of the councillors were designated as Moderates, they allowed the few others their share of responsibility; Dougan, for example serving as magistrate and convener of the housing committee. Those who were chosen to be provost were all substantial business men. John Davidson, Glasgow auctioneer and a councillor since 1910, was appointed in 1919 but died after less than a year as provost. James Meikle of Powbank farm, a councillor only since the first postwar election in November 1919, followed; a native and freeman, he was continued in office until in 1926 Thomas McClure, who had returned to the council in 1920, became provost for a second time. When he resigned in 1928 for health reasons, he was awarded the Freedom of the Burgh and presented with a burgess ticket and casket, the first to be so honoured. Subsequent provosts were David Bryson, garage owner, from 1928; Thomas Howie, land valuer, from 1931; D.H.Marr, timber merchant, from 1934; after whose death in 1936, David S. Govan, building contractor, succeeded; then Alexander Ferguson from 1938.

Prestwick town council in the immediate postwar years was primarily concerned with maintaining and modernising existing services. Water mains and sewers had to be replaced or extended. Sam Clark with his team of Clydesdale horses got the

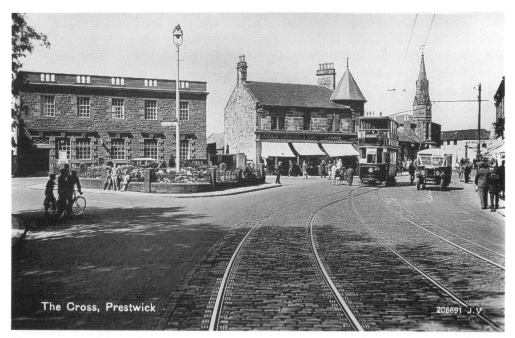

The Cross, Prestwick · 206691 J.V.

The town centre became busier, with buses passing through the town, and in 1931 superseding the trams.

cleansing contract for £800 in 1921. Electricity was installed at the Beach Pavilion (1922) and the Burgh Chambers (1924) and those main thoroughfares where cables had been laid were illuminated with 100 watt street lamps – in 1926 there were 70 electric and 151 gas street lamps. The main road between Pow Burn Bridge and the Toll required major renovation, and in 1924 it cost £20,000 to do so, applying a surface of bituminous asphalt. To widen the main street, ground in front of some of the old cottages had to be acquired, often involving lengthy negotiations. The burgh still had to rely on the services of Ayr fire brigade – local provision in 1921 remained the burgh workmen with one barrow and six lengths of hose totalling 130 yards. There were some modest outlays. In 1920 the bell in the Freemen's Hall was recast (£37 10s); in 1921 the burgh coat of arms was matriculated (£19) to allow display on the war memorial, and on the glass panels of the street lamps. A suggestion by Bailie D.S. Govan in 1920 that a museum be established to exhibit the burgh relics was sadly not followed up, though a glass case in the Burgh Chambers housed the records and other items – like the key of the old tolbooth presented by James A. Morris in 1925. Little was spent extending holiday attractions. The Beach Pavilion was renovated, the kiosk nearby at the south end of the esplanade was partnered by another kiosk with tea room at the foot of Links Road (as the western part of Station Road was now known). The municipal golf course was restored, a second putting green at the sea front laid out. A horse and man were hired in July 1921 to operate the bathing boxes, let at sixpence each, and six bathing costumes and six towels were purchased for hire at twopence each. Burrows and Co. renewed publication of annual guides to Prestwick.

One committee was at this time sufficient to cope with golf, public parks, shore, and attractions. When Aero Photos Ltd in 1920 asked for a site for exhibition flights, it was refused, indicating some reluctance to innovate. But by 1924 to improve Prestwick's attractions a Parks Ranger was employed at £3 3s a week, whose work would include planting and care of plots of shrubs and flowers. One resident complained about this extravagance, so the burgh surveyor Frank Pritty did a mental calculation and offered to refund him one shilling, which was each ratepayer's share of the annual cost.

When a Prestwick Cinema Company which operated in the former Unionist Hall went bankrupt in 1922, opportunity was taken by the town council, which offered £2,500 for the property and converted it into a Town Hall. This became available for the popular whist drives and dances, and could seat up to a thousand persons at meetings, concerts, and otherwise for lease to the New Cinema, which with the other in Bridge Street provided the town with two picture houses. This latter cinema, the Bug Hut, was for a time managed by Alex. Lauder, brother of Sir Harry Lauder. Another hall seating 300 persons, suitable for weddings and other social functions, became available when the Kilmarnock Equitable Co-operative Society opened its new suite of shops in 1921. Smaller halls were erected by the Order of the Eastern Star (which was formed in 1918), the Y.M.C.A. (1920), the Salvation Army (1923), and the United Services Club for ex-servicemen (1925). Likewise in Monkton the Carvick Webster Memorial Hall was donated in 1929 by the owner of Orangefield to commemorate two deceased sons.

The splendid Bathing Lake opened in 1931.

By 1927 the council could afford to address a disturbing problem. Because of the rapid growth of the burgh, especially in the last five years, there was an increased flow of sewage, which was contaminating the foreshore. The outfall installed in 1908 required supplementing with a sewage screening plant, which was built by a local contractor Richard Dumigan, and became known locally as Dumigan's Castle. While the council was planning thus to improve the beach, they instructed their burgh surveyor to prepare a more general report, and Frank Pritty suggested a bathing pool.

William Cowie was commissioned to design what would be the largest swimming pool in Scotland, at an initial cost of £22,000, plus another £13,000 to enhance the esplanade. Of Olympic standard, the pool was one hundred yards long, forty-three yards wide at the centre, and held one million gallons of water, purified by a filtration plant installed in 1934. Prestwick Bathing Lake was opened on 13 June 1931 by Secretary for Scotland William Adamson, in the presence of a crowd of five thousand. Among them were guests Prestwick town council was proud to invite to view this jewel of the Clyde coast, and the occasion was recorded on film by Daniel Paterson, owner of the Picture House. The pool could accommodate 1,200 bathers and 3,000 spectators, and proved immensely popular with residents and visitors. Single admission cost sixpence for adults, threepence for juveniles under sixteen, two shillings for spectators; there were weekly, monthly and season tickets, these last costing 12s 6d and 6s, reduced to 7s 6d and 5s for members of the swimming club. Throughout the season there were swimming galas, demonstrations by world champion swimmers, mannequin parades, evening occasions with illuminations, fireworks, and moonlight bathing. In the first season there were eight galas, each of which attracted around three thousand persons, and that year

The Bathing Lake was popular until the fifties, then closed in 1972.

a total number of 321,855 were admitted to the pool. The 1936 *Guide* could advertise Prestwick also as "The Children's Paradise" with paddling, donkey-rides, castle-building competitions, sea bathing, and rowing and motor boats for hire.

During the 1920s the burgh population of 6,500 increased by some 2,000. Over 400 new houses were erected, mostly by private builders. A Royal Commission of Housing had reported in 1917, and to provide "Homes fit for Heroes" an Act of 1919 offered state subsidies for local authority housing. Prestwick town council decided in December 1918 that there was no local need for a housing scheme. When pressed by the Local Government Board in January 1920 the Medical Officer and Sanitary Inspector "did not consider that houses for the working classes in Prestwick was an urgent case." The census report for 1921 confirmed the county average of 1.56 persons per room was bettered by 1.37 in Prestwick, even when holiday visitors were there. Though there were still sixty-four single-apartment households, these formed only 4.1% of the total, the lowest proportion of any Ayrshire burgh, and favourably comparing with 13.2% for the entire county. The town council affirmed its dependence upon "private enterprise in house building". There were half-a-dozen local builders whose firms were kept busy, for even yet building houses to let was profitable. Nevertheless there was some concern, for in 1920 when William Baird & Co. were asked if they planned to build more houses for miners at Glenburn they queried why they should spend money on this when taxes they were now paying were being used to to build houses for others. In 1923 the council took advantage of government money available to subsidise private builders with £100 per house. They then also began to operate as a kind of building society, offering loans to those wishing to build houses, covered by money from other persons who had money to invest in safe and profitable local authority bonds. Not till 1925 did Prestwick town council initiate a housing scheme by purchase of two plots, each of two acres, at a total cost of £600. The following year thirty-six houses were commenced at Shaw Road near Glenburn, and another thirty-six at Waterloo Road near New Prestwick, and £25,500 was borrowed from the Public Works Loans Board to cover the average cost per house of £354. Though the annual rents were relatively high – £18 for two-apartment, £25 for three-apartment house – 224 applications were received, and the first tenants took occupation in February 1927. The following year another 76 houses were built, 36 flatted houses in Wellington Street off Waterloo Road, 40 in Newdykes Road and Manson Avenue off Shaw Road. The purpose of such early housing schemes was to accommodate better-off working class families, whose rented houses when vacated could be occupied by poorer families. A survey made in 1927 revealed forty-three households in Prestwick without an indoor water supply, and only seven without a water closet, though 281 (including 184 at Glenburn) had to share with other families. The 1931 census indicated that Prestwick, like Largs and Girvan, had 0.9 persons per room, better than other places in the county, whose average was 1.33 per room. The number of single-ends in Prestwick had been reduced to thirty-two, fewer than in any other Ayrshire burgh; 72% of the population lived in households with two per room or fewer, only 3.7% in households with more than four persons per room, bettered only in Largs (79%, 1.4%), Girvan (76%, 4.6%), Troon (75%, 2.3%), and not to be compared with a really badly-housed burgh like Galston (47%, 10.9%). In 1931 the town council decided that another hundred new houses would meet all needs, eleven to replace unfit houses, forty-nine to abate overcrowding, and the rest to meet further increase in population. New legislation was directed towards providing council houses for persons living in slums or overcrowded conditions and empowered councils to impose closing orders upon unfit properties. To implement such policies, Prestwick town council in the thirties built 78 new council houses, 6 of them in 1932, 36 in 1933, another 36 in 1938.

Because Prestwick's population had grown so much, an application to the sheriff was made in 1929 by the town council for an increased number of councillors and magistrates and for a division of the burgh into wards. In May 1930 Sheriff W.Lyon MacKenzie judged (mistakenly) that the population of Prestwick was greater than 10,000; entitling an increase to twelve in the number of councillors, with five magistrates including the provost. As requested, there should be four wards, which would provide the council with a more balanced representation. Ward One comprised the area west of the main road, as far south as Grangemuir Road. Ward Two covered the north eastern area beyond the line of Crofthead and Briarhill roads and included Glenburn. Ward Three was to the south of this and extended to Bellevue Road. Ward Four lay to the south of Grangemuir and Bellevue Roads and took in New Prestwick. Each ward would be represented by three councillors, retiring annually in rotation. In November 1930 all nine councillors of the previous council were required to retire to allow a first election to the enlarged council. Ward One chose three who sought re-election; Ward Two produced two new men, one of them representing the Labour Party; Wards Three and Four, one new man each. With eight re-elected and only four new councillors, continuity was maintained, which was particularly important for a wider reorganisation was in process of implementation.

The Local Government (Scotland) Act of 1929 was introduced to rationalise a system of local government which had developed in haphazard fashion over the previous century. Municipal authorities were now classified as cities, large burghs, or small burghs, without regard to previous status, but according to population. Prestwick with fewer than 20,000 inhabitants became a small burgh and as such certain powers previously exercised by its town council were transferred to the county council whose responsibilities were considerably enhanced. Ayr County Council retained control over the police force, except in the large burghs of Ayr and Kilmarnock; took charge of education throughout the county, superseding the Ayrshire Education Authority; became responsible for poor relief (renamed public assistance) in the small burghs and landward areas, involving abolition of parish councils and their replacement by district councils which dealt with cemeteries and little else. Prestwick burgh handed over to Ayr Council the main road, retaining responsibility only for side streets; lost control over most aspects of public health; and though the dean of guild court continued to monitor building standards, overall planning passed to the county council, whose powers in this respect were vastly extended by an Act of 1932. Prestwick retained its management of the minor environmental services, namely water, drainage, cleansing; its local authority housing; and could complement such mandatory responsibilities by continuing to use permissive powers to cater for the requirements of this holiday resort. Financing such expenditures was facilitated by the steadily increasing number of households paying rates. The rateable value of the burgh increased from £26,000 in the first decade of the century to £100,000 in 1939. Over this period, income from rates grew from £4,000 (plus another £2,000 collected by the parish council) to £63,000 in 1938. £39,000 of that had to go to the county council but with exchequer grants of nearly £8,000 there was £32,000 available to be spent by the town council.

After the Bathing Lake was opened in 1931, Prestwick town council continued to improve the amenities of the sea front. The esplanade was widened and resurfaced in 1936; toilet facilities were improved; beach chalets were erected for letting; the old beach pavilion was demolished in 1938 and plans were considered for other forms of entertainment on that site. To extend attractions, in 1939 a pageant was organised, with characters chosen from the local schools, and on 24 June Jenny Wilson was crowned as Prestwick's first Holiday Queen, with Donald McNiven in attendance as Robert the Bruce. Elsewhere there was the municipal golf course, in 1930 designated St Ninian's. In 1934 the town council extended municipal ownership by purchasing St Nicholas Ladies Course, which was threatened by private building, and St Nicholas continued to be the only ladies' club in Britain with its own course. The public park beside the high school acquired a sports pavilion and facilities for playing cricket; equipment was supplied for the

Prestwick hosted the Open Golf Championship for the last time in 1925.

several small playgrounds for children. In 1933 Provost Howie suggested a public bowling green might be created in Bridge Street, generously offered personally to defray costs of forming it, and so the following year the Howie Municipal Bowling Green was opened.

The town council, whose meetings were held in the Freemen's Hall, felt that more up-to-date accommodation was desirable. In 1929 Boydfield was purchased for £3,000 and demolished in 1933 to make way for a projected new Civic Centre, which would comprise burgh chambers, municipal offices, and public baths. Designs were invited, and no fewer than ninety-seven architects submitted plans. But money was tight, and the ambitious scheme was abandoned, as was a planned reconstruction of the concert pavilion. On the site of Boydfield, gardens were laid out. These, incorporating the war memorial, the Smith Memorial fountain, and a newly-erected bandstand, formed an appropriate centre piece to the other small garden plots which beautified the central area of the town. For meetings of the town council an alternative was found at the Links Hotel, which was purchased for £2,500 in 1938, renovated and taken over in 1940.

There was considerable public interest in affairs of the town. In 1920 there were sufficient signatures to require the council to organise a poll, in terms of the Temperance (Scotland) Act, at which 850 who wished a "dry" Prestwick voted for "No licence" and another 53 voted for "Limitation"; but 1,012 confirmed "No change". In 1926 and again in 1933 Ayr town council made overtures for an amalgamation with Prestwick, whose council on the latter occasion held a plebiscite,

Private building in the thirties, as advertised in 1939.

Boydfield House was demolished in 1933; plans for a civic centre here were abandoned.

with 170 voting in favour, and 3,622 against! There were contests at every council election throughout the twenties. After the burgh was divided into wards, in the nine elections from 1930 to 1938, there were fourteen occasions when seats for particular wards went uncontested, mostly in Wards One and Three when a challenge seemed unlikely to succeed. Ward committees kept a close eye on what affected the interests of their areas, and annual ratepayers' meetings in the town hall became particularly lively in the later thirties. In 1935 at a packed town hall meeting which lasted till nearly 11 p.m., concern was expressed at continuing losses at the pool, and the expenditure on illuminations which brought evening visitors at no profit to the town. At the 1937 meeting there was pandemonium and the magistrates had to leave the platform following angry complaints over licensed premises. Drinks licences had since 1903 been held only by three public houses, three grocers, and the three (private) golf clubs. In 1935 the Queens Hotel had an application refused for the seventh time. In 1936 three hotels were granted permisssion to sell alcohol, and in 1937 two more. Some of those at the ratepayers' meeting loudly objected to the latter additions, others were incensed because a third hotel had been turned down. In 1938 housing was the principal issue, with council tenants concerned at being charged half the cost for installation of electric lighting. Some private householders were by this time objecting to low rents in the most recent council houses, though the charge on the rates was as yet insignificant. Outlay in refurbishing the Links Hotel for conversion into council chambers produced an outcry and a noisy indignation meeting in 1939. Rates increased from 11s 5d in the pound (1932) to 13s 1d (1938). There were repeated grumbles because of the steadily increasing annual amounts Prestwick had to contribute to the county council. Ayr County Council was composed of ninety-one members, among whom were two town councillors from Prestwick to represent the burgh interests. In 1938 the county requisition from Prestwick included £22,000 for education, £12,000 for public assistance, £8,000 for roads, £7,000 for public health, and with other services amounted to £56,000 less £17,000 share in exchequer grants, requiring payment of £39,000. This took away 62% of the rates collected by Prestwick town council.

Prestwick's own services cost £32,000, which exchequer grants reduced to a net £24,000. While £7,000 of that went on parks and other amenities, the bulk was spent on the those mandatory services for which the town council was responsible. £7,000 was devoted to maintaining and augmenting the water supply. Between 1925 and 1938 nearly three miles of new mains were laid, and 5 miles were renewed between 1932 and 1936. The Raith reservoir, storing 40 million gallons, supplied 170 million gallons annually; supplemented by 140 million gallons from Loch Bradan; and from 1938 another 35 million gallons from Ayr town council's Loch Finlas. £2,500 was required for drainage, with 5 miles of new sewers laid between 1925 and 1938. Cleansing cost £4,000 for street sweeping and refuse collection and disposal. Collections were made daily in the town centre and Glenburn, thrice weekly elsewhere. The council supplied three trailers, the contractor provided horses and men at a cost of £976; to which was added £448 for haulage of over three thousand tons of refuse into Ayr, and £651 charged by Ayr town council for its incineration at Lochside. £4,000 was spent on roads and pavements, a major expenditure after 1936 being widening of Maryborough and Station Roads. Street lighting cost another £4,000. The council required £3,000 for those public health responsibilities not transferred to the county council. £2,000 was devoted to miscellaneous services, less than half of that being chargeable to the rates for housing, and including fire brigade charges by Ayr town council. Of the figures quoted as expended on particular services a part, sometimes substantial, was devoted to paying off part of £166,000 outstanding debt incurred by loans which had been taken over the years to fund the council's various major capital projects. What made it possible to finance such expenditure was that the larger number of properties in the growing town steadily augmented the rateable value of the burgh, which reached £100,000 by 1939.

Each of the councillors was closely involved in administration, as all were members of the dean of guild court and of the eight major committees – Finance; Water and Drainage and Public Health; Roads and Footpaths; Lighting and Cleansing; Housing; Halls; Attractions; Golf Course, Shores and Public Parks. William Shaw, who continued as town clerk, and James A. Kinghorn, who in 1930 succeeded Hugh Boyd as burgh treasurer and collector, were still part-time officials. The busy full-time burgh surveyor and sanitary inspector Francis Pritty has been described by his successor as a "larger than life character", a familiar figure with his purple plus-four suit and walking stick.

Education had become the most expensive public service, costing Prestwick ratepayers £22,000 in 1938 as compared with £4,000 in 1918, the last year of the

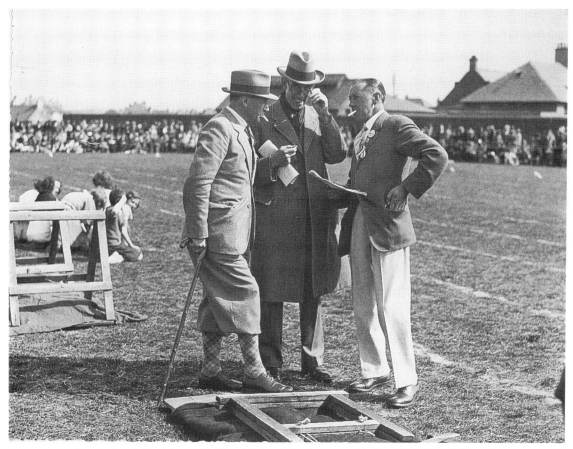

Coronation School Sports, 1937, with local headmasters, Mathew F. Foulds, Adam Duncanson, and James G. Russell. (*IF*)

school board. Ayrshire Education Authority between 1919 and 1931 established a uniform system of schooling throughout the county and introduced various improvements, removing any remaining school fees, making more satisfactory provision for post-elementary pupils, and enhancing opportunities for those able and willing to continue beyond school leaving age. These policies were continued after 1931 when Ayr County Council became responsible for education. There was continuity in management: at Glenburn, Mathew Foulds remained headmaster throughout the period; at Prestwick Public School, Adam M. Duncanson was headmaster from 1920 until 1945; James G. Russell was appointed to Prestwick High School in 1921 and continued until his retirement in 1941. In 1931 Heathfield School was opened to cater for children from the south end of Prestwick as well as those within the adjoining part of Ayr burgh. Almost all local children went to one or other of these schools; few went to the St Nicholas School for Young Ladies in Marina Road and other "private kindergarten and preparatory schools" mentioned in the 1936 *Prestwick Guide*.

Educational provision was extended by additions made to Prestwick High School in 1926, which then acquired an art room, gymnasium, and extra classrooms. In the same year Prestwick Public School got a science room, this its third addition, which brought the school's original four classrooms up to eleven; and also in 1926 central heating was installed in place of open fires. Pupils enrolling at the age of five were, if they made sufficient progress, promoted twice yearly through Infants 1 and 2, Junior 1 and 2, Senior 1, 2, and 3, in which last class they sat the qualifying examination entitling them to attend supplementary classes for three years, at the end of which they might gain a Day School Certificate (Lower) on leaving school. In 1931 a major reorganisation was made whereby the "quali" was superseded by a primary promotions examination. Pupils in the Prestwick schools and those from Monkton, St Quivox, and Symington were thereafter allocated, those considered fit to undertake academic studies to Prestwick High School for a three year "secondary" course in this "higher grade school", after which they might continue at Ayr Academy; the others to Prestwick Public School for a three year course in the "advanced division" until they left school at the age of fourteen.

How schools were changing is evident from the log book of Prestwick Public School in which the headmaster was required to insert details ranging from teachers' absences to events of the school year. There were summer holidays of eight weeks in July and August; Easter and New Year holidays of one week (this last always including Christmas day after 1927); midterm holidays of one day; local holidays as in Ayr September Race week and when the school was required for polling at elections. There were national holidays like Empire Day each May and on special occasions when there were royal weddings and funerals; at the Jubilee of George V in 1935, when the town council presented each pupil with a shilling; at the coronation of George VI in 1937 when their gift was chocolate, and twenty trees were planted in the public park by local pupils. There was a half-day in 1932 to commemorate the centenary of Sir Walter Scott's death; other half-days when the weather was inclement and occasionally in frosty weather when there was ice for skating. The New Year holiday in January 1921 had to be extended for a fortnight because of an epidemic of scarlet fever, which with measles and mumps periodically affected attendance. There were regular inspections of pupils by the schools medical officer, joined now by a school dental officer, an oculist, and (after 1940) by a schools psychologist. In 1922 the teeth of 124 pupils were examined, 93 required treatment, the parents of 42 agreed, and the school dentist undertook 111 extractions and 42 fillings. On a national basis, in 1934 a scheme of milk distribution was commenced, and most pupils paid one halfpenny daily for a bottle containing one third of a pint of Grade A tuberculin-tested milk. School meals were not yet available on a regular basis, but eighty children were provided for during the miners' strike of 1921 and again in 1926. At Glenburn school, where most of the pupils were miners' children, to cook meals members of staff and parents purchased ex-army equipment, which could not be provided officially, and Mathew Foulds insisted that cocoa was the most nutritious beverage for children.

There was continued emphasis on academic merit. By the 1930s Prestwick Public School was staffed by twelve teachers, all now required to be college-trained, and half of them also university graduates. Standards were set by frequent visits of His Majesty's Inspectors, by the county Director of Education, by term examinations, issue of report cards. and presentation of prizes each June, with Provost Howie in 1933 instituting a gold medal for the dux pupil. Widening of the curriculum was encouraged by county advisers of art and physical education and the appointment to Prestwick Public School of visiting teachers in these subjects. Pupils in local schools were treated to occasional radio broadcasts and film shows even before the county council supplied schools in 1935 with wireless sets, and in 1938 with loan of a film projector. From time to time visiting lecturers gave talks on such subjects as temperance and hygiene, and pupils were encouraged to invest weekly in national savings. Horizons at the public school were widened in 1928 by a teacher from Canada – Miss Macdonald who went in exchange married there; if she had returned she could not have been employed, for women were as yet debarred from teaching after marriage. Annual school sports were instituted here in 1935. Pupils were now sometimes taken outwith the classroom, for physical training in the playground in good weather; on 8 April 1921 at 9.45 a.m. to view the solar eclipse; in December 1936 to hear the proclamation of George VI at the mercat cross; and throughout the 1930s for swimming lessons at the Bathing Lake. More outings followed. In 1934 the school closed early so that pupils might attend Bertha Waddell's Children 's Theatre in the Town Hall; next year some pupils were taken to visit Auchincruive college; and annually from 1935 a party went to the Agricul-

St Quivox Roman Catholic Church, one of several new places of worship provided in the inter-war years. (*KA*)

tural Show at Ayr. For those who could afford it, there were trips to Edinburgh in 1935 and 1939, to the Borders in 1937, to the Empire Exhibition at Bellahouston in 1938, and week-end excursions to London in 1936 and 1938. Parents were involved in 1935 in a sale of work for school funds (£47 was raised); and in 1939 were invited to visit the school one Wednesday afternoon. From 1919 one annual occasion was universally honoured – on the anniversary of the armistice, pupils assembled on 11 November to remember at 11 a.m. by two minutes' silence those who had died in the war.

In the aftermath of the war, the churches in Prestwick continued to flourish. At St Cuthbert's, Rev. D.A.Reid's death in 1923 marked the end of his long ministry of thirty-five years. Rev. Luke McQuitty who followed occupied the charge until his own death in 1947. During his ministry, the church was in 1925 enlarged and enhanced with a chancel designed by Jeffrey Waddell, all costs covered by Robert L. Angus of Ladykirk. 150 more sittings accommodated an increasing membership until 1937 a further addition was necessary, this being accomplished to celebrate the centenary of the opening of this church. The church hall was also extended in 1930, to provide for the various organisations connected with the church – the Sunday School and Woman's Guild were joined by a Mothers' Union (1926), Young Men's Guild (1923), Girl Guides (1923), Boys Brigade (1924), and Life Boys (1930). To assist with pastoral duties, an anonymous donor presented the minister with a motor car in 1924, and the congregation helped him to replace it with another in 1932. From 1933 the first of a series of assistant ministers was appointed. In 1932 the church tower was floodlit, the first church in Scotland to have such a permanent installation; in 1935 a new bell was donated by R.L.Angus. There were expanding activities also at St Nicholas Church, whose first minister Rev. J.M Crawford died in 1927, to be succeeded by Rev. George MacLeod Dunn, who staged popular annual congregational concerts in the town hall. The United Free congregations were also attracting new members, so rapidly was the town growing. Prestwick North's Rev. G.F.Forbes was translated to Leith in 1921, and Rev. W.R.McKinnon held the charge thereafter until 1949. Prestwick South was served by Rev. Alexander Gibson until 1934, then by Rev. George A.T.N.Christie, formerly of Bombay, until 1947. In 1929 the Union of the Churches brought all those four congregations together within the Church of Scotland, and a fifth was added by formation of a new congregation. This originated in New Prestwick mission hall of St Nicholas Church, which in 1934 was recognised as Prestwick Kingcase Church, a church extension charge to which Rev. Peter A. Ferguson was ordained.

The former U.P. and Free congregations had their own distinctive traditions, but theological dissension was a thing of the past, and all were committed to offering, each Sunday, church services which were more joyful than in the past, and throughout the week attracting adherents to their organisations which catered for recreational activities of particular groups. The churches were an important medium by which incomers were assimilated into the community. Membership of a congregation was a mark of respectability, and sometimes of prestige. There were still those who wore top hats and morning suits when attending Communion services. But the role of the church in supervising behaviour was becoming less effective. Observance of the Sabbath was steadily being eroded. Those who in 1901 argued successfully in favour of Sunday trams pointed out that some opponents, including several ministers, travelled to church in private or hired carriages. Sunday newspapers, first published during the war, became established institutions. To cater for the swelling number of Sunday trippers, cafes and tea rooms were allowed to open. The bathing lake, too, was open on Sundays, though during hours which did not impinge on church services. When the members of Prestwick Golf Club in 1932 voted to introduce golf on Sundays, they were denounced by Ayr presbytery and by newspaper correspondents.

To counter such secularism, the Salvation Army and the Christian Brethren each held Sunday afternoon services on the beach. Both showed continuing support – the Salvation Army built a hut in Berelands Road in 1923; the Christian Brethren in the Bute Hall were joined by another (less affluent) assembly at Glenburn, whose Bethany Hall was a hut with a corrugated iron roof; a separate group set up their own New Prestwick mission hall at Waterloo Road. New Prestwick Baptist Church continued under the pastoral care of Revs. Joseph Burns from 1923, and Benjamin Bridges from 1933 until 1943. Two more prominent denominations established themselves in Prestwick. Until the twenties, local members of the Scottish Episcopal Church and Anglicans of the Church of England worshipped in Holy Trinity Church, Ayr. In 1915 services were provided in Prestwick for soldiers stationed here, who were joined by some local people and summer visitors. A temporary hut was erected and Rev. J.C.Melville apppointed curate. A more permanent mission was formed in 1923, with Rev. John Knox as curate, and plans made to build a church. In 1926 St Ninian's Episcopal Church was consecrated. Erected in Maryborough Road near the the ancient chapel remains, this handsome building was designed by James Hay as a smaller replica of St Margaret's in Newlands, Glasgow. Its parish extended as far south as Tam's Brig, was served by Rev. Gordon Sylvester, then by Rev. James Gait from 1937 till 1940 when he became an army chaplain and the incumbency became temporarily subject to Holy Trinity. Roman Catholics in Prestwick also had to go to Ayr for worship until 1926 when, on Sunday mornings, Mass was celebrated in the Town Hall, or occasionally in the public school, and once in a loft over a garage. In 1933 this was made a separate parish, under charge of Rev. Laurence F. Breen, and a church designed by James A. Carrick was built in St Quivox Road. With eleven places of worship within the burgh, Prestwick by the end of the thirties was a well-churched town.

The number of households, around 1,800 in 1918, increased to 3,000 by 1938. During this period over 1,300 new houses were erected. Those 326 provided by the town council formed only 25% of the total, and in some cases replaced older properties which were demolished. In the twenties nearly 300 were constructed by private builders. There was less building in and around 1930, because of the world economic crisis, but in the thirties over 600 private houses were built in Prestwick. Most of these were sited in Wards Three and Four. Reduction of building costs by 20% between 1925 and 1933 meant that bungalows could be sold at prices ranging from £300 to £800; a fall in interest rates from 6 to 4.5% and a rise in real wages meant that persons of modest means could afford to pay a mortage of a few shillings a week for a new three-bedroomed home. Into these bungalows of Prestwick flitted local people, skilled workers and lower middle class, and incomers retiring to this pleasant seaside venue. At the same time, costs of maintaining the older large villas had grown so much that one was converted into a nursing home and ten turned into hotels and boarding houses.

For the growing number of consumers, there were new shops, including chain stores ranging from Kilmarnock Equitable Co-operative Society's new suite of shops (1921) to Woolworth's (1936); a new post office (1928); the Bank of Scotland and Clydesdale Bank were joined by the Royal Bank (1923), then the Union Bank and the National Bank. Of around 160 shops listed in the Valuation Roll for 1939/40, 10 were located at the Cross, 108 in Main Street, 17 at Prestwick Toll, and another 23 mainly in the eastern housing areas. In the twenties milk was still sold from farmers' carts; by 1937 most of the milk was being bottled; of twenty-seven registered purveyors of milk, fifteen had premises within the burgh; only one of these kept cows, a last relic of the burgh's agrarian past.

New recreational facilities catered for residents as well as holidaymakers. The cinema became increasingly popular with the introduction of talking pictures in 1929. Until then the Picture House (and two others in Ayr) satisfied demand, but in the thirties four more cinemas were opened in Ayr and Prestwick acquired the Broadway. This was officially opened on Monday 29 April 1935 with "The Barretts of Wimpole Street" starring Charles Laughton, Frederic March, and Norma Shearer. It was indeed a "Modern super cinema", designed by Alister Macdonald, son of the prime minister, and financed by John C. Sword, pioneer of bus transport and general manager of Western SMT. Appropriately the Broadway was chosen by the Ayrshire Film Society for its Sunday evening meetings. More occasional entertainment in the town was provided by the circus, whose venue in the thirties was the public park; previously the circus and shows were held at the Bog – on the first visit of the circus an elephant sank in the mud and had to be hauled out by cart horses. Throughout the year young people were catered for by the various uniformed organisations which were now at their peak of popularity. When Mathew Foulds in his capacity of councillor went in 1924 on the water trip to Loch Bradan, he found a site by Straiton which as scoutmaster he retained for the troop as a summer camp. The various halls where youth organisations met were also in use for the whist drives, dances, and badminton which were so popular. There were even dances in the granary above Gardiner's bakery. The Town Hall also catered for such functions, for the annual flower show, the shows of the Ayr and District Canine Club, the Prestwick Choral Union, and for dramatic shows – in 1936 the town council discovered a licence was necessary before the Prestwick Players Club could stage their first performance – and there was a summer show in the town hall in 1938 following demolition of the beach pavilion. Outdoor sports flourished. In 1922 the high school acquired a hockey pitch and a tennis court, and hockey and lawn tennis clubs were formed. Football enjoyed a temporary local revival. In

1919 Glenburn Rovers was formed, with its own pitch and pavilion. In 1920 another club was started at New Prestwick, for whom the town council provided a pitch, but refused permisssion for a pavilion. Glenburn Rovers competed in junior football, but their only notable success was in 1929 winning the Stirling Trophy, which had been presented in 1927 for competition by John Stirling of the Red Lion Hotel in Prestwick. With limited local support there were difficulties in times of economic depression. To raise funds, from 1928 dances were held in the Town Hall on Saturday nights, but with £2 2s rent nightly and sometimes rowdy elements they could not be continued, and Glenburn Rovers was one of five Ayrshire clubs which had to disband in 1936. Prestwick Cricket Club was formed in 1929, with a pitch where Angus Avenue is now built, moved to Shaw farm in 1933, and to Powmill Road from 1935 until 1939 when outbreak of war forced the club to disband. Golf still flourished, with all the five courses well patronised. But 1925 was the last occasion when the Open was played at Prestwick: with increased numbers of spectators attending such events there were difficulties in crowd control, especially here where a public right-of-way crossed the course. Apart from organisations relating to sport or connected with the churches, there was an obvious dearth of other voluntary associations in the town; people with special interests found these conveniently provided in Ayr. There was however a Prestwick social and welfare association which continued to organise the annual children's gala day. In 1926 a group of older men who met at the sea front formed themselves into the Prestwick Shore Old Cronies Club, which organised lecture meetings, and by 1932 with a membership of 130 they were able to acquire their own premises in the Riggs. During this period there were two unsuccessful attempts to launch a local newspaper. For a few years after 1926 the *Prestwick Press* was promoted by J.R. Mungo, the town council's publicity officer. In 1931 the *Prestwick News* was initiated by James Shields and his son, but proved equally short-lived.

The town was still small enough for those who grew up in it to be on familiar terms with many of their fellows, and one who was a schoolboy in the thirties has listed over ninety persons whose nicknames he has recalled, and some of the many others who of necessity left Prestwick to pursue careers in the professions. That emigration of some of the young folk coupled with a greater influx of older incomers had its effect on the composition of the population. The census report of 1931 showed that, of Prestwick's population of 8,538, 16% were aged 60 and over, and the average age of 33.9 was higher than elsewhere in Ayrshire, exceeded only in Largs. The sex ratio of 137 females to 100 males was also more unequal than elsewhere in the county except for Largs. Because the population was older, in the years between 1931 and 1938 the birth rate of 14.0 (per thousand of population) was similarly lower than 18.6 for the county. Despite the ageing population, Prestwick was a healthy place, for between 1931 and 1938 the death rate was 12.9 per thousand (13.3 for the county) and infantile mortality 67 per thousand births (79 for the county). In the same period, 5.3% of the births in Prestwick were illegitimate. It would be interesting to speculate why Prestwick like Ayr and Kilmarnock were between 5% and 6% – while all the other burghs in north

Ayrshire were below 5%; and Cumnock, Girvan, and Maybole were much higher than the county average of 6%.

A distinguised historian has written of the inter-war years: "The nineteen-thirties have been called the black years, the devil's decade. Its popular image can be expressed in two phrases: mass unemployment and 'appeasement' ... Yet, at the same time, most English people were enjoying a richer life than any previously known in the history of the world: longer holidays, shorter hours, higher real wages. They had motor cars, cinemas, radio sets, electrical appliances." Most of the people in Prestwick benefited from such social advances. In the twenties few houses were lit by electricity, and in 1927 the first council houses had only a gas supply. BBC radio commenced broadcasting from Glasgow in 1923 and "wireless sets" (powered by rechargeable wet batteries called "accumulators") were still a novelty in 1927 when council house tenants required permission to erect aerials. By the thirties those in council houses as well as occupants of new bungalows could enjoy a more spacious family life as bad housing and overcrowding were being elimi-nated. Health was improving, helped by expansion after 1918 of the schools medical service and by Ayrshire General Medical Service established in 1935 by the general practitioners of the county, whereby small weekly subscriptions guar-anteed provision of medical treatment. Coincidentally, in 1935 Dr Hewitt died, the town's first doctor, of whom it was said, "Better the wee doctor drunk than any other sober". In 1929, aged 78, after practising for fifty years in Prestwick, the town council had sponsored a public testimonial and he was then presented with a gold watch and chain and a wallet of notes.

Despite social progress, there were problems. For some, local employment was lacking, and not all able young people could afford higher education. Harry Gardiner recalled that one girl who was dux of the high school found work only in scrubbing floors. Things were particularly difficult at times for the miners of Glenburn. Their housing was superior to that in miners' rows elsewhere, and in 1933 pithead baths were provided. But they formed a community which was in some respects separate, and in some quarters resented. Glenburn's principal recreations were football, quoiting, and gambling at pitch and toss at a spot just over the burgh boundary. Glenburn had its own annual gala, and there was Glenburn Pipe Band. And there were buses which took them directly into Ayr. For their neighbours in Prestwick who relied on the holiday trade, the miners were something of a nuisance. There were smells from the burning Glenburn bing (1935); the Pow Burn, where flounders might be caught and kingfishers admired, was becoming polluted with effluent from Glenburn and Mossblown pits (1937); backshift miners loitering at the town centre spoilt the image of the place. If Prestwick had been a different sort of community the Glenburn folk might have been more effectively assimilated. But, as was later observed, "A good many things have conspired to prevent the development of a healthy community spirit". Many of the incomers were strangers, some retaining links with their former homes, some too old to become involved in local affairs, except as owner-occupiers concerned about public expenditure and the rates. Those long settled in Prestwick were themselves divided, for there were some who profited from the holiday trade, and well-to-do residents whose lives were disturbed by the summer crowds.

Most of the holidaymakers found lodgings in private houses. In 1926 the Chief Constable reported that others had set up tents in "holiday camps" at Glenburn, St Quivox Road, Waterloo Road, Pleasantfield Road, Crandleyhill Road, with caravans near the Biggart Home. There were Boys Brigade camps "more or less under military discipline and properly conducted"; other "respectable people of the working class" whose conduct was also exemplary; but in Crandleyhill Road especially there were "young men of an undesirable class". Burgh bye-laws were enacted to control such visitors, and latterly houses were built on these sites. To provide for others who could afford a more expensive holiday, the *Burgh Guide* of 1926 listed six of the larger villas which had been converted into hotels or boarding houses; increased to ten by 1936. But in the thirties the major development was a vast increase in the number of day trippers.

There were changing fortunes for those in the landward part of the parish. Monkton village experienced modest expansion, with some new bungalows, and a couple of dozen houses erected by the county council. Situated as it was at the convergence of two major roads, it suffered from increased motor traffic. In the early thirties a new road was planned to bypass Monkton and Prestwick, and to capture anticipated traffic Messrs Austin and McAslan of Glasgow purchased a piece of Rosemount land and opened the Dutch House Tea Room. This was an era when many Ayrshire estates were being broken up, with farms sold off to tenants, and such trends were affecting Monkton and Prestwick parish. Adamton after the death of William Weir was occupied by his widow, but purchased by William Whitelaw from Kirknewton, then in 1929 by William Lindsay Carlow. The five Adamton farms were sold off, Adamton Mains, Woodside, East Bogside, Brieryside, Newlands, the first three to occupiers. However, Ladykirk and its three farms, Ladykirk Mains, Shawhill, South Bogside, remained in the hands of Robert Angus until his death in 1925, to be inherited by his only surviving son, Robert L. Angus. R.L.Angus continued his father's mining interests, principally as chairman of William Baird & Co., which in 1931 was extended to become Bairds and Dalmellington Ltd. Fairfield house continued to be leased by trustees of W.G.Campbell, who retained ownership of the farms of Fairfield Mains, Monktonmill, Muirhouse, West Orangefield, and Orangefield Mains. Elsewhere in the parish, Monktonhill and Whitehaugh were owner-occupied, but Aitkenbrae, Hobsland, and Whiteside were rented, like most of the farms in the parish. Orangefield had earlier lost its lands; Harry and Agnes Carvick Webster owned the mansion house until 1933 when it became a fully-licensed hotel. Auchincruive estate, which extended into this parish, was sold in 1925 after the death of R.A.Oswald. Its mansion house in Ayr parish became the West of Scotland Agricultural College which opened in 1931, which, with the nearby Hannah Dairy Research Institute, would significantly contribute to agricultural advances throughout Ayrshire. The Land Utilisation Survey of 1937 revealed that Monkton and West Kilbride were the most intensively tilled parishes in the county, with more than 40% of the farmland under crops, and between 50% and 60% on the lighter soils near the shore, forming "stretches of arable land equal to any in Scotland". On these relatively dry and frost-free farms of Monkton nearest the coast, potatoes formed a principal crop, with wheat grown sometimes to break the routine. Inland there was the more typical Ayrshire farming with most of the land kept in grass for pasture, and oats was the main crop, grown to feed the dairy cattle. Two memories appropriately reveal increasing concern for milk hygiene: during the twenties an outbreak of foot and mouth disease required the slaughter of infected animals, and Thomas Lindsay of Aitkenbrae saved his herd through three months in quarantine; and in the thirties Hugh Sillars of Whiteside was the first local farmer to sell his milk in bottles. Throughout the period the annual cattle shows were held, for a time in a field near Biggart Home, latterly in the park beside the high school. But the milling of grain in the parish ceased with the closure of Powbank Mill, and James Kennedy, the last miller, died in 1936.

There were remarkable developments in transport during the inter-war years, many of which had significant social consequences. On 1 January 1923 by amalgamation the Glasgow and South Western Railway Company became part of the London Midland and Scottish Railway Company, and the lines became busier than ever. There were increasing numbers of business men settled in Prestwick and travelling daily to Glasgow. The 5.10 p.m. train from Glasgow was always busy, and for a time carried two dining cars which the G. & S.W. had introduced – bearing the names of "Bonnie Jean" and "Lass of Ballochmyle". In the 1930s there were twenty-five trains daily from Glasgow St Enoch. To Prestwick station was brought an increasing volume of newspapers, mail, and goods traffic. Special excursion trains brought day trippers each Saturday in summer from inland towns, some of which were emptied on the occasion of the annual Sunday School jaunt to the coast. Prestwick was particularly popular for the station was so near the shore. One Saturday in 1938 an estimated 50,000 trippers arrived by train at the Ayrshire resorts, and Prestwick took at least a fifth of these. Prestwick also shared in the "Evening Breathers" which that year carried nearly 400,000 passengers who paid a few pence each for a few hours at the coast. All this despite competition from the buses.

In 1919 Matthew Brown of Ayr instituted a service of motor charabancs "to all Places of Interest within Twenty Miles of the Town" and obtained from Prestwick town council permission to have a "stance at the Cross for Pleasure Cars". In 1923 James Dodd began a bus service between Troon and Ayr. In 1924 the Scottish Transport Motor Services began to operate between Kilmarnock and Ayr. There followed long distance services to Ayr which passed through Prestwick – O'Hara's Southern buses from Newton Mearns and Sword's Midland buses from Airdrie also coming across the Fenwick Moor; Currie and Thomson's service from Airdrie via the Irvine Valley. In 1927 the Midland and Southern companies provided the first direct services between Glasgow and Ayr. Other local services, competing with the trams, followed. In 1928 William Young of Ayr began to operate between Prestwick Cross and Burns Monument; Frank Kerr instituted a similar service from

Glenburn; other services into Ayr were offered, from Prestwick Toll by William Law, from Glenburn by Rolph brothers. In 1930 James Dodd and some smaller owners formed the A.A.Motor Services Ltd, with their principal trade on the route between Ardrossan and Ayr. In 1932 the Scottish Transport Motor Services combined with other major operators and established the Western Scottish Motor Traction Company Limited, whose services from Glasgow and Kilmarnock augmented the summer holiday traffic. In the same year their associated Edinburgh-based SMT bought out Ayr burgh's tramways system, to replace it with a local bus service. The trams ran for the last time on 31 December 1931. The final scheduled run was from Burns Monument to the depot at Newton Park. But Tram No.9 from Prestwick Cross, which should have arrived earlier, deliberately ran slowly to be the last tram home, in the first hour of 1932. Within three years the SMT also took over the local services previously operated by Young, Kerr, Law, and Rolph. By 1934 through Prestwick were passing buses at fifteen-minute intervals on the Ayr-Glasgow route and every thirty minutes between Ayr and Troon. Also in summer there were bus trips from inland places to Prestwick; and for those holidaying in Prestwick tours were available, provided latterly by Law, by Dodds of Troon and by Western SMT. The roads were busier not only with buses but with

The airfield established at Monkton in 1935. (*JH*)

182

Pilots were trained for the RAF in Tiger Moth planes. (*JH*)

lorries and private cars. The number of vehicles registered in Ayrshire rose from 37 in 1903 to 5,438 in 1923, and 14, 518 in 1938; they were joined in summer by motorists from elsewhere taking trips to the coast. The busiest road within Ayrshire was from Monkton passing through Prestwick into Ayr: traffic censuses reported that on this stretch the average daily number of vehicles passing was 1,203 in 1925, 4,467 in 1938. To try to ease the flow through the town, traffic lights were installed in 1933, and pedestrian crossings in 1935; plans were drawn up in 1932 for a new road bypassing Monkton and Prestwick, revised in 1935, but the county council was unable to proceed with the scheme.

Prestwick was to become involved in a spectacular way in the 20th century's newest means of transport. From 1931 flights were offered from the north shore. First was the 'Prince Henry', a fourteen-seater air liner operated by Aviation Tours Ltd. In subsequent years there were flying boat excursions (1932), flights by Midland and Scottish Air Ferries Ltd. (1933), and Coburn's flights. Earlier, during the First World War, it is said that a Captain Callaghan of the Royal Flying Corps, based at Ayr racecourse, landed his plane near Redbrae to visit Mrs Collins who lived there. Around 1934, after John C. Sword's Midland and Scottish Air Ferries commenced a regular service between Renfrew and Belfast, and the weather was bad on Clydeside, planes were diverted and landed on a field near Monkton village which was rented for that purpose. Nearby, an airfield was laid out in 1935. David F. McIntyre and the Marquess of Clydesdale (later Duke of Hamilton) were both members of No. 602 City of Glasgow Auxiliary Air Force Squadron based at

Scottish Aviation Limited

request the honour of your company on the occasion of the

Empire Air Day Flying Display,

which is being held at Prestwick Aerodrome
on Saturday, 21st May, 1938,
between the hours of 2.30 and 5.30 p.m.

This card is required for admission to the Aerodrome and should be retained throughout the afternoon for admission to Refreshment Rooms reserved for private guests.

Note.—Empire Air Day is 28th May, but it is being held one week earlier at Prestwick in order
to avoid disturbance to the British Amateur Golf Championship Finals at Troon on 28th May.

The first Prestwick Air Show.

Renfrew; and had been selected to make an epic flight over Mount Everest in 1933. They were aware that the RAF, anxious to increase its supply of pilots, would contract with private firms which supplied flying training. On 9 August 1935 Scottish Aviation Ltd. was formed by McIntyre and Clydesdale in association with the De Havilland Aircraft Company, and with R.L. Angus of Ladykirk as one of the directors. Heathfield, their first choice for an airfield, could not be sanctioned so Monkton proved a satisfactory alternative. When prospect of a local aerodrome was discussed by Prestwick Town Council in June 1934, the first reactions were favourable. Ex-Bailie Milligan pointed out that "planes should not cross over a city" so "Renfrew was entirely unsuitable"; and "Prestwick was near enough Glasgow" so "might get the cream of the business". Ex-provost Bryson remarked that now "Prestwick was on the map." But some residents who were resolutely opposed to the proposed aerodrome persuaded the council to change its mind. In September 1935, "Councillor Smith drew attention to the fact that an aerodrome was to be erected immediately outside the Burgh of Prestwick, which might injure the amenity of the Burgh, and moved that the Town Council should enter their protests to the Ministry of Transport requesting them to have the same removed further from the Burgh. This was agreed to." Nevertheless Scottish Aviation Ltd was able to go ahead, purchasing 157 acres for an airfield just north of Orangefield Hotel, and another 191 acres to allow for future expansion. A terminal building with hangars and control tower was built by the end of 1935, fields which had grown wheat and turnips were seeded with grass, and on 17 February 1936 No. 12 Elementary Flying Training School was inaugurated. There were eight instructors; thirty-four pupils; twenty Tiger Moth planes, painted orange with silver wings; and a second-hand ambulance. With Prestwick's fog-free climate, training could be carried on without interruption, in 1937 weekend training of volunteer reserve pilots was introduced, in 1938 training of navigators, in 1939 wireless operators, so that Scottish Aviation had become the country's largest training school under contract to the Air Ministry. There was now a fleet of one hundred aircraft of various types; Orangefield Hotel had been enlarged to provide messes for officers and men; and Powbank Mill was converted to become a social club. There were complaints about disturbance to the environment, when hedges and trees were removed to form the flying field; and there were objections to the noise of aircraft. But it was conceded that flying on Sundays should commence only after church service, and similar reasonable measures were taken to allay local opposition. In May 1936 there was a successful Empire Day Display of Flying. The name of "Prestwick Aerodrome" was already in use and proved acceptable, even though it was actually located in Monkton, outwith the burgh boundary. In five years Prestwick trained 1,334 pilots, 1,994 air observers, 1,200 wireless operators, and over 400 members of the volunteer reserve. Also, giving a welcome boost to the local economy, early in 1939 Scottish Aviation Limited commenced work on modification of aircraft and manufacture of parts, employing 370 persons in this initial stage before the outbreak of war.

CHAPTER TWELVE

The Second World War

IN 1933 H.G.Wells' novel *The Shape of Things to Come* described the current "phase of dismayed apprehension ... that comes at times before the breaking of a storm." He forecast outbreak of war between Germany and Poland in January 1940, characterised by destructive bombing of cities and extensive use of poison gas. Everyone assumed that airpower would be a decisive feature of the next war. Stanley Baldwin in 1932 gloomily assumed that "the bomber will always get through". The public, informed as never before of international affairs by cinema newsreels and BBC news bulletins, was aware of the Japanese attack on Manchuria (1931); the Italian conquest of Abyssinia (1935) with the aid of bombers and mustard gas; the Spanish Civil War with the devastating bombing of Guernica (1937). Liddell Hart, a military expert writing early in 1939, estimated "nearly a quarter of a million casualties ... in the first week of a new war". Threat of a second world war from resurgent Germany appeared after 1933 when Hitler came to power and in 1936 sent in troops to occupy the demilitarised Rhineland. In 1935 a government white paper entitled *Statement Relating to Defence* initiated a British programme of rearmament. Later that year Scottish Aviation Ltd was formed and (as detailed in the previous chapter) laid out the flying field at Prestwick for training of RAF pilots. In the same autumn Prestwick town council received from the Scottish Office a first circular relating to air raid precautions.

Hitler moved into Austria (1936) and Czechoslovakia (1938). Already in 1937 the programme of rearmament was giving increased priority to aircraft production and training of pilots. Provision for air raid precautions was enacted, a conference of local authorities met in Ayr, and Prestwick town council arranged for St Andrew's Ambulance Association to provide first-aid classes in the town hall. In the spring of 1938 Ayr County Council authorised appointment of air raid wardens, volunteers who were fit men over military age, not employed on key work and so available in any emergency. Respirators (gas masks) for all civilians were supplied by the government, those for Prestwick stored in the United Services Club, and later distributed. The log book of Prestwick public school for 30 September 1938 notes "Staff instructed in fitting gas-masks". On that date there was also a national registration for issue of identity cards, prelude for distribution of ration books, which would come into use from January 1940. Preparation for war (which seemed almost inevitable following the Munich crisis of September 1938) involved also the introduction of conscription for military service, and the first of these militia-men were called up in July 1939. Locally, special constables were enrolled; the number of air raid wardens brought up to strength to man five wardens' posts – in Boyd Street, at the Howie bowling green, Ladies St Nicholas and St Ninian's clubhouses, and Glenburn recreation block; a first-aid casualty station was set up at the Bathing Lake, rescue and decontamination services located in the burgh yard; training provided for an emergency fire service; plans were made for four air raid shelters. Meanwhile everyday life was continuing. Ayr County Council was planning an extension to Prestwick High School and construction of a Roman Catholic primary school. The town council was considering tenders for erection of 174 houses in Adamton Road. The Scottish Amateur Golf Championship was contested in March and the Holiday Queen crowned in June. Prestwick public school took a party of pupils to Edinburgh in May and participated in the inter-schools swimming gala in July. The Scouts went to Arran for their annual summer camp.

When Hitler invaded Poland, the prime minister Neville Chamberlain declared war on Sunday 3 September 1939. Anticipating massive air raids, evacuation plans were implemented, and since Prestwick was designated a safe area special trains that weekend brought 1,564 school-children and their teachers from Glasgow, St Paul's R.C. School, Whiteinch and Bankhead School, Knightswood. They were billeted with local families, and shared part-time education with local pupils in the three schools and church halls. There followed those relatively quiet months designated the "phoney war", during which most of the evacuees returned to their own homes. In April 1940 intensive military action commenced with fighting in Norway, and Prestwick aerodrome, now an RAF station, was a staging post for planes participating in that campaign. Failure in Norway brought in Winston Churchill as prime minister of a coalition government; German invasion of the Netherlands; evacuation of the British forces from Dunkirk; capitulation of France; and threatened invasion of Britain. To immobilise potential landing sites, posts were erected on the shore; tank traps were formed on golf courses, road blocks erected, and all signposts and placenames removed to hinder the invader. Local defence volunteers were recruited, to become the Home Guard which, under Major Leitch, took over the town hall for indoor training of a company of nearly 150 men. A separate company was formed to defend the aerodrome, composed of SAL workers led by Ronald Howgarth. Older local Scouts formed War Service Patrols to assist ARP, Fire and Ambulance services by message-carrying and other duties. Because of the emergency, bells were to be rung only as warning of imminent attack, so the one on the Freemen's Hall was silenced, and Willie Wilson was last of the bellringers who by tradition called inhabitants to and from work at 7 a.m. and 6 p.m. daily.

Though in March 1940 the county council insisted that Prestwick as a safe area required no air raid shelters, in July twelve brick public shelters were authorised, augmented in November by 150 steel shelters "in view of the proximity of the Aerodrome". Volunteers trained as auxiliary firemen were in May supplied with one large and two small trailer pumps, located at Prestwick Laundry in Briarhill Road and Hamilton's Garage in Ayr Road. This Auxiliary Fire Service was (in 1941) incorporated within a National Fire Service; with a new fire station established in

1943 at the ladies' golf course to accommodate four pumping units. The prospect of invasion was diminished by success in the Battle of Britain, fought by the RAF in the skies above southern England from July to September 1940; but bombing of London and other cities intensified. In 1941, on the nights of 13-14th March, Clydebank was blitzed. One trailer pump with six firemen was sent from Prestwick to assist. A party of twenty-eight Glenburn miners went to clear a shelter where relatives of a workmate were buried. Some of those there rendered homeless were received at Prestwick High School, recently designated as an Emergency Rest Centre. A survey made in April reported Prestwick as having 778 evacuee children, including 148 who were homeless and 69 from England. The Rest Centre had to be re-opened on 7-12 May after Greenock was bombed, to take in 173 persons. As before, some returned home; those who could afford it found lodgings for themselves; others were allocated accommodation by the billeting officers; in May the remainder had to make do with the clubhouses of the two municipal golf courses.

Stray bombs which fell in Ayrshire in April and May 1941, with deaths in Irvine and Kilmarnock, emphasised the need for continued vigilance. In September 1941 all men between eighteen and sixty, unless otherwise exempted, were required to register for duties in Civil Defence (ARP). As incendiary bombs were now causing as much damage as high explosives, fire watching of premises (introduced in October 1939) was more effectively organised, and stirrup pumps supplied to fight localised fires. In November 1941 John S. Morrison, the Head Warden, was appointed full-time Fire Guard Staff Officer, and in April 1942 installed in headquarters at 53 Main Street. By the end of 1943 there were 994 men and 880 women involved in fire-watching rotas. To ensure supplies of water for the National Fire Service, the mains were linked with those of Troon and Ayr, and static water tanks were set up for emergency use. Fear of gas attack persisted and in November 1941 local authority workers were urged to copy the armed forces by practice in wearing respirators for a half-hour once a month. Also because the possibility of enemy landings was still not ruled out, road blocks were rebuilt in Prestwick in February 1942 and an Ayrshire invasion committee formed in April 1942. Work continued providing air raid shelters – by the end of 1943 Prestwick had twelve public shelters capable of protecting 600 persons, 294 domestic communal shelters for 4,058, 66 Morrison table shelters, and also four special shelters suitable for 176 at the Biggart Home. As a final precaution, in May 1942 a mortuary was established in the stables of the Red Lion. By this time, in fact, there was less danger, and the character of the war changed in 1942 as Britain gained allies, the USSR after German invasion (June) and the USA after Japanese attack on Pearl Harbour (December). Yet there remained, in Prestwick, a particular urgency about civil defence because developments at the aerodrome made it seem an inviting target.

At the outbreak of war in September 1939 the aerodrome was requisitioned by the Air Ministry to become an RAF Station, with Wing Commander David F. McIntyre as commanding officer until the summer of 1941. It continued its important work in training pilots while also serving as base for a succession of

Prestwick aerodrome from 1941 until 1945 was busy with transatlantic military flights. (*JH*)

fighter squadrons. For training there was now a fleet of 45 Tiger Moths plus a four-engined Fokker Airliner acquired from KLM and flown out of Holland just before the German occupation. Scottish Aviation expanded its manufacture of aircraft parts and the maintenance, repair, and modification of planes, principally Hurricane and Spitfire fighters – which were ferried to and from Prestwick by a locally-based Air Transport Auxiliary unit. In 1940 Lord Beaverbrook as minister of aircraft production, while the Battle of Britain was being won by RAF fighter planes, sought to obtain from the USA a supply of bombers for raiding Germany. These were manufactured in California and a bold decision was taken. Transatlantic flights were still a hazardous novelty, but it was planned to fly the bombers from Gander in Newfoundland to the nearest UK landing field, which was the RAF station at Aldergrove in Northern Ireland. The first flight of six planes landed there on 11 November 1940. Later that month another formation of Hudsons was en route when one plane lost contact and landed at Prestwick – on 29 November, after a flight of 2,100 miles taking 10 hours 54 minutes. The advantage of a terminus on mainland Britain was realised, and one which was especially suitable because of its fog-free record and with an airfield which was capable of major expansion.

In February 1941 the Atlantic ferry route was switched from Aldergrove to Prestwick and the first five "lease-lend" bombers arrived for delivery to the RAF. To begin with, the aircrews of such planes returned to America by ship, because

Control Tower set up on Orangefield House in 1943.

east-west flights were more difficult. But in July 1941 Liberators operated by British Overseas Airways Corporation commenced a return service, with six flights weekly to Montreal. Ferry pilots were by this means swiftly transported back across the Atlantic, and also RAF personnel for training as pilots in Canada, allowing disbandment of flying schools in this country, that at Prestwick closing in March 1941.

Work was commenced in extending Prestwick's main runway, to provide safe landing for pilots who were tired after a long transatlantic trip. By September 1941 it was ready, a concrete landing area 2,200 yards long and 100 yards wide; and a second runway of 1,500 yards was added in 1942. Four-engined bombers were now flown in directly from Montreal. Smaller planes refuelled at Gander – as on 8 August 1943 when the first Canadian-built Mosquito arrived after a record flight of 5 hours 37 minutes. Some planes were manned by RAF personnel, others by civilian crews of Air Transport Auxiliary and British Overseas Airways Corporation. Flights were organised by RAF Ferry Command (formed July 1941) which was incorporated in RAF Transport Command (March 1943). In the course of the war, 5,600 bombers for the RAF were brought into Prestwick, including Liberators which were adapted at Prestwick for Coastal Command operations against German U-boats. Also, after the USA entered the war, on 1 July 1942 there arrived at Prestwick the first of 12,357 aircraft for the US 8th Force – Dakotas, Mitchells, Liberators, and Flying Fortresses. At peak periods up to 300 planes arrived on a single day, and a record 7,847 landed during the month of August 1944. By that time, following invasion of Europe, Prestwick was handling also traffic in US casualties evacuated from the continent on their way home. It is estimated that altogether there were 37,000 aircraft movements through Prestwick between 1941 and 1945.

To direct the ever-increasing number of flights, the Transatlantic Area Control Centre was moved from Gloucester to Prestwick, acquiring Rebrae to set up an operations room which exercised by radio the direction of all aircraft flying over the North Atlantic. To handle movements in and out of Prestwick a new control tower was erected in August 1943, incongruously perched upon the roof of Orangefield House, whose interior was converted to become the terminal building of the aerodrome. On the opposite (northern) side of the runway, a US Air Force base was established in 1942, adjacent to the factory buildings of Scottish Aviation Ltd. In the early months of the war that firm's manufacturing work was rapidly expanded. To provide large-scale factory premises, the Palace of Engineering was in 1940 moved from Bellahouston Park near Glasgow, where it had been erected for the Empire Exhibition of 1938. It was dismantled and re-erected at Prestwick in less than four months. It was therefore available to service transatlantic ferry aircraft and to prepare incoming planes for their operational roles. By the end of the war Scottish Aviation Ltd occupied more than a million square feet of factory space, and employed a labour force of 6,000 – 3,203 males, 2,691 females, and 449 juveniles – servicing aircraft and manufacturing jigs, tools, and aircraft components.

Some disruption resulted from this massive expansion of Prestwick aerodrome to 631 acres, and the creation in September 1940 of a lesser Heathfield airfield which was used by RAF Fighter Command and later by the Fleet Air Arm. Westward extension of the main runway interfered with free flow of traffic on the main road passing from Monkton to Prestwick. Several minor roads were blocked, those from Monkton to Sandyford, Glenburn to Adamton, Prestwick to St Quivox – to compensate, a new road was opened in 1943 on behalf of the Air Ministry by Lord Sherwood, and named after him. Farmland was lost, Aikenbrae and Mid Sanquhar disappeared, and there was encroachment on St Cuthbert and St Ninian's golf courses. Into Prestwick flooded personnel based on or passing through the airport; in the streets of the town Scots voices were mingled with English, Canadian, and American accents. The Royal Hotel, though a fairly small establishment, provided billets for Poles, Czechs, Russians, French, Dutch, Norwegians, and Americans; for the proprietors William and May Bryce it was "like an Allied Family at times under one roof." Troops of a Polish unit were based in army huts near the Monkton shore, while Commandos exercised all along the Ayrshire beaches. Workers travelled in daily from other parts of Ayrshire to work in the Scottish Aviation factory, and some from further afield sought accommodation in the town. A civil defence census made in January 1942 found 12,000 living in the burgh, and, with 3,036 houses providing 11,505 rooms, there was obviously more overcrowding than appeared at the last official census in 1931. Two years later, by the end of 1943 the population was estimated as more than 12,500. The town clerk as Billeting Officer reported that in fifteen months accommodation had been found for 1,980 war workers and 400 American troops. There were then, in December 1943, more than 2,000

In 1940 the Palace of Engineering was transferred from Bellahouston to provide factory space for Scottish Aviation Ltd. (*KA*)

currently provided for. These comprised 591 male war workers with 255 wives and children; 224 female war workers; 67 BOAC and ATA personnel with 37 dependants; 213 from the RAF with 293 dependants; 27 from the army with 35 dependants; 362 men of the US forces and 3 dependants. Separately, under the evacuation scheme, there were 173 mothers and children in requisitioned houses and private households, nearly all being families of men serving overseas. All this caused inconvenience. As early as February 1941 there were protests to Sir Thomas Moore, the local MP, at "the inadequacy of the payment to householders who have members of the forces billeted on them", which included threepence for a tea and fivepence for a supper. But it was ruled that the billeting rates, whether for lodging or meals, were statutorily determined by Army and Air Force Acts, and could not be increased. In 1942 a Lodging Restrictions Order introduced compulsory billeting. This served only for workers at the aerodrome, so in 1942 one unfortunate miner at Glenburn could not find a room locally and had to cycle daily to and from Maybole. Travel of any kind was difficult. Those few who had private cars might obtain some petrol only for essential purposes. Trains were often cold and usually overcrowded: one student travelling home daily from Glasgow remembered that in the blackout "the trains were black in every sense – blue bulbs dimmed the carriages, blinds were drawn, and we were filthy from the sooty smells." There were long queues at bus stops and those buses passing though Prestwick to Glasgow and elsewhere were all too often already filled to capacity. Despite an appeal from the town council in 1943, Western SMT regretted it was impossible to reserve seats for the convenience of Prestwick passengers.

There was a range of minor inconveniences – the blackout (throughout the war); carrying of gas masks in little cardboard boxes (in the early years); testing of air raid sirens (weekly); rationing of food (from 1940) extended by a points system to clothing (1941) and other items (1942); introduction of double summer time (1941). More seriously, there was always concern for the safety of relatives who had been conscripted (or volunteered for service, especially in the RAF). Leisure time was curtailed by duties in the Home Guard or civil defence, by working on allotments and in other ways serving the war effort. One student remembers working on holiday as a labourer building the new main runway at the aerodrome; and at home only a bath of cold water to get rid of cement dust. His sister cycled daily to Hobsland farm to work as an unofficial land girl and able to augment her rations with fresh eggs. A "Dig for Victory" campaign launched in November 1940 was followed by closure of St Ninian's golf course for areas to be ploughed and cultivated; and some of the flower plots in the town were turned over to growing of vegetables. The town council showed concern (*AP* 31 July 1942) at depredations by children; when Provost Dunsmore suggested erecting a notice, Bailie Govan jocularly recommended it read "Please do not steal the beans and peas." Waste materials were rescued for salvage. During three months in 1942 as part of a national contest, Prestwick produced fifty-four tons of waste paper, which included fourteen tons collected by the high school. Money was raised for various good causes – victims of the Clydebank blitz, the War Relief Fund (1941), an ambulance to serve Prestwick and district (1942), Aid to Russia (1943), merchant navy comforts (1944). Throughout the war there were campaigns to encourage national savings – as the Spitfire Fund (1940); War Weapons (1941); Warships (1942); Wings for Victory (1943), Salute the Soldier (1944). In the Wings for Victory Week, for example, Prestwick's target was £76,000 and £84,751 was invested. Less spectacular but much appreciated were the efforts of local ladies who served on such bodies as the Women's Voluntary Service, Voluntary Aid Detachment, Red Cross, and the Prestwick and Monkton Works Depot which made garments and hospital supplies. Miss Anderson of the Homestead converted her home into a Forces Canteen and Rest Centre which catered for a quarter of a million servicemen throughout the war, and at one peak period served four thousand per week. WVS responsibilities included collecting in the town hall comforts for the forces, operating canteens in the South Church hall and Monkton, and distributing cod liver oil and fruit juices for young children at the Carvick Webster Hall in Monkton, the church hall in Alexandra Avenue, and St Ninian's clubhouse. Throughout the war, the churches provided spiritual comfort in difficult circumstances, and the schools were able to operate with the assistance of superannuated teachers and (for the first time) married women. It might be supposed that the established local youth organisations suffered because so many leaders were in the forces or on war work; but in fact they flourished. Their rolls were swollen with evacuee children, and evacuee teachers and a number of servicemen from local bases volunteered to help; as they did also in newly-formed organisations like the air training corps, army cadets, and sea cadets. Though the blackout posed difficulties, younger children like the Cubs met on Saturday mornings rather than Friday evenings; and the Scouts were able to overcome rationing and transport problems and (except for 1940) organise weekend camps and hold a summer camp at Straiton in 1944.

Polish War Memorial, later relocated at the RAFA Club at Stonegarth; their wartime camp at Monkton became a caravan park. (*KA*)

Most adult organisations, like the Cronies Club, continued functioning with restricted activities.

There was as elsewhere in Britain a wartime camaraderie. Members of the civil defence services cemented friendship in 1941 by the first of their annual suppers. Everyone listened to the BBC, and enjoyed the Brains Trust and Tommy Handley in ITMA while also keeping abreast of the war by the evening news broadcasts. From 1940 war commentaries by distinguised speakers were provided by the Ministry of Information and delivered to packed audiences in the Broadway Cinema on Sunday evenings. Throughout the war various local happenings are worthy of passing note. In February 1940 Sir Harry Lauder sang to a capacity audience in the Broadway to raise funds for evacuee schoolboys; in June, when Mussolini declared war on Britain, windows of Italian ice-cream shops were smashed; in July the town council provided relaxation for war workers by allowing Sunday play on the St Nicholas Ladies municipal golf course and the burgh putting green. In February 1941 there was indignation when it was revealed that the new council chambers in Links Road had cost a total of £8,176 to purchase, renovate, and furnish; a captured Junkers 88 bomber was displayed in Boydfield gardens. In February 1942 a proposal to move the mercat cross ten feet was refused authorisation; arrangements were made for removal of railings within the burgh to provide scrap iron for war industry. In March 1943 Sir Thomas Moore MP opened Britain's 2001st British Restaurant in the former United Services Club at Templerigg, with places for 250 diners. One day in October 1943 Clark Gable and Irving Berlin landed at Prestwick; and later Bob Hope gave three shows here (one in the Broadway cinema) on his way to entertain US troops in North Africa. When publicity was given to Prestwick aerodrome by the *Glasgow Herald* (29 Oct. 1943) and the BBC (Feb. 1944) there was alarm that it might attract German bomber attack. Tragically, there were victims of air accidents. One plane crashed at Whitletts in 1941 with twenty-two deaths, and another at Prestwick in 1944 when twenty-five were killed. Early on Monday morning 29 August 1944 a low-flying plane struck a chimney of No. 59 Berelands Road, hit No. 60, then crashed into Nos. 4 and 6 Hillside Avenue. Fortuitously, No. 4 was temporarily vacant, and eleven persons escaped from the others before all the houses were engulfed in flames. Four workers lodging in No. 6 were killed, and five-year-old Irene Haswell died on the way to hospital. Those twenty others who were crew and passengers on the plane also died. One eye-witness recalled the scene: "I was wakened by the loud roar of a low aircraft, looked out of my bedroom window and saw the plane skimming past the Laundry chimney. Dashing through to the back bedroom window I saw the horror of the flames where the plane had demolished the houses in Hillside Avenue." A month later there was a happier occasion, when Bailie James Dunlop's daughter arrived back in Prestwick. She had been on a physical education training course in Denmark when war broke out and unable to leave before Denmark was occupied by the Germans; in 1943 she and two other Scots girls escaped to Sweden and finally reached home in September 1944.

Throughout the war Prestwick town council, with eight Moderate and four

Labour members, played an important role in representing the efforts, the fears, and the aspirations of the community. In 1939 there was concern at the effect the war would have on the holiday trade upon which so many residents depended. Housing evacuees was much less profitable than taking in holidaymakers as boarders, and as so many of the former returned home, there were in the early months of 1940, while the phoney war continued, continued hopes of attracting visitors. The Bathing Lake remained open, and the Attractions committee planned the usual programme of galas there, engaged brass bands to play at Boydfield gardens, and renewed the franchise of taking photographs of holidaymakers on the esplanade. By 1941 the Attractions committee met less regularly for often there was "no business requiring the attention of this Committee". Yet throughout the war the Bathing Lake remained open, and there was a curtailed programme of swimming galas and band concerts. These served to refresh war workers and servicemen stationed locally and day visitors who could manage a trip to the coast. The council continued routine work, though it was difficult to complete partially-built houses because of shortage of materials and labour, and to maintain services when council workers were called up or volunteered – in February 1940 James Melrose and three others of Frank Pritty's staff enlisted in the Royal Engineers. Money was saved in cleansing when in January 1940 the arrangement with Ayr town council for disposal of refuse was terminated and tipping was commenced beside the north foreshore and at East Sanquhar farm. There was much additional work in organising billeting, fire-watching, salvage, allotments, constructing air raid shelters, cooperating with the county council in civil defence, planning and managing the British Restaurant. All such reponsibilities were initially handled by the Water, Drainage, and Public Health committee but a separate ARP committee had to be formed in November 1941. From time to time the council had to concern itself with matters of less consequence. Pollution of the Pow Burn was still a cause for complaint in 1940. Annually, tickets for free coal were distributed to necessitous persons, 120 of them in 1943. The council continued to collect feu duties on behalf of the freemen, and in 1943 handed over £3,200 received in coal royalties. In November 1942 after much discussion Mr William Hewitson was allowed access to the old burgh records. The Council for Encouragement of Music and the Arts was granted use of the town hall in May 1944 for two performanaces of "Mr Bolfry" by James Bridie, with a young actor called Duncan Macrae in the cast; and in August 1945 was paid £5 to stage an art exhibition in the North Church hall. In February 1945 the council was presented with a brass ladle which had belonged to Robert Manson, freeman. In April 1945 Provost Dunsmore suggested discussions with Ayr on possible amalgamation. Extension of the runway at the aerodrome required consent to closure of two roads and (until 1946) a right of way beyond Powmill Road. When St Cuthbert golf course was let for grazing of sheep the council protested in May 1941 at obstruction of "the Highlandman's Pad" leading from Kirk Street towards Orangefield; the secretary of the golf club denied it was a right of way; claiming that the said Highlander was a gardener who lived in a cottage near the Orangefield byre at the foot of Kirk Street and used this path on tolerance; it was added that "There are other interesting facts in connection with the matter, but these need not be gone into meantime, more especially during the war when everyone's rights, real or imaginary, are more or less restricted". Rights of way would continue as a vexed issue in Prestwick.

Councillors felt obliged to involve themselves in numerous activities associated with the war effort – the series of national savings campaigns, charitable concerts, church parades, and the like. Since elections were suspended for the duration of the war, there was no respite, and they were all older men, as were those five who were coopted to replace casual vacancies caused by death or resignation. There were obvious signs of stress. In November 1941 when the provost and magistrates were reappointed en bloc, two councillors who objected walked out. Provost Ferguson who had earlier planned to resign from the council did so in April 1942 along with Bailie Boylan Smith. Robert H. Dunsmore, appointed provost in May 1942, continued in that office till after the war. Some of the burgh officials had to be replaced. The burgh prosecutor Stephen Cosh died in November 1939. William Shaw, the town clerk, died in April 1944, and the council in an obituary appreciation noted that his work was always "meticulous" and that he was "an authority on the ancient history and customs of this town and had a unique knowledge in all things pertaining to the freedoms of the burgh." Frank Pritty, since 1913 serving as burgh surveyor, water engineer, and sanitary inspector, soldiered on in this full-time post until he died, aged sixty, in February 1946. Because of the increased volume of local authority work, the vacant post of town clerk was converted into a full-time appointment. John L. Jones, 35-year-old depute town clerk of Kilmarnock was in June 1944 selected, by Provost Dunsmore's casting vote, and engaged on an annual salary of £600 rising to £800. Before the end of the year his recommendations were accepted for reorganisation of committees with precise definition of their responsibilities – finance, housing, public health, streets and planning, parks and recreation, and war emergency services, which last disappeared a year later, when recreations were transferred to an entertainments committee.

People anticipated a better postwar world as early as 1942 when the Beveridge Plan proposed a welfare state based upon social security; and as the war advanced local authorities commenced preparing for the future. After initial reverses the tide of war began to turn with the US naval victory at Midway in the Pacific (June 1942), the British victory at El Alamein in Egypt (October 1942) and the Russian recovery of Stalingrad (January 1943). Troops trained in this area left the Clyde in December 1942 to land in North Africa and thereafter invade Italy. In June 1944 those landings were made in Normandy which would lead to the liberation of Europe and German capitulation in May 1945. In November 1942 Prestwick town council appointed a committee to prepare plans for postwar development of the burgh. Between 1925 and 1939 the council had built 326 houses, and it was possible to complete 32 which were under construction when the war began. In December 1942 it was estimated that 205 houses were required in addition to those 142 whose construction had been postponed because of the war. In September 1943 thirty acres off Adamton Road were earmarked for building and in March 1944 the council was authorised to begin advanced site preparation. The council was promised, in November 1944, 85 temporary houses and, in April 1945, 50 Swedish timber houses. But there were lengthy delays. It was November 1945 before work commenced on 144 houses at Marchburn. Delivery of 82 prefabricated aluminium houses was scheduled later that month for erection on the south side of St Quivox Road; and it was expected that the 50 Swedish houses would be put up in December between Wellington and Waterloo Roads. There were 500 applicants on the waiting list for council houses.

Towards the end of 1944 things began to wind down on the home front, except in London which was now subjected to attack by flying bombs. Here in September 1944 the evacuation scheme was terminated; in December fireguard duties were abandoned. In February 1945 the wardens posts were closed; in May the Civil Defence services were disbanded and the Home Guard stood down; in September the billeting office and the fire station both closed. Defeat of Germany in May was celebrated by a short service of thanksgiving at Boydfield gardens, then dancing in the streets. In June the town council planned its first water trip since 1939; and permitted a showground to be held between Crandleyhill Road and Waterloo Road. To raise funds for Prestwick Welcome Home and War Commemoration Fund, a Welcome Home Week was held in July. A four-day garden fete and fancy fair in Boydfield Gardens was organised by the WVS and opened by Mrs R.L.Angus of Ladykirk; elsewhere there were bowling, swimming, and pin-up girl competitions; dancing nightly in the town hall and in the open air at Grangemuir Road. Organised dancing was continued throughout July and August, and an estimated ten thousand persons participated. Eventually just over £5,000 was raised, and ten per cent of this would be devoted to refurbishing the war memorial and adding 64 names to the roll of 113 who had fallen in the earlier world war. The Welcome Home fund did not reach its anticipated target, for there was some uncertainty about how the money raised should be expended, and apparent overlapping with other funds already established in Prestwick, Glenburn, Prestwick Toll, and Monkton which provided comforts for the troops, distributed gifts to prisoners of war who had returned home, and continued to do so to other servicemen when they were demobilised. The war came to end in August with the surrender of Japan. There was spontaneous rejoicing, more dancing in the streets, and bonfires. American troops organised an impromptu victory parade. With assorted musical instruments and drums, the GIs marched from Adamton into Ayr, and were brought back by trucks at five o' clock next morning.

When the Americans left in October 1945 the future of Prestwick was uncertain. Could it survive as an airport? David McIntyre had in the thirties envisaged a major aiport located in central Scotland, near Glasgow and Edinburgh. When Prestwick began to expand he became convinced that this should after the war become an international civil airport. In August 1942, in his capacity as manager of Scottish Aviation Ltd he submitted to the Air Ministry his plans for such an airport. There would be a main runway of four miles extending to the shore where a marine base would handle flying boats; a secondary runway towards Heathfield; a new terminal with control tower, reception area, hotel; and an integrated railway station and freight depot. The plan was approved by the Scottish Council for Industry which was that year set up by Tom Johnston, Secretary of State for Scotland in the wartime government. Tom Johnston, himself supportive of Prestwick, recommended that Scottish Aviation Ltd should become a public utility company to own, manage, and develop Prestwick. In November 1943 when Lord Sherwood, Under Secretary of State for Air, opened the new road at Glenburn he declared that it had already been "proved that this was one of the great airports of the world" but what the future held it would be "inopportune" for him to intimate.

When a Ministry of Civil Aviation was formed in October 1944 the future of Prestwick was in the balance, as was that of Scottish Aviation Ltd whose activities embraced airport control, airline operation, and aircraft manufacture. Early in 1945 Lord Swinton as minister decided to construct a main international airport near London, and a grass field at Heath Row was selected. British Overseas Airways Corporation, formed in 1939, was to be joined by British European Airways, with prospects for private operators uncertain. British refusal to subscribe to international civil aviation agreements formulated at Chicago in November 1944 left foreign airlines uncertain if they could use Prestwick. In the meantime there were public meetings on the future of the airport, held in Prestwick (December 1944) and in Ayr (February 1945). At the Prestwick meeting, Sir William Darling as chairman of the Scottish Council on Industry emphasised that "it must remain the cross-roads of the world's airways if Scotland was to get its full share of post-war prosperity." There were debates in parliament in February, March, and April, and private meetings with Lord Swinton, at which MPs of all parties urged support for Prestwick, led by Sir Thomas Moore (Conservative, Ayr Burghs) and Alexander Sloan (Labour, South Ayrshire). In March, debating the government white paper on civil aviation, Sir Stafford Cripps as Minister of Aircraft Production announced that "One cannot afford to have more than really first-class airport. As the House knows, it has been decided that the Heathrow Aerodrome, which is in course of construction and will cost a very large sum of money, is to be utilised as the main central Transatlantic airport of this country". Prestwick, like other airfields, might be used if and when Heathrow was not available. In May the war coalition was dissolved and, until a general election could be held, Churchill continued as prime minister of a Conservative "caretaker" government. In June it announced that "Pending the completion of Heathrow and its use as the main international terminal in the United Kingdom, the Government will arrange that British land-based aircraft in passage to and from Canada and the United States shall stop to pick up and set down at Prestwick." There was an addendum: "Even when Heathrow is in operation, Prestwick will continue to be designated, which will enable air lines of any nationality to pick up and set down passengers and freight at Prestwick." Later that month, on 27 June 1945 Prestwick town council paid tribute to Group Captain David F. McIntyre and the Duke of Hamilton by conferring upon them the freedom of the burgh "in appreciation of their achievements and of their foresight and acumen in founding the Prestwick Airport".

David F. McIntyre and the Duke of Hamilton were in 1945 awarded the freedom of the burgh. (*JH*)

The Labour government under Clement Attlee which took office in August discussed at cabinet level in October the status of Prestwick airport. Lord Winster, Minister of Civil Aviation, wished to depart from the terms of the June statement, to the disadvantage of Prestwick. Tom Fraser, Scottish Office Under-Secretary of State, pointed out in a confidential memorandum: "Prestwick was selected and has maintained its position throughout the war as the main airport in this country for trans-Atlantic traffic. The undertaking given by the Caretaker Government ... implicitly recognised this and was regarded in Scotland as providing a reasonable working arrangement. If the proposal now submitted by the Minister – as it seems to imply – means that on operational grounds the undertaking may not be implemented, then Scottish people, without distinction of Party, will not readily appreciate why the airport should suddenly be found operationally unsuitable unless more convincing reasons than have yet been adduced are in evidence." Following debate in parliament, Lord Winster met a deputation, promised that Prestwick would not be shut down, and that even after Heathrow was ready, Prestwick would be available for such operators as wished to use it. This ended the period of uncertainty, when some airlines initiating services between New York and London (which they could not reach directly), were touching down at Shannon in the Irish Free State rather than at Prestwick. In November Lord Winster announced that BOAC was to introduce a transatlantic service via Prestwick. In December the Ministry of Civil Aviation announced compulsory purchase of Scottish Aviation's holding and on 1 April 1946 Prestwick was designated as an International Airport.

CHAPTER THIRTEEN

The Mid 20th Century

*T*HE end of the war was officially marked by Victory Day celebrations on Saturday 8 June 1946. In Prestwick each child was presented as a souvenir with a kind of "ration book" containing vouchers allowing admission to a film show, bathing gala, other beach facilities, and one free ice cream. There were inter-school sports, a fancy dress parade, performances by the Cadet Pipe Band, bonfires, and a carnival dance in the town hall. Such an event momentarily brightened the period of austerity which marked the post-war years. Rationing continued; indeed from 1946 until 1948 bread was added to the list; other items would be removed in 1948, 1950, and 1953; but not till July 1954 could ration books be discarded. The other continuing shortage was of housing, which made things difficult for those 500 applicants who in 1945 were on the burgh's waiting list for council houses.

Prestwick town council at the end of the war comprised eight Moderates (five of whom had been co-opted to fill casual vacancies) and four Labour members. Following Labour victory in the General Election of July 1945 and the formation of a government under Attlee, local supporters anticipated similar gains at the first post-war municipal election in November. In fact two seats were lost, and among the Moderates elected was Mrs Annie Crawford, Prestwick's first lady councillor. A year later Bailie Dougan lost his seat after sixteen years' service, leaving Gilbert Steele as Labour's sole representative. Older councillors were steadily being replaced. Typical was James Dunlop who died in 1946 in his 79th year. A noted breeder of Ayrshire cattle, he came from Fenwick to Prestwick in 1933 and became a councillor in his retirement. An obituary notice described him: "His dress and outlook were both those of the countryman, and his pawky, knowledgeable speeches were characteristic of the older type of Scots farmer." Another stalwart was Bailie Govan, who retired from the council in 1946 after more than twenty years, and was to be honoured with the freedom of the burgh, but he died in January 1947. Local government was in process of change. To increase popular involvement, from 1945 the franchise was extended from ratepayers to all adults, and municipal elections, held annually in November until 1947, were transferred to May in and after 1949. Throughout the fifties, candidates in Ward One were returned unopposed on seven occasions, and eight times in Ward Four. By contrast, there were always contests in the other two wards, except 1957 in Ward Two. These elections were fiercely fought, there was a high turnout of electors (sometimes more than 60%), and often the result was a close one. In 1949 Labour recovered one seat and a third in 1954, but the council continued to be dominated by Moderates, with a few who preferred to be known as Independents. In 1947 when Provost Dunsmore retired, they chose as his successor Frank M. Milligan, a 64-year-old veteran of the Boer war described as a "delightful Irishman". Provost Milligan presided over a council which he described as "made up of young men" who formed "an excellent cross-section of the community". On the council, as in the elections, personal worth was respected despite political differences. So in 1954 Gilbert Steele, representing Ward Two for Labour since 1938, was appointed provost. Like all the others he was an incomer, a former professional footballer who found work at Glenburn and Mossblown pits, and after forty years in Prestwick he was accepted as "almost a native". He was followed in 1957 by John Kerr, an oil company representative; and in 1960 by William S. Moir who was a grocer.

The council, meeting since 1941 in their grand new municipal chambers in Links Road, had their dignity further enhanced in 1948. When Frank Milligan became provost in 1947, his friend R.R.Stalker of Broughty Ferry suggested a chain of office should be acquired. His donation of ten guineas was supplemented by even more generous contributions from local gentlemen, so that provost, magistrates, and town clerk could be appropriately attired for ceremonial occasions. Henceforth provosts would appear in a robe of scarlet trimmed with white fur and ermine tails, and a chain of office bearing the burgh arms. The four magistrates were similarly robed in purple, and the town clerk in a wig and gown. These robes, presented to the civic chiefs in the Queen's Hotel in November 1948, would be worn on 3 July 1956 when there was a royal tour of nine Ayrshire burghs. Queen Elizabeth and the Duke of Edinburgh arrived from Kilmarnock in a gleaming maroon Rolls Royce car to be greeted outside the Burgh Chambers by Provost Gilbert Steele. 800 local school children were given pride of place among the assembled crowd of spectators. Overhead a Prestwick Twin Pioneer plane gave a special salute. After magistrates and several others were presented, portraits and visitors' book were signed, and the royal party sped on towards Ayr. A few months earlier one councillor had proposed to revive "the old custom of ringing curfew at 7 a.m. and 6 p.m." but no action was taken, so the bell on the Freemen's Hall remained silent. In 1955 the mercat cross was officially designated as an ancient monument, but £160 on conservation work could not be spared. However in that year the burgh coat of arms was re-matriculated, with addition of a motto suggested by Rev. Donald M. Caskie – "Loyalty, Vigilance, Foresight".

In the difficult years after the war, the council had to attend to those environmental services which had of necessity been neglected in wartime – water, drainage, streets, and lighting. Scarce materials and available labour were devoted to pushing forward the housing programme. The burgh was restricted to a fixed quota of houses, and private building was limited. In 1948 there were ten local building firms and others in ancillary trades – 7 joiners, 8 plumbers and slaters, 4 electricians, 12 painters, 1 plasterer, 4 contractors. The housing problem was a main concern of the town council. In 1945 there were 358 council houses; in the next few years progress was slow; in 1948 there were still only 432. Thereafter the building programme accelerated, especially after 1952 when controls were lifted.

Between 1948 and 1961 there were constructed 230 council houses and 475 new private houses. At the latter date the burgh contained 862 council houses and 3,231 others, a total of 4,093. But there remained a severe housing shortage. In 1961 there were 550 names on the council waiting list. The Census Report of 1961 revealed the extent of the problem. In the previous ten years burgh population had increased from 11,387 to 12,562. There were now 4,093 households, but 234 families (nearly 6%) were living in shared dwellings. There were few houses to rent, and small houses of two apartments with kitchen and WC were fetching £1,600, twice what they cost in Ayr and four times as much as in Kilmarnock. Some families (54) were able to rent rooms in the 2,379 owner-occupied houses which formed 58% of the total in the town. Most found lodgings with tenants of the 518 privately-rented houses (126) or as sub-tenants in houses belonging to the town council (47) or the coal board (7). For the burgh as a whole in 1961 the number of persons per room (0.8) was bettered only by Troon (0.77) and Largs (0.72). But Ward Two could only equal the county average (0.91). If census figures are scrutinised more closely, it becomes evident that 14% of all Prestwick households were then overcrowded with more than 1.5 persons per room. Around a hundred families were living in single rooms, most of them in other people's houses, a score in caravans, and there remained eleven old single-end dwellings. All houses in the burgh were now supplied with piped water, but 327 lacked a hot water tap, 415 were without a fixed bath, and 14 had no water closet. Apart from those 234 families living with others, there were 259 other households where lavatories had to be shared with neighbours, and nine older houses with communal cold water taps.

Because there were so many applicants for council houses, in 1947 a points system had to be introduced, and apparent anomalies caused vexation for dissatisfied applicants, and heated debate at council meetings. Ex-servicemen might expect priority, but some civilians had undertaken work as important for the war effort. Residents of long standing should have precedence, but what of natives returning from war work elsewhere, or incomers who were key-workers in local industry? How should choice be made between a large family in overcrowded conditions and a smaller family in worse circumstances in an unfit house? As one councillor put it in 1947, "It would take a Solomon to create a system that would give fairness and satisfaction to everyone." In 1948 when the council granted a vacant house to a new employee, seven hundred protesters attended a town hall meeting, and the housing convener (who agreed with them) resigned from the council. Finance was another sore point concerning council housing at a time when costs were escalating. Tenants were faced with bigger rent bills. In 1948 charges were increased to £21 for a house of two apartments and £36 for one of five apartments. When tenants found difficulty in paying, an "iron fist" collection policy was introduced, so that by 1957 there was a no-arrears record. Among others there was complaint that council houses were being subsidised by the rates.

Until 1957 rates were levied on owners and occupiers of property; thereafter only on occupiers. By 1960 the burgh rate was 17s 6d in the £ plus one shilling water rate. The rateable value of the burgh was now around £155,000. Annual expenditure by the town council was £94,000, the county requisition had risen to a massive £202,000, there were government grants amounting to £141,000. Of outlays by the town council, environmental services required £59,000 (in thousands of pounds, for water, 10; lighting, 7; cleansing, 22; sewers, 4; public health, 2; streets, 14). Some other services cost £22,000 (for parks, 13; bathing lake, 2; miscellanous items, 7). Housing required £13,000 from the rates. To effect economies a Special Committee on Administration and Finance was formed.

The council met one evening each month except August. It is said that the town clerk John L. Jones could write the minutes in advance, for at the committee meetings on previous Tuesday evenings all councillors were members and there made decisions which normally had only to be ratified at the subsequent full council meeting. Of the six committees, that of finance was of increased importance and its convener was designated as Treasurer following upon the Local Government Act of 1947. That act also authorised an annual allowance for the provost, initially of £150. This enabled the provost, among other things, occasionally to entertain councillors and officials, a fitting reward for their work, supplementing the water trip which was reintroduced after the war.

Management of the burgh was in the hands of full-time officials and their staff. In 1947, the town clerk and the burgh chamberlain each required three assistants; the burgh surveyor needed five; and a burgh factor had to be employed to look after the council houses. In 1945 Frank Pritty, burgh surveyor since 1913, died at the age of sixty. He was remembered as "a notable figure in the daily life of Prestwick ... played a prominent part in the making of the Prestwick we know today". He was replaced by James Melrose, who was appointed as Pritty's deputy in 1938 and returned in 1945 after war service. In 1954 the town clerk John L. Jones resigned and went off to Canada; Allan Inglis came from Milngavie to fill the post. When James A. Kinghorn died in 1956, Lewis D. Stewart came from Newmilns as burgh chamberlain. In the same year the burgh officer James Hoy retired after twenty-four years' service and his successor George Craig was fitted out with the customary working dress, ceremonial uniform, and a bicycle.

The holiday trade suffered during the war, and from 1945 efforts were made to revive Prestwick's attractions, though no major expenditure on improvements could as yet be contemplated. Indeed in 1947 the town council considered selling off the town hall and even proposed amalgamation with Ayr. Yet it proved possible to repair the sea wall and other areas which had been ravaged when armed forces practised beach landings. The Bathing Lake was reinstated, and a programme of galas organised. The council made arrangements most years for boat hiring, pony rides, Punch-and-Judy shows, taking photographs, motor cycle races on the north shore, publication of a burgh guide; and sometimes for a model railway, roller skating, summer shows in the town hall. In 1948 £800 was expended to institute an annual Bathing Beauty contest. In the summer of 1950 weekly competitions in putting, golf, bowling, and tennis were sponsored, and the sea front was illuminated; in 1953 an Information Kiosk was set up in Boydfield gardens. To cater for an increased number of private motorists, the car park on the north

LAW'S MOTOR TOURS

WEEK COMMENCING SUNDAY, 16th MAY 1948

	Leaving at	Returning at	Fare
SUNDAY, 16th—			
Ballantrae	2.15 p.m.	7.00 p.m.	5/-
Straiton Circular	7.15 p.m.	9.30 p.m.	3/-
MONDAY, 17th—			
Southern Highlands	2.15 p.m.	7.00 p.m.	6/6
Turnberry Circular	7.15 p.m.	9.30 p.m.	3/-
TUESDAY, 18th—			
Ballantrae	2.15 p.m.	7.00 p.m.	5/-
Mauchline Circular	7.15 p.m.	9.30 p.m.	3/-
THURSDAY, 19th—			
Village of Barr	2.00 p.m.	6.00 p.m.	4/-
Clyde Coast	2.15 p.m.	7.00 p.m.	6/6
Dundonald Circular	7.15 p.m.	9.30 p.m.	3/-
FRIDAY, 20th—			
Southern Highlands	2.15 p.m.	7.00 p.m.	6/6
Portencross	2.15 p.m.	6.00 p.m.	4/-
Turnberry Circular	7.15 p.m.	9.30 p.m.	3/-

BUSES LEAVE FROM FOUNTAIN. TOP OF SANDGATE

Seats booked at STANCE or LAW'S GARAGE. PRESTWICK TOLL.   Phone 7669

Bus tours in 1948 continued popular with visitors.

esplanade was extended. In 1955 there was an ambitious plan to introduce major improvements at the beach, in three phases over the next seven years, to cost £40,000 in all. A preliminary to this project was removal of sand dunes at the north shore; which left that area somewhat spoiled when current government restrictions on local authority borrowing meant that the expensive scheme for beach improvement had to be shelved. There were those in the council who were quite pleased

Air Cruises
OVER
Firth of Clyde
FROM
PRESTWICK AIRPORT
Starting 11th JULY.

TUES. — WED. — SUN.

Fare, 30s.   Children, 15s

BOOK NOW WITH
SCOTTISH AIRLINES
PRESTWICK AIRPORT
Phone 7281
Or Your Local Travel Agent.

Air trips for visitors in 1948.

at this, wishing for economy on such things as developing recreational facilities and planting of tulip bulbs in the town's flower borders, objecting to the cost of the bathing beauty contests, restricting the summer programme of music to the Prestwick Youth Pipe Band, divided over allowing a fairground on the north esplanade and circus performances at Prestwick Toll. Expenditure on holiday attractions was particularly resented by residents in Ward One who were most incommoded by summer crowds. The seat for that ward was uncontested from 1946 until 1954, but in 1955, 1956, and 1960 retiring members were ousted by Independent candidates pledged to oppose "unwarrantable expenditure". In 1960 there was formed a Prestwick Citizens Association, succeeding the Ratepayers Association which had lapsed in 1952. In 1960 the council hired consultants who made a seven-month study of organisation, methods and work, and recommended cutting staff for a saving of over £6,000.

The population of 11,386 in 1951 was reckoned to rise beyond 20,000 at the height of summer. There was now much less letting of private houses to summer visitors, but more villas were converted into boarding houses and hotels. There were fifteen of these in 1951, the largest providing twenty-four bedrooms. Six were licensed to dispense alcoholic drink, while in the rest of the town there were only four public houses and four licensed grocers. There was more generous provision of other refreshments in seven restaurants and ten cafes selling ice cream and fish and chips. For visitors and residents Prestwick was a good shopping centre. There were (in 1951) for foodstuffs 26 grocers, 11 butchers, 9 bakers, 7 dairies, 6 fruiterers, 6 confectioners, 4 fishmongers; for dress goods 13 drapers, 7 shoemakers, 1 wool shops, 1 tailor; 11 hairdressers; 8 newsagents; there were also 3 shops selling china, 2 hardware, 2 jewellery, 2 antiques. All six of Scotland's national banks which then existed had branches in the town, as well as the Glasgow Savings Bank. The Post Office also operated a savings bank, and in 1954 a Sub Post office was opened in Berelands Road. But while the town remained busy in summer, things were changing in all the Ayrshire holiday resorts. In the fifties and afterwards more people were taking charter flights for holidays abroad. The Ayrshire coast remained popular for day trips, by train, buses, and increasingly by private cars. A census of traffic at Glasgow Fair in 1955 recorded in one hour 1,300 vehicles crawling through Prestwick. The *Prestwick Standard* in 1958 reported on "the seriousness of Prestwick's traffic problems", noticing that "rarely a weekend passes without scapes or collisions of varying seriousness". That year the police introduced radar traps to cut down speeding and the town council helped through an active Road Safety committee and improved street lighting. Yet in December 1959 there were twelve road accidents, with two deaths. In 1960 the Easter weekend brought first of a series of traffic jams; in June there were frequent and lengthy delays when jet planes practising landings held up traffic on the road crossing the airport runway; at the end of the Glasgow Fair in July vehicles returning home took fifty minutes to travel from Ayr through Prestwick. Partial relief came with opening in 1961 of a dual carriageway from Monkton to Whitletts as first stage of a Prestwick-Ayr by-pass.

Life in the postwar years was in many ways affected by the innovations of the Labour government under Attlee (1945–51), creating nationalised industries and a welfare state, which were maintained during the subsequent Conservative administrations of Churchill (1951–55), Eden (1955–57) and Macmillan (1957–63). The National Health Service was established in 1948, involving Prestwick's 6 general practitioners, 4 dentists, 6 chemists, and one optician. In the same year the Ministry of National Insurance extended its scope, and a National Assistance Board removed from local authorities administration of what had once been called poor relief. There was nationalisation of the railways (1948), fire service (1948), electricity (1948) and gas (1949). Of special local impact was nationalisation of the coal industry. During and after the war there was great demand for coal. Production at Glenburn was sometimes interrupted by strikes. From 1944 until 1946 there were disputes between miners and the owners, Bairds and Dalmellington Ltd, over payments for working dirty coal (seams where the coal was interspersed with layers of dirt). On 1 January 1947 the National Coal Board took over, and its flag was raised at Glenburn by 76-year-old James Johnson. One incidental consequence of nationalisation was that a lump sum had to be paid by the NCB to the Prestwick freemen to compensate for their loss of royalties. Thereafter they relied on those miscellaneous feu duties which the town council collected on their behalf. In 1954 these were purchased by the Prestwick Investment Trust. The freemen, who until then were registered in town council minutes when they entered their freedoms, in 1955 lost their identity as such, and so ended a tradition of seven centuries. Glenburn, under Coal Board management from 1947, was one of the most productive of Ayrshire's thirty-six pits. Working beneath a large part of the parish and under the sea, by 1950 there was an annual output of around 230,000 tons of coal, mainly for industrial use. About 700 men were then employed. 180 of them lived in Glenburn and Prestwick, where there were another 106 miners who worked at Mossblown. The Coal Board, with its area headquarters initially in Ayr, had one of its three sub-area offices at Glenburn. Company-owned houses became NCB property, and those at Glenburn required renovation. Electricity was installed to supplement the unsatisfactory supply of gas. It even proved possible to erect some new houses. But there were problems for the NCB. Industrial disputes continued: at Glenburn there were twenty stoppages in the first five months of 1948. And the NCB shared responsibility for continued pollution of the Pow Burn, caused by washings from Glenburn colliery, effluent from the county council's sewage plant at Mossblown, and discharges of oil from the airport.

Prestwick was designated as an International Airport on 1 April 1946. Before the end of that year five airlines inaugurated regular transatlantic services using Prestwick as a convenient staging point. First, commencing in May, was KLM Dutch Airlines; followed in June by Trans Canada Airlines; then in July Scandinavian Airlines System and British Overseas Airways Corporation; and in October American Overseas Airlines, which later became Pan American. Continental and internal flights were introduced by Air France, Norwegian Airlines, British European Airways, and Scottish Aviation Ltd. By 1948 there was a daily arrival and departure

AIR TRAVEL
Single Fares from Prestwick

Paris	£16	0	0
Amsterdam	£14	0	0
Athens	£58	10	0
Alexandria	£73	0	0
New York	£81	8	0
Reykjavik	£25	14	0
Copenhagen	£20	19	0
Johannesburg	£172	13	0
Australia	£277	8	0
Brussels	£15	13	0
Zurich	£24	0	0
Cyprus	£74	0	0
Cairo	£75	0	0
Montreal	£77	18	0
Oslo	£20	19	0
Geneva	£23	0	0
Rome	£37	8	0
New Zealand	£264	8	0

FOR DETAILS and RESERVATIONS
Apply to:—

Scottish Aviation
Limited
Prestwick Airport. Phone 7281

Prestwick was designated an international airport in 1946, and two years later offered a wide variety of flights.

THE PUBLIC ENCLOSURE, PRESTWICK AIRPORT:

The busy airport attracted spectators. (*JH*)

of about thirty aircraft, and about 2,000 passengers passed through weekly. For that entire year there were 5,400 arriving and 5,429 departing planes; 19,995 passengers arriving and 27,703 departing; 100,988 pounds of mail and 438,721

Until a bypass was opened in 1962, traffic on the main road was held up whenever planes landed or took off. (*KA*)

pounds of other freight brought in, 39,373 pounds of mail and 467,610 pounds of other freight taken away. Increased traffic brought risks. On 20 October 1948 a KLM Constellation on its approach to the airport crashed at Auchenweet farm between Mauchline and Tarbolton where forty lives were lost. Then on Christmas day 1954 a BOAC Stratocruiser crashed beside the airport runway and twenty-eight died.

Prestwick had become one of the world's busiest airports. To cope with the volume of traffic, extension of runways was undertaken. The wartime secondary runway was unsatisfactory because it crossed the main runway; various alternatives were considered and rejected, and long delays when nothing seemed to being done. The local Prestwick Airport Consultative Committee was frustrated at its lack of powers, and the Ministry of Civil Aviation appeared to be giving priority to expanding Heathrow and planning a second London airport, which would open at Gatwick in 1958. The line of a new second runway for Prestwick was eventually decided in 1953. This was to run south towards Heathfield, and involved revision of Prestwick town council's housing plans, reduction of the Glenburn bing, and closure of the railway from there to Mossblown. This second runway was opened for use on 31 September 1955. The main runway was provided with an improved surface, but still crossed by the A77 road, so that whenever planes were landing or taking off, traffic was halted at traffic lights. In 1954 it was planned to provide a tunnel under the runway; in 1958 the alternative of a loop road was proposed, to the consternation of Monkton residents who objected to losing their direct route into Prestwick, as occurred when that loop road was eventually opened in 1964.

Scottish Aviation Ltd, the company which had pioneered the airport, in 1946 had to hand over its land and buildings to the Ministry of Civil Aviation, who established their Scottish headquarters in Adamton House, which had been requisitioned early in the war. Their compulsory purchase of the airport was followed by long arguments as to price, and not till 1953 was settlement reached, with the company awarded £450,000 and a 99-year lease of the premises they occupied. SAL (as the company became commonly known) had other difficulties to surmount. David McIntyre as managing director had the noble vision of establishing SAL as a major international airline and in 1945 chose from Robert Burns the motto "The World O'er" to accompany the company's new coat of arms. To operate in this sphere, SAL formed a subsidiary company called Scottish Airlines. In 1946 when SAL had to relinquish control over the airport it had managed so efficiently during the war, it hoped to develop the airline as its principal enterprise. It purchased Liberators, Dakotas, and other planes for conversion to civil use and formed a fleet of twenty aircraft. But that was the year when the government nationalised Britain's scheduled air services, granting monopoly to BOAC, BEA, and British South American Airways. As a result SAL was not allowed to operate scheduled services in its own right. It was however able to obtain contracts with these companies to provide services which they could not as yet themselves undertake; it established air services in various European countries until local operators could take over; it offered charter flights and set up travel agencies; it handled freight traffic through its subsidiary Scottish Air Express Limited. Scottish Airlines also supplied aircraft for a Pakistan airlift in 1947, the Berlin airlift of 1948, and for troop carrying on various occasions. Independent operators were in 1949 offered opportunity to operate certain scheduled services, a facility extended by the Conservative government after 1951. BEA granted Scottish Airlines a franchise to operate on several internal routes. Nevertheless, the number of passengers carried on Scottish Airlines dropped from 44,000 (1947) to 30,000 (1952) and 24,000 (1954). The Liberators were withdrawn from service in 1950, most of the Dakotas in 1952, and the Avro Yorks which replaced them proved unreliable. By 1956 SAL was in financial difficulties. On 7 December 1957 David McIntyre was killed in Libya on a demonstration flight, and with the loss of his driving force Scottish Airlines could not long continue. At the end of 1958 the trooping and freight contracts came to an end. One Dakota remained in use. It operated a seasonal scheduled service to the Isle of Man until September 1960. On 9 November 1960 a flight from Belfast ended the fifteen years' career of Scottish Airlines. There also came to an end in 1960 those pleasure flights over the Firth of Clyde from Prestwick which SAL had advertised since 1947, and which latterly were provided by an independent operator, Louie Wood in his 8-seater

From 1946 until 1960 Scottish Airlines operated "the World O'er", here taking up passengers in Pakistan. (*JH*)

Rapide plane. Such flights were no longer practicable for an international airport handling jet planes.

What had been ancillary work now became Scottish Aviation Ltd's principal business. During the war, servicing and conversion of aircraft had expanded to employ more than 6,000 workers by 1944. Cancellation of government contracts reduced the labour force to 1,750 in 1948. SAL was forced to diversify into building buses. But plans were then being implemented to commence a more appropriate enterprise, the construction of a new type of aircraft. The Prestwick Pioneer was designed in 1946 for SAL by Robert McIntyre (no relation of the managing director) who came to Prestwick in 1942 with twenty years' experience in the aircraft industry. This small plane, to carry a pilot and four passengers, was primarily intended for military use. Its engine and metal body had to be sturdy enough for work in difficult conditions, and capable of being easily maintained and repaired. A special requirement was the ability to operate on rough ground and landing strips only one hundred yards long – the Pioneer could land in twenty-six yards. With its steep angles of approach and climb, and able to manoeuvre at speeds of less than forty miles per hour, it could operate within very confined spaces, and would prove ideal for RAF operations in Malaya. A prototype took to the air in 1947. In 1953 the RAF took delivery of their first Pioneer and purchased forty of the fifty-eight manufactured over the next ten years. In 1955 a larger twin-engined version was designed, for a crew of two and sixteen passengers, suitable for short-range inter-city trips or for under-developed areas with small airfields. This Twin Pioneer made its first flight in 1955, when it proved possible to land in sixty yards. But there were difficulties. The earliest version was underpowered. Metal fatigue contributed to several crashes, most notably that of the Twin Pioneer on a demonstration tour in Libya, in which David McIntyre lost his life. By the end of 1958 seventy Twin Pioneers had been sold, too few to show profit, and there were poor prospects for further orders. In the last three months of 1958 SAL had to dismiss around 400 workers, and for those 1,950 remaining there was threat of closure at the beginning of 1959. SAL was heavily in debt to the Finance Corporation for Industry, which had invested £3million in the Twin Pioneer. Fortunately it was possible to maintain a reduced production programme (by 1963 a total of 87 Twin Pioneers had been sold); and contracts were obtained for servicing aircraft and aero engines. In 1961 just over 1,000 were engaged in aircraft manufacture and repair, and among another 1,450 working at the airport a proportion were employed in SAL's subsidiary enterprises. Scottish Air Express Limited, formed in 1946, continued to handle freight for most of the airlines operating through Prestwick, and indeed established air freight branches at other airports. In 1954 the travel agencies which had been part of Scottish Airlines were taken over; in 1958 the firm began dealing with freight by land and sea, and changed its name to Scottish Express. SAL was also involved in catering since the days it arranged meals and accommodation for its trainee pilots; its Airport Hotel in Orangefield House was busy throughout the war and afterwards. Its restaurant – providing a twenty-four hours' service – gained an international reputation, which an American visitor contrasted with "service at London airport, which is

Prestwick Pioneers in Malaya. (*JH*)

about as indifferent and icy cold as the North Pole". In 1959 Prestwick became the first UK airport offering duty-free sales for airline passengers. The profitable catering and sales business would develop further when the new terminal was opened in 1964.

The Ministry of Transport (responsible for civil aviation since 1953) commenced work in 1959 on that new terminal, with a new control tower, new freight buildings, and a loop road around an extended main runway. The main runway of 3,300 yards was completed in 1960; supplemented by the second runway of 2,000 yards which had been opened in 1955. Prestwick was now well equipped to handle the newer, larger, faster, and heavier aircraft which were coming into use. In April 1951 the first Comet jet aircaft visited Prestwick, and the massive Bristol Brabazon four months later. Passenger-carrying Comets came twice the following year, unable to land at London and diverted to Prestwick. In February 1953 a Vickers Viscount left Prestwick for the first commercial transatlantic crossing by a turbo-prop plane. In October 1958 a Boeing 707 jet airliner belonging to Pan Am made a first landing at Prestwick on a test flight. The first scheduled flights into Prestwick by these new planes were operated from 1960 by BOAC, and one travelled from

A Twin Pioneer over the airport. (*JH*)

213

New York in a record 5 hours 3 minutes on 22 September 1962. Compare that with the first non-stop civilian flight from New York to Prestwick on 11 September 1946, which took 11 hours 2 minutes. In 1951 128,000 passengers passed through Prestwick; in 1960 nearly 300,000 passengers were handled, over 92,000 of them starting or finishing their journey here. Transatlantic services were operated by BOAC, TCA, Pan-Am, KLM, and SAS.

As well as transatlantic commercial traffic, Prestwick was busy with Unites States planes and military personnel serving in continental Europe as part of the North Atlantic Treaty Organisation. In 1951 an air base squadron of the US Air Force established itself at Prestwick to handle such flights in transit. In 1952 the USAF decided also on an air-sea rescue unit here, in May two of their helicopters made a first transatlantic crossing (via Iceland), and in 1953 the 65th Air-Sea Rescue Unit was installed. On the north fringe of the airport Greensite was built to accomodate 600 servicemen and their families. This "Little America" had its own air terminal, housing, church, school, cafeteria, jukebox, bowling alley, cinema, gymnasium, post office, dentist, hospital. Nearby, Adamton House, badly affected by dry rot, was completely restored to provide an Officers' Mess. Altogether about 250 local workers found employment. It was at this American base that, on the evening of 2 March 1960, Elvis Presley made his only visit to Britain when, returning from military service in Germany, the DC 7 carrying him touched down at Prestwick to refuel.

Prestwick burgh's population of 11,386 in 1951 increased to 12,562 in 1961. The Census Report of 1961 described 5,150 of these (3,690 male, 1,460 female) as "economically active", many working within Prestwick but some employed else-where. The total number of persons actually employed within the burgh, including some travelling in to work, was 3,250 (2,430 male, 820 female). There were 850 employed by the Coal Board at Glenburn; 420 in the building trade; 570 in distributive trades, mostly shop workers; another 230 in hotels and restaurants; and 470 in professional and administrative work. Around 700 others were esti-mated as involved in a wide range of other trades including laundry work (70), garages (80), hairdressing (60), domestic service (70). There were small firms engaged in light engineering and manufacturing pre-cast concrete, but no space was available for any major industry to become established within the burgh, even if such had been considered desirable. Prestwick remained a residential area, a dormitory town for many who worked elsewhere. Of those 390 coal miners who lived within Prestwick, some travelled daily to other pits in central Ayrshire. A large number of the 540 classified as working in engineering and electrical trades were employed by SAL at the airport. Some of those engaged in sales (690), office work (680), teaching (240), and transport (420) did so in Ayr, elsewhere in the county, or in Glasgow. With only 820 local jobs for women, many of the 1,460 women residents in employment had to go out of the town to find work. Of the men living in Prestwick and gainfully employed within or outwith the burgh, the 1961 Census Report provided statistics of their socio-economic status. 14.9% were employers, managers, or administrators; 5.5% were in the professions; 23.1% were other non-manual workers. Kilmarnock and Ayr had of course greater numbers of each, and Troon was home for more of those who controlled large establishments. But with 43.5% in those higher socio-economic groups, Prestwick was surpassed only by Largs (45.4%), and well above the county average (24.6%).

The Census Report of 1961 featured further characteristics of Prestwick's population. Over the previous ten years the population had increased by 0.98% annually; 0.35% of this attributable to natural increase by excess of births over deaths; so that there was a net inward migration of 0.63%. Prestwick was continuing to attract large numbers of incomers. The published statistics do not specifically indicate how many were born locally, but included within those 56% who had been born in Ayrshire, they formed a minority. Another 31% had come from other parts of Scotland, the main groups being 1,468 born in Glasgow, 619 in Lanarkshire, 338 in Renfrewshire. Discounting 123 visitors from outside Scotland at the time of the census, there were 887 residents who were English by birth, 124 Irish, 33 Welsh, 5 from the Isle of Man, 130 from Commonwealth countries, and 453 from other foreign countries of whom 364 were defined as aliens. Many of these (193 male, 171 female) were of course among the 993 Americans resident in the county at the time of the census. With such diverse origins, Prestwick was a heterogeneous community.

If the reader can suffer a further paragraph of statistical information, the population of the burgh may be further dissected. The ratio of the sexes in 1961 was 1.20 males for every female, a less pronounced disparity from 1931 when the ratio of 1.37 was influenced by the presence of so many domestic servants, of whom there were now few. The continuing female preponderance (compared with 1.09 for the county) was because of the large number of retired persons who had settled here, and among those aged 65 and over there were in Prestwick twice as many women as men. They were 1,629 in number, 543 men and 1,086 women. There were 359 married men and 277 married women (some of the men had younger wives); 140 widowers outnumbered by 503 widows; 1 man and 4 women divorced; 43 bachelors as against 302 spinsters. That group of persons aged 65 and over formed 13% of the burgh population, as compared with a 10% county average. There were higher proportions in the other residential coast towns – Largs 25%, Troon and Girvan 14%; and in the Irvine Valley – Darvel 14%, Newmilns just over 13%. But while in these and most other places the percentage of older people was increasing, in Prestwick the predominance of older persons was reduced from 14% in 1951 by an influx of younger persons.

The large number of older persons, especially women, and the high proportion of relatively well-off residents in the higher socio-economic groups meant that the churches continued to occupy a prominent role in local life. A survey of church membership made in 1948 by the present author in the *Third Statistical Account* discovered that in Ayrshire just about half the adult population aged 16 and over were members of some denomination. In that volume the section relating to the parish of Monkton and Prestwick showed a dozen congregations of various religious bodies had a combined membership of about 5,300, and there were then probably 9,750 adults aged sixteen and over. This gives a parish percentage of around 54%, higher than the county average. As elsewhere, the Church of Scotland was most widely supported, with a combined membership of nearly 4,000 in its five congregations: St Cuthbert's, 1,600; St Nicholas, 1,000; South, 400; North, 450; Kingcase, 440. St Quivox Roman Catholic Church had approximately 720 adults on its roll; St Ninian's Scottish Episcopal Church had 250; perhaps half of the New Prestwick Baptist Church's 100 members came from this parish. Nearly 300 persons were members of the three Christian Brethren assemblies, the Salvation Army had 65, and there was a small group of Christadelphians who met in Glenburn.

In the Church of Scotland, continuity was maintained by Rev. George MacLeod Dunn who ministered at St Nicholas from 1927 until he retired in 1959. New men came to serve the other four charges. When Rev. Luke McQuitty died in 1947 after twenty-three years in Prestwick, Rev. Donald Murdoch Caskie (aged 39) was called and inducted to St Cuthbert's, following wartime service as a chaplain to the forces. In 1947 there was also a vacancy at Prestwick South, when Rev. George Christie left for another parish, and Rev. James Burgoyne Yorke (41) was inducted as his successor. In 1948 Rev. Peter Ferguson of Kingcase also left, followed by ordination of Rev. George Paterson (34), who had worked in insurance before wartime military service. The fourth vacancy was at Prestwick North when Rev. William McKinnon, inducted in 1921 when this was a United Free Church, demitted the charge in 1949 and died in 1952; Rev. John Wallace Patterson (27) was in 1950 inducted to succeed him, followed by Rev. Charles Raymond Vincent (30) in 1958. All the new ministers were comparatively young men, three had previously held other charges, two had served with the forces, two had young families and the others were recently married. The five Church of Scotland congregations were in good hands. The most recent, Kingcase, erected as a church extension charge in 1934, was granted full status in 1950. An auxiliary hall was built by voluntary labour in 1949 and the main church extended in 1955. When Rev. Peter Higgins succeeded to the charge in 1958 membership had increased to 1,000.

There was vitality also in the other churches. St Quivox Roman Catholic Church had a building which was originally used both for worship and social activities. Rev. Laurence Breen who was appointed parish priest in 1938 was insistant that the latter function was inappropriate, and in 1947 it proved possible to obtain a separate hall capable of holding over 200 people. St Ninian's Scottish Episcopal Church, which during the war had to operate as subsidiary to Holy Trinity, Ayr, got its own minister again in Rev. Dr Ernest Jauncey, followed by Rev. R.L. Armitage, then Rev. E.W. Buswell from 1957. New Prestwick Baptist Church, whose pastors were Rev. William Brown from 1944 and Rev. George Maitland from 1948, was able to provide a new manse for Rev. Walter Main (1952–57) and Rev. Walter Lang who followed him. The *Third Statistical Account* published in 1951 revealed the smaller sects in Prestwick as particularly active. The three assemblies of Christian Brethren were especially successful with Sunday schools attracting 210 children, of whom 120 attended at Glenburn. The Brethren, like the Salvation

Army, complemented their own meetings with open-air summer services at the shore. At St Quivox Roman Catholic Church, each Sunday there was a morning service attended by almost all the 720 adults and 280 children; there were four other services that day and others throughout the week; there were also youth clubs for boys and girls, guilds for men and women, and a Catholic Ex-servicemen's association. All the other churches also operated Sunday schools and various social meetings. St Cuthbert's had two Sunday schools – one in Monkton, and a Prestwick one with 350 children. The South Church had its own dramatic society, which benefited from the new church hall opened in 1960. But certain weaknesses were evident in the Church of Scotland congregations. Only a third of those on their rolls were men. And a minority of members were regular attenders. Around two-thirds of all the members came to the communion services. But the usual attendance on a Sunday morning was usually less than one-third. At St Cuthbert's for example, out of the roll of 1,600, there were 1,000 at communion, 270 on other Sunday mornings, and around 50 at evening services. It was much the same at St Ninian's Scottish Episcopal Church, with its roll of 68 men and 181 women – 50 on Sunday mornings, 11 in the evenings.

For most of the people, religion obviously meant much less than it had been for their predecessors. The annual kirking of the council continued as a formality. In 1947 the town hall was let for Sunday evening variety concerts. despite protests from the churches. Sunday golf was permitted on St Ninian's municipal golf course. If Sunday observance was being widely ignored, so also were other commitments. While the 1931 census reported only three divorcees in Prestwick, by 1961 there were forty-six, and the number would continue to increase. There were other signs of the times. The once powerful temperance movement had for long limited the number of licensed premises in the town. By 1961 nine local hotels had acquired licences, as well as the four public houses; the private golf and bowling clubs were joined as licensees by SAL Social Club and the RAF Association Club; and permission was now readily granted for a bar at dances in the town hall. Gambling of one kind or another was becoming more common. When in 1946 a local branch of the Lions Club was formed to raise money for handicapped children, they sought a let of the town hall on Thursday evenings "for the purpose of a game called Bingo." After the town clerk was called upon to explain the game, the councillors granted the application. Then, when more serious gambling was legalised by the Betting and Gaming Act of 1960, there were six applicants from Prestwick seeking to set up as bookmakers. Another indication of standards becoming more lax appeared in 1958 when vandalism was reported at the public park and at the high school. More seriously, in 1960 five Prestwick youths were gaoled for murder of a Kilmarnock man at Monkton.

If the religious way of life seemed to be disappearing, there was, by contrast, an expansion of education. In 1947 the school leaving age was raised from fourteen to fifteen, which created problems of overcrowding. Monkton and Glenburn schools for primary pupils were not affected, and in 1948 their rolls were 119 and 284. There were also 224 primary pupils in Prestwick Public School and 305 in

Prestwick High School, which catered as well for 151 and 110 in their secondary departments, including pupils from Symington, St Quivox, and Heathfield primary schools. Allocation to secondary school was determined by primary promotion examinations. Prestwick Public School was designated a junior secondary school with practical courses for pupils intending to leave school at fifteen. Those others considered capable of benefiting from an academic course went to Prestwick High School for transfer to Ayr Academy after the age of fifteen. In 1945 Ayr County Council Education Committee acquired responsibility for Biggart Memorial Home, which provided residential accommodation for convalescent children from Glasgow and Ayrshire, one hundred of them in 1949, reduced to sixty-nine by 1961. Before the war plans had been made for a new school in Prestwick, a so-called "transferred" denominational school, but for those 280 children of all ages from Roman Catholic homes there was as yet no local provision. Those of school age had to travel to Troon or Ayr for primary schooling, and to Irvine or Kilmarnock thereafter. A very few children of Catholic parents were sent to boarding schools, and a greater number from other families.

With a post-war increase in the birth rate and Prestwick continuing to attract families of incomers, there was a new pressure on schools. In the three years between 1948 and 1950 the number of pupils within the three schools in Prestwick burgh had increased by 26% to 1,192. In the immediate post-war years the policy of Ayr County Council was to give priority to house-building, and schools had to take second place so long as labour and materials were scarce, making do with prefabricated huts erected in playgrounds. In 1958 it was possible to open a major £90,000 extension to Prestwick High School, whose roll could be doubled to 800 by taking in all secondary pupils. Glenburn would get additional rooms as a two-stream primary school, with two classes for each age group. Prestwick Public School, built seventy years before and needing replacement, would continue as a one-stream primary school. Monkton school acquired an extension in 1954, but plans for a Roman Catholic school were still on the drawing board, and proposals for a nursery school and technical college in Prestwick would never be realised. Meantime inadequate accommodation, over-size classes, shortage of staff, and innovations in curriculum – all had to be coped with by the head teachers. At Prestwick High School, after J.G.Russell retired in 1941, James A. Scott was appointed, followed in 1956 by Joseph Murdoch. At Prestwick Public School, Adam Duncanson was followed in 1945 by Thomas Blackwood, and in 1951 by John Harrison. Also in 1951, an era ended at Glenburn Public School when Mathew Foulds retired after thirty-three years as headmaster, to be followed by Alexander P. Adams. At Monkton there was change in 1957 when John A. Morgan was appointed. He replaced John Wilson who like Mathew Foulds had trained as a pupil teacher, and was headmaster at Monkton for forty-one years until his retiral. He is otherwise remembered for, only a few years after his appointment in 1916, he was winner of the first Scottish Amateur Golf Championship in 1922. By the time of his retiral in 1957 there were 200 pupils in Monkton school which, like the other local schools, was experiencing additional enrolments from a new source.

After the United States Base was established in 1953 its Greensite accommodated families of servicemen who were normally stationed here for three years. A school was set up at the base in 1957, with three teachers from USA teaching 120 pupils from six to fourteen years. But even after that, another 200 American children were enrolled in local schools. At the time of the 1961 census, there were within Prestwick burgh altogether 2,081 children aged five to fourteen, among a total of 3,060 under-fifteens who formed 24% of the population. The importance attached to education may be gauged from the fact that in that year ratepayers in Prestwick were contributing £150,000 for education, as compared with £51,000 for other county council services, and £94,000 for those provided by Prestwick town council.

In the years after 1945 the County Education Committee extended its responsibilities for further education and youth service. Evening continuation classes held in the high school covered not only school subjects but also in 1948 dress-making, model-making, physical training, country dancing; and there was a youth group meeting weekly in winter and organising cycle trips in summer. In 1946 the Education Committee took over the former British Restaurant for conversion into a Youth Club. In 1948 it had a programme of discussions, drama, arts and crafts, cookery, and physical training for 62 girl and 51 boy members. By contrast, football and athletics were the sole activities of clubs at Glenburn (30 boys) and New Prestwick (20 boys). The *Third Statistical Account* confirmed the continued popularity in 1948 of voluntary organisations for youth: Boys Brigade, three Scout groups, three of Girl Guides, with Cubs and Brownies for younger children; there were also a Girls' Training Corps, and young people's groups associated with South Church, St Cuthbert's, and SAL Social Club. The strength of one particular body was confirmed in 1959 when the 14th Ayrshire (1st Prestwick) Scout Group celebrated its fiftieth anniversary by presenting the burgh with a sun-dial erected in Boydfield Gardens, and its founder Mathew Foulds was made a Freeman of the Burgh in recognition of his services to young people. A handbook for 1961 indicated there were by then no fewer than five scout groups and four of Girl Guides; there continued the Boys Brigade company, boys' clubs at Glenburn and Prestwick, youth clubs at the high school and the South Church; there was now a youth club attached to St Quivox R.C. Church (as well as one of the Scout groups), British Red Cross cadets, Women's Junior Air Corps, a drama group called the Junior Prestwick Players. At Monkton there was a youth club in the school and the Young Women's Christian Association meeting in the Church hall. Altogether twenty youth groups were affiliated to the District Youth Panel which was formed in 1953.

For team sports Prestwick could offer only a small playing field, which had to be given up to allow extension of the high school. But opportunity was taken to provide a better alternative. In 1953 the St Ninian's golf course was closed and on its central site a recreation centre was formed in 1954, a public park with facilities for tennis, cricket, hockey, athletics, and football. This was particularly welcome for local members of Ayr Craigie Cricket Club, which had to close down in 1954, so a Prestwick Cricket Club was then formed. The public park provided a much better pitch than those of the former cricket club which had lapsed in 1939; and the former St Ninian's golf clubhouse was available as a pavilion. Elsewhere other sports flourished. There was football at the park and at New Prestwick, bowling on two greens, and a sailing club was formed in 1959, with twenty boats and 130 members paying £2 annually. The three private golf clubs maintained their well-established reputation. In 1951 Prestwick Golf Club celebrated its centenary. St Nicholas Club was as old, though only sixty years on its present course. The youngest, St Cuthbert Club, had its fiftieth anniversary in 1949. The municipal St Ninian's course was closed in 1953 for conversion of eighteen acres into a public park; in 1955 it was reopened as a nine-hole course on adjoining thirty-one acres which the town council held on lease. But in 1958 it had to close; though the council planned compulsory purchase of the land to allow it to continue, after four years of legal dispute the owners were allowed to dispose of it for building of private houses. St Cuthbert club was also threatened when in 1959 its course was claimed for the planned extension of the airport; but £51,000 compensation allowed purchase of ground in 1961 for a new course at Heathfield beside the East Road. For visitors and others who could not afford the high golf fees, there were four putting greens, and a pitch-and-putt course near Prestwick Toll.

The *Third Statistical Account*, published in 1951, after listing Prestwick's various facilities devoted a paragraph to community life, based on information supplied by a local committee whose members included solicitors, teachers, banker, minister, a councillor, and the burgh's two principal officials. It was concluded that "A good many things have conspired to prevent the development of a healthy community spirit." What these were have already been noticed in Chapter Eleven. Hope was expressed that social cleavages would be narrowed: "There was promise of that in the fine co-operation of men and women of all classes in the A.R.P. and the W.V.S. during the War." For a time some of those in the Home Guard and in civil defence arranged annual reunions, and the wartime Army Cadet Pipe Band was in 1951 converted into a Prestwick Youth Pipe Band. The community which shared in the Victory celebrations came together again at the time of the Coronation of Queen Elizabeth in 1953. On 2 June the streets were decorated, commemorative trees were planted, children were provided with sports (and souvenirs from the county council), 600 old age pensioners watched the coronation ceremony on television in the town hall, and in the evening there was a coronation ball. As in other years there was also a Children's Day with free cinema, fancy dress parade, and inter-school sports. But efforts to sustain the community spirit by a local newspaper were not successful: the *Prestwick News* was resuscitated in 1953, ran for several years, then failed, as did a *Prestwick Standard* of 1958 and 1959.

There were of course plenty of organisations for those who chose to participate. Clubs which been dormant during the war were revived, and once again enthusiasts arranged in the town hall their shows of flowers, dogs, or cage birds. For a time there was support for a Literary and Debating Society, a Scientific Film Society, an Ayrshire Cine Club, a Model Aero Club, the Prestwick Players, an

Athletic and Boxing Club, and the Gardening Club was revived. In 1951 a Townswomen's Guild was formed, so popular that those who could not be admitted formed their own Boydfield Townswomen's Guild. Some organisations had a restricted membership, like the SAL Social Club. A Rotary Club was formed in 1948, on the pattern of one individual from each trade or profession. The Royal Air Force Association, open to former service airmen, in 1948 acquired Stonegarth as a club house (and transferred there the Polish War Memorial from the former army camp at Monkton). The Freemasons also obtained their own premises. They had since 1909 met in various locations until a hall in Berelands Road came on the market. This had been acquired by the Order of the Eastern Star to replace their former hall which burned down during the war. This was in 1965 purchased to become the Masonic Hall, where Lodge 1060 could meet, and where a Masonic Club was formed in 1969. A Toastmasters' Club of 1953 and a Burns Club of 1954 were open to all who were interested. The Prestwick Old People's Welfare Association showed concern for the growing number of older residents, and in 1960 an Evergreen Club began to meet in the OES Hall. Certain areas retained local loyalties. Glenburn had its own range of organisations (including an Orange Lodge) and provided a Christmas treat for its own old folk. So did the Third Ward Social Welfare Association, which arranged various social activities, and staged its own pantomime in 1949. Prestwick Toll also retained a separate identity, which

Provost Gilbert Steele welcomed Queen Elizabeth at the Burgh Chambers in Links Road, on the royal visit of 1956.

seemed to be threatened in 1960 by a major redevelopment project. Monkton felt itself increasingly isolated from Prestwick. At the end of the war it chose to organise its own celebrations, and as the airport was extended the physical links between that village and Prestwick became even less close.

Monkton remained small, with fewer than a thousand inhabitants. There was no work in the village itself, which was mostly of old houses, and otherwise spoilt by the heavy traffic passing through. It had its school, a church hall, and the Carvick Webster Hall, a public house, and a licensed grocer, but it now served as a parish centre only for meetings of the Women's Rural Institute. The landowners who had once dominated the scene had all but one gone. Fairfield was sold in 1950 and the house demolished by its new owner, whose plans for a scheme of villas and racing stables came to nothing, and only the old family cemetery survived. Orangefield and Adamton mansions were now each used in connection with the airport. Ladykirk alone remained, occupied by Robert L. Angus until his death in 1949. A year later his widow married Sir Thomas Moore, MP, himself a widower since 1945 and recently (in 1956) created a baronet. Most of the thirteen farms in the parish were still rented, on fifteen year leases, and there were few changes in tenancy. This remained Ayrshire's premier arable parish, with 45% of the farmland in 1946 under crops, and growing oats, wheat, and early potatoes. Those farms on higher ground kept dairy herds of around forty Ayrshire cows, and the arable farms nearer the coast raised beef cattle for sale and for the sake of the manure they produced. At Hobsland farm Alan Barr, who had established Ayrshire's first herd of tuberculin-tested cattle, built up a business exporting breeding bulls by air to America. To pay around £4 per acre for an arable farm of some 120 acres, and make a profit, all local farmers had to be business men and in the second half of the 20th century invested heavily on new machinery – tractors, combine harvesters, milking machines. The old farmhouses were also renovated and equipped with modern conveniences. But for the farmers and farmworkers it remained an isolated life. The former however had now their own private cars and opportunity to travel into town for shopping and on social occasions. For them Ayr was a magnet, as it was for many of the townsfolk within Prestwick itself.

Leisure time was increasing. Some workers were now enjoying a forty-hour five-day week. Shopkeepers and their staff had a half-day each Wednesday; in 1959 the Merchants' Association's 110 members decided that a change to Thursday would be beneficial. Housewives, with no days off, had their burden somewhat eased, for items like washing machines, electric irons, vacuum cleaners, and refrigerators were becoming common. Modern homes were easier to keep, and half of Prestwick houses in 1948 were less than thirty years old. Sandfield Cottage, built about 1780 and the town's last thatched house, was demolished in 1958. Homes were more comfortable and less overcrowded. From 1947 those who enjoyed reading could borrow books from the new branch library which the County Council established in Kyle Street in a former billiard hall. The introduction of television to Scotland in 1952 had a dramatic effect on family life, for it was no longer necessary to escape from the home in search of entertainment. After forty-three busy years, the Picture House had to close down on 3 August 1957. The more modern Broadway survived as a cinema until 1976. The *Prestwick Standard* observed (6 Nov. 1958) that the advent of television did not seem to have reduced the number of children out guising at Hallowe'en. In this year television sets were advertised at a cash price of 69 guineas or 156 weeks at fifteen shillings. Television, as well as offering diversion, provided information. National and international events and issues acquired a new immediacy. In the General Elections of 1945, 1950, and 1951, voters had to rely on the press before making their choice. In 1959 and 1959 TV cameras brought the national campaigns into the living room. After the count the result in each constituency was immediately available on the screen. On every occasion Sir Thomas Moore was re-elected to represent Ayr Burghs in straight contests with the Labour Party. Though television occupied many hours in the home, there was more leisure time also available to travel further afield. More and more people had their own private cars; more and more people could afford foreign holidays. Within Prestwick itself there was also particular opportunity to meet a wider range of people from different backgrounds. Christmas, though still not a public holiday, was more widely celebrated. In 1958 the Parkstone Hotel was offering Christmas dinners at 12s 6d per head. Each year the Rotary Club set up a Christmas tree at the Cross and solicited donations for the needy. The novelty of illuminating the windows of private houses with little Christmas trees was attributed by the *Prestwick Standard* of 1958 to American custom. Americans, accustomed to central heating – which was unknown here – had high heating bills which astonished local people. The presence of so many young American servicemen had special impact in Prestwick when some local girls found romance, which was followed by married life in the USA. In ways which could not have been contemplated earlier in the century, Prestwick was brought into direct connection with the rest of the world.

CHAPTER FOURTEEN

The End of the Burgh

IN the 1960s party politics more noticeably intruded themselves into local affairs. Nationally, the Conservative ministries of Macmillan (1957–63) and Home (1963–64) were followed by Wilson's Labour government (1964–70), Conservative rule again under Heath (1970–74), then Labour administrations led by Wilson (1974–76) and Callaghan (1976–79). In local municipal elections, rivalry between Labour and Moderates was confused by intervention of candidates of the Liberal Party in 1963 and the Scottish National Party in 1969. In Ward One a Liberal took a seat from an Independent and held it from 1963 until 1969; but otherwise the balance was not disturbed. Labour achieved four seats between 1963 and 1965 but the Conservatives (as all Moderates designated themselves from 1968) retained their ascendancy. In 1969 they held eleven of the twelve seats, and Labour was able to recover only one more in 1972. Nevertheless, members of the council continued to respect worth and seniority, so that in 1963 at the end of Moir's provostship, the Moderate nominee Hugh Chapman withdrew his nomination to allow unanimous choice of Labour councillor Iain Foulds as provost. A teacher of history, he was member of a long-established local family and the second native of the burgh to hold the office of provost. Hugh Chapman, who was a draper, had his turn in 1966; followed in 1969 by Fred Horton, airport commercial manager, who would continue to represent Prestwick in local government until 1992. In 1972 John D. Watt succeeded him; he worked with a Kilmarnock commercial firm, but ill health forced his resignation from the provostship in 1974. William Harkiss, a retired building contractor, became the last of Prestwick's twenty-two provosts, the third native to hold that office.

Though the council was dominated by one party, the members of that group were not always of one mind, which contributed to what were sometimes quite violent disagreements. Some examples can be quoted from the local press: a "storm" over tenancy of the former St Ninian's Clubhouse (March 1962); a "blazing argument" when the provost's allowance was raised to £300 (May 1962); a "row" over council minutes (Oct. 1967); and "near uproar" over approving the accounts (Dec. 1967). Other issues were disputed: there were three-and-a-half hours of debate before a motion to dismiss the burgh surveyor was thrown out (March 1961); heated discussions of rents policy (May 1964, April 1967); allocation of lets of the town hall (March 1962); allowing council tenants to display political party posters at elections (Oct. 1964); arguing about a betting shop in Main Street (Sept. 1967); curtailing the water inspection (May 1966); dealing with the trust funds which the council administered (Dec. 1967). There were other topics which caused some irritation. Before 1965 when a five-day week for council staff was introduced, cleansing workers were (May 1961) offered a 42-hour week without overtime; this caused a backlog in collection of refuse and a dispute which was settled by an increase of wages to £11 11s 6d per week, making them Scotland's highest-paid bin men. Shopkeepers who had voted in 1959 for a Thursday half-day sought to have annulled an order of 1935 for early closing on Wednesdays; it was discovered (Jan. 1961) that there was no such order, the council (Feb. 1964) left shopkeepers to make their own arrangements, and Wednesday was continued. The annual kirking of the council had always been to St Cuthbert's church: Provost Moir, an elder at St Nicholas, wanted a change and the council decided (March 1961) that there should be a rota of the five Church of Scotland charges; but the ministers were aggrieved that they had not been consulted. Yet on many other occasions council decisions were unanimously approved and deemed acceptable. The practice of installing lamps outside the provost's residence was continued: new ones had to be purchased (Apr. 1963) to replace the antiquated standards dating from the age of gas. There was a function (Dec. 1963) to commemorate the sixtieth anniversary of the town council, when a scroll was presented to Gilbert Steele for his twenty-five years of service. There was a civic welcome (Nov. 1964) for Alistair Wilson, the 24-year-old local finalist in the kayak singles at Tokyo Olympic games. These miscellaneous snippets illustrate, among other things, the range of council business.

Prestwick Town Council, 1964. (*IF*)

Council houses and finance continued to exercise much of the councillors' attention. In 1961 the town chamberlain revealed that Prestwick burgh had borrowed £1 million pounds for house building, and to provide fifty houses more at £20,000 each with a sixty years' loan at 7% would cost a further half-million pounds. That year rents were increased to a maximum of £51 for a five-apartment house, and plans had to be formulated for future building, for there were still 474 persons on the waiting list, including subtenants. In 1962, housing applications were described as "a tangled mess", so, to assess requirements, a survey was made of tenants of the 996 council houses. There were 44 recently occupied in East Road, 23 for old people under construction at Templeriggs, 20 let to SAL and 4 to police. Apart from these and several who did not reply, it was found that of 857 remaining there were 103 houses over-occupied and 234 under-occupied, and most of these were willing to exchange, which enabled a more precise definition of housing needs. From 1960 council houses specially designed for occupation by older persons were constructed at Templeriggs, Waterloo Road, Bellevue Road, and Sherwood Road. The council also realised that their older houses required modernisation, particularly as regards electrical installations. Improvement grants were now available for owners of older private houses to bring them towards standards of new houses being built. Further attention was directed towards sub-standard houses. It was noted in 1965 that there were 333 such houses in the burgh (including 184 at Glenburn and 58 at Prestwick Toll) and 96 of these were scheduled for demolition within the next two years. Throughout the sixties the Prestwick Toll area was redeveloped, by compulsory purchase and removal of old properties, and building of new houses and shops. In 1967 the Glenburn houses (and the communal wash-house) were disposed of by the Coal Board to the town council. These were all demolished by 1971, providing scope for renovation of that area now that the Prestwick Toll redevelopment was almost complete. In 1971 a new phase commenced when, as recommended by the Conservative government, council houses were offered for sale to sitting tenants, and by 1974 a score had been sold, at an average price of £4,000. The 1971 Census revealed a decade of progress, with the number of households in the burgh increased from 4,093 to 4,720 and the population continuing its growth from 12,562 to 13,437.

The Census of 1971 revealed also improvements in living conditions. The report for 1971 was not published till after reorganisation of local government, so provided no figures for the burgh, but those supplied for the parish of Monkton and Prestwick indicate the general local picture. Of 5,076 households, 60% were owner-occupied, 31% were council houses, only 9% privately rented. There was still some overcrowding, with 3% at more than 1½ persons per room and another 8% from 1 to 1½ per room; but only 2% were now having to live in shared dwellings. 95.6% of households were supplied with all specified amenities – hot and cold water, bath, and inside toilet. What the census could not quantify was the acquisition of other domestic facilities – more had washing machines, refrigerators, fitted carpets, telephones. In 1961, 279 council house tenants indicated a desire to rent refrigerators. In 1968 two sought permission to instal central heating.

In 1960 the town council was in the comfortable position of having no arrears in rent or rates. The burgh rate of 18s 6d in the £ was lowest among Scotland's fifty largest burghs. In 1961 it proved possible to reduce the rate to 15 shillings in the £, thanks to a surplus accumulated over previous years and despite a county requisition increased that year to £230,000. Rates in Prestwick continued low, and a decade later in 1971 (the year when decimalisation was introduced) the levy on domestic ratepayers was 58p in the £ – less than twelve shillings in the former currency. Council policy was always to maximise collection of rates and rents and to promote revenue-producing enterprises. But by this time the county requisition exceeded £1 million a year and was continuing to increase annually; some council house tenants were finding it difficult to pay their rents (after 26% increase in 1971) so that at the end of 1973 more than a hundred of them were in arrears. In 1974, for the last year of the town council, rates were increased from 78p to 90p in the £.

One disappointment, common to all coastal resorts, was a failure to restore the holiday trade to its pre-war level. The council continued to issue a guide book, publicise the bathing lake, organise the annual beauty competitions and children's events, provide band concerts, and introduce novelties like a postmark advertising Prestwick (1964) and souvenir copperware table mats (1965), and thought for a time in 1964 of spending £12,000 to improve the south esplanade. Disappointed at the council's lack of success, the hoteliers and merchants in 1965 set up a Tourist and Development Association. Local societies were involved in providing a range of activities which might attract a new clientele. In 1967 a first Prestwick Week was organised, with sports, concerts, and other shows. But all to no avail. There were still day visitors as in the hot summer of 1960 when British Rail ran extra trains to Prestwick and Ayr, and one Sunday there were over 2,000 swimmers in the bathing lake, bringing the total that year to 40,000. But people were now preferring to go further afield for their holidays. Prestwick bathing lake had lost its former magnetism. To heat the pool, as considered in 1967, would cost £10,000. Some brief publicity was obtained when BBC television chose it to stage "It's a Knockout" in May 1971, broadcast in August. But the following season the Bathing Lake had to close. Annual maintenance costs of £10,000 were not being covered by takings which were annually declining, made worse by bad weather (in 1971 and 1972 the bathing beauty competitions had to be held in the town hall) and by counter-at-tractions (Ayr Indoor Pool opened in 1972). Thereafter the annual bathing beauty competitions were discontinued, and other events like the Prestwick open golf tournaments for young players. The town council concentrated on providing facilities which might attract some visitors but which were principally directed towards the benefit of the local community.

The report of the census of 1971 showed 19.5% of the parish population aged 65 and over. The proportion within Prestwick burgh, though not listed, was certainly higher, and much greater than ten years before when it was 13%. Prestwick town council, in cooperation with other agencies, made appropriate provision. From 1960 onwards, council houses designed for older persons were built and support was offered by schemes like grass cutting for unfit older house-holders. In 1962 the council decided that premises it owned at 65 Main Street might be renovated for use of the Prestwick Old People's Welfare Committee, and there in 1964 the appropriately-named 65 Club was opened; the council charged an annual rent of £100 but donated that sum to cover it. Meanwhile Bailie Hugh Chapman instituted a campaign to raise £700 to provide a minibus for transporting old people, and in 1962 a purple and gold twelve seater named the Pioneer was acquired; the council provided driver and garaging. In 1965 the town in association with the county council subsidised Meals on Wheels for old folk, and by the end of 1967 ten thousand meals had been served. The Old People's committee continued to raise funds by public concerts, and in 1967 sponsored an Old Prestwick exhibition in the 65 Club. In 1971 a survey discovered 574 old persons living alone, and visitations and advice were offered. The following year the town council offered concessionary bus tickets to 1,900 older people, and 1,700 took advantage of the scheme. In 1973 the 65 Club was extended to provide a hall for evening meetings and daytime classes in country dancing and keep fit for older persons.

For another 22% of the population, those 2,957 in the burgh who were under the age of fifteen, the town council sponsored annual Children's Weeks. For the general populace, an annual town fete was organised. A most ambitious project was construction of an indoor bowling club; though it cost £63,000 it was expected to bring in £6,000 profit in its first year. It provided eight rinks, adaptable to six for national contests. It was opened in 1964 and enhanced by murals rescued from the former airport terminal in Orangefield House. In 1967 Councillor Clifford Westcott, a keen musician, proposed construction of a multi-purpose arts centre, suitable for local clubs and also to host national conferences. The idea was revived in 1972; but with closure of the bathing lake, and indoor bowling proving so popular, preference was given to planning a leisure complex with an indoor swimming pool. In other ways the town council sought to improve the town. In 1960 the antiquated underground lavatories at the cross were closed, filled in, and the mercat cross was moved to this new site in 1963. At the same time Bruce's Well at Kingcase was also renovated. Public rights were defended in 1964 when St Nicholas Golf Club closed up a path leading north from Maryborough Road; and the Air Ministry was required to restore a stile on another right of way over the old St Cuthbert golf course; earlier in 1961 Ayr District Council had required to take similar action against Prestwick Golf Club regarding a pathway from Monkton to the shore; across that same course runs another right of way providing a route from Seagate to the shore, though golf balls in flight render it hazardous. In course of these disputes, Provost Foulds was approached by the police who brought to his attention as a justice of the peace the destruction of a wire fence erected by a golf club; in his other capacity as scoutmaster he had led a party of his boys to undertake its removal; but he had the assurance of the town clerk that there was a right of way. The council's attention in 1972 turned towards the possibility of town-twinning. The idea, first mooted in the council in 1959, was at that time turned down.

But now negotiations were commenced and a link with Lichtenfels established in 1974. Lichtenfels, an industrial town and holiday resort in north Bavaria, is about the same size as Prestwick and, chartered in 1206, is almost as old.

Meantime the town council's routine work continued. William Alan Morton came from the County Buildings in Ayr to become town clerk in 1968 after Allan Inglis retired, dying in 1969; Lewis Stewart continued as town chamberlain to control burgh finances; James Melrose as burgh surveyor managed the various services. In 1967 a programme to improve street lighting was completed. Throughout the 1960s, the cleansing department collected 5,000 tons of household refuse annually. Each year more than 200 million gallons of water was supplied to consumers. Increased housing created greater demands. In 1961 Prestwick town council had to call upon Ayr to augment the supply of water. In 1968 an Ayrshire and Bute Water Board was formed, which took over from the various local authorities. Drainage continued to be a local problem, with periodic flooding in times of heavy rain; and disposal of sewage became critical as more houses were built. Again Prestwick and Ayr town councils collaborated in attempts to solve a common problem, which would for long remain intractable. Increased centralisation was being introduced to deal, not only with water but other public functions: in 1968 the police forces of Ayr, Kilmarnock, and the county were amalgamated; in 1974 Ayrshire and Arran Health Board took over those public health duties previously undertaken by local authorities. Ayr County Council, responsible since 1932 for planning throughout the county outwith the two large burghs, undertook between 1963 and 1966 the compilation of a Prestwick Town Development Plan. But while subject to oversight by the county planning department, Prestwick town council made its own significant contribution to shaping the town's future.

In 1962 the town council considered the desirability of extending the burgh boundaries by taking in 12 acres at Heathfield. This apparently straightforward exercise turned out to be a lengthy one, complicated because the town clerk could find no precise record of the existing boundaries, and because a more ambitious enlargement became desirable. Ultimately in 1968, with county council consent and legal approval, 380 acres were added to the burgh's eastern border between Glenburn and Heathfield, extending the areas of Wards 2, 3, and 4. The purpose of this burgh extension was to provide additional land for housing and industrial purposes. The latter was influenced by developments at Glenburn colliery.

The Ayrshire coal industry was contracting. In 1959 the NCB area office in Ayr was given up; a West Area headquarters was established at Glenburn in a new three-storey building; after only three years this was in 1962 abandoned when administration was concentrated at Lugar. Glenburn colliery, employing a thousand miners in 1964, was scheduled for run-down. In 1965 the NCB workshops which employed a hundred men were closed; production of coal was reduced and finally ceased in 1973. Those 149 employees remaining were transferred to other pits or offered redundancy. Glenburn was one of the last pits to extract coal by the traditional stoop-and-room method; mechanical cutting had been tried with limited success between 1959 and 1962. The colliery, in operation since 1910, had

TERMINAL BUILDING, PRESTWICK AIRPORT, SCOTLAND   D 8697

The new Airport Terminal was opened in 1964.

its pithead sited outwith the burgh, as the freemen in 1903 insisted. Now the town council, anticipating the colliery's eventual closure, realised the site's potential as an industrial estate on the fringe of the airport. In 1967 the council acquired the 184 Coal Board houses, which were located within the burgh; and between 1969 and 1971 these houses and the old wash-house were demolished – ironically it took £50 to knock down houses which had cost £40 to build. In 1968 when the burgh was allowed to extend its boundary other Coal Board properties were acquired. Glenburn House was leased to Prestwick Circuits Ltd. in 1969; by 1973 it had 44 employees manufacturing circuit boards for the electronics industry until, requiring to double its staff, it then moved to Mosshill industrial estate near Ayr. The former NCB area offices were acquired in 1972 by National Air Traffic Services to become Atlantic House. There were those in the town who were not too keen on new industry – throughout the sixties there were numerous complaints about W. P. Lawrie's pre-cast concrete works in Berelands Road. Yet there were hopes for the industrial estate laid out at Shaw farm on the edge of the airport, and eventually modern factory buildings would be erected alongside the Shaw Tower – a feature now within the burgh, which had been built in the 18th century (possibly), by a landowner (identity unknown) for observation in falconry (supposedly).

Government plans announced in 1958 for development of Prestwick Airport were fully implemented. In 1960 the runway extension was completed; in 1962 a new control tower became operational; in 1964 the loop road was opened; on 11 June the splendid new terminal came into use and on 22 September was officially opened by Queen Elizabeth the Queen Mother. Costing £5 million, it was designed by Glasgow architect J.L. Gleave. Purpose-built for the new jet age, its apron could accommodate twelve of the largest aircraft, and the terminal building provided admirable facilities for passengers. Within, a plaque commemorating the memory of David L. McIntyre, 1905 – 1957, founder of the airport, was presented by the town council, who commissioned a Kirkcudbright artist Tim Jeffs to design it. Later there would be added (1973) a nine-foot square ceramic mural by Bob Stewart; then, to celebrate the airport's jubilee (1985) a tapestry by ladies of the SWRI. In 1966 the Ministry of Civil Aviation transferred to British Airports Authority responsibility for running Prestwick, Heathrow, Gatwick, and Stanstead. In 1970 the spectators' gallery was packed when a crowd of five thousand watched the first landing of a Jumbo-jet, a Boeing 747 on a demonstration flight. To meet regular use by such heavy aircraft, the runway was in 1971 strengthened, speedily completed in fourteen weeks of night work. In 1972 the National Air Traffic Services, a civil-military partnership, took over the former Coal Board headquarters at Glenburn to establish as Atlantic House the Oceanic Air Traffic Control Centre with responsibility for all aircraft movements over north Britain and the north-east Atlantic, including (from 1978) those previously handled at Redbrae.

Throughout the sixties Prestwick was busy with transatlantic flights, and dignitaries on arrival were welcomed by the airport's official piper, Jimmy McCallum, in full Highland dress. Those who passed through the airport included members of the royal family, world politicians, film stars and pop stars, sportsmen, astronauts, and assorted other celebrities. For lesser mortals, there were in 1961 over a hundred flights some weeks, more in others when London was closed by fog or strikes. The number of passengers passing through Prestwick continued to increase to more than 500,000 annually, while freight had an even more specatacular rise to just under 20,000 tons in 1970, requiring a 40-acre cargo centre to be opened in 1973. But as the decade advanced there was concern over certain developments. In 1966 the USAF left Prestwick, and though the airport continued to be used by their mail and cargo flights to Europe, the American base remained unoccupied until 1970 when the Royal Navy commissioned it as HMS Gannet to operate a squadron of Sea King helicopters. The first HMS Gannet had been a sloop registered in 1800, replaced by others in 1814 and 1857, and the resurrection of the name was appropriate for an establishment whose purpose was anti-submarine surveillance and air-sea rescue. With the arrival also of RAF personnel the camp gained an establishment of 350 servicemen. A continuing concern was the lack of internal air services acting as "feeders" for the transatlantic flights. Prestwick had to rely largely on a forty-five minute journey from Glasgow by railway, on which diesel locomotives were introduced in 1959; and in 1961 a coach service to Edinburgh was inaugurated. It was a serious threat when Glasgow town council began planning to establish its own rival airport at Abbotsinch after closure of the RAF station at Renfrew, rejecting in 1964 the alternative suggestion of locating at St Enoch's railway station a Glasgow terminal for Prestwick airport. After Abbotsinch was opened in 1966 the British Airports Authority and Glasgow

Corporation agreed (1967) that Abbotsinch should handle short and medium-haul traffic while Prestwick would retain intercontinental flights. But aircraft could now fly direct from America to London and European cities without requiring to make a stop at Prestwick for re-fuelling. Ayrshire local authorities, chambers of commerce, and others formed a Prestwick Airport Development Association which for several years promoted vigorous campaigns to "Fly the Prestwick Way". However, by 1974 KLM, SAS, and Pan Am had abandoned Prestwick, leaving three major operators: Air Canada; British Airways, formed in 1973 by merging BEA and BOAC; and British Caledonian Airways, which inaugurated services from Prestwick in 1973. The airport was quiet enough at times to allow use for other purposes. In 1967 the local branch of the Royal Air Force Association staged at Prestwick the first ever Scottish Air Show, which became a biennial event, each contributing several thousand pounds to charities. Short pleasure flights were reintroduced in 1972 by Forth Air Services. The airport was used regularly for training flights. In 1971 a crowd of more than 13,000 surrounded the airport to witness Concorde's first visit, on a low-flying display; it touched down for the first time in 1973 to begin an initial series of training flights. Meanwhile Abbotsinch was being preferred by operators of chartered holiday flights, so that travel agents in 1971 were advertising in the Ayrshire press, "Jet direct from Glasgow". In 1974 plans were shelved for a luxury airport hotel, which the current level of traffic would not justify. In 1975 the British Airports Authority took over Abbotsinch, which was continuing to expand passenger and cargo traffic at the expense of Prestwick. That year Prestwick airport, after nine years of profit under management by British Airports Authority, showed a deficit for the first time. This was bad news for those 1,500 persons employed at the airport – 422 BAA staff, 468 government employees, 127 employed by airlines, 450 in shops, bank, and restaurants, 20 working on maintenance and repairs; not counting another 2,700 employed by SAL.

There was continued concern for Scottish Aviation Limited in the years after it celebrated its silver jubilee in 1960. There was work on aircraft conversion and maintenance, with important contracts from the Canadian Air Force, Rolls Royce (for engines), and the Lockheed Aircraft Corporation (manufacturing parts). But necessity forced SAL in 1963 to diversify into general engineering, with a separate division seeking markets for items ranging from hospital beds to electric cars, The Finance Corporation for Industry which had rescued SAL in 1959 became anxious to recover its investment and in 1966 sold off its controlling interest to Cammel Laird, a long-established shipbuilding and engineering group which was broadening its concerns. Takeover by Cammel Laird ensured survival of SAL at a time when other aviation companies were foundering, and offered necessary finance for new projects in aircraft manufacture. The long-established Handley Page Limited, producing in 1967 a prototype of its HP137 Jetstream, engaged SAL to undertake subcontract work; and the Beagle Aircraft Company was hoping for SAL cooperation in manufacture of its B125 Bulldog whose prototype made its first flight in 1969. In 1970 those two companies went into receivership, and SAL acquired the rights to manufacture both these planes. The Bulldog, a 2/3 seater primary trainer, went into production at Prestwick; in 1971 twenty were supplied to the Swedish army; and ultimately 325 Bulldogs would be sold to customers in Europe, Africa, and Asia. In 1972 work was commenced on the Jetstream, an 18-seater turboprop plane, when the RAF ordered 26 for a military role. 1973 became a vintage year when the first of 132 Bulldogs was handed over to the RAF, who the same year took delivery of the first Jetstream manufactured by SAL. But while this year marked a new beginning, it was also the end of an era, with the death of the Duke of Hamilton who had been associated with SAL since its inception in 1935. The company, adding manufacture to its maintenance work, could now employ 2,700 people. But there were strikes over pay in 1972 and 1973, and dark clouds on the horizon: the oil crisis of 1973; a world-wide recession in the aerospace industry; and the prospect of nationalisation following Labour victory in the 1974 general election.

The census of 1971 reported that of those 13,437 persons resident within the burgh 5,800 (43%) were economically active persons, as compared with 5,150 (41%) ten years before. The number of employed men remained virtually the same; but there were more women at work, and the majority of them (1,245 out of 2,135) were married women. Also, the population's sex ratio of 1.18 females for every female (1.20 in 1961) was becoming more balanced. The 7% growth in general population over the decade was largely due to a continuing influx of incomers, and despite the departure of most Americans – while in 1961 nearly 5% were natives of foreign countries, that proportion had dropped to 2% in 1971.

The High School was elevated to become Prestwick Academy in 1968, with extensions added in 1972. (*KA*)

Those 2,937 children under the age of fifteen were fewer then before, reduced from 24% to 22% of the total. The census further revealed that the population of Monkton and Prestwick parish included 15.3% (about 2,200) school children between the ages of five and fourteen, and a further 3.7% (about 520) students aged fifteen and over.

This was a period of innovation in education – introduction of the O-grade certificate in 1961; abolition in Ayrshire in 1967 of primary promotion examinations and introduction of comprehensive secondary schooling; raising of the school leaving age to sixteen in 1973. It proved possible for Ayr County Council Education Committee to undertake a major programme of school building. In Prestwick the Roman Catholic community was at last catered for when St Ninian's School opened in 1962, with secondary provision from 1966 at the new St Margaret's Academy in Ayr. In 1972 pressure on Prestwick Public and Glenburn schools was relieved when Ayrshire's first open-plan school was built at Kingcase in 1971. This allowed closure of the antiquated Public School, which continued breifly as an annexe to the new school at Kingcase. The 16th century bell from old St Nicholas Church which had been installed in the Public School after it opened in 1882 was now appropriately handed over to Kingcase school. Prestwick High School, which took all secondary pupils from the burgh, Monkton, and Symington, provided new fourth year classes for pupils sitting O-grade examinations; the opening of Kingcase allowed it to shed the primary department it had maintained since 1902. After introduction of comprehensive education the high school was elevated in 1968 to become Prestwick Academy, offering full secondary courses, ending the tradition by which senior pupils had to proceed to Ayr Academy. To provide for its 900 pupils and others expected when the school leaving age was raised, five new blocks were added to the academy in 1972, at a cost of £700,000. New subjects were being added to the curriculum in all schools, and pupils' horizons were being widened in various ways, as some random examples illustrate: in 1959 Prestwick Burns Club instituted the first of several annual festivals in the town hall where capacity audiences appreciated Scottish songs and recitations by pupils of the local schools; in 1965, when television sets in classrooms were still a novelty, BBC produced a twenty-minute schools programme on tourism in Ayrshire featuring Prestwick bathing lake; in 1966 Prestwick High School published its first magazine, and after it became an academy produced in 1971 Gilbert and Sullivan's "The Pirates of Penzance". The sports complex included in the 1972 extension at Prestwick Academy was available after school hours for youth and adult activities organised by the Community Development Service. Further Education evening classes for adults at the academy comprised traditional subjects like woodwork, dressmaking, and typing, and extended by 1973 to include motor car maintenance, conversational French, hostess cookery, beauty culture, gem stone art, and wine-making. In the sports complex, coaching was provided in football, hockey, volleyball, basketball, table tennis, badminton, trampolining, archery, golf, and there were also sessions of country dancing, and keep fit for canoeists. Biggart Home, maintained by the Education Committee since 1945 as a special school for handicapped children, was in 1966 transferred to the Hospitals Board for care of geriatric patients; among new facilities provided by the county council was a hostel erected in 1972 at Blackford Crescent to house ten mentally-handicapped persons.

Expansion of education required an augmentation of staff, and from time to time new head teachers. Joseph Murdoch, headmaster of the high school since 1956, managed its conversion into an academy and was succeeded in 1974 by A. Douglas Monnickendam. At Glenburn school, Hugh Paterson who followed Alexander Adams in 1969 was promoted to become county primary adviser in 1971, when he was replaced by Francis D. Welsh. Also in 1971 Alfred J.W. Simpson was appointed to the new Kingcase Primary School. Prestwick Public School continued under John Harrison from 1951 until its closure. At Monkton, John Morgan was followed by John H. Steele in 1967 and Miss Ellen Smart in 1974. St Ninian's R.C. School was opened in 1962 with Hugh Hasson as head teacher for its first eleven years, then Patrick McGuire was appointed in 1973 to succceed him. Now that travel to work was becoming much more common, only some of those head teachers and their staff chose to reside locally and so had less involvement in the community than many of their predecessors; though conversely, a number of those who taught elsewhere had their roots in Prestwick, and a few of them became members of the town council, most notably Provost Iain Foulds, head teacher of Irvine Royal Academy.

While the ministers of the local churches retained their local role, their influence in the community was diminishing as society became increasingly secular in character. Rev. Donald M.Caskie continued his long ministry at St. Cuthbert's, as did Rev. James Burgoyne Yorke at the South Church, but there were changes in the other Church of Scotland charges. Rev. George MacLeod Dunn retired after serving for thirty-two years at St. Nicholas and died in 1963; in 1961 Rev. William Humphrey Hamilton was inducted as his successor. Rev. Charles Raymond Vincent left the North Church in 1965, followed by induction of Rev. Philip Wilfred Powell Petty. When Rev. Peter Higgins left Kingcase Church in 1958, Rev. James Logan was inducted as his successor. At St Ninian's Episcopal Church, Rev. Canon Charles Paton was followed by Rev. E.W. Buswell in 1964 and Rev. Joseph Burrows in 1970. Father Laurence Breen of St Quivox R.C. Church retired in 1960 and died in 1964; his successor was Father Vincent Walker. New Prestwick Baptist Church was served by Revs. Walter Lang (1958–65), John Moore (1966–68), Ken Mc Dougall (1969–73), and showed a modest increase in membership. The Christian Brethren of the Bute Hall continued their evangelism, as with a "Christ is the Way" campaign in 1961. Completion of St Ninian's Episcopal Church in 1962 after 35 years' delay was an indication of continued support. In the Church of Scotland congregations new halls were acquired by the South Church (1960), Kingcase (1965), and St Nicholas (1968). Kingcase was the only one which showed increase in membership. While most of the congregations continued to maintain youth organisations, membership of many Sunday schools was falling, and a new Friendship Club formed at St Nicholas in 1962 and similar efforts to attract adult adherents to weekly evening meetings proved of limited success. Most people preferred to pursue secular interests in their leisure time.

Organisations for men like Rotary, Burns Club, and Toastmasters, formed locally in the post-war years, were joined by others like the Round Table and a Probus Club. For the opposite sex, as well as the Townswomen's Guilds there were now also a Business and Professional Women's Club, a Ladies Circle, a Ladies Speakers Club, and a Women's Junior Air Corps. For those with special interests, an Ayrshire Cine Club formed in 1960 was centred in Prestwick; there were the Prestwick Players, also an Amateur Operatic Society formed in 1964, and an Arts Guild in 1970. For those with various interests in aviation there were the RAFA in Stonegarth, a Prestwick branch of the Royal Aeronautical Society, the Prestwick Flying Group, an Airport Club in the old St Cuthbert clubhouse, and the SAL Social Club which abandoned Powmill for new premises. Sports enthusiasts benefited from extended facilities at the public park, now commonly known as the Oval. There was a football field and pavilion for use by local and visiting amateur and juvenile teams; municipal tennis courts; a cricket pitch with a pavilion modernised in 1967; and children's playground. Bowling greens were busy in the summer, and the indoor bowling club opened in 1964 attracted devotees from a wide area. Other sports were also flourishing. The long-established angling club was joined by a sea angling club in 1966, while the sailing club remained popular. Prestwick Golf Club and that at St Nicholas continued to flourish. Though the municipal St Ninian's course had gone, the St Cuthbert club commenced play in 1963 on its new course at Heathfield, with a clubhouse for its 600 members opened the previous year. Among other pastimes, there was still an active gardening club, and from 1971 a new commercial venture was a garden centre established near the Towans Hotel.

Decline of the cinema continued. The Picture House which had closed down in 1957 was demolished in 1963. By that time too the Broadway was introducing bingo for several nights in the week, and film performances ceased there in 1976. The cinema could not compete with television, especially after colour was introduced in 1967 and a mast erected at Darvel in 1973 improved local reception. Outside the home, young people were catered for by the uniformed organisations and by the youth service of the county education committee. In 1960 the youth club in the former British Restaurant had to close when the premises were demolished to make way for old people's housing; an alternative was provided by the Tiki Club (named after a Pacific good-luck talisman) which met in the town hall, then in the former Kingcase golf clubhouse. Pop music made its appeal to teenagers via TV, records and tapes, and the twist introduced a new style of dancing, so that they crowded into what were originally called discotheques, becoming commonly known as discos. The local press in the seventies recorded disturbing developments among a minority of those attending – fighting among rival gangs of youths, instances of under-age drinking, and evidence of drugs.

There was much more drinking among adults. By 1961 alcoholic drinks were on sale in four public houses, nine hotels, and four licensed grocers. That year two other grocers in housing areas were awarded licences to meet demand for drinks for home consumption. More hotels would obtain licences and equip their premises to attract new customers, matching facilities available to members of the golf and other licensed private clubs. In 1964 the long-established Royal Hotel in Main Street was in 1964 demolished to make way for the Golden Eagle. Public houses, formerly male preserves, now welcomed patrons of both sexes to their lounge bars. Meals out were becoming popular, and in 1964 a restaurant in Main Street was first of those to obtain a table licence. Outwith the burgh, Adamton House, after lying empty since the Americans left, was in 1973 licensed as a hotel with banqueting facilities and a park for 100 cars. In this period, when closing-time in Ayr was 10 p.m., in Prestwick it was 10.30 p.m., an advantage for customers of the Carlton Hotel at Prestwick Toll, for the hotel was within Prestwick and its car park over the boundary in Ayr burgh. Breathalysing of motorists was not yet introduced, so that cars were extensively in use for evenings out, as well as more properly for travel to work and holidays. Cars were increasingly use for shopping at the new style of superstores, typified by Massey in Main Street (1962) and Safeway in Ayr Road (1971).

The census inquired for the first time in 1971 about possession of a car. 52.4% of households in the parish had at least one, which indicates about 2,500 cars within Prestwick. The result was that, even though the entire length of the Prestwick-Ayr bypass was completed in 1971, a traffic problem persisted. Holidaymakers in cars and coaches might no longer form a steady stream on their way through the town at peak periods. But now, throughout the year, the main street and those adjoining were almost permanently congested with parked cars. This was something which the town council could not solve. Along both sides of the Main Street, the Valuation Roll listed for 1975 over one hundred shops, branches of four banks, several restaurants, offices of various firms, two betting shops, and five public houses.

During the sixties, people were brought into close contact with the outside world through television, experiencing the Cuban missile crisis (1962), assassination of J.F. Kennedy (1963), the first men of the moon (1969). National affairs were punctuated by the general elections of 1964 and 1966 which awarded Harold Wilson the premiership; continued in the seventies when Edward Heath won in 1970 and Harold Wilson returned in 1974. The local constituency continued to return a Conservative member. Sir Thomas Moore who held the seat since 1925 retired in 1964, and died in 1971. His successor was George Younger, whose grandfather had been MP for Ayr Burghs from 1906 till 1922. He obtained a majority of two thousand in 1964, reduced to 384 in 1984, and this continued to be a marginal seat when the franchise was extended to eighteen-year-olds, though in the general elections of 1970 and 1974 the Labour opposition lost some of its support to Scottish National Party candidates. Throughout the early seventies, popular concern was focussed briefly on decimalisation of the coinage (1971), more consistently on economic problems, industrial unrest, troubles in Ireland, arguments over entry into the European Common Market, and a growing demand for Scottish devolution. Limited popular interest was shown when the Wheatley Report in 1969 recommended reorganisation of local government, and when the new Local Government (Scotland) Act was passed in 1973, its implications made little immediate impact upon the general populace. There was regret that Ayrshire would become absorbed within a massive Strathclyde region; but few seemed aware how Prestwick would be affected by abolition of town councils.

In the last twelve months of Prestwick burgh's existence, the local press reported a variety of events of local concern. In May 1974, the new blocks at Prestwick Academy showed signs of subsidence; pupils were sent home and experienced part-time lessons until end of the session in June. In June, St Cuthbert Golf Club celebrated its 75th anniversary. In July, Monkton had its first-ever gala week. In August, plans were approved for 210 new private houses at Heathfield. In September, the town council determined the burgh rate for the last time. In October it was announced that a recent boom in charter flights had, for the time being, compensated for the loss of various scheduled services. In November, schools were disrupted by a teachers' strike. In December, a Gospel musical, "Time for Christmas", was staged in the town hall by Unity, an interdemoninational Christian group of twenty-five performers, mostly from Ayr and Prestwick. Also, for Christmas, 650 grocery parcels were distributed to old folk by Prestwick Old People's Welfare Committee, in co-operation with Rotary, Round Table, and St Vincent de Paul Society. In January 1975 another charitable venture headed by the Round Table

After the last meeting of the town council in 1975, tribute was made to surviving dignitaries: Ex-Provost W. Iain Foulds; Honorary Burgess Mathew F. Foulds; Ex-Provost Gilbert Steele; Ex-Provost Fred Horton; Ex-Provost John Watt; Provost William Harkiss; Ex-Provost Hugh Chapman. (*IF*)

was fulfilled when a specially-designed minibus costing £4,000 was presented to the Biggart Home. In February, George Younger MP was appointed to the shadow cabinet as defence spokesman. In March, HMS Gannet initiated a course for six general practitioners to establish an emergency flying doctor service. In April a kitchen porter in a local hotel murdered the head waiter, and the following month was jailed for life.

To prepare for takeover by the new local authorities in May 1975, elections were held the previous May. Prestwick was entitled to three of the twenty-five seats on Kyle and Carrick District Council, and one of the 103 members of Strathclyde Regional Council. For the district council Fred Horton was elected to represent Kingcase, Edward Darley for St Nicholas. and Clifford Westcott returned unopposed for St Cuthbert. A fourth Conservative, Mrs Joan Ferguson, was elected to represent Prestwick and Coylbank on the regional council. Following the death of Councillor Darley, he was replaced in August by William Harkiss, after an uncontested election. Four of the twelve members of Prestwick town council were thus involved in the initial stages of the new authorities, while continuing to manage the burgh in its final year.

Prestwick town council had, after closure of the Bathing Lake, prepared ambitious plans for a £750,000 leisure centre incorporating an indoor swimming pool. These plans were submitted for government approval in 1973, but restrictions on public expenditure in 1974 meant that the scheme could not yet be implemented. That summer there were fewer visitors than ever and the *Ayr Advertiser* reported that "Prestwick takes a beating in tourism slump." It was pointed out that there was "no night life for young people". It was noticed that a discotheque club opened the previous year had closed down when its application for a liquor licence was turned down. Councillors were reluctant to provide facilities for unruly teenagers. There were complaints about "noisy brats" at band concerts. There were reported sightings of nude "streakers" on the beach. Permission was refused for a hot-dog stand at the esplanade, which might attract "an unwanted type of clientele". However, a final grant of £1,500 was awarded to Prestwick Tourist Association. The council pressed ahead with Lichtenfels town-twinning. A deputation from that German town visited Prestwick in July 1974, and a return visit was arranged in November, when formal compact was concluded. To ensure that this link would be maintained, and to ensure survival of burgh tradition, Prestwick town council sponsored formation of a Community Council in 1973, rather than wait for such a body to be established by statutory authority following local government reorganisation. The town council in 1974 considered the possibility of marking the end of an era with a Prestwick Civic Week, but reluctantly decided against. In 1975, the last months of the town council were spent in routine work, especially concerned with slow progress in construction of old people's houses at Sherwood Place; advocating proportional representation in a proposed Scottish Assembly; referring for future decision by the district council an application for an open-air market at the railway station car park.

On 13 May 1975 Prestwick town council met for the last time. Representatives of the Community Council handed over an illuminated scroll "to express the thanks of the comunity to past and present councillors." To the chairmen of the district and regional council who were present, Provost Harkiss handed over to these new authorities "with reluctance", and one of the bailies opined that the change would prove to be "utter disaster". The formal meeting was followed by a special function attended by councillors, officials, past-provosts, ministers, and representatives of the community council. Each councillor left with a photograph of the last council as a memento. So Prestwick, after eight centuries, ceased to exist as a burgh.

CHAPTER FIFTEEN

The Late 20th Century

WHILE it is impossible exactly to assess public opinion, it is certain that many local people regretted the demise of Prestwick town council which accompanied reorganisation of local government in 1975. Some major services like education, roads, police, fire service, water, drainage, and social work previously operated by Ayr County Council were taken over by Strathclyde Regional Council, and the more centralised administration from Glasgow sometimes seemed less satisfactory. Of special local concern were those other functions including housing and environmental services which were transferred from the town council to Kyle and Carrick District Council. Previously, when anyone mentioned to the burgh surveyor that a pavement needed repair, the work could be undertaken by his men with little delay. Now, however, a formal report had to be made, the matter remitted to anonymous officials, and only after some time might the work be undertaken. Complaints and suggestions could be made to the local councillors at "surgeries" which were instituted for that purpose. Under the old regime there were twelve councillors any one of whom might be consulted; one ex-provost recalled how he was always available for informal approaches during his regular Saturday morning walks along the main street. In 1985 another who regretted the changes remarked that Prestwick was no longer "our town". On a district council of twenty-five members, the three local representatives were in the minority. Something which proved galling was that in selecting a provost for the district, choice went to Troon (Alexander Paton, 1975–80), Girvan (James Boyle, 1980–84), Ayr (Gibson Macdonald, 1984–88 and from 1992), and Maybole (Dan McNeill, 1988–92); Prestwick was the only burgh in the district never to have a member chosen as civic chief of the district. In the years immediately after 1975 there were complaints that Ayr was unduly favoured in allocation of resources. In particular, Prestwick Merchants' Association protested at expenditure on establishing a district headquarters there. Householders in Prestwick felt inconvenienced when a new system of refuse collection was introduced in 1977. In the same year, Prestwick Amateur Operatic Society had to cancel its production because the district council would not subsidise it as had the former town council. In 1978 youngsters were using Maryborough Road for the current craze of skate-boards; suggestions for a proper track at the Oval were turned down. There was much concern at delay in implementing plans the town council had made for building an indoor swimming pool. The former bathing lake at the sea front was allowed to decay, when schemes to convert it into a seal sanctuary (1977–80) or

The sea front, with the former Bathing Lake landscaped. (*KA*)

fish farm (1982) proved unsuccessful. In 1980 Prestwick was described as "the district's forgotten town", and "negative planning policies" were said to have resulted in "running down of the sea front" and "general deterioration of Prestwick as a residential and holiday centre". As time passed it was discovered that memorabilia had disappeared, like the visitors' book with autographs of celebrities like the cosmonauts Yuri Gagarin and Valentina Tereshkova whom civic dignitaries had welcomed at the airport; and it was suspected that the freemen's records too had been unwittingly destroyed around the time of regionalisation. The district council continued to attract criticism whenever rates and council house rents were increased, though in fact inflation and government cut-backs were contributory factors.

Though politics had played a part in the work of Prestwick town council, party divisions and factional disputes formed a principal feature of the district council. The local Labour Party which had been virtually defunct since the early 1970s was resuscitated, and its candidate Jim Murray captured St Nicholas Ward in 1980 when his party took control of the district council for the ensuing four years. That seat was held for Labour by Ian Welsh in 1984, though the Conservatives then recovered a majority in the council. In 1988 he was joined by Patricia McLellan who narrowly defeated Clifford Westcott in St Cuthbert Ward and shared in Labour's second

The main street, congested with motor traffic. (*KA*)

district administration. In 1992 St Cuthbert Ward was recovered by Christina Young; in Kingcase Ward, Fred Horton did not seek re-election and was succeeded by Pamela Paterson; St Nicholas Ward continued to be represented by Ian Welsh, who became Leader of the Council in 1990 and continued from 1992 as leader of the Labour group in opposition. But despite intense political rivalries on the council, the district elections were never so keenly contested as those for the town council had been, and the turn-out was rarely more than 50%. Similarly with the regional council, whose 103 members included one representing Prestwick – Mrs Joan Ferguson was elected in 1974, a member of the Conservative group in opposition; followed in 1986 by John Baillie who won the seat and joined the continued Labour majority on Strathclyde Regional Council. Public interest throughout the period was focussed rather on national issues, especially when the Labour government of James Callaghan (1976–79) was followed by the Conservative ones of Margaret Thatcher (1979–90) and John Major (since 1990). George Younger continued to represent the Ayr constituency as he had done since 1964, serving from 1979 as Secretary of State for Scotland, then as Secretary for Defence, retiring in 1992 to enter the House of Lords and taking the title of Lord Younger of Prestwick. In successive general elections he had retained a majority of votes against a divided opposition, though the contests had become increasingly marginal. In 1992 his successor Phil Gallie obtained 22,172 votes, only ninety-five more than his Labour opponent, with another thousand shared by Liberal-Democrat and Scottish National party candidates. Throughout the eighties, the operations of local authorities were more closely monitored by central government: rates were replaced by a community charge then by a council tax; expenditure was more rigorously restricted.

Despite the loss of local control, a number of significant improvements were made. The regional council converted the disused public school into a community centre in 1979, and continued to extend educational provision in the town; established a much-needed sewage pumping scheme at the north end of the promenade, whose construction was impressive enough to win a Civic Trust Award in 1986; opened in 1983 a dual-carriageway road to Irvine and the north, complementing those others by-passing Prestwick and leading to Kilmarnock which had been made by Ayr County Council. The district council after many difficulties was able to open in 1984 the long-awaited indoor swimming pool adjacent to the indoor bowling rinks, at a cost of nearly £400,000. In 1992 work commenced on a £250,000 renovation of the sea front: the bathing lake was landscaped to provide a safe play area – originally set securely on piles, it was too expensive to remove. Another £9,000 was expended improving the area round the cross. There was some regret when the district council sold off the Town Hall in 1991, though the regional council's community centre offered some alternative facilities. The district council showed proper concern for economic development, supportive of the claims of Prestwick Airport – as compared to the Glasgow-based regional council which tended to favour Abbotsinch. The district council in 1980 took over the Shaw Farm Industrial Estate, and that year the Caledonian Airmotive plant was opened there on a twenty-acre site, refurbishing aero and industrial gas turbine engines. Established by the Caledonian Airways Group, it was taken over in 1987 by the US-based Ryder System. Renamed Aviall Caledonian in 1993, it overhauled a large range of engines used by world airlines, with a work force which steadily increased from 120 in 1980 to 820 in 1993, working in shifts round the clock seven days a week.

It has been estimated that in the 1980s more than ten thousand families in Ayrshire were directly or indirectly dependent upon Prestwick Airport, so that its fluctuating fortunes have been a continuing concern here and hereabouts.

In 1977 Prestwick was designated as the Gateway to Scotland, confirming its role for transatlantic flights. Scheduled services were then being operated by British Airways, British Caledonian, and Air Canada, and they were joined by Northwest Orient in 1979, with daily flights to Boston. Several smaller Canadian and US companies providing charter flights were tempted to make transit stops at Prestwick, and from 1978 the newly-formed Laker Airways initiated charter flights from Prestwick, extended in 1980 to providing direct scheduled services to Los Angeles and Miami. But the 1980s brought setbacks. In 1982 Laker Airways went out of business; others providing transatlantic charters found it more profitable to use English airports; while Scottish tour operators chose Abbotsinch for flights to European resorts. Prestwick also lost its scheduled services. Air Canada withdrew flights in 1979, British Caledonian ceased to survive as an airline, and British Airways abandoned Prestwick in 1981. The airport handled 418,000 pasengers in 1980, only half that number three years later. In 1984 a campaign was initiated to

"Keep Prestwick Flying", which however failed to halt demands for an "open skies" policy which would allow Abbotsinch to operate transatlantic flights. In 1985 the status of Prestwick as Gateway to Scotland was confirmed, but despite vigorous efforts in 1989 by Kyle and Carrick District Council government restrictions were removed, and British Airways and Air Canada introduced transatlantic services from Abbotsinch. Northwest alone remained at Prestwick, until 1990 when its transfer also to Abbotsinch left Prestwick without any remaining scheduled services. The airport continued in occasional use for diverted aircraft, for a very few chartered flights, for Concorde as a quiet location where pilots could practise landings. In 1987 British Aerospace took over and extended Adamton House to establish a flying college which could train 120 students at a time, thus reintroducing Prestwick's original function. HMS Gannet continued to operate its Sea King helicopters, complementing anti-submarine practice with much-appreciated rescue work. In 1993, 819 Squadron undertook 232 such sorties from Prestwick, searching for missing ships and aircraft, recovering stranded climbers and hillwalkers, transporting seriously ill patients, once airlifting from a 250-foot chimney a steeplejack suffering from a heart attack, once saving a blind dog which had started swimming towards Arran. The airport still proved a convenient base for freight flights. In 1984 approval was granted to establish a Freeport, where goods could be landed and not required to pay duty before they were prepared for depatch. This allowed in 1985 some 12,000 tons shipped by air from Prestwick, and as much by road. But the busiest time at the airport was at the biennial Scottish Air Shows. For most of the time, the airport terminal remained an empty shell.

From 1990, after introduction of the "open skies" policy which favoured Abbotsinch, there were fears that the privatised British Airports Authority was intent on running down Prestwick Airport. The possibility arose of Prestwick being more effectively promoted by local enterprise. The district council, with cross-party support from local MPs George Younger (Conservative: Ayr) and George Foulkes (Labour: Cumnock, Carrick and Doon Valley), and in cooperation with the local management of British Aerospace, created conditions for a local consortium to take over the airport. A successful bid was made by this consortium, headed by George Youmger, now Lord Younger of Prestwick. Taking its name from the airport's international call sign, PIK Ltd assumed ownership in February 1992. Freight traffic continued as a healthy business – in PIK's first nine months, 21,000 tons of cargo passed through, and there were fifteen regular freight flights weekly. A concerted effort was made to re-establish the airport's passenger traffic, and a local newspaper commented that "Like Sleeping Beauty the Airport is coming to life". In October 1993 it was announced that six tour operators would the following summer provide 200 flights to eight holiday destinations. Customers would be attracted by cheap rates, and easy transport to the airport – the railway line between Glasgow and Ayr had been electrified in 1986, and a new railway station alongside the airport was opened in September 1994. With a tradition of smooth transfer of passengers through the spacious terminal, Prestwick promised to become "Scotland's Leisure Airport".

Scotland's Leisure Airport: the first charter flight of 1994 from Prestwick. (*PIK Ltd*)

Closely associated with the airport, the manufacture of aircraft also experienced a period of change. While in 1945 there had been twenty-seven such British firms, by 1977 SAL was one of the six still surviving. In that year the Labour government nationalised the aircraft industry and in 1978 the SAL works became part of British Aerospace. Then at a low ebb, the workforce of 2,700 employees in 1975 was reduced to 1,400 engaged in repairs and manufacture of parts. But a new market was emerging for smaller civil planes, and British Aerospace had the resources to develop an improved version of those Jetstream planes previously manufactured by SAL, and could concentrate on this as work on repairs and engine overhaul dried up. Production commenced in 1980 of Jetstream 31, a roomy nineteen-seater pressurised aircraft, a miniature airliner rather than a magnified small plane. By 1985, Prestwick's fiftieth anniversary, more than one hundred had been sold, and the Queen's Award for Export Achievement received. This award was repeated on two later occasions, for by 1991 more than 320 Jetstream 31 and Super 31s had been delivered to airlines worldwide. Also in 1991, in the presence of HM the Queen, the first Jetstream 41 was rolled out, a twenty-nine-seater plane which has proved equally successful. From 1981, following denationalisation, the new owners were British Aerospace PLC, which in 1984 incorporated Prestwick in its Civil Aircaft Division, then in 1993 formed Jetstream Aircraft Ltd as a separate subsidiary company. Production of an advanced turboprop design was transferred to Prestwick. This Jetstream 61 could take up to sixty-eight passengers and carry them for longer distances. By now, 2,500 workers were employed by Jetstream, though the world-wide recession brought cancellation of orders in 1993 and prospect of 630 redundancies. Of the original Scottish Aviation Ltd., there survived Scottish Express International, a major freight company with more than two hundred employees centred at Dundonald, Prestwick, and Ayr.

Catering for visitors, once Prestwick's premier industry, was now a shadow of its former self. By the 1990s the number of hotels was reduced to seven. Others had closed, some converted into nursing homes for the elderly as a more profitable enterprise. Those which survived provided altogether fewer than 150 beds, and the principal business of the larger ones was hosting wedding receptions and other functions. A Visitors' Guide to Ayrshire showed in the 1980s twenty smaller establishments offering bed and breakfast accommodation, adding sixty other rooms to the total. St Andrew's Caravan Park at Monkton and lesser sites in the neighbourhood offered a more attractive alternative for some summer visitors. The number of day trippers was also reduced, with pollution of the Ayrshire beaches a powerful disincentive. Similarly the oldest occupation in the district, that of agriculture, was also much reduced. Land was lost as the airport was extended and new houses and roads built. Only nine farms continued to operate within the area of the former parish, nearly all rented still, several still owned by the Angus family of Ladykirk, the one remaining local estate.

The population of Prestwick at the census of 1981 was 13,532, hardly increased in the previous decade. The number of houses was now just over 5,000, including more than 1,400 which had been built by the town council and transferred to district council ownership in 1975. Older council houses were modernised, but few new ones were henceforth built, here or elsewhere. Private building continued, mostly undertaken by large outside firms. This was limited by shortage of remaining building plots, and houses were erected on former nursery gardens, the old burgh yard, even on the disused railway branch line to Glenburn. Despite protests, a piece of ground near the railway station was taken over which it was claimed had been common land. By 1993 building extended beyond East Road to reach the edge of the airport's secondary runway. With Prestwick's population swollen towards 15,000, the town centre was busier than ever and the main street congested with parked cars. By contrast, Monkton had become a much quieter place now that it was bypassed by through traffic. There in 1981 nearly a thousand people lived in just over 300 houses. With older houses modernised, the village had become a much more attractive place. Here as everywhere, domestic life was further improved; central heating and double-glazing became commonplace; fridges were joined by freezers and microwave ovens; with washing machines in common use, the Prestwick Laundry closed in 1982; video-recorders now took their place alongside television sets; children listened to pop music on ghetto-blasters and played computer games.

Provision of education by Strathclyde Regional Council involved management of the four primary schools and Prestwick Academy. Glenburn had, as head teachers, Francis D. Welsh (from 1971), John H. Steele (1979), Mrs Freda Wilson (1992); Kingcase had A.J.Simpson (from 1971), then Mrs Anne Nutt (1984); Monkton had Miss Ellen Smart (from 1974), Kevin Gavin (1977), Mrs Ina-Mae Dickinson, then Mrs Margaret McCluskie (1984); St Ninian's R.C. school was headed by Patrick McGuire (from 1973), then Mrs Helen Hilley (1984) who continued after marriage as Mrs O'Hagan. It is noteworthy that women (included married ladies) were now being appointed to such posts; and because the local primary schools were comparatively small, there was a rapid turnover as some head teachers moved elsewhere to gain further promotion. Kingcase was the largest, able to accommodate 462 pupils, with a roll of 440 in 1993; Glenburn could take 429 and had then 370 pupils; Monkton with 80 pupils was only half full; and St Ninian's had a roll of 150 out of a possible 230. At Prestwick Academy, A. Douglas Monnikendam, appointed head teacher in 1974, was followed in 1987 by Roy G.Storie. The academy had capacity for 1,588 pupils, and its roll surpassed 1,200 in 1972, but following national demographic trends, fell to 750, though numbers rose again to 900 in 1992, the 90th anniversary of the school. In that year 39% of pupils in S4 year gained three or more awards at levels one and two in the new Standard Grade examinations, while 33% in S5 gained three or more Higher grade passes at levels A – C. These figures were .well above the average in Ayr Division, and to some degree an index of teaching efficiency, though also reflecting pupils' abilities and social background. A year later numbers had risen to 971, and other published statistics revealed expenditure on Prestwick Academy in 1993 was £2,397,000, a cost of £2,469 per pupil. Altogether, local schools catered for around two thousand pupils, compared with some eight hundred early in the century. While the school board in 1919 had a staff of thirty-one teachers, the regional council in 1993 required forty-six in the primary schools and eighty-seven in the academy. To all these must be added ancillary staff, school secretaries, auxiliaries, janitors, cleaners, dining hall attendants, and "lollipop ladies" for street crossings; as well as school doctors and dentists, educational psychologists, speech therapists, and attendance officers. In addition to outlay on salaries, there was increased expenditure on equipment for a widening range of studies. Within the academy there were departments responsible for English, Mathematics, Modern Languages, Social Studies, Science, Business Studies, Art and Design, Technical Subjects, Home Economics, Music, Physical Education, Religious Studies, and Library. In primary and in secondary schools there were extramural activities like sports and excursions (including foreign trips), and academy pupils had not only a string orchestra but a jazz band. There was increased parental involvement in school work and activities, and the premises of each school provided facilities for adults to share in what was called community education. This era of educational development was not without its problems, Curriculum changes brought stress to teachers. Reduction of school rolls brought an end to overcrowded classes, but teacher shortage resulted in composite classes being formed in primary schools. This was always acceptable in small schools like Monkton where three or four teachers were responsible for sharing the work of seven year-groups; but caused indignation in other cases, and parental protests at St Ninian's in 1977. This was an era of discontent among Scottish teachers, who were involved in strikes in 1965, 1974, 1980, and 1985. In the year 1977–78 Francis D. Welsh, head teacher of Glenburn, was national president of the Educational Institute of Scotland, the largest teachers' union. For most of the time, however, schooling went on quietly and effectively, in an age when many pupils were under various external pressures. From 1968 guidance teachers were appointed in secondary schools and after 1982, when corporal punishment was abolished, their efforts were particularly necessary in supervising the behaviour and welfare of their pupils.

There was as yet no nursery school within Prestwick, but several playgroups for toddlers were formed under private auspices. For older age groups, young people were still catered for by various organisations. Particularly popular was Prestwick Boys Club which commenced in 1977 as a juvenile football team sponsored by the Cricket Club; ten years later it had 300 members. There were other groups for those with sporting interests, even a Prestwick Girls Football Club formed in 1988. Other girls joined the majorettes. Pastimes like chess and drama also had junior groups. The long-established uniformed organisations continued to attract members, as did others associated with the churches, but they provided for a smaller proportion of teenagers and, despite efforts of the Prestwick Youth Panel, to which eighteen groups were affiliated in 1988, many young people belonged to no organisation at all.

This was an increasingly secularised society. Membership of churches was everywhere declining, and indeed in Prestwick the majority of adults now had no church connection. Yet within the increased population, the number of church members in the town was little changed from what it had been in mid-century, so that the various denominations were able to maintain vitality. Within the Church of Scotland, Kingcase Church emerged to become the largest congregation under Revs. James Logan (from 1958), D. Muir McLaren (1977), Alexander B. Douglas (1985), then Ian Purves (1992). With 1,400 on the roll it served the southern and now more-populous part of the town. The northern part with four other charges was deemed by Ayr Presbytery in 1976 to be "over-churched"; an attempt to reduce the number by uniting the North and South churches proved abortive, but an alternative proved possible in 1981. In that year Rev. Donald M. Caskie retired from St Cuthbert's. He had ministered here since 1947, the last minister to be inducted to what had been the parish church of Monkton and Prestwick, and when he died in 1992 at the age of 84 he was eulogised as "the quiet man who always possessed the voice of authority". After his demission in 1981, Rev. Arthur F.S. Kent was appointed to serve both St Cuthbert's and the North Church, where Rev. Philip W.P.Petty had been minister since 1965, and a merger of the two congregations was consummated in 1986. The new Monkton and Prestwick North Church, with a roll in 1993 of 840, was established within the North Church under Rev. Arthur F.S. Kent, and St Cuthbert's as the older building sold in 1987. The South Church, within the town centre, celebrated its centenary in 1984. Under the Revs. James Burgoyne Yorke (from 1947), Jack Brown (1976), Thomas B. Girdwood (1981), and Kenneth C. Elliott (1989) its membership increased to 640. St Nicholas Church with 950 members in 1993 experienced little change in numbers under Revs. W. Humphrey Hamilton (from 1961) and George R. Fiddes (1985). While in these four Church of Scotland congregations there were around 3,800 communicant members, fewer than 400 were attached to the Woman's Guilds, and just over 500 young people attended Sunday schools and Bible classes. Most of the other denominations remained without dramatic change. St Ninian's Episcopal Church was served by Revs. Joseph Burrows (from 1970), Alisdair Petrie (1978), Dr John McKay (1981), then Philip D.Noble (1984), and in 1994 had 120 communicant members. St Quivox R.C. Church continued with just over a thousand members of all ages (some 800 of these being adults). Father Vincent Walker, later Canon Walker, retired in 1988 and died in 1993; his successor from 1988 was Father Francis P.G. Moore. New Prestwick Baptist Church continued, with as ministers Revs. Ken McDougall (from 1969), Tom Lawson (1975), Ian King (1985), James Neilson (1986), then Foster C. Wright (1993). It retained around 200 members and adherents, half of them from Prestwick and Ayr, the rest from other parts of the county. This membership continued despite a schism which resulted in formation of a Kyle Community Church which from 1985 held Sunday services in Prestwick Community Centre. That doctrine for some people remained an important issue appeared also with formation of another new congregation. In 1987 the former St Cuthbert's Church was purchased to become the New Life Christian Centre for a group already established locally. This was a Pentecostal church belonging to the Assembly of God, and Saturday, Sunday, and mid-week services attracted some 200 adherents from various parts of Ayrshire. Meanwhile the Christian Brethren of the Bute Hall and at Glenburn continued active, though with fewer adherents now. The Salvation Army retained some members, but had to sell their local hall and become attached to the unit in Ayr. One welcome ecumenical development was the formation of a Prestwick Council of Churches with Church of Scotland, Episcopal, and Roman Catholic involvement. There was an annual week of Christian Aid, and seaside missions in summer continued as a reminder that religion was still alive in Prestwick.

The town itself succeeded in retaining its distinct identity, despite the reorganisation of local government in 1975, and despite the former Prestwick burgh appearing in later census reports only as postal districts KA9 1 and KA9 2. Prestwick town council had anticipated its demise by sponsoring in 1973 formation of a Prestwick Community Council of thirty elected members, which in 1977 was statutorily constituted with eighteen members. Though with no mandatory powers, it proved more effective than similar bodies in many other places. It manfully asserted Prestwick's interests, and provided a focus for expression of local opinion. In 1983 it organised celebration of "Prestwick Millennium" with a programme extending from 11 May to 4 September. This ambitious project included election of a Millennium Queen, a Prestwick Princess, a Prestwick Junior Miss, and there were a pageant, displays, sports tournaments, competitions, organised games at the shore, variety shows, band concerts, musical recitals, as well as the usual town fete. Altogether more than sixty local organisations were involved.

A remarkably wide range of activities was now on offer. The three golf courses remained busy, despite rising costs of playing. Prestwick Golf Club remained select with around 550 members of various categories, including some enthusiasts living overseas who chose to belong to this prestigious club. St Nicholas and St Cuthbert had now each around 800 members. Bowling acquired extended popularity when older outdoor greens were complemented by the indoor rinks, which from 1964 made Prestwick a mecca for devotees. The adjoining pool, opened in 1984, revived and widened enthusiasm for swimming. Prestwick Cricket Club retained its popularity; not far away on the football pitches Prestwick Amateurs and Glenburn Welfare played on alternate Saturdays, while juvenile and schools teams shared these facilities. The Sailing Club and those others for sea angling and fishing at the reservoir continued to attract members. New groups were formed for other sports: Adamton Clay Pigeon Shooting Club, an Aviation Archery Club at Atlantic House, a Ladies Volleyball team, and one old sport was revived when a Glenburn Quoiting Club was instituted in 1982. Curlers and skaters had to go into Ayr, though there were plans to accommodate them in the Centrum complex being built near Prestwick Toll. This was a privately-funded project: it was located on ground acquired by a former town council which was regarded as common land by those who opposed loss of this open space; and financial problems hampered its completion. There was a widening range of organisations for those with other interests. In 1979 the regional council converted the old public school into a community centre, and the Community Association elected to manage it sponsored various activities. Parts of the town retained something of their separate identity, as witnessed by Glenburn Miners Welfare Club, Prestwick Toll Senior Citizens Club, and Kingcase Community Association. But nearly all catered for the entire community and most of those listed in previous chapters continued to flourish. In 1988 the local Women's Royal Voluntary Service celebrated its fiftieth birthday, while in 1993 Boydfield Townwomen's Guild had its fortieth and Monkton WRI its seventieth anniversary. The Town Twinning Association had proved so succcessful in establishing the association with Lichtenfels since 1974 that in 1993 a link was formally established also with Vandalia in Ohio. Well-established organisations were joined by several new ones, like a Speechmasters Club, a dog training club, Amity Luncheon Club, a Wine Circle. Following the "Millennium" celebrations, a History Group was formed in 1984 whose series of winter lectures and annual exhibitions proved immensely popular. The community centre, the academy, smaller halls, and several hotels provided meeting places not only for local societies, but attracted organisations with a wider membership who found Prestwick a convenient centre. These included groups as diverse as the Ayrshire Chess Association, Kyle Fencing Club, Ayr Photographic Society, Ayrshire

Video-Cine Club, Kyle Mountain Club, Ayrshire Spanish Society, British Sugarcraft Guild, Embroiderers Guild, Royal Aeronautical Society, Royal Naval Association, an Association of Wrens. In 1977 the Ayrshire Bridge Club acquired its own premises in Prestwick by purchasing the Old Cronies Club at the Riggs.

One notable feature of local organisations in Prestwick has been their charitable efforts. This is worth particular emphasis because in the latter part of the 20th century attention of the media is often focussed on less desirable aspects of human behaviour. Prestwick, like everywhere else, has suffered from anti-social activities. The local press has reported vandals damaging bus shelters (1976), thefts of drugs from surgeries and chemists' shops (1978), a local drugs ring (1982), assault on a 72-year-old woman by a teenager breaking in (1984), a 60-year-old widow murdered by a burglar (1992), complaints that homosexuals were picking up partners at the sea front (1992). As against these may be recorded the Christmas efforts when Rotary annually led other local groups in collecting donations and distributing gifts to elderly residents. The Biggart Hospital was recipient of numerous gifts of equipment, and when the Old Cronies Club was wound down in 1977, its funds went towards laying out a garden there. In 1989 there was opened in Links Road a Malcolm Sargent House to provide holidays for children suffering from cancer; local organisations helped finance conversion of the former family house, and continued to contribute to running costs. Prestwick Friends of Ayrshire Hospice was formed to organise fun-runs and other means of supporting that hospice which opened in Ayr in 1989; and in nine years up to 1993 £100,000 was raised in Prestwick for that specific purpose. The Hansel Village at Symington for the medically- handicapped was another local good cause; an Oxfam shop opened in 1987 was only one example of the numerous national and international charities otherwise benefiting from the generosity of Prestwick folk.

Exactly one hundred years ago Rev. Kirkwood Hewat published the book he called *A Little Scottish World*. Since then Prestwick has changed much. But the words he then wrote in his introduction are quite appropriate for repetition by the present writer:

"If he has been successful in rescuing many interesting traditions and pictures of old Scottish life from passing into oblivion the Author will be much gratified. He will feel too that his labours have been amply rewarded if this volume be the means of stimulating others to study and put on record the history of their own districts, and also if it should give natives and visitors – and their friends — a fresh interest in the ancient Ayrshire parish of Monkton and Prestwick."

Sources of Information

The bibliography lists books, articles, and records relating to Prestwick, with cue titles used in the Chapter Notes, where more detailed references are given, as well as more specialised sources.

Principal Printed References

Records: Records of the Burgh of Prestwick 1470–1782, Maitland Club, 1834, with an Introduction by John Fullarton.

OSA: The |Old| Statistical Account of Scotland, Vol. XII, 1793, Parish of Monkton and Prestwick by Rev. Andrew Mitchell, pp. 394-403; references are from Vol. VI, Ayrshire, 1982 reprint, cited as *OSA Ayrshire*, pp. 458-67.

Chalmers: George Chalmers, *Caledonia*, 4 vols., 1807–24; 8 vols., 1887–1902; Vol. 3, 1824 has Ayrshire pp. 445-566, Monkton and Prestwick pp. 505-08; references are from Vol. 6, 1890, pp. 445 – 566, pp. 505 – 08; also extracts in William Robertson, *Historic Ayrshire*, 2 vols., 1891, 1894.

NSA: The New Statistical Account of Scotland, Ayrshire, 1847; Parish of Monkton and Prestwick by Rev. Thomas Burns, pp.169-78.

Paterson: James Paterson, *History of the Counties of Ayr and Wigton*, 2 vols., 1847, 1852; in 5 vols., 1863–68; in 2 vols. with addenda, 1871; references are to Vol. 1, Part 2, 1863, Parish of Monkton, pp. 574-602.

Hewat: Rev. Kirkwood Hewat, *A Little Scottish World*, 1894; second edition,1908.

Murray: David Murray, *Early Burgh Organization in Scotland*, Vol. 2, 1932,Chapter XXV, The Burgh of Prestwick, pp. 55-165.

Pryde 1958: G.S.Pryde, 'The Burghs of Ayrshire', *Ayrshire Collections*,Vol.4, 1958, pp. 8-49.

Other References

ACL: Ayr Carnegie Library.

AA: *Ayr Advertiser*, from 1803, files in ACL.

AO: Ayr Observer, 1832–1930, files in ACL.

AP: Ayrshire Post, from 1880, files in ACL.

Andrew: Ken Andrew, *Guide to Kyle and Carrick District*, 1981; also *Discovering Ayrshire*, 1988, 1994.

Ayrshire Collections: Collections of the Ayrshire Archaeological and Natural History Society, 12 vols., 1951–83, and subsequent monographs, published by AANHS.

Ayr: John Strawhorn, *The History of Ayr, Royal Burgh and County Town*, 1989.

ATB: *Ayrshire at the Time of Burns*, ed. John Strawhorn, AANHS, 1959.

Book of Wallace: C. Rogers, *The Book of Wallace*, Grampian Club, 2 vols.1889.

Boyd: William Boyd, *Education in Ayrshire Through Seven Centuries*, 1961.

Census Reports: Issued decennially since 1801 (except 1941).

Corbet: *Ayr, Prestwick, and District Historical Guide*, ed. R.Y.Corbett,1965.

Close: Rob Close, *Ayrshire and Arran Architectural Guide*, 1992.

Edgar: A. Edgar, *Old Church Life in Scotland*, 2 vols., 1885, 1886.

Fasti Scot.: *Fasti Ecclesiae Scoticanae*, ed. Hew Scott, Vol. 3, 1868; alsoVol. 8, 1950; Vol. 9, 1961.

Groome: F.H.Groome, *Ordnance Gazetteer of Scotland*, 6 vols.,1885–86, esp.Vol. 5, p. 48 (Monkton); Vol. 6, p. 231 (Prestwick).

Guide Books: ACL has collection in 652 BY; see also below, Steven.

McCarter: *Reminiscences of the County and Town of Ayr*, 1830; second edition entitled *Ayrshire*, 1832.

McQuitty: Rev. Luke McQuitty, *The Book of St Cuthbert's*, 1938.

Paisley Charters: *Registrum Monasterii de Passelet*, ed. Cosmo Innes, Maitland Club, 1832, reissued, New Club, 1877.

G.S.Pryde, *The Court Book of the Burgh of Kirkintilloch*, Scottish History Society, 1963, Introduction.

G.S.Pryde, *The Scottish Burghs*, A Critical List, 1965.

Sanderson: Margaret Sanderson, *Mary Stewart's People*, 1987, pp. 149-165 for'Robert Leggat, Parish Priest, and the parishioners of Prestwick'.

SRAA: Strathclyde Regional Archives, County Buildings, Ayr.

SRO: Scottish Record Office, Edinburgh.

Steven: Helen J. Steven, *Guide to Prestwick and Vicinity*, 1897.

TPT: *Troon and Prestwick Times*, from 1904; only complete file in British Library, Colindale, London; ACL has copies from 1970.

Welsh: Ian Welsh, *Prestwick in the 40's*, 1992.

Local and National Records

Prestwick Freemen's Records, 5 vols., 1726–1906, and Instruments of Sasine since 15th century: noted in Records Survey of July 1970 as in possession of Prestwick Town Council, but since disappeared. Some items, including Account Books 1824–1903. have survived, stored in ACL 652 GB; see also above under Principal Printed References for *Records*.

KS: Kirk Session Records of Monkton and Prestwick Parish, from 1615,in SRAA, ref. CH2/809.

SB: Monkton and Prestwick School Board Minute Books, 1873–1919, in SRAA, ref. CO3/10.

Log Book: Log Book of Prestwick Public School, 1882–1971, in SRAA, ref. CO3/10.

Monkton and Prestwick Parish Council Minute Books, 1903–29, in SRAA ref. CO3/51.

PTC: Prestwick Town Council Minutes, 1903–1975, in ACL except final volume in Burns House.

Ayrshire Commissioners of Supply Records, from 1713, in SRAA, ref. CO3/2.

Ayrshire Road Trustees Records, from 1767, in SRAA, ref. C03/4.

T1-T70: Tape recordings of Prestwick History Group lectures, 1984–92: especially useful are contributions from persons with local knowledge, K.Andrew (T37, 51, 60, 61), A.W.R Cochrane (T3, 4, 23, 24, 25, 42, 48, 49, 60, 61, 63, 64, 67, 68), W.Iain Foulds (T26, 27, 65, 66), H.Gardiner (T59), R.M.Gardiner (T5, 6, 19, 20), G.Giles (T10, 11), H.C.Law (T1, 2), D.McConnell (T35, 36), J.Melrose (T7,8), D.W.Rowan (T1, 2, 21, 22, 23, 24, 25, 42, 48, 49, 60, 61, 63, 64, 67, 68), D.C.Smail (T32), I. Welsh (T33, 34), W. Welsh (T1, 2, 51, 52), J.M.Wilson (T17, 18, 31, 41).

APS: The Acts of the Parliament of Scotland, ed. T.Thomson and C.Innes, 1814–75.

RMS: Registrum Magni Sigilli Regum Scotorum (Register of the Great Seal) ed. J.M.Thomson et al, 1882–1914.

RPC: The Register of the Privy Council of Scotland, ed. J.H.Burton et al., 1877–

Treasurers Accounts: The Accounts of the Lord High Treasurer of Scotland, ed. T.Dickson et al., 1877–

Bain: *Calendar of State Papers relating to Scotland*, ed. J.Bain, 1898–

General Works

Source Book: A Source Book of Scottish History, ed. W.C.Dickinson et al., 3 vols. 1952–54.

Edinburgh History of Scotland, 4 vols., 1965–75:
    A.A.M.Duncan, *Scotland, The Making of the Kingdom*, 1975;
    R.Nicolson, *Scotland, The Later Middle Ages*, 1974;
    G.Donaldson, *Scotland, James V – James VII*, 1965;
    W.Ferguson, *Scotland 1689 to the Present*, 1968.

T.C.Smout, *A History of the Scottish People, 1560–1830*, 1969; and *A Century of the Scottish People, 1830–1950*, 1986.

New History of Scotland, 8 vols., 1980–84:
    A.P.Smyth, *Warlords and Holy Men, A.D. 80 -1000.* 1984;
    G.W.S.Barrow, *Kingship and Unity, 1000 – 1306*, 1981;
    A.Grant, *Independence and Nationhood, 1306 – 1469*, 1984;
    J. Wormald, *Court, Kirk, and Community, 1470 – 1625*, 1981;
    R.Mitchison, *Lordship to Patronage, 1603 – 1745*, 1983;
    B. Lenman, *Integration, Enlightenment, and Industrialization, 1746 – 1832*, 1981;
    S. & O.Checkland, *Industry and Ethos, 1832–1914*, 1984;
    C.Harvie, *No Gods and Precious Few Heroes, 1914 – 1980*, 1981.

Sunday Mail Story of Scotland, 52 issues, 4 vols., 1988.

Michael Lynch, *Scotland, A New History*, 1991.

Maps and Plans

Blaeu 1654: 'The province of Kyle' from Vol. 5 of the *Atlas Novus*, published by W. and J. Blaeu, Amsterdam, 1654; reprinted by John Bartholomew and Son, Edinburgh, 1967. Scale 1.75 miles to one inch, 1:79200.

Roy 1747–55: Military Survey of Scotland by William Roy, manuscript maps in British Library; photocopies and colour slide in ACL. Scale 1.75 inches to one mile, 1:36000.

Armstrong 1775: *A New Map of Ayrshire* by A. and M. Armstrong, in six sheets.; reprinted by AANHS, 1959. Scale 1 inch to one mile, 1:63360.

Crawford 1780: 'Plan of Prestick Arable Lands and Peat Holes', by W. Crawford, 1780? Scale about 12 inches to one mile, 1:5280.

Prestwick 1780: 'Plan of the Town of Pristick', author not indicated, 1780? Scale about 16.5 inches to one mile, 1:3900. Copy in SRO (RHP 607).

Prestwick 1814: 'Plan of the Lands of Prestwick' A. and R. Kenneth, 1814. Scale about 8.5 inches to one mile, 1: 7500.

McDerment 1831: 'Plan of the Lands of Prestwick belonging to the Freeholders', by James McDerment, 1831. Scale about 16.5 inches to one mile, 1: 3900.

McDerment 1838: ditto, showing line of proposed railway. Scale about 30inches to one mile, 1:2000.

McDerment 1842: ditto. Scale about 15 inches to one mile, 1: 4000.

McDerment 1852: *Map of the Turnpike Roads of Monkton and Prestwick* by James McDerment and Sons, 1852. Scale 1.3 inches to one mile, 1: 48000.

OS 1857 and later editions: *Ordnance Survey maps*, various scales.

Copies of all these held in ACL.

Miscellaneous Notes

(a) Currency. Before decimalisation in 1971, £1 was divided into twenty shillings, and each shilling contained twelve pennies; thus £1 2s 6d, 12s 6d, 10/-, 6d equalled respectively £1.12, 62p, 50p, 2p. For earlier currency, £1 Scots was valued at one twelfth of £1 Sterling, and a mark or merk was worth two-thirds of £1 Scots.

(b) Dates. Before 1600 in Scotland the New Year commenced on 25th March, which has required conversion of certain earlier dates to conform with modern usage. Uncertainty regarding an exact date is variously indicated: c. 1750, circa 1750, signifies about 1750; Walter Fitzalan established Prestwick burgh, 1136 x 1173, sometime between those two years.

(c) Spellings. Quotations from earlier periods have been given in original spellings, to preserve the flavour of the times, but with occasional amendments for the sake of clarity.

Chapter Notes

For brevity in these notes, certain books and articles frequently referred to are cited by author's name (e.g. Hewat) or shortened title (e.g. *OSA Ayrshire*). See Bibliography above for such cue titles.

Chapter 1 – Origins

Prehistory is covered by two monographs, Alex. Morrison and Isobel Hughes, *The Stone Ages in Ayrshire*, AANHS, 1989, and Alex. Morrison, *The Bronze Age in Ayrshire*, AANHS, 1978. Though John Smith, *Prehistoric Man in Ayrshire*, 1895, pp. 126-27, noted "few remains of antiquity", a fuller range of sites is reported in *Archaeological Sites and Monuments of Scotland, 25: North Kyle*, 1985, esp. nos. 4-13, 27, 30, 41, 51, 56, 60, 61. For Mitchell's imaginative reference to Romans, *OSA Ayrshire*, p. 466. For place name interpretation, W.F.H. Nicolaisen, *Scottish Place Names*, 1976, Chapter 5, esp. p.79. For the year 750, A.O. Anderson, *Scottish Annals from English Chroniclers, A.D. 500 to 1286*, 1908, p. 56. For Sts. Cuthbert and Nicholas, D.H. Farmer, *The Oxford Book of Saints*, 1978, pp. 94-96, pp. 292-93. For the supposed establishment of a burgh in 983, see Chapter 4 for commentary on the Charter of 1600. For the early medieval period W.J.Dillon, 'The Origins of Feudal Ayrshire', *Ayrshire Collections*, Vol. 3, 1955, pp. 65-85; supplemented by G.W.S.Barrow, several of whose works interpret the feudalism of Kyle within a wider context: *Regesta Regnum Scottorum I: Acts of Malcolm IV*, ed. G.W.S. Barrow, 1960, p. 286 for Kyle grant to Walter Fitzalan; Barrow's *The Kingdom of the Scots*, 1981, with details of Walter on pp. 285, 326, 337, and of his lands in Kyle on pp. 347-50. For church lands in 1114, John Durkan, 'The Bishops Barony of Glasgow', *Scottish Church History Society Records*, Vol. 22, 1986, p. 278. For earliest references to Prestwick, *Paisley Charters*, esp, pp. 5-6, 7, 70-72, 308-314; several quoted by Chalmers, *NSA*, and Paterson, I.ii, p.660. For other references, two Scottish Record Society volumes, Ian Cowan, *The Parishes of Medieval Scotland*, 1967, and D.E.R.Watt, *Fasti Ecclesiae Scoticanae Medii Aevi*, 1969; *Records of the Regality of Melrose*, Scottish History Society, Vol. 3, 1917, ed. C.S.Romanes; G.W.S. Barrow, 'The Gilbertine House at Dalmilling', *Ayrshire Collections*, Vol. 4, 1958, pp. 50 – 67; W.J.Dillon, *Catholic Ayrshire*, Catholic Truth Society, 1958, pp. 12, 13 on Ladykirk; McGibbon and Ross, *Ecclesiastical Architecture of Scotland*, 3 vols., 1896, for Monkton and Prestwick churches.

Chapter 2 – The Medieval Burgh

Most of the information is derived from the printed burgh *Records* which commence in the year 1470, with two documents from 1446 in appendix, pp. 112-116. These *Records* have been already examined by Paterson, I.ii, pp.569 – 71; Murray, pp. 55-165; Pryde 1958, pp. 24 – 25, with his estimate of population in 1470; and by Sanderson, pp. 154 – 58. For burghs in Scotland, see Pryde 1958, 1963, 1965; Barrow, *Kingship and Unity*, pp. 84 – 104; *Scottish Urban History*, ed. G. Gordon and B. Dicks, 1983; *The Scottish Medieval Town*, ed. M. Lynch et al., 1988; Lynch's *History*, 1991; *Ayr*, Chs. 2 – 4. In determining the layout of Prestwick, the Puddock Sheugh's course can be traced on Plans of 1814 and 1831, with mention in T1, T4, and further considered in Chapter 9. For quotation from Walter of Newburgh, *Source Book*, Vol. 1, p.40. For Wallace's dream, Blind Harry's *Wallace*, ed. M. McDiarmid, Scottish Text Society, Vol. 1, 1968, Book VII, lines 58 – 169; Vol. 2, 1969, pp. 199 – 201. For Bruce's leprosy, G.W.S.Barrow, *Robert Bruce*, 1976, 1982, pp. 444-45. For Kingcase, *OSA Ayrshire*, p. 467; Chalmers, pp. 495 – 97; *Records*, notes on pp. 127-28; *NSA*, p. 173; Paterson, I.ii, p. 575 – 76; W.J. Dillon, 'The Spittals of Ayrshire', *Ayrshire Collections*, Vol. 6, 1961, pp. 12 – 30. For establishment of Newton burgh, Paterson, I.i, p. 157; Murray, p.171; Pryde 1958, pp. 20 – 21. For the plague, Grant (cited among General Works) pp. 72-75. For sand inundation, *Ayr*, pp. 33 – 34. McQuittie, pp. 9, 10, provides a list of vicars of Monkton and chaplains at Prestwick.

Chapter 3 – 16th Century

For the Blair family, Paterson, I.ii, pp. 577 – 82; II, pp. 393, 409; III.i, pp. 158 –89; G. Robertson, *Cunninghame*, 1820, p. 235; *RMS*, I, no. 157 (1363) and II, no. 1945 (1490); J. Hunter, *The House of John Blair of Adamton*, AANHS. 1976, and in *Ayrshire Collections* Vol. 11, 1976. For Our Lady Kirk of Kyle, Chalmers, pp. 497-98; *Records*, 1470, p.9; Paterson, I.ii, pp. 573-75, where Robert II's marriage is cited from *The Historie and Descent of the House of Rowallan*. For letter to Pope, Dillon, *Catholic Ayrshire*, p.13. For royal donations, references in *Treasurers Accounts*, Vol.1, 1872. For the Wallace family and Sir William Hamilton, R. MacKenzie, *A Scottish Renaissance Household: Sir William Hamilton and Newton Castle in 1559*, AANHS, 1990. Genealogy of the Wallaces of Craigie and their cadet branches remains confused because of their preference for Adam, Hugh, John, and William as forenames; Paterson I.i, pp. 163-70, 264, 269, 283-297, may be supplemented by *The Book of Wallace*, Vol. 1, pp. 35-57. There are Wallace references in protocol books (listed below) and in the Prestwick *Records*, including appendix, pp. 117, 118; there is also mention (p.47) that Adam Wallace was alderman of Ayr, 1515, not included in 'List of Provosts', *The Royal Burgh of Ayr*, ed. A.I. Dunlop, 1951, p. 317, nor in *Ayr*, p. 283, where James Chalmers and Adam Wallace were inadvertently omitted. In designating priests, the abbreviation "Sr" for "sir" – though rarely used by contemporaries – has been chosen to avoid confusion; according to Dr Sanderson, clerks of the time made a distinction by using an ornate upper-case "S" for a knight and a lower-case "s" for a priest. Sanderson's account of Leggat may be pursued in published protocol books: *Protocol Book of Gavin Ros*, ed. J. Anderson and F.J. Grant, 1908 (for years 1512–51, esp. nos. 717, 736, 896, 1123, 1152 for Leggat; nos. 1069, 1073, 1074 for Simpson quarrel; no. 1067 for boundary dispute in 1530); 'The Protocol Book of Henry Prestoun', ed. Sir J. Fergusson, *Ayrshire Collections*, Vol. 3, 1955 (for 1547–51, esp. no. 6 for Leggat as witness); 'Protocol Book of James Colvill', ed. A.I. Dunlop et al., *Ayrshire Collections*, Vol. 10, 1972 (for 1545–78, with Blair and Wallace references); abstracts from John Mason's 'Protocol Book'. ed. J.S.Dobie, *Archaeological and Historical Collections of Ayrshire and Galloway*, Vol. 6, 1889 (for 1576–93, esp. no. 114 for Leggat's tenement in Newton, and references to Prestwick, pp. 150, 168, 182). Leggat is also mentioned in *Charters of Ayr Friars Preachers*, Ayrshire and Wigtonshire Archaeological Association, 1881, p.92. For Leggat, see also *Ayr*, 56, 58 (where his Newton tenement is incorrectly located in Ayr), 59, 60. For Kingcase, see Chapter 2 notes. For Paisley Abbey and its lands in Ayrshire, Chalmers, Vol.6, pp. 823-827; for Hamiltons of Bothwellhaugh who feued Monktonmains, *Records*, pp.139-143, and Hewat, pp. 80-83. Sanderson pp. 152, 163, for quotations and p. 155 for estimate of mid-16th century population. Also Margaret Sanderson, 'Some Aspects of the Church in Scottish Society in the Era of the Reformation', *Records of the Scottish Church History Society*, Vol. XVII, part 2, 1970, pp. 81-98. For later protestant ministers, *Fasti Scot.*, Vol. 3, p.55; also C.Haws, *Scottish Parish Clergy at the Reformation*, Scottish Record Society, 1972. For assassination of John Mure, Paterson, I.i, p. cviii. References in the burgh *Records* are supplemented by *Paisley Charters*, p. 48 (Prestwick mill), and pp. 364-366 (Monkton Mill). For Wallace versus the freemen of Prestwick and Newton, Pryde 1958, pp. 32, 33; Murray, p. 196; and for charters, *RMS*, Vol. 6, nos. 359, 972, 1042, 1048. For economy of Prestwick, *Records*, esp. (for mills) pp. 42, 45, 48, 117.

Chapter 4: The Charter of 1600

Copy of the Charter ... taken from the original MS was published in 1794 by Robert Miller, town clerk (copy in ACL, ref. 652 CL), and reprinted in 1864 (copy in ACL, ref. 652GB large box); this contains a translation upon which the present version is based. The Latin form was again published in the Burgh *Records*, appendix, pp. 120-124; and an abbreviated version in *RMS*, Vol.6, no. 1042, pp. 353-354. ACL has what may be the original charter held by the freemen, as well as several other near-contemporary originals.

Chapter 5: 17th Century

The printed burgh *Records* end in 1616 and resume in 1726, with two items for 1693 engrossed in 1733, "Copied out of the old book" which, covering the period 1617 – 1725, no longer survives. For this chapter there is consequently heavy reliance on General Works (as cited above); acts of parliament quoted from *Source Book* and *APS*. 17th century events in Ayrshire are covered by Paterson, I.i, cxxxv – ccxii. Paterson also deals with the lairds of Adamton, Ladykirk, and Monkton (I.ii, 579-580, 582, 582-583) and the Wallaces of Craigie (I.i, 289-294); the *Book of Wallace*, Vol. 1, pp. 57 -72 seems more reliable. For details of Sir William Wallace versus the freemen, *RPC* Vol. 6 (1678–80), pp. 590-592, and *Historical Notices of Sir John Lauder of Fountainhall*, Vol. 1 (1661–1683), Bannatyne Club, 1848, pp. 276, 277. For parish ministers, *Fasti Scot.* Vol. 3, pp. 55, 56; for further details of Hamilton, Paterson I.i. clxi – clxiv, Hewat, pp. 59-64; for Muirhead, Hewat, pp. 181-183. For other Covenanters, Hewat, pp. 58, 63; *RPC* Vol. 1 (1625–27), p. 25 for Dunbar, and Vol. 5 (1676–78), pp. 543, 556 for 1678. For church bells, R.W.M.Clouston in *Ayrshire Collections*, Vol. 1, pp. 239, 240. For Crosbie, Paterson, I.ii, pp. 422, 463-465. For schools, McQuitty, p. 27; J.J.Fowler, 'The Presbytery of Ayr: Its Schools and Schoolmasters, 1642–1746', *Ayrshire Collections*, Vol. 6, esp. pp. 152, 153; Boyd, p. 3 for William of Prestwick; Edgar, Vol. 2, p. 102 for 1651. KS from 1615, quoted by Edgar, Vol. 2, pp. 102 and Boyd, p. 25 (school); Hewat, pp. 96, 110 (witch, beggars); McQuitty, pp. 12, 24 (collections, Newton). For Kingcase, Dillon in *Ayrshire Collections*, Vol. 6, pp. 27, 28. The final paragraphs on social changes are derived from Lynch (cited in General Works), pp. 171-184, 252-256. Local references come from Murray pp. 168-170 (boundaries); *Ayr*, pp. 43, 95 (fishing), p. 82 (coal and highways), pp. 70, 71 (plague); *RPC* 1672, p.502, and 1690, p.18 (levies of seamen); *APS* Vol. 10, appendix p. 132 (proposed levy on burghs).

Chapter 6: 18th Century

'Description of some parishes in Kyle, May 1723' appears in *Macfarlane's Geographical Collections*, ed. A. Mitchell, Scottish History Society, 1906, Vol. 1, pp. 409-414. The printed Burgh *Records* include extracts from the years 1726 – 1780; but the manuscript Freemen's Minutes have disappeared (as noted above under 'Sources'). For Sir Thomas Wallace who lost control of the burgh after 1730, Paterson, I.i, p. 295; *Book of Wallace*, Vol. 1, pp. 78 – 86; *Ayr*, p.98; and *ATB*, p.102 for 1770 as date of death; for the Neills of Barnweill, Paterson, I.i, p. 266. The disputed election of 1770 finds mention in Frank Brady, *James Boswell, the Later Years 1769–1795*, 1984, pp. 43, 508; and in KS 30 Sept. 1770. The Constitution of 1780 is included in the *Records*, pp. 105-111, and the accompanying plans of 1780 are in ACL; for 1780 see also 'Freemen v. Town Council 1903–08' in ACL 652 GB large box. *OSA Ayrshire* is quoted for tenurial system in Newton (p. 501) and Prestwick (p. 462), and desribes agrarian advances in Monkton (pp.462-464); William Fullarton, *General View of the Agriculture of the County of Ayr*, 1793, has statistical table at end; though he was chancellor of Prestwick at date of publication, he mentions the burgh only briefly under 'State of property'. Estate owners are noted for Ladykirk (Paterson I.ii, p. 582), Fairfield (Paterson I.ii, p. 601; Hewat, p. 83); Adamton (Paterson I.ii, p. 580-581; F.A.Pottle, *James Boswell, The Early Years 1740–1769*, 1966, p. 322 foll.); Monkton, renamed Orangefield (Paterson I.ii, pp. 594-600; J.T.Wheeler, *Annals of James Macrae*, Madras, 1832, in ACL with other items, 651 CH, 651 JB). For Prestwick town, *OSA Ayrshire*, pp. 464, 465; market cross, pp. 24; tolbooth, Paterson I.ii, p. 569 and note. For Richard Oswald of Auchincruive, his saltpans, coalworks, and roads, W.S.Robinson and J. Kirkwood in *Ayrshire Collections*, Vol. 3, 1955, pp. 119-135; *Records*, pp. 95, 96, which last reference indicates terminus of the waggonway noted by Harry Broad, *Rails to Ayr*, AANHS, 1981 (also in *Ayrshire Collections*, Vol. 12, 1983), pp. 105, 109; the principal authority for the Craigie and Maryburgh saltpanss is C.A.Whatley, *The Scottish Salt Industry: an Economic and Social History*, 1987; his lecture recorded on T15, T16; and extracts he generously supplied from National Library of Scotland Acc 5381, Caddell of Grange MSS, Box 39. For smuggling, Hewat, pp. 12, 13, 103; Paterson, I.ii, p. 571; Paterson, *Autobiographical Reminiscences*, 1871, p. 87. *Source Book*, Vol. 3, pp. 357-359 has Act of 1669 for repair of highways and notes subsequent measures; SRAA has County of Ayr Road Trustee Records for turnpike roads; with maps, *ATB*, pp. 152-158; the coastal route is not shown on Roy's manuscript map c.1755 but indicated in the Armstrong Map of 1775 and is noted in *OSA Ayrshire*, p. 171; the Plan of Prestwick in 1780 shows line of bypass. As mentioned, Monkton had a masonic lodge (*ATB*, p. 132), a dancing school (KS 6 May 1771 referring to 1769), and its Wreck Society (Hewat, p.112). For schools, J.J.Fowler in *Ayrshire Collections*, Vol. 6, pp. 152, 153; KS 14 Nov. 1762, 30 Mar. 1772, 14 Nov. 1773, 27 Mar. 1776, 22 July 1781; *OSA Ayrshire*, p. 465; McQuitty, p. 27, for list of session clerks, who were also schoolmasters and (until 1822) precentors. For poor relief, KS 27 July 1767, etc.; *OSA Ayrshire*, p. 466; *Records*, p. 129 (Kingcase). For wages, *OSA Ayrshire*, p.466. *Fasti Scot.*, Vol. 3, pp. 56, 57 lists parish ministers. For manse in 1737, Edgar, Vol. 1, p. 41. For Mitchell, *Fasti Scot.*, also Hewat, pp. 69-71, 157, 158; Robert Chambers in *Life and Work of Robert Burns*, ed. Chambers and Wallace, Vol. 3, 1896, p.94; I.S.Lustig and F.A.Pottle, *James Boswell, The Applause of the Jury 1782–1785*, 1981, p.283; *OSA Ayrshire*, pp. 458-467 for 'Parish of Monktown and Prestik, By the Rev. Andrew Mitchell, D.D.'; KS 25 Oct. 1810 quoted. Disjunction of Newton-upon-Ayr is reported in *OSA Ayrshire*, pp. 458-459, 461, 491-492. The work of the Kirk session is revealed in KS, and considered by Hewat, pp.66, 70, and (for marriages) pp. 138-140; also Edgar, Vol. 2, pp. 80, 103n, 157. Hewat reports various customs, pp. xii, 7, 90, 94-113; his story of David Rankine (pp.100-101) is derived from William Aiton, *General View of the Agriculture of the County of Ayr*, 1811, p.96. Hewat's account of Boswell's links with Prestwick (pp. 183-186) may be amplified from Boswell's *Tour to the Hebrides* 1 Nov. 1773; *Life of Dr Johnson* 29 Jan. 1774, 27 Oct. 1779; Frank Brady, *James Boswell, The Later Years*, pp. 125, 522 on the proposed history; Boswell's (unpublished) Book of Company lists his visits.

Chapter 7: Early 19th Century

Population statistics are taken from *Census Reports*, 1801 and decennially thereafter; unpublished Census Returns 1841-1891 are held in New Register House, Edinburgh, with microfilms in ACL. Note that numbers in the Returns were occasionally adjusted to give slightly different parish totals in the published *Census Reports*. Quotations and other details for 1834 from *Records*, pp. ix, x, xiii, xv – xvii, and list of provosts 1784–1830 on p.146. For Withrington, see Hewat, pp. 107-109; J.K.Hunter, *Retrospect of an Artist's Life*, pp. 68 – 71. For the Prestwick Drum, Hewat, p. 25, and James Paterson, *The Ballads and Songs of Ayrshire*, second series, 1847, pp. 35-38. For Smith, see William Aiton, *General View of the Agriculture of the County of*

Ayr, 1811, pp.349, 350; *Pont's Cuninghame*, ed. J.S.Dobie, 1871, pp. 250, 251; Paterson III.i, pp. 190-91. For changes in land tenure and use, Murray, ii, p. 73; plans of 1814 and 1831; *NSA*, pp. 175, 178; *Records* p.x. Excerpts from minutes of 1780, 1832, 1837, and 1849 relating to tenure are included in 'Freemen v. Town Council 1903–08' in ACL 652 GB large box. *NSA*, p. 174 is quoted for housing development in Newton. For coal, *Ayr*, p. 146; *NSA*, p. 171. *Fasti Scot.*, p.57 for ministers; also Hewat, p. 86 (Oughterson), p. 199 (Burns), p.87 (new church); *NSA*, p. 176 (for quotations), p. 177 (poor relief, education); *Answers to Queries on Parochial Education*, for Monkton in 1824, in ACL 650 PC. Account Book 1824–1870 in ACL 652 GB lists schoolmasters. For dissent, Hewat p.71 (quoted); *NSA* p. 177; *ATB* and *Ayr* for available other places of worship. For Landowners, *NSA*, p. 173, and 'Land Tax Roll, 1837' in SRAA, ref. CO3/3/3. For the estates, Paterson, I.i, p. 267 (Barnweil); I.ii, pp. 582, 582, 600, 602, 667 – 668, 747 (Adamton, Ladykirk, Orangefield, Fairfield, Auchincruive, Rosemount). Ayrshire freeholders and Prestwick freemen are listed in William McCarter's *Ayrshire*, 1830 and 1832 editions; Hewat, p.25, mentions local involvement in 1819 demonstration; for this and 1832, *Ayr*, pp. 153, 157; for elections, *British Parliamentary Results 1832–1885*, ed. F.W.S.Craig, 1977; *Ayr Directory*, 1845–46, lists persons in Prestwick, but the *Ayrshire Directory*, 1851, has the earliest information found regarding county electors in the period after 1832; there is also a *List of Voters for the County of Ayr*, 1857, in ACL, 400 AK. Prestwick is mentioned in A. Wilson, *The Chartist Movement in Scotland*, 1970, p. 84. For roads, *NSA*, p. 176; Hew Ainslie, *Pilgrimage to the Land of Burns*, 1822, 1892 edition, pp. 53 – 55, at Black Bull in Monkton; Hewat, p. 210 for Waterloo; *AP* 28 Apr. 1967 for Burke and Hare. 'Prestwick in 1825', *AP* 4 Dec. 1931, has extract from Pigot's *Directory*.

Chapter 8: Mid 19th Century

Population statistics and Census Returns as noted for Chapter 7. *The Glasgow and South Western Railway*, Stephenson Society, 1950, provides details about Prestwick station. For the Town House and quotation, Hewat, p. 24; bridges as on OS Map of 1857. Hewat, p. 20, reports the important tenurial change: "Formerly the Freedoms could only be sold to the Community, which again had the right to sell them to whom they pleased; but in the year 1850, all restrictions were abolished and the land is now held in the same way as other heritable property in Scotland"; see also excerpt from Freemen's Minutes for 1849 under 'Freemen v. Town Council 1903–08' in ACL 652 GB large box. There are two histories of *Prestwick Golf Club*, one by J.E.Shaw, 1938; another edited by D.C.Smail, 1989, from whom also information on T32; William Galbraith, *Prestwick St Nicholas Golf Club*, 1950, and "125 Years of Golf at St Nicholas", *AP* 5 Nov. 1976 and *AA* 4 Nov. 1976. For the church and the Disruption, *Fasti Scot.*, pp. 57, 58; *Annals of the Free Church of Scotland*, ed. W. Ewing, 2 vols., 1914; Hewat, pp. 71-75, 112; with 'Prestwick Names', *AP* 9 Feb. 1934, mentioning Tippery's Brae. Information on Prestwick connections with New Zealand from Professor David Purdie, a native of Prestwick, who supplied extracts from Tom Brooking, *And Captain of Their Souls*, Otago Books, Dunedin,

1984 (on Burns) and *The Advance Guard Series II*, ed. G.J.Griffiths, Otago Daily Times, 1973 (on Wilson), these now deposited in ACL; also Margaret Harper, 'The Farthest Journey' in *Sunday Mail Story of Scotland*, Vol.3, p. 930. Hewat, pp. 199-204 for further details of Burns and Lawrie, (and pp. 156-174 for Robert Burns connections); also Hewat, 'Fifty Years of Church Life' in *Half Hours at the Manse*, 1904; McQuitty, pp. 13-16; KS 1837–1867, especially 27 Jan. 1844 ("sin of uncleanness"), 29 Dec. 1844 (Cowan replaces Gibson as schoolmaster), 14 Dec. 1845 (Hillas), 13 Apr. 1846, 26 Sept. 1850 (Poor Law); schoolmasters from Freemen's Account Book 1824–1870 in ACL 652 GB. Some other details of this period in J.H.Dawson, *Abridged Statistical History of Scotland*, 1853. For glimpses of social life, Hewat, pp. 112; KS 14 Dec. 1848 (Sacraments); Minutes of Monkton and Prestwick Library Society, CH2/809.34 in SRAA. Comments on Census Returns derived from Margaret Swain, 'Ayrshire Needlework', *Ayrshire Collections*, Vol. 3, 1955, pp. 174-184; quotation from *NSA Ayrshire*, p. 612; Hewat, pp. 9-11, 242 (needlework), pp. 11 (fishing, shipbuilding, colliery, kail), pp. 160, 161 (Aikenbrae); for Isabella Bruce's mother, Hewat, p. 160; for her father, Yale MSS, and especially the Boswell family oath of 1767 (M 22) for "the continuance and prosperity of the ancient family of Auchinleck, and that the Family of Bruce might ever flourish there". For the Neills of Barnweil, Paterson, I.i, pp. 267-268.

Chapter 9: Late 19th Century

For this era of rapid change, ACL provides *Census Reports* and Returns; *Ayrshire Directory* for 1851 and *Slater's Directory* for 1867; *Return of Owners of Lands and Heritages, 1872–73*, 1874; OS Maps for 1857 and 1897; files of the local press, *AA*, *AO*, and (from 1880) *AP;* 'Prestwick Names', *AP* 9 Feb. 1934; 'Old Prestwick' by A.C.H., *AP* 4 Feb. – 4 Mar. 1938; Hewat and Steven as contemporary sources; and recollections mentioned in several Prestwick History Group tapes, T1-66. For the early part of this chapter, R.Mackenzie Fisher, *Poems and Sketches*, appendix (Crimean War veterans); Steven p. 11 (kail); Hewat p.9 (weavers), p.209 (Maryburgh), p.209 (incomers, with *AO* 8 May 1883 for James Keppie), p.208 (resort), p.212 (railway, also *Glasgow and South Western Railway*, Stephenson Society, 1950, pp. 18, 56), pp. 212-3 (roads, with *AA* 18 Jan. 1900 for dimensions of railway bridge); Iain Foulds in T27 on his great-grandfather Dr Foulds; Harry Gardiner in T59 on Queens Terrace, Regent Park. The Burgh School is noticed in *Slater's Directory* and *AA* 28 Feb. 1867. For police, Commissioners of Supply Police Committee Minute Book, 1841–57, 1872–87, CO3/2/7,8 in SRAA; and T.Hamilton, 'The Ayrshire Commissioners of Supply' in *Ayrshire Collections*, Vol.1, 1950. For water supply, 'The Sanitary Condition of Prestwick', *AO* 26 July 1881; also *AO* 14 Jan., 12 Apr., 3 May 1881; *AA* 18 May 1882, 13 Nov. 1884, 12 Feb., 24 Sept. 1885; *AO* 16 June 1891; and for the Water Famine, *AA* 24, 31 Aug. 1899, 11 Jan. 1900. For burghs, Pryde 1958; councils, Hewat quoted p. 214; parliamentary reform and extension of franchise, *AA* 4 July 1850, 14 Mar. 1861, 22 Aug. 1867, 3 Sept. 1874, 28 Aug. 1884, 22 Oct. 1885; riot act deposited in ACL; for McLellan, also Census Returns; F.W.S.Craig, *British Parliamentary Election Results, 1832–1885*, 1977, *1885–1918*, 1974; *List of Voters for the County of Ayr, 1857*, 400 AK in ACL; *Voters in South Ayrshire*, 1878–79 and 1883–84, both with addenda and annotations, also in ACL 400 AK; *Register of Voters for South Ayrshire*, 1884–85, CO3/9/7/2 in SRAA; *AA* 18 Dec. 1885 for Liberal Association. For main and parish roads, Hewat p. 208; *AA* 28 Mar. 1867 (Prestwick toll, also *AP* 11 Feb. 1938); Ayr District Trust, Conversion Money, 1892, enclosure within CO3/3/3 in SRAA. For Local Improvement committee, Hewat p. 213, *AO* 24 Feb., 14 Apr. 1891. For church, *Fasti Scot.*, McQuitty, and KS; *Annals of the Free Church of Scotland, 1843–1900, Fasti of the U.F. Church*, ed. J.A.Lamb; Hewat pp. 72, 237; for Rev. Kirkwood Hewat, *AO* 11, 18 Nov. 1881, also *AP* 3 Apr. 1925, 1 July 1927; for U.P.Church, *Prestwick South Church*, centenary brochure, 1984, also *AA* 6 July 1882, *AO* 8 May 1883, *AA* 12 June 1884, Hewat p.72; Steven p.66 (church services); *New Prestwick Baptist Church*, centenary booklet, 1989. For schools, C.D.Legge, 'Ayr Working Men's College', pp. 20-22, 672 PK in ACL; SB Minutes from 1873; Freemen's Account Books 1824–70, 1872–1903, in ACL 652 GB; Iain Foulds in T65, T66; 'A Prestwick Jubilee' in *AP* 27 May 1932. For shops, etc., 1851 and 1867 directories; also for postal service, Hewat p.111 and Groome; inns, *AP* 9 Feb. 1934; *Voters Roll* as above; Census Returns 1891; Valuation Roll 1899–1900; F.W.Sears, *Ayrshire, Historical, Commercial, and Descriptive*, 1894. For trades, Census Returns, and for nurseries, T5, T17. For golf, Shaw, Smail, and Galbraith as in Chapter 8, Hewat pp. 223-230, Steven p.63, *AO* 3 July 1883, *AA* 3 Sept. 1885 (ladies links course). Other references from *AA* 3 Jan., 27 June, 12 Dec. 1861; *AO* 12 July 1881; *AA* 3 Sept. 1885; Steven p.11 and Hewat p.225 (quoted); Hewat pp. 223, p.261, and also for 'A Veteran Golfer' Hewat, *Half Hours at the Manse*, 1904; *AP* 9 Feb. 1934 (John Gray); J.E.Shaw, p.138 (Charles Hunter). Other sports in Steven p.66; Hewat pp. 214, 143, 214; *AA* 14 Nov. 1867, *AO* 4 Nov. 1881; also references in T17, T22 (location of tennis courts), T17 (bowling club). For the Puddock Sheugh's course, plans of 1814 and 1831, references in T1, T4. For the shore, Steven, p.3; *AO* 7 Aug. 1883 (donkeys); Hewat pp. 213-215, 146 (charabancs); *AO* 16 Jan. 1883 (tramway proposal). Other recreational facilities, Hewat p. 215; *AO* 17 Mar., 20 Mar., 3 Apr., 14 Apr. 1891, 29 Aug. 1884 (concerts). For superstitions and legends, Hewat pp. 94-115, and especially items on pp. 106, 110, 137, 103, 127, 131, 105, 7, 216; *AA* 4 July 1850; *AP* 9 Feb. 1934, 11 Feb. 1938. R. Mackenzie Fisher, *Poems and Sketches*, 3rd edition (1898). 4th edition (1906) in ACL 672 NG; published by Ayr Observer, but not listed in Careen Gardiner, *Printing in Ayr and Kilmarnock*, AANHS, 1976. For telephones, J.E.Shaw. *Prestwick Golf Club*, 1938, p. 94; and for coal mining, Hewat, p. 237. For estates, M.C.Davis, *Castles and Mansions of Ayrshire*, 1991; J.T.Ward, 'Ayrshire Landed Estates, 19th Century', *Ayrshire Collections*, Vol. 8, 1969, pp. 130, 140-141; Census Returns and Valuation Roll as above. Also (for Adamton) Hewat, pp. 204-5 and *AA* 21 May 1885; (for Ladykirk) Hewat, p. 136, Paterson I.ii, p. 574, KS 25 Mar. 1894; (for Fairfield) R.M.Gardiner in T19, T20. For houses in town and country, Andrew and Close as noted in 'Sources'; also J.M.Wilson in T17, T18, T31, T41. Useful details for this and subsequent chapters were provided by Iain Foulds.

Chapter 10: Early 20th Century

For establishment of the police burgh, *AA* 1 July 1897, 13 Nov. 1902; *AP* 20 Feb., 30 Oct., 6 Nov. 1903; G.S.Pryde, 'The Scottish Burgh of Barony in Decline, 1707–1908', *Proceedings of the Royal Philosophical Society of Glasgow*, 1949, pp. 62-63 for Blairgowrie case; R.M.Gardiner in T5, T6, also for a lucid account of Freemen v. Town Council; see also Freemen's Minutes 1908–16 in ACL 652 GB, and Papers relating to Freemen v. Town Council in ACL 652 GB large box; List of Freemen in 1904 and other documents held by McCosh and Gardiner (now Lawson and Russell), solicitors, Prestwick; also Prestwick Investment Trust. PTC Minutes in ACL from 1903 are supplemented by J.Melrose on 'Civic Government 1903–75' on T7, T8; also *AA* 5 June 1903 (nigger minstrels) and 3 July, 16 Oct. 1903 (Matthew Smith). For schools, SB Minutes in SRAA; *Prestwick Academy 1902–1992*, Yearbook, 1992; Iain Foulds on T26, T27, T65, T66; quotation from William Boyd, *Education in Ayrshire through Seven Centuries*, 1961, p. 175; for James Howat, *AP* 24 Jan. 1941; Mathew Foulds' career is covered in a brochure *The Haka*, commemorating the 14th Ayrshire (1st Prestwick) Scout Group 1909–1979. The only guide of the period found in ACL is *Prestwick Illustrated Guide*, sixpence, 1908; published by W.Somerville, printer, the Cross; letter press by H.J.S(teven?). Michael Davis, *Castles and Mansions of Ayrshire*, 1991, for Ladykirk; *Kilmarnock Standard* 25 Aug. 1906 for Orangefield; Valuation Rolls in ACL and SRAA for owners and occupants; also Dane Love, *Auchinleck*, 1991, pp. 99, 116, 139 for Lugar connections. For Glenburn, William Welsh on T52, T53, Close, p. 35 quoted on town centre. For traffic, Ronald Brash, *The Tramways of Ayr*, 1983; Robert Grieves, *Motoring Memories*, 1988, p. 40. For churches, see Ch.9 notes. For Boer War and First World War, local press and passing references in sources noted above. Additional information on residents is obtainable from *Ayr and District Directories* from 1900, which include Prestwick among 'Outlying Districts'. Fred Horton supplied information on Lodge 1060 of the Freemasons, as contained in his 'Brief History of Prestwick', now deposited in ACL.

Chapter 11: Between the Wars

PTC minutes recording decisions must be supplemented by local press reports, which more fully reveal divisions of opinion (as well as notable events); James Melrose covered 'Civic Government' on T7 and T8, with description of Pritty; *TSA* Part 3 gives an account of public administration in Ayrshire after the 1929 Act; PTC for most years included financial statements, and sometimes separate Sanitary Inspector's reports are bound in. Supplementary information from *Census Reports* for 1921 and 1931. Official *Guides to Prestwick*, 1926 and 1934, are in ACL. For schools, see local press, some of the sources for Ch. 10, and Prestwick Public School Log Book. For the churches, *Fasti*, including 1950 and 1961 supplementary volumes; McQuitty; Prestwick South Church *Centenary Brochure*, 1984; *Kingcase Parish Church 1934–1984*, ed. Leslie Duncan; *History of St Ninian's Episcopal Church* by a Layman (F.Cromar) c.1957; J.E.Shaw, *Ayrshire 1745–1950*, 1953, chapter 3. For housing, *Census Report* for 1931; Lynch p. 439 on bungalow development in the thirties; *TSA* p.180. Shops from Valuation Rolls. Analysis of population from *Census Reports* and *TSA* p. 238. On the thirties, quotation from A.J.P.Taylor, *English History 1919–1945*, 1965, p. 317; Harry Gardiner on T59, T27; William Welsh on Memories of Glenburn, T52, 53, also T21 and T60; *TSA* p.573 on community life. For landward area, Valuation Rolls; *AP* 25 Feb. 1949 for R.L.Angus; R.M.Gardiner on Monkton, T19 and T20; J.H.G.Lebon, *Land of Britain, Land Utilisation Survey, Ayrshire*, 1937, esp. pp. 39, 40, 45, 48, 54. T1 and T55 for railway; T43 for buses; R.W.Brash, *Tramways of Ayr*, 1983, pp. 31-33, and pp. 52-54 for bus services; *TSA* pp. 111, 116 for rail and road statistics. PTC, *AP*, and T1, T19, T37 for early flights; *AP* 8 June 1934, PTC 3 Sept. 1935, and *AA* 13 Feb. 1936 for Prestwick Aerodrome; T35 for Scottish Aviation; also a collection of reports, brochures, and documents held in ACL 652 MP, especially Jim Ewart, *Prestwick Airport Golden Jubilee 1935–1985* and Alan Robertson, *Lion Rampant and Winged*, 1968, on SAL. A variety of topics is covered by Bob Blane in 'Proud Prestwick', supplement to *AA* Feb. 1993.

Chapter 12: Second World War

PTC minutes provide useful details which could not in wartime be reported in the press, though sometimes published after the war. *Prestwick in the Forties*, by Ian Welsh, published by the District Council in 1992, is a most useful collection of newspaper cuttings from *AP*. For the airport, books as noted for Chapter 12; for controversy over postwar development, see *Glasgow Herald* as well as local press; *Keesing's Contemporary Archives* for government policies; and Dr Ian Levitt has supplied information from confidential records for 1945 now accessible at the Public Records Office. Other information from Willfred Collins, Margaret Foulds, John Hope, Muriel Macaulay,

Chapter 13: Mid 20th Century

PTC minutes and local press, with Welsh as in Chapter 12 notes. ACL has copies of *Prestwick News*, 1951, 1953; and *Prestwick Standard*, 1958, 1959. Invaluable are *Census Reports* for 1951 and 1961, esp. 1961 *County Report* and 1961 *Occupation and Industry Tables for Ayr and Bute*. *TSA*, pp. 566- 580 provides much information about the Parish of Monkton and Prestwick just prior to publication in 1951. Note in particular *TSA* pp. 180, 571 on housing; pp. 121-124, 569-570 on the airport; pp. 262, 578-580 on religion; pp. 576-578 on schools, children and young people; pp. 573-574 on community life; pp. 527, 574-576 on Monkton and farming. For youth groups later, *Youth at Fifteen*, Education Committee handbook, 1961; for churches and airport, see also Chapter 11 notes. Dr Ian Levitt, who contributed material as indicated in Chapter 12 notes has provided other items from the Public Records Office relating to Cabinet Economic Policy Committee discussions concerning SAL's difficulties in 1948. Quotations are from *AA* 30 May 1946 (Dunlop), *AP* 19 Dec. 1947 (Milligan), T6 (Steele), *AP* 28 Feb. 1947 (points system), *AP* 15 Feb. 1946 (Pritty), *TSA* p. 573 (community life).

Chapter 14: The End of the Burgh

PTC minutes and local press, including *TPT* in ACL from 1970; *Census Report* for 1971; for airport and SAL as in Chapter 11 notes; contributions from Ex-provost Foulds.

Chapter 15: Late 20th Century

ACL holds minutes of Kyle and Carrick District Council and Strathclyde Regional Council. The local press is a principal source, particularly of criticisms of district council, as *AA* 2, 30 June, 8 Sept., 10 Nov. 1977, 19 Jan., 5 Oct. 1978; *TPT* 2 Jan. 1976, 28 Nov. 1980; also T8. For airport, local press updates concluding chapters of books listed in Ch. 11 notes. Ayrshire and Arran Tourist Board *Visitors Guides*, 1984 and later, provide details of holiday trade; Valuation Rolls for farms; *Census Report* of 1981 for population. For education, Schools Handbooks and *Prestwick Academy 1902–1992*; for religion, Yearbooks of Church of Scotland and other denominations, plus information from several ministers. *Prestwick Millenium* official brochure, 1983, provides programme and list of participating organisations. For all organisations and events, the files of the current local press (*AP, AA, TPT*) have been supplemented by information from various residents, including Fred Horton and Ian Welsh; also Alasdair Cochrane and Iain Foulds, both of whom have also kindly read drafts of Chapters 9-15; any remaining errors are those of the author.

List of Provosts

The Burgh of Barony

The burgh was for long periods controlled by neighbouring landowners, who were designated as oversmen. The first so recorded was David Blair of Adamton, oversman in 1473, who held the office until his death in 1487. He was followed by John Blair of Adamton, 1487 – c.1513; Adam Wallace of Newton, 1515 – 1532; David Blair of Adamton, 1533 – 1540; David Blair of Adamton, 1540 until 1570. The new title of provost was adopted by John Wallace of Craigie, 1571 – 1592. During a brief interlude of independence, John Mertene was elected chancellor in 1600, followed by Lambert Hay and William Blair. Control was reasserted by Sir William Wallace of Craigie, 1605 – c.1610; Sir John Wallace of Carnell, 1610 – 1631; Hew Wallace of Craigie, 1631 – 1665; Thomas Wallace of Craigie, 1665 – 1680; Sir William Wallace of Craigie, 1680 -1700; Sir Thomas Wallace of Craigie, 1700 – c.1729. His son, another Sir Thomas Wallace, lost control over Prestwick in 1731. Thereafter chancellors were elected by the freemen: James Neill, 1731 – 1743, also 1750 – 1754 and 1760 – 1769; James Blair. 1743 – 1748 and 1766 – 1770; David Andrew, 1748 – 1750; Charles Dalrymple of Orangefield, 1754 – 1760; William Fullarton of Rosemount, 1770 – 1780; James Campbell, 1780 -1782; Robert Doak, 1782 – 1784; Captain John Hamilton, 1784 – 1786; Colonel David Boyd, 1786 – 1792 and 1806 – 1810; William Fullarton of Fullarton, 1792 – 1802; James Hunter, 1802 – 1806; William Fullarton of Skeldon, 1810 – 1814; John Guthrie, 1814 – 1818 and 1827 – 1830; John Boyd, 1818 – 1827. There are only passing references to some later chancellors (or provosts as they were now more commonly known): Major William Neill of Barnweill, 1830, 1834; Andrew Caldwell, 1841; William Smith, 1851; David Boyd, 1864; Gray Edmiston, 1897, 1903.

The Burgh of Prestwick
designated as Police Burgh 1903 – 1929, Small Burgh 1929 – 1975.

JOHN WILSON WEIR, 1903 – 1905
ROBERT H. STEEDMAN, 1905 – 1906
GRAY EDMISTON, 1906 – 1912
THOMAS McCLURE, 1912 -1916, 1926 – 1928
ALFRED JAMES COCHRANE, 1916 – 1919
JOHN DAVIDSON, 1919 – 1920

JAMES MEIKLE, 1920 – 1926
DAVID BRYSON, 1928 – 1931
THOMAS HOWIE, 1931 – 1934
DUGALD HAMILTON MARR, 1934 – 1936
DAVID S. GOVAN, 1936 – 1938
ALEXANDER FERGUSON, 1938 – 1942
ROBERT H. DUNSMORE, 1942 – 1947
FRANK M. MILLIGAN, 1947 – 1954
GILBERT STEELE, 1954 – 1957
JOHN KERR, 1957 – 1960
WILLIAM S. MOIR, 1960 – 1963
W. IAIN FOULDS, 1963 – 1966
HUGH CHAPMAN, 1966 – 1969
FRED HORTON, 1969 – 1972
JOHN D. WATT, 1972 – 1974
WILLIAM HARKISS, 1974 – 1975

List of Events

PRESTWICK	ELSEWHERE
	1115 St Bernard founds Clairvaux abbey
1136	1136 Walter Fitzalan comes to Scotland
Burgh established	
	1162–1227 Genghis Khan in China
1173	1190 Richard I on Crusade
	1197 Castle built at Ayr

	1205 Ayr burgh established
	1215 Magna Carta in England
	1230–49 Irvine burgh established
	1263 Battle of Largs
1297 Wallace at Monkton	1275 Marco Polo in China

	1314 Battle of Bannockburn
1329 Bruce at Kingcase	1314–1371 Newton burgh established
	1338 Hundred Years War begins in France
1347 Stewart wedding at Ladykirk	1350 Black Death reaches Scotland
1380 Inundation with sand	1381 Peasants Revolt in England

	1431 Joan of Arc burned
	1445 Gutenberg prints first book
1470 coal worked for saltpans	1452–1519 Leonardo da Vinci
1474 Burgh taken over by Adamton	1478 First czar of Russia
	1492 Columbus crossses Atlantic

1525 Leggat as St Nicholas curate	1513 Battle of Flodden
1527 Earl of Cassillis murdered	1517 Martin Luther begins Reformation
1560 Leggat as protestent minister	1564–1616 William Shakespeare
1571 Burgh taken over by Craigie	1588 Spanish Armada
1592 Revolt of the freemen	1592 Kilmarnock burgh established

1600 James VI charter	1603 Crowns united under James VI and I
1605 Craigie rule re-established	1606–69 Rembrandt
1616 Parish school opened	1638 National Covenant
1646 Parish minister deposed	1666 Pentland Rising
1678 Parish conventicles	1688 Glorious Revolution

1731 Craigie rule ends	1707 Union of Parliaments
1733 Macrae acquires Orangefield	1715, 1745 Jacobite rebellions
1765 Oswald's new saltpans	1740–95 James Boswell
1766 Runrig abandoned	1759–96 Robert Burns
1770 Riotous election	1767 1st Ayrshire Turnpike Act
1777 Market cross restored	1769 James Watt's steam engine
1779 Newton to be separate parish	1770–1827 Beethoven
1780 Constitution for 36 freemen	1776 American Revolution
1780 Tolbooth rebuilt	1779 John Galt born in Irvine
1783 Adamton sold to Robert Reid	1789 French Revolution

1814 New Prestwick formed	1808 Kilmarnock-Troon railway
1814 Division of common lands	1815 Battle of Waterloo
1833 Freemen take 999 years' tenure	1832 Reform Act
1837 New parish church	1837–1901 Reign of Queen Victoria
1840 Opening of railway	1840 Penny postage introduced
1844 New Freemen's Hall	1843 Disruption; Free Church formed
1850 Freemen now heritable owners	1848 Rev. Thomas Burns at Dunedin
1851 Prestwick Golf Club formed	1854 Crimean War
1882 Public School opened	1861–65 American Civil War
1883 Water from Raith reservoir	1885 Motor car built by Karl Benz

1902 High School opened	1901–31 Ayr tramways
1903 First Town Council elected	1903 Wright brothers' flight
1912–73 Glenburn colliery	1914–18 First World War
1926 First council houses built	1926 General Strike
1931 Bathing Lake opens	1928 Fleming discovers penicillin
1935 Broadway cinema opens	1933 Hitler becomes German chancellor
1935 Airfield formed by SAL	1939–45 Second World War
1946 International Airport	1952 Television comes to Scotland
1964 New Airport terminal	1966 Abbotsinch airport opens
1975 End of town council	1973 U.K. joins EEC

Index

1. Page numbers in italic refer to illustrations.
2. Subheadings under any given heading are in chronological (not alphabetical) order.
3. Centuries mentioned in subheadings are given thus:
   c16 (= sixteenth century, i.e. 1500-1599)

A.A.Motor Services Ltd. 182
Adamton 8
   C16 27–8
   C17 51
   C18 65
   C19 79, 103, 134–5
   C20 150, 180, 222, 237, 245
adult education 121
agriculture *see* farming
air accidents 195
air raid precautions 186, 187, 188
air traffic control 191, 231
airport *2, 182,* 183–5
   World War II 188–91, *189,* 198–200
   air trips *205*
   post-war 207–14, *208, 209,* 230–32, *230,*
      244–7, *246*
alcohol consumption 132, 169, 170, 217, 236–7
Alison, Archibald (*d.*1900) 119
animals *see* livestock
arms (Prestwick Burgh) *162*
associations 155–6, 220–21, 236, 249, 251–2
Atlantic House 230, 231
Auchincruive 180
Auxiliary Fire Service 187
Ayr
   creation 9
   effect on Prestwick 22, 138
Ayr County Council 114, 171
Ayrshire Education Authority 149
Ayrshire Needlework 78, 97–8, 108

Baird, John George Alexander
   (*d.*1917) 134–5
Baird, Matthew (*fl.*1688) 51
Baptist Church 176, 216, 250
baronial burghs 44
Bathing Lake *164,* 165–6, *165,* 196, 204, 227
Beaton, Walter (*d.* 1917) 122, 148
Bellrock quarries *35*
Biggart Memorial Home *155,* 218, 234

billeting, World War II 191–3
Black Death 24
Blair. *Family*
   C16 27–8, 29
   C17 49, 51
Blair, Catherine 65
Blind Harry 23
Boer War 158
Bonfire Monday 132–3
Boswell, James 59, 77
boundaries 44–5, 53, 229
bowling 130, 169, 228, 251
Boy Scouts 149, 155, 219
Boydfield House *170*
Boys Brigade 155
Broadway cinema 177, 223, 236
Bruce, Robert 23
Bruce's Well 23, *24,* 145, 228
Bulldog aircraft 232–3
burgesses 46
   see also freemen
burgh of barony 45
Burgh Police (Scotland) Act 138
burgh records v, 14–15, *25*
Burns, Thomas (*d.* 1871) 84–5, 92–3, *96*
bus services 181–2, *205*

cars 151, 183, 206, 237, *243*
Caskie, Donald M. (*d.* 1992) 249
Catholic Church see Roman
   Catholic Church
Centrum leisure centre 251
Chapman, Hugh *238*
Charabancs 131
Charter (*1600*) 38–47
Chartist Association 88
Christian Brethren 157, 176, 216–17, 235, 250
Christmas 156–7, 223
Church
   C8–14 4, 6–9
   C15 17–20

C16 30–33
C17 48–51, 54–5
C18 73–5, 76
C19 84–7, 92–6, 97, 117–20
C20 156–7, 175–6, 215–17, 235–6, 249–50
cinema 156, 164, 177, 223, 236
circuses 177
Civic Centre 169
Civil Defence 188, 198
cleansing 143, 171
climate 25
coal industry
  C16 35–6
  C18 68, 70
  C19 83, 98–9
  C20 150, 207, 229–30
commerce *see* trade
Common Good fund 46
Community Council 239, 250–51
concerts 132
conventicles 50
corn mills 34
Coronation (1953) 220
councillors *see* elections
courts 45, 46–7, 145–6
  see also crime and public order
Covenanters 49, 50
cricket 178, 219–20
crime and public order
  C15 16–17
  C16 34, 36
Cross, The *145, 163*
curling 104, 130
Cuthbert, *St.* 4

Dalmilling Charter 7, 8
Dalrymple, James (*d.* 1795) 66
Damnonii 3
Dark Ages 3
demography *see* population
devil, folk tale 76–7
Disruption 92
dissenters 86–7
domestic servants 125
drainage
  C19 113, 114, 143, 229
  C20 165
drinking 132, 169, 170, 217, 236–7
Dumigan's Castle 165
Duncanson, Adam *172*
Dundonald 5
Dunlop, James (*d.* 1946) 201
Dykes, Andrew 134

Edmiston, Gray 137, 138, *139*
education
  C17 53–4

C18 72–3
C19 86, 97, 120–23
C20 146–50, 171–5, 217–19, 234–5, 248–9
Education (Scotland) Act
  (1872) 121
elections
  early C20 138–9, 141–2
  inter-war 161–2, 167, 170
  suspended 197
  post-war 201–2, 223, 224, 237, 239, 242–3
  see also franchise
electricity 163
Elizabeth, *Queen 221*
embroidery 97–8
emigration 93–5, 108
employment *see* jobs
Episcopal Church 176, 216, 235, 250
esplanade *142, 144, 242*
evacuees 187

Fairfield 104, 135, 150, 180, 222
farming
  C13 9
  C15 14
  C16 34
  C18 64–5
  C19 83, 102–3, 133–4
  C20 180–81, 222, 247
  see also land
fees, schools 147
finance
  C19 82–3
  C20 171, 203–4, 227
fines *see* punishment
Fire Service 187–8
First World War 159–60
Fisher, R. Mackenzie (*b.*1840) 133
Fitzalan, Walter (*d.*1177) 5–6, 7
Fitzalan, Walter (*fl.*1220) 9
Flowering Web 78, 98, 108
football 130, 177–8
Foulds, Matthew F.(*d.*1979) 149, *172, 238*
Foulds, W. Iain *238*
franchise
  Charter (1600) 46
  C18 61
  C19 87–8, 115–16
  C20 161, 201, 237
Free Church 92–3, 118–19, 120
North Church *118*
Freemasons 155, 221
freemen v–vi
  C15 21
  C16 37
  C18 61, 63
  C19 80–82, 89, 108–9, 125
  C20 *139*, 141, 207

Freemen's Hall 89, 145–6
further education 219

Gallie, Phil 243
gambling 217
Gannet, HMS 231, 245
gaol 36, 80
gas lighting 117
gateways 10–12
Glenburn
  school 148, *154*
  colliery 150, *152*, 179, 207, 229–30
  village 150, *153*, 226
  "steamie" *154*
Glenburn Rovers 178
golf
  C19 89, 91, *126*, 127–9
  C20 145, *168*, 178, 219, 220, 251

halls 156, 164
Hamilton, D. Douglas-Hamilton, *14th*
  Duke of 183–4, 199, 200, 233
Hamilton, Robert (*d.*1647) 49–50
Hamilton, *Sir* William
  (*d.*1560) 29
handloom weaving 98
Harkess, William *238*
Heathfield airfield 191
Hewat, Kirkwood v, vi, 119, 133, 156
  quoted 108, 109, 110, 111–12, 112–13, 116,
  130, 131, 132, 252
Hewitt, *Dr.* (*d.*1935) 179
HMS Gannet 231, 245
holidaymakers *see* tourism
holidays, schools 173
Home Guard 187, 198
Hope, Bob 195
Horton, Fred *238*
hospital (Kingcase) 17, 23, 55–6
housing
  C19 110–11, 112–13
  early C20 150
  inter-war 166–7, *169*, 170, 176–7
World War II 197–8
post-war 202–3, 226, 247
Howat, James (*d.*1941) 148, 149
Howie Municipal Bowling
  Green 169
Hunter, Charles (*d.*1921) *128*, 129
Hutchison, Alexander ((*d.*1898) 129

immigration *see* migration
indulgences 51
inflation
  C17 56
  C18 73
Invercargill (New Zealand) 94–5

Jetstream aircraft 232–3, 246–7
jobs
  C19 78–9, 97–8
  C20 179
Johnson, Samuel 77
Jones, John L. 197, 204

Kingcase
  foundation 8
  hospital 17, 23, 55–6
  church 175, 216
Kirk St. 10, *12*
Knights Templars 19
Kyle and Carrick District
  Council 241–3

Lady Kirk, chapel 27, *31*, 33
Ladykirk *62*
  C16 33
  C17 51
  C18 65
  C19 79, 104, 135
  C20 150, 180, 222
land
  summary v–vi
  medieval burgh 13–14, 15, 20–21, 21–2
  Charter (1600) 45–6
  C18 59–60, 61–4
  C19 81–4, 108–9, 134–5
  see also farming
laundry *151*, 153
Lawrie, George James (*d.* 1877) 95
laws *see* courts
legends 132–3
Leggat, Robert (*d.*1571) 31–2, 33
leisure time 222–3
Liber Communitatis 43
libraries 97, 132, 222
lighting, streets 117, 143
livestock 15, 35, 62–3
local government
  C18 61
  C19 80, 113–15
  early C20 137–42
  inter-war 161–6, 167–71
  World War II 195–8
  post-war 201–2, 204, 224–5, 229, 237–8,
  239–40, 241–3
  see also franchise

McClure, Thomas (*b.* 1877) 141–2, 160,
  162
McIntyre, David F. 183–4, 188, 199, *200*, 210,
  231
McLellan, Hugh Dunlop 115
Macrae, James (*d.* 1746) 65–6
Main St. *243*

maps
  Stewart Kyle 6
  early burgh 11
  Ayrshire Burghs (1600) 41
  Kyle (1654) 52
  Ayrshire (1775) 60
  Prestwick Burgh (1780) 67
  arable lands (1780) 69
  lands of Prestwick (1814) 81
  Prestwick (1857) 90
  Monkton (1857) 101
  town centre (1903) 140
  town plan (current) 273
Marina Rd. *110*
markets *see* trade
marriage customs 76
Masons 155, 221
Maxwell, Robert (*d.* 1686) 50
"Mechanics, The" 91
Members of Parliament 115, 161, 223, 237,
  243
mercat cross *18*, 46, 66, 228
migration, C19 80, 93–5, 99–102, 108, 127, 215
Milligan, Frank M. 202
mills 34, *45*, 181
miners, Glenburn 179
Mitchell, Andrew (*d.* 1811) 74–5, 86
Monkton
  church 7
  C16 33
  C17 51
  school 54, 122, 123, 148
  C18 63–5, 66, 72
  C19 79, 99–100, 126, 133
  map 101
  C20 180, 222, 247
Monkton House *see* Orangefield
Morris, Tom 91, *95*, 127, *128*
motor vehicles 151, 182–3, 206, 237, *243*

National Covenant 49
needlework 97–8
Neill. *Family*. C18 58–9
Neill, James George Smith (*d.* 1857) 104–5
New Life Christian Centre 250
New Prestwick 78, 79, 80, *84*, 86, 99, 126
New Zealand, emigration 93–5
newspapers 158, 159, 178, 220
Newton-upon-Ayr *29*
  foundation 8, 23–4
  C16 37
  C18 58, 66, 75–6
  North Church *118*

officials 141, 197, 204, 229
old people 227–8
Open Golf Championship *126*, 127, *168*

Orangefield *64*
  C18 65, 66
  C19 79, 104, 135
  C20 150, 180, *190*, 191, 222
organisations 155–6, 220–21, 236, 249,
  251–2
Oswald. *Family*. 135
oversmen 27, 28, 36, 37

Paisley Abbey
  foundation 7
  C13 9
Palace of Engineering 191, *192*
Parish Council 146
parliamentary elections 115–16, 161, 223, 237,
  243
Parochial Board 113–14
pavilion *144*
pay *see* wages
peat-holes 63
Picture House 156, *159*, 223, 236
'Pioneer'' aircraft 211, *212, 213*
plague 24
police 113
Police Burghs 138
Polish War Memorial *194*
politics
  C19 87–8, 115–16
  C20 161–2, 237, 243
poor relief 73, 85, 96, 146, 207
population
  C15 20
  C17 56
  C18 66
  C19 78–80, 99–100, 108, 111, 125–6, 133
  early C20 137
  inter-war 166, 178–9
  World War II 191–2
  post-war 206, 214–15, 233–4, 247
Post Office 157–8
Pow Burn, derivation of name 36
Powbank Mill *45*
presbyteries 32–3
Presley, Elvis 214
press (journalism) 158, *159*, 178, 220
Prestwick
  derivation of name 3–4
  spelling of name 44
Prestwick Academy *233*, 234, 248
  see also Prestwick High School
Prestwick Airport *see* airport
Prestwick Bowling Club 130
Prestwick Circuits Ltd. 230
Prestwick Citizens
  Association 206
Prestwick Council of
  Churches 250

Prestwick Golf Club 89, 91, *126*, 127, *130*, *158*, *168*, 220
Prestwick High School 147–8, *147*
see also Prestwick Academy
Prestwick Pioneer 211, *212*, *213*
Prestwick Public School *121*, 122–3, 146–7
Prestwick St. Nicholas Club 91
Prestwick Toll 71, 78, 83–4, *84*, 116–17, 221–2, 226
prison 36, 80
Pritty, Frank (*d.* 1946) 197, 204
property *see* land
provosts
  C16 36
  list 268–9
public houses 88, *94*
public order *see* crime and
  public order
punishment, C15 17

quarries *35*, 36

railways 89, *91*, 112
  station *158*
Ratepayers Association 206
rates 141, 168, 170–71, 203–4, 227
rationing 201
Records of the Burgh of Prestwick v
Red Lion Hotel *94*
Reform Acts 87, 116
Reformation 30, 32
refuse collection 143, 171
religion *see* Church
rents
  land 65, 83
  houses 203, 226, 227
riggs 14
rights of way 196–7, 228
roads
  C17 56
  C18 71–2
  C19 88, 116–17
  see also streets
Robert I, King of Scotland 23
Robert II, King of Scotland 27
Roman Bridge *71*
Roman Catholic Church *174*, 176, 216, 217
  schools 218, 234
Royal Air Force, World War II 188–91
Royal Air Force Association 221
Royal Hotel 124, 237
Royal Navy 231, 245
Royal visit 202, *221*
  runrig 59–60
Russell, James G. *172*

Sabbath observance 176
St. Cuthbert Golf Club 128–9, 220
St. Cuthbert's Church *4*, *85* (new) 156, 175
St. Nicholas Church 7, *8*, 19, 53
  bell *53*
  C20 156, 175
St. Nicholas Golf Club 127–8, *131*, 220
St. Nicholas Ladies Club 128
St. Ninian's Chapel *20*
St. Ninian's Episcopal Church 176, 216, 235, 250
St. Ninian's Golf Club 145, 219, 220
St. Ninian's School 234, 235
St. Quivox Roman Catholic
  Church *174*, 216, 217, 250
saltmaking 16, 66–70, 83, *142*
Salvation Army 176, 250
sand, effect in C14 25
Sandfield House *74*
sasines 22, 46
schools *see* education
Scott, Ernest F. (*d.* 1954) 120
Scottish Air Express 212
Scottish Airlines 210, *211*
Scottish Aviation Ltd, 184–5, 191, *192*, 210–13, 232–3, 246, 247
Scottish Express 212
Scout movement 149, 155, 219
Seagate 12, *13*
Second World War 186–200
senior citizens 227–8
servants 125
sewage *see* drainage
Shaw Tower 230
Shaw, William (*d.* 1944) 197
Shields, Tommy 146
ship-building 98
shops *see* trade
  65 Club 228
Skene, *Sir* John 43
Smith, John (*fl.* 1785) 80
smuggling 70
societies 155–6, 220–21, 236, 249, 251–2
soum 14, 62–3
South Church *119*
sports 236, 251
see also bowling; cricket; curling; football; golf;
  swimming
Steele, Gilbert 202, *221*, 225, *238*
Steven, Helen Jane 133
Stewart Kyle 6
Stone Age 2–3
Strathclyde, Kingdom of 5
Strathclyde Regional Council 241, 243
  streets 142–3
  lighting 117, 143
  see also roads

suffrage *see* franchise
Sunday observance 176
Sunday Schools 86
superstitions 132–3
swimming
    pool *164*, 165–6, *165*, 196, 204, 227, 239, 244

taxes 47
    see also rates
telephones 133
television 222–3
temperance *see* drinking
Templars 19
tennis 130
territorial army 159
textiles 35, 66, 98, 108
threshing machines 134
tofts 10, 13
tolbooth 36, 46, 66
tourism
    C19 130–31
    early C20 143–4, 153
    inter-war 163–4, 180
    World War II 196
    post-war 204–6, 227, 239, 247
Town Council
    early C20 137, 138–46
    World War II 195–8
    post-war 201–2, 204, 224–5, *225*, *238*, 239–40
Town Councils (Scotland) Act 138
Town Hall 164
Town House *92*
town-twinning 228–9, 239, 251
trade
    C15 15–16
    Charter (1600) 45
    C17 56
    C19 78, 98, 124–5
    C20 152–3, 177, 206
traffic *see* motor vehicles
tramway 151, 157, *157*, 182
transport
    C19 88
    C20 151–2
    see also airport; bus services; railways; roads;
      tramway
truancy 122

turnpike roads 71–2, 88, 116–17

United Free Church 120, 156, 175
United Presbyterian Church 119–20
    South Church *119*
United States Air Force 190, 191, 214, 219, 223

Valuation Rolls 111, 124, 152
vehicles *see* motor vehicles
Vikings 4–5
visitors *see* tourism
voting *see* franchise

wages
    C18 73
    C19 86, 122
Wallace. *Family*
    C16 28–30
    C17 48, 51–2
Wallace, *Sir* Thomas (*d.* 1770) 57–8
Wallace, *Sir* William
    (*d.* 1305) 23
Wallace, *Sir* William
    (*d.* 1700) 52
Walter (Fitzalan) (*d.* 1177) 5–6, 7
Walter (Fitzalan) (*fl.*1220) 9
war memorial 160
wars
    effect on early Prestwick 23, 26
    Boer War 158
    World War I 159–60
    World War II 186–200
water supply
    C19 113, 114
    C20 143, 171, 229
Watt, John *238*
weaving *see* textiles
Western Scottish S.M.T. 182
Wilson, James (*d.* 1898) 94–5, 99
Women's Voluntary Service 194
Working Men's College 121
World War I 159–60
World War II 186–200

Younger, George, *Baron*
    Younger 38, 237, 243, 245
Youth activities 219, 236, 249

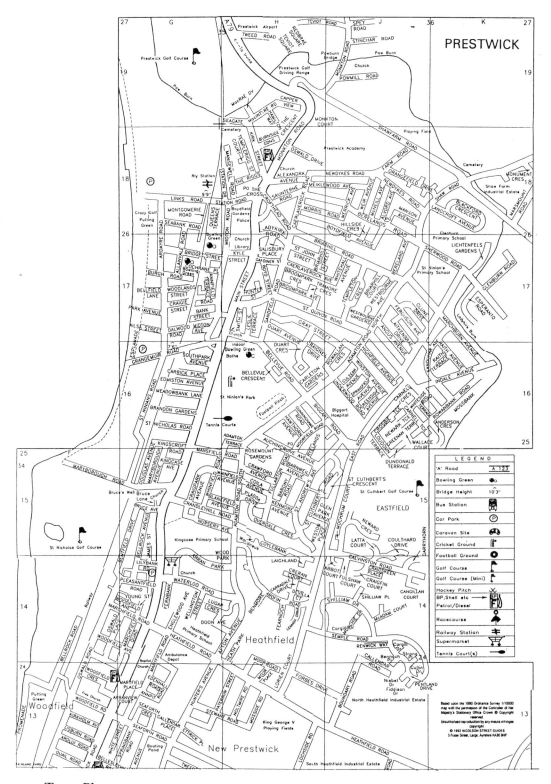

Town Plan.